KT-519-561

Integrated HTML and CSS:

A Smarter, Faster Way to Learn

KT 0735180 1

Integrated HTML and CSS:
A Smarter, Faster Way to Learn

Virginia DeBolt

San Francisco   London

Publisher: Dan Brodnitz
Acquisitions Editor: Willem Knibbe
Developmental Editor: Pete Gaughan
Production Editor: Leslie Light
Technical Editor: Molly Holzschlag
Copyeditor: Sally Engelfried
Compositor: Laurie Stewart, Happenstance Type-O-Rama
Graphic Illustrator: Jeffrey Wilson, Happenstance Type-O-Rama
CD Coordinator: Dan Mummert
CD Technician: Kevin Ly
Proofreaders: Nancy Riddiough, Amy McCarthy, Jim Brook
Indexer: Nancy Guenther
Cover design and photo-illustration: John Nedwidek, Emdesign

KINGSTON UPON THAMES LIBRARY	
KT07351801	
Browns Books	24/02/05
005.72	16.99
NM	

Copyright © 2005 SYBEX Inc., 1151 Marina Village Parkway, Alameda, CA 94501. World rights reserved. The author(s) created reusable code in this publication expressly for reuse by readers. Sybex grants readers limited permission to reuse the code found in this publication or its accompanying CD-ROM so long as the author(s) are attributed in any application containing the reusable code and the code itself is never distributed, posted online by electronic transmission, sold, or commercially exploited as a stand-alone product. Aside from this specific exception concerning reusable code, no part of this publication may be stored in a retrieval system, transmitted, or reproduced in any way, including but not limited to photocopy, photograph, magnetic, or other record, without the prior agreement and written permission of the publisher.

Library of Congress Card Number: 2004109318

ISBN: 0-7821-4378-4

SYBEX and the SYBEX logo are either registered trademarks or trademarks of SYBEX Inc. in the United States and/or other countries.

Screen reproductions produced SnapZ Pro X. © 1994–2004 Ambrosia Software, Inc. All rights reserved.

The CD interface was created using Macromedia Director, COPYRIGHT 1994, 1997–1999 Macromedia Inc. For more information on Macromedia and Macromedia Director, visit http://www.macromedia.com.

Mozilla is a trademark of the Mozilla Foundation.

TRADEMARKS: SYBEX has attempted throughout this book to distinguish proprietary trademarks from descriptive terms by following the capitalization style used by the manufacturer.

The author and publisher have made their best efforts to prepare this book, and the content is based upon final release software whenever possible. Portions of the manuscript may be based upon pre-release versions supplied by software manufacturer(s). The author and the publisher make no representation or warranties of any kind with regard to the completeness or accuracy of the contents herein and accept no liability of any kind including but not limited to performance, merchantability, fitness for any particular purpose, or any losses or damages of any kind caused or alleged to be caused directly or indirectly from this book.

Manufactured in the United States of America

10 9 8 7 6 5 4 3 2 1

Software License Agreement: Terms and Conditions

The media and/or any online materials accompanying this book that are available now or in the future contain programs and/or text files (the "Software") to be used in connection with the book. SYBEX hereby grants to you a license to use the Software, subject to the terms that follow. Your purchase, acceptance, or use of the Software will constitute your acceptance of such terms.

The Software compilation is the property of SYBEX unless otherwise indicated and is protected by copyright to SYBEX or other copyright owner(s) as indicated in the media files (the "Owner(s)"). You are hereby granted a single-user license to use the Software for your personal, noncommercial use only. You may not reproduce, sell, distribute, publish, circulate, or commercially exploit the Software, or any portion thereof, without the written consent of SYBEX and the specific copyright owner(s) of any component software included on this media.

In, the event that the Software or components include specific license requirements or end-user agreements, statements of condition, disclaimers, limitations or warranties ("End-User License"), those End-User Licenses supersede the terms and conditions herein as to that particular Software component. Your purchase, acceptance, or use of the Software will constitute your acceptance of such End-User Licenses.

By purchase, use or acceptance of the Software you further agree to comply with all export laws and regulations of the United States as such laws and regulations may exist from time to time.

REUSABLE CODE IN THIS BOOK

The author(s) created reusable code in this publication expressly for reuse by readers. Sybex grants readers limited permission to reuse the code found in this publication, its accompanying CD-ROM or available for download from our website so long as the author(s) are attributed in any application containing the reusable code and the code itself is never distributed, posted online by electronic transmission, sold, or commercially exploited as a stand-alone product.

SOFTWARE SUPPORT

Components of the supplemental Software and any offers associated with them may be supported by the specific Owner(s) of that material, but they are not supported by SYBEX. Information regarding any available support may be obtained from the Owner(s) using the information provided in the appropriate read.me files or listed elsewhere on the media.

Should the manufacturer(s) or other Owner(s) cease to offer support or decline to honor any offer, SYBEX bears no responsibility. This notice concerning support for the Software is provided for your information only. SYBEX is not the agent or principal of the Owner(s), and SYBEX is in no way responsible for providing any support for the Software, nor is it liable or responsible for any support provided, or not provided, by the Owner(s).

WARRANTY

SYBEX warrants the enclosed media to be free of physical defects for a period of ninety (90) days after purchase. The Software is not available from SYBEX in any other form or media than that enclosed herein or posted to www.sybex.com. If you discover a defect in the media during this warranty period, you may obtain a replacement of identical format at no charge by sending the defective media, postage prepaid, with proof of purchase to:

SYBEX Inc.
Product Support Department
1151 Marina Village Parkway
Alameda, CA 94501
Web: http://www.sybex.com

After the 90-day period, you can obtain replacement media of identical format by sending us the defective disk, proof of purchase, and a check or money order for $10, payable to SYBEX.

DISCLAIMER

SYBEX makes no warranty or representation, either expressed or implied, with respect to the Software or its contents, quality, performance, merchantability, or fitness for a particular purpose. In no event will SYBEX, its distributors, or dealers be liable to you or any other party for direct, indirect, special, incidental, consequential, or other damages arising out of the use of or inability to use the Software or its contents even if advised of the possibility of such damage. In the event that the Software includes an online update feature, SYBEX further disclaims any obligation to provide this feature for any specific duration other than the initial posting.

The exclusion of implied warranties is not permitted by some states. Therefore, the above exclusion may not apply to you. This warranty provides you with specific legal rights; there may be other rights that you may have that vary from state to state. The pricing of the book with the Software by SYBEX reflects the allocation of risk and limitations on liability contained in this agreement of Terms and Conditions.

SHAREWARE DISTRIBUTION

This Software may contain various programs that are distributed as shareware. Copyright laws apply to both shareware and ordinary commercial software, and the copyright Owner(s) retains all rights. If you try a shareware program and continue using it, you are expected to register it. Individual programs differ on details of trial periods, registration, and payment. Please observe the requirements stated in appropriate files.

COPY PROTECTION

The Software in whole or in part may or may not be copy-protected or encrypted. However, in all cases, reselling or redistributing these files without authorization is expressly forbidden except as specifically provided for by the Owner(s) therein.

To my two favorite distractions: Montana and Gabriela

Acknowledgments

Thanks to Mark Longley for inviting me to join his first HTML class. No one at the local community college had heard of HTML back then, and Mark had to invite people to take the class to prove he could fill it before the administration would let him offer it. He planned a great curriculum that remained strong for many semesters after that. When he decided to stop teaching the class, he passed it on to me, and I taught basic HTML for several years. That teaching experience led to the new approach to teaching integrated HTML and CSS that you'll find in this book.

I am grateful to the following wonderful Sybex staffers for their invaluable help in making this book. Thanks to Acquisitions Editor Willem Knibbe for believing in the project and getting it approved. Thanks to Developmental Editor Pete Gaughan for making sure my content was its maximum best and for getting permission to include screen shots of other folks' software or websites. Thanks to Copy Editor Sally Engelfried for fixing my writing errors and holding my horrible passive voice habit in check, and thanks to our proofreaders for giving us all a reality check. Thanks to Production Editor Leslie Light for finding me help from illustrators and keeping me on schedule. And special thanks to Technical Editor Molly E. Holzschlag for agreeing to take on this book and for her outstanding expertise that helped me make sure all the information in the book is correct.

The beautiful photograph of Austin's famous Highway 360 bridge was taken by John Seibel of John Seibel Photography (`www.johnseibelphotography.com`) in Austin, Texas. I also appreciate the permission to use a sound clip by the jazz trio The Beat Divas (`www.madykaye.com/divas`).

Contents at a Glance

Contents

Introduction

This book combines the learning of Extensible Hypertext Markup Language (XHTML) and the learning of Cascading Style Sheets (CSS) into an integrated and unified experience.

I taught HTML classes at a community college for several years. The books available for teaching HTML generally teach you all about HTML first and all about CSS later. I believe that the two go hand-in-hand and should be learned at the same time. There are several reasons I chose this approach:

♦ Almost the instant that students manage to get one word to appear on a web page, they start demanding to know how to make it look better: how to change the color or the font or the placement. The only way to meet those demands with standards-based code is by using CSS.

♦ Having the awareness of what you intend to do with CSS as you create XHTML helps you write web pages that are CSS-ready. It helps you structure your pages with various hooks, handles, and holders meant for styling with CSS.

♦ Learning to write XHTML with CSS in mind helps you design pages that work in modern browsers, download quickly, are accessible, and hold up well over time. These are design skills that help students when they reach the job market.

A Brief History of HTML and CSS

Go back in history a few years to HTML 4 and CSS1, both of which were drafted by the standards group the World Wide Web Consortium (W3C) in order to enable the separation of structure from presentation. In terms of what you are learning in *Integrated HTML and CSS*, structure is the XHTML, and presentation is the CSS.

Before HTML 4 and CSS, presentation was built into the HTML code in the form of elements, attributes, and values defining things now defined instead with CSS rules. An *element* in XHTML is something on a page such as a heading, a paragraph, an image, a list, a table, or a block quote. On any given page, there might be hundreds of attributes and values assigned to elements in the HTML that are strictly there for presentation, making web pages very large and bandwidth heavy to download. One of the goals in the movement toward using current standard specifications is to simplify HTML pages, reduce bandwidth costs, and reduce download times.

Before CSS, controlling the placement of elements on a web page was nearly impossible. Most designers learned to use tables to position elements on a page, but there was a problem with that. Many devices, such as the aural screen readers used by people with vision problems, made an incomprehensible mess of jumbled text out of the contents of a page laid out in a table, particularly if tables were nested one inside another. Another goal of CSS and the movement toward standardization is to make web pages accessible to any device by providing new methods of positioning elements on the page.

Another aspect of accessibility that CSS and XHTML is meant to solve is the illogical use of elements. Before CSS, many elements were misused in the sense that the elements were not used for their intended purpose.

For example, there was no way, pre-CSS, to indent text for presentation. Elements such as lists and block quotes, which are indented, were used to give text an indented appearance. If the indented text was not really a list or a block quote, there was a loss of logic between what the element actually was and the way it was used (or misused).

The world of the Web has progressed since those early days to a point where a web page might be displayed in a browser, a hand-held device, or even a cell phone. For the content of the web page to work sensibly in any Internet-capable device, the elements must be used for their logical purpose only: headings must really be headings, lists must really be lists, tables must really organize tabular data, and so on. CSS provides a method for controlling presentation while preserving logic with the proper use of the XHTML elements.

Who Should Read This Book

Integrated HTML and CSS is for beginners who don't know anything about XHTML or CSS. It is also for beginners in CSS who already know HTML.

This book will get you off to a strong start, although it does not teach you everything about XHTML or everything about CSS. When you finish this book, you will be more than ready for the books that do teach you everything about these tools. In fact, scattered throughout this book you will find notes and tips that point out good books and online resources that will help you build on what you learn here.

What You Will Learn

This book will teach you the basics of writing standards-based, accessible web pages that you can style with CSS.

You will learn the latest version of Hypertext Markup Language (HTML), which is called XHTML.

There were several versions of HTML prior to XHTML. The version known as HTML 4.01 is still in widespread use and creates web pages that work quite well. The differences between XHTML and HTML 4.01 are small, and you will be capable of writing either one after reading this book.

XHTML was chosen for this book because it is the current specification. Using current specifications (also called *standards*) allows you to design web pages with a more consistent display across browsers and devices.

There are also several versions of CSS. You will learn CSS 2, again because it is the latest standard or specification.

The emphasis here is on learning to write XHTML and CSS according to standard specifications. I will touch very lightly on techniques that are not part of the standards. Such nonstandard techniques are called hacks, filters, or workarounds. Only those hacks or workarounds that are absolutely essential will be mentioned.

You will be prepared to make your website accessible after reading this book. *Accessibility* can be defined as a lack of barriers to the accessing of your content. You will learn to write web pages that are accessible to all platforms, browsers, and devices.

What Is Covered in This Book

Integrated HTML and CSS is organized in a sensible progression that matches the process of web-page design and construction. Each chapter will add to your knowledge so that by the book's end you will be adept with web page building. As you learn each new XHTML element, you will learn to style your efforts with CSS. You will create actual pages in each chapter to practice your skills.

Chapters 1 and 2 give you some background and basics about the Web and the tools used to build web pages. By Chapter 3 you will be creating a simple web page. Chapters 4 through 11 each walk you through a new aspect of web page design and construction, from headings to paragraphs to links to images to forms and more.

Chapter 12 describes the first and basic steps in getting your web pages onto the World Wide Web. Chapter 13 teaches how to specifically style a weblog (or "blog"), and Chapter 14 presents some fundamental principles on designing web pages.

At the end of most chapters are a few suggestions to challenge you to attempt things on your own using the new information you learned in the chapter.

Real World Examples

Many chapters give you examples of web pages from the real world that are outstanding instances of the material discussed in the chapter. To get the most out of the real world examples, you need to take a look at the source of the page. In most browsers, there is a View menu with a Source or View Source option that allows you to see how the page was written. By viewing the page source, you can learn how any web page was created.

Resources on the CD

The CD contains a Style Me Challenge Page. After you have completed the book, you can create stylesheets to control the presentation of this simple HTML page. Getting successful stylesheets written for the Style Me page will prove to you that you are ready for a real-world website of your own design.

Several browsers for both Windows and Mac are included on the CD. The browsers included are all the latest and most standards-compliant versions available from the various browser manufacturers. Install all of them on your computer so you can look at the pages you make in many different browsers.

Trial versions of several HTML and CSS text editing software tools for both Windows and Mac are also provided on the CD. These sample software tools are not required to write HTML or CSS— any basic text editor will do—but they have handy features such as color coding and indenting that make writing HTML easier.

Visibone (`www.visibone.com`) has allowed us to include their color pop-ups on the CD. These are color palettes you can keep open on your computer desktop in order to choose colors and color names while you write your HTML.

Files that you need to work along with each chapter are included on the CD. You will use these files to do the real work of learning the HTML and CSS, because you will actually be typing and working through the material as each chapter progresses. You will immediately see the effect of what you have done in a browser.

Contacting the Author

Comments from readers are always welcome. You can reach me by e-mail at `virginia@vdebolt.com` or by visiting my Web Teacher site at `www.webteacher.ws`.

Chapter 1

How to Write XHTML and CSS

XHTML and CSS are two different animals, or specifications used to create web pages. Each has a distinct look and purpose. When used together, the combination can produce a useful, information-rich, and highly attractive web page.

If you see an example here or in any later chapter typed in a particular way, you should copy that exactly as you type along with the exercises in the book. The rules defining how a language is put together are its *syntax*. In this chapter, you will learn the syntax of XHTML and CSS. You will learn what each of these specifications does, how each looks, and how to write both. Basic rules for typing both XHTML and CSS, such as when to use the spacebar, when to type a semicolon, or when to type a bracket, will also be explained in this chapter.

Anatomy of a Website

For those of you who have never built a website before, a summary of what goes into a site may help you understand what HTML/XHTML and CSS do and how they can work together to implement your vision. (If you've already worked with one of the "visual tools" like Dreamweaver or FrontPage, you're a little further along the learning curve, but this recap will still help to put what you're about to learn into perspective.)

If you have explored the World Wide Web, you know that a web page may contain text, images, links, sounds, and movies or moving images. You may also be aware that some pages use scripts written in various languages such as JavaScript, PHP, or ASP to create interactivity, to connect the page to a database, or to collect information submitted in a form.

The glue that holds all those pieces and parts together and displays it in a browser such as Internet Explorer or Netscape Navigator in a readable or useable manner is HTML or XHTML. The browser is your window on the World Wide Web; XHTML is the language used to tell the browser how to format the pieces and parts of a web page.

CSS enters the scene by adding style to the formatted elements on a web page. The style might involve color, placement, images, fonts, or spacing, but it would not change the underlying pieces and parts formatted by the XHTML.

NOTE   The Internet is a vast collection of interconnected computer networks from all over the world. The World Wide Web (WWW) is a part of the Internet but is not the Internet itself. The Internet has many parts besides the WWW, such as e-mail.

What Are XHTML and HTML?

Hypertext Markup Language (HTML) is the programming specification for how web pages can be written so they will be understood and properly displayed by computers. XHTML is an acronym for

Extensible Hypertext Markup Language, a specification that grew out of HTML. You'll see what "extensible" means in a moment, but to understand the role of HTML and XHTML, you need to understand the three terms in HTML.

Hypertext is simply text as it exists in what is called "hyperspace"—the Internet. It is plain text that carries the content of your web page and the programming information needed to display that page and link it to other pages. Hypertext is formatted via a *markup language*—a standardized set of symbols and codes that all browsers can interpret.

NOTE   The organization devoted to creating and publishing the standardized rules for various web technologies, including XHTML, is the World Wide Web Consortium, or W3C, at www.w3.org. See also the Web Standards Project, a grassroots coalition fighting for the adoption of web standards, at www.webstandards.org.

Markup is used to convey two kinds of information about text or other content on a web page: first, it identifies what kind of *structure* the content requires. If you think of a web page as simply a whole lot of words, the HTML is the markup, or framework, that specifies that certain words are headings or lists or paragraphs. The way you mark up the text on the page structures the page into chunks of meaningful information such as headings, subheads, and quotes.

Markup may also define the *presentation* of those elements; for example, the different fonts to be used for headings and subheadings. When it was first developed, HTML was the only tool for defining visual presentation on screen. When the World Wide Web began, the only information transmitted using the *Hypertext Transfer Protocol (HTTP)* was text. As the capability to transfer images, sounds, and other information was added, presentational markup was added to HTML to help format the new information. After a few years of amazing growth, the HTML that was being used to mark up individual elements reached burdensome proportions. It became apparent that markup for presentation was an inefficient way to define what every item of text or graphics on a website should look like, and the web community developed Cascading Style Sheets (CSS) as a better way to handle presentation.

What's the Difference between XHTML and HTML?

XHTML actually *is* HTML—it is the most recent standard for HTML recommended by the W3C. XHTML was chosen for the basis of the codes used in this book because it is the current recommendation. You will be learning HTML when you learn XHTML. It is a two-for-the-price-of-one bargain. There are a few basic differences in writing XHTML versus writing HTML, and these will be pointed out to you at appropriate times in the book.

XHTML is more than HTML, because it is extensible. XHTML uses the syntax rules of the *Extensible Markup Language (XML)*. An extensible markup language can be extended with modules that do things such as make math calculations or draw graphical images. Web pages written in XHTML can interact with XML easily.

What Is CSS?

CSS is an acronym for Cascading Style Sheets, another programming specification. CSS uses rules called *styles* to determine visual presentation. The style rules are integrated with the content of the web page in several ways. In this book, we will deal with style rules that are embedded in the web page itself, as well as with style rules that are linked to or imported into a web page. You will learn to write the style rules and how to import, link, or embed them in the web pages you make.

In HTML, styles can be written into the flow of the HTML, or *inline,* as well.

CSS can also be integrated into web pages in other ways. Sometimes you have no control over these rules. Browsers allow users to set up certain CSS style rules, or user styles, according to their own preferences. The user preferences can override style rules you write. Further, all browsers come with built-in style rules. Generally the built-in styles can be overridden in your CSS style rules. Built-in browser display rules are referred to as *default* presentation rules. Part of what you will learn is what to expect from a browser by default, in order to develop any new CSS rules to override those default display values.

Getting Started with XHTML Syntax

The building blocks of XHTML syntax are *tags*, which are used to mark up *elements*. A tag is a code that gives an element its name. For example, the tag used to format a paragraph is a p tag, which is called either a "paragraph tag" or "a p tag." When text is marked up with a p tag, it is an instruction to the browser to display the element as a paragraph.

Elements in XHTML, such as paragraphs, can also have attributes and values assigned to them. But before you find out about attributes and values, let's dig into tags just a bit more.

Opening and Closing Tags

Opening and closing tags are used to specify elements. Here is a marked up paragraph element:

```
<p>This is the text of the paragraph.</p>
```

The paragraph is opened with a p tag. Tags are enclosed by angle brackets (< and >). So the markup <p> instructs the browser that a paragraph starts now.

A closing tag </p> indicates the end of the paragraph. Notice that the closing tag is the same as the opening tag, with the addition of a forward slash (/) before the tag. Tags are rather like on and off switches: turn on a paragraph here and turn it off there. With a few more sentences added to make the paragraph show up, and a second identical paragraph added, this element would appear something like Figure 1.1 in a browser.

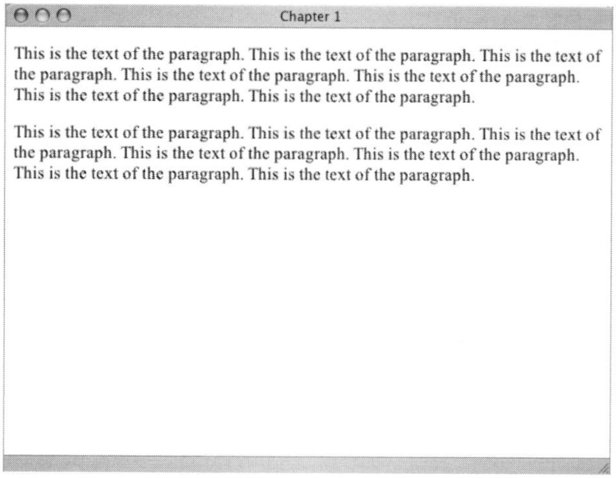

FIGURE 1.1
Two paragraph elements

Notice that the browser left a blank line between the two paragraphs and that there is no indenting. This is an example of a *default* paragraph. A default display is the browser's built-in interpretation of what the element should be. One way to change the browser's default interpretation of an element is to include additional instructions in the form of *attributes* and *values* that further define the element.

An attribute is information about the element. An example of an attribute that might define a paragraph is alignment. Text in paragraphs can be left-aligned, right-aligned, centered, or justified. As you can see in Figure 1.1, the browser default for text alignment is left-aligned. In XHTML, the type of alignment you choose is the value. The exact attribute is `align`. The value of this attribute could be `left`, `right`, `center`, or `justify`.

An attribute is written as part of the opening tag. The attribute name is followed by an equal sign (=) and the value in quotation marks (").

Here is a marked up paragraph element with an attribute name and value.

```
<p align="right">This is the text of the paragraph.</p>
```

By adding `align="right"` to the first paragraph element in Figure 1.1, you can see the alignment change to an appearance similar to Figure 1.2.

There are two important things to take note of in this example. First, there is a space between the tag and the attribute name, `align`. The attribute is followed by an equal sign and the attribute value `"right"` is enclosed in quotation marks with no surrounding spaces. Attribute/value pairs in XHTML always follow this syntax. Also notice the closing tag. It does the job of ending the paragraph and the effect of the paragraph's attributes merely by using the forward slash (/) and the p again. When the paragraph ends, all of its attributes and values terminate with it.

One of the distinctions between XHTML and HTML is that closing tags are *required* by XHTML. In HTML, closing tags are not always required.

Empty Elements

Before I describe empty elements, let me quickly define nonempty elements. An element with text in it, such as the previous paragraph examples, is considered nonempty.

FIGURE 1.2
The first paragraph
with `align="right"`

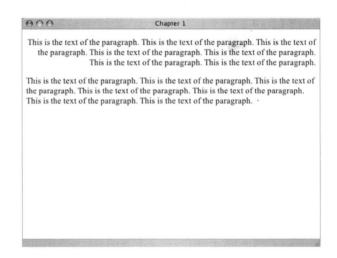

Sometimes you put something on a web page that does not contain text. Such elements don't need closing tags and are referred to as *empty elements*. An example would be an image or a line break. But before I get into the requirements for empty elements in XHTML, here's an example in HTML:

```
<p>Jingle bells, jingle bells,<br>
Jingle all the way...</p>
```

The HTML tag `<br>` (for break) is used for a line break in formatting this paragraph. The line break doesn't have to open and close, it merely has to *be*. A line break moves down to the next line, without any intervening white space, which you would get by default if you put the second line in a new paragraph element.

Formatted with a break in the first line, this paragraph would display like Figure 1.3 in a browser.

However, XHTML uses syntax based on the rules of Extensible Markup Language (XML) to write HTML. One of the requirements of XML is that every element must be terminated whether it is empty or not. You may be asking how an element can be "terminated" if there is no closing tag. The solution for XHTML is to add the closing forward slash to the empty tag itself. Empty tags in XHTML look like this example.

```
<p>Jingle bells, jingle bells,<br />
Jingle all the way...</p>
```

Notice the space between the `br` and the forward slash (/). Even empty tags with attributes and values can be closed in this way.

NOTE The space before the closing forward slash is not required by XHTML. In other words, `<br/>` would be considered correct. However, inserting a space enables older browsers to correctly display the document, so I will use the space here. (Older browsers are those versions earlier than 5, such as Netscape 4.7.)

FIGURE 1.3
The line break

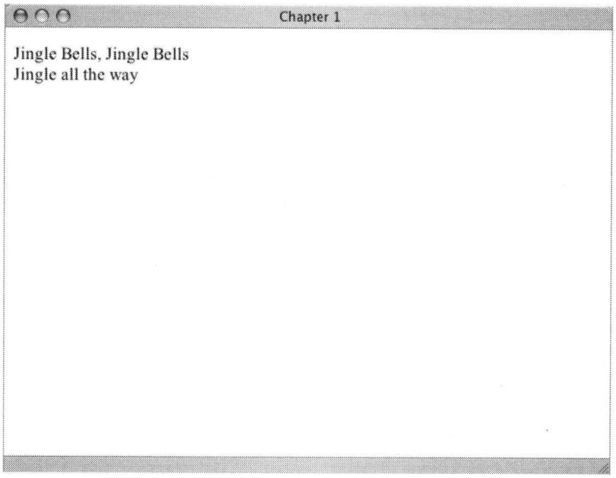

The img (for image) tag is another empty element. Look at this example:

```
<img src="photo.gif" />
```

This empty element places an image on the page, and the source of the image is given as an attribute of the img tag. The space and forward slash at the end give the empty element the required XHTML closing.

There are not many empty elements in XHTML. Others include horizontal rules, the link element, and meta elements. Most of the time you will mark up text with both opening and closing tags. Even if you are writing HTML, where closing tags are not always required, it is considered good practice to include closing tags whenever possible.

XHTML: Specific Requirements

As mentioned previously, XHTML use XML syntax rules. In addition to the requirement that every element be terminated, there are several other specifics about writing XHTML that are different from HTML requirements:

◆ Specific DOCTYPE declarations are required, which you will learn about in Chapter 3.

◆ All elements, attributes, and values must be in lowercase.

◆ All values must be enclosed in quotation marks. Values can be quoted with single or double quotation marks, but you must be consistent about using the same type each time. The examples in this book will consistently be in double quote marks (").

◆ Every attribute must be given an explicit value.

Although these rules are not required when writing HTML, they all work just fine in HTML. The only XHTML syntax rule that does not produce valid HTML is using the forward slash to terminate an empty element. Should you decide to use HTML instead of XHTML, you will need to make only this minor adjustment to your coding habits to write an HTML page.

TIP Throughout this book you'll learn the most important XHTML tags and attributes, but as you begin working on your own you'll find it valuable to have a complete reference to the language. You can find that reference in *HTML Complete* (Sybex, 2003), a compilation of useful information that also contains a command reference for CSS.

Getting Started with CSS Syntax

Cascading Style Sheets (CSS) are used to add presentational features to elements within your markup. CSS can set colors, fonts, backgrounds, borders, margins, and even the placement of elements on the page.

A stylesheet can be either placed directly in an XHTML document or linked to it as a completely separate file. In Chapter 2 you'll explore both these approaches, but most of the time CSS is linked to the XHTML page. In one document, you'll have your XHTML page, which you will learn to plan in a clean, logical structure of the headings, paragraphs, links, and images needed to present your ideas. In another file, you'll have your stylesheet, which gives color, emphasis and pizzazz to your display. This way, you can change the way your web page looks simply by changing the stylesheet and without changing the content at all.

The power to change a site's complete appearance by changing the stylesheet gives you great flexibility in its appearance. It also saves enormous amounts of time on maintenance and upkeep, since style rules are in a file that is apart from the content. Any number of web pages can be linked to a single stylesheet, so it becomes merely a matter of minutes to make sweeping changes to the appearance of all those pages. Once a stylesheet has been downloaded by a browser, it is saved in a special folder called *cache*. The next time the browser downloads a page using that stylesheet, there is no wait for the user while it downloads because the browser already has it in cache. So every page that uses that stylesheet will download very quickly, saving waiting time and bandwidth charges.

NOTE Visit www.csszengarden.com to see inspirational examples of the same content styled in many different ways using CSS.

Styles and stylesheets look very different from XHTML, and a different set of syntax rules is used for writing styles.

Selectors and Declarations

Style rules are written with *selectors* and *declarations*. Selectors, well, *select*. That is, they select which elements of an XHTML page the style will apply to. The most basic selector is the element selector. For example, the selector p selects all the paragraph elements on a page.

For each selector, you write a set of declarations that govern how the selected element will be displayed. Together the selector and declarations make up a style rule or, more simply, a style. Here is a set of style declarations for the selector p:

```
p {
font-family: Arial, Helvetica, sans-serif;
font-size: small;
color: blue;
}
```

Let's examine that bit by bit. You already know that the p is the selector. Everything that comes between the two curly braces ({ }) is the declaration block, which contains three different declarations.

A declaration consists of a *property* followed by a colon, a space, and then the *value*. A semicolon follows the value. As you can see in this example, a property in CSS is similar to an attribute in XHTML. They both identify a characteristic of the element you are formatting. The first property I declared in this example is the font family to be used for text in the paragraphs. I specified Arial as my first choice, if the user's computer has it. If not, Helvetica will do, and if neither is available, the system's default sans-serif font will have to do. See Figure 1.4 for examples of these font families.

TIP *Font family* is the slightly fussy typographical term for what we usually call a *typeface* or just a *font*. Strictly speaking, every variation in size and weight within a typeface is considered a separate font, and the whole set of these variations is considered the font family.

It is considered good practice to include more than one font family in a declaration because not all computer systems come equipped with the same set of fonts. As in this example, the fonts are normally listed in the order of preference.

FIGURE 1.4
Sans-serif font families

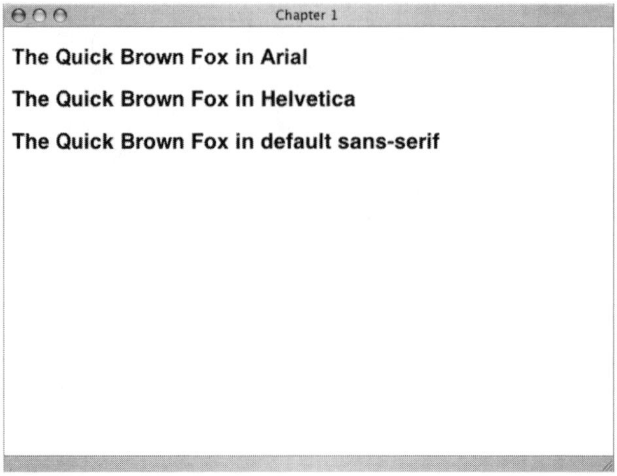

Generally, if no font family is specified, a browser will use Times as the default. See Figure 1.5 for examples of serif fonts.

TIP   You'll learn more about fonts and font families in Chapter 4. Typography and fonts are the topic of many books, including *The Non-Designer's Design Book* by Robin Williams. CounterSpace at `http://counterspace.motivo.com/` provides a good introduction to the topic.

The second declaration in the preceding rule is `font-size: small`. You will learn about the various options in font sizes in Chapters 4 and 5, but I'm sure you can guess that this declaration sets the font for all the p elements to a small size. The final declaration sets the color to blue.

NOTE   Unless a user has changed the browser default settings, the default font-size setting in most browsers is medium.

This style rule has the effect of making every paragraph on that page appear in a font that is slightly smaller than normal, blue, and Arial.

In the examples in this book, each style declaration is written on a separate line, and the closing curly brace is on its own line as well. This makes the style easier to read. However, style rules don't have to be typed in exactly that form. For example, you could write it like this:

```
p {font-family: Arial, Helvetica, sans-serif; font-size: small; color: blue;}
```

If you do put more than one declaration on a line, be sure to leave a space after the semicolon.

Some styles can be written in shorthand form. For example, `font` can be used as shorthand for all the font properties including `font-style`, `font-variant`, `font-weight`, `font-size`, `line-height`, and `font-family`. That allows you to combine the two declarations about fonts into one shorthand declaration like this:

```
p {
font: small Helvetica, Arial, sans-serif;
color: blue;
}
```

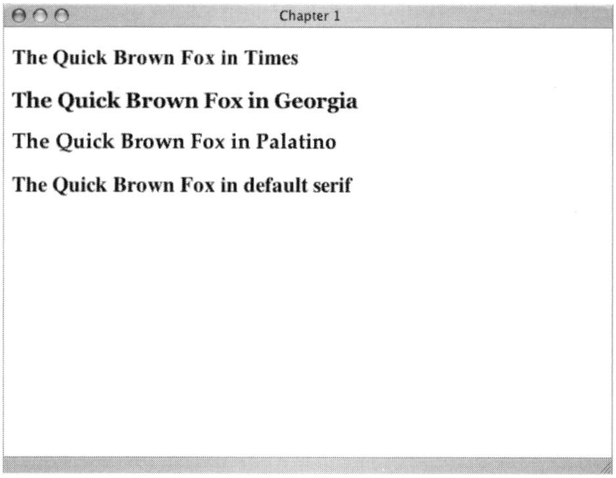

FIGURE 1.5
Common serif font
families

The Quick Brown Fox in Times

The Quick Brown Fox in Georgia

The Quick Brown Fox in Palatino

The Quick Brown Fox in default serif

Color is not considered a property of font. The `color` property expresses a foreground color, meaning that the text in the foreground of the page will be in the color named. Color is distinguished from `background-color`, which, as you can probably guess, sets a background color for the entire element.

SELECTORS GET SPECIFIC

Often you'll need to be more explicit in styling elements in the XHTML than the first example shows. CSS does allow for more specific selectors than the general element selector just described. Since the selector distinguishes what element in the document will be affected by the style rule, an element selector such as the p selector in the example above will affect all the p elements. There are times when you want particular (or what CSS terms *specific*) instances of paragraphs to follow different rules from those assigned to all p elements in general. Two of those types of selectors are the *ID selector* and the *class selector*. These two selectors allow you to write style rules for elements in a particular context. For example, instead of styling all the paragraphs on a page, you can style only the paragraphs of a certain class or ID.

NOTE   The types of selectors included in this book are element selectors, class selectors, ID selectors, contextual selectors, pseudo class selectors, and group selectors.

ID Selectors

IDs can only be used once per XHTML page. They are usually used to identify content that you style as a structural unit, such as a header, footer, content block, or menu. We will be working with this concept in almost every chapter of this book, but for now, you will simply see how ID selectors look in the stylesheet.

ID selectors are preceded by this symbol: #. The correct term for this symbol is "octothorpe," but most people in America call it a pound sign or hash sign. In this book, we will use the term hash sign for this symbol. An id rule in a stylesheet looks like this:

```
#footer {
font-size: x-small;
}
```

NOTE   In XHTML id is in lowercase.

This rule would make everything in the section (or division) of the page identified as footer extra small. Notice that there is no space between the hash sign and the ID name.

But suppose you don't want everything in the footer to be extra small—you want only the paragraph in the footer to be extra small? You could accomplish this using a *contextual selector* that applies to only a paragraph in the division of the page identified as footer:

```
#footer p {
font-size: x-small;
}
```

Notice the space between the #footer and the p. This font-size value won't apply to other paragraphs on the page, only to paragraphs placed within the context of the footer section. This use of the ID selector followed by the element selector is very specific to only particular paragraphs in particular parts of the page.

The selector #footer p is a contextual (or *descendant*) selector. You can build contextual selectors into your XHTML with named IDs that allow for finely drawn CSS selectors. In the upcoming chapters, you will use descendant selectors to create many CSS styles.

You create the names for the id selectors yourself. They don't have to relate to any XHTML tag. It is good practice to create a simple and meaningful name that reflects the structural purpose of the content of the section identified with an id. The id selector #footer is a good example of a name that reflects some meaningful purpose on the page. If you worked on a stylesheet and went back to it after several months, the id selector #footer would still make sense to you as you reviewed and changed the stylesheet.

Class Selectors

Class selectors can be used as many times as you want per XHTML page. Class selectors are preceded by a period (.). As with id selectors, you create the class name yourself. If you want a style that will highlight certain terms on your page, you can create a class and name it term.

```
.term {
background-color: silver;
}
```

This style rule would put a silver background behind any words or phrases that were identified as being in the class term. Notice that there is no space between the preceding period and the name of the class.

NOTE   One of the reasons CSS is popular is because a page's whole look can change almost instantly. It is good practice to choose class names that express purpose rather than some momentary choice such as a color, which might be changed later. So a class named .term is a better choice here than a class named .silver because the name term will continue to make sense no matter what color is used.

You can use complex combinations of selectors, IDs, and classes to style specific sections of your pages. The following selector would apply only to paragraphs of a class called term in a division of the page called footer.

```
#footer p.term {
background-color: gray;
}
```

Notice that when writing a style declaration for an element found in XHTML such as the p element, which is assigned to a particular class, there is no space between the element and the period and class name: p.term.

NOTE SelectORacle is a free tool at http://gallery.theopalgroup.com/selectoracle/ that will translate complex CSS selectors into plain English to help you understand exactly what CSS rules are selecting.

GROUPING SELECTORS

You may want to use the same style for several elements on your page. Perhaps you want all the paragraphs, lists, and block quotes on the page to have the same font size. To achieve this effect, list the selectors, separated by commas, and give the font-size declaration:

```
p, li, blockquote {
font-size: medium;
}
```

This rule makes the text in any paragraph, list, or block quote have the font size medium. Notice that there is a space between each item in the comma-separated list of selectors.

In this example, the comma sets up a rule for every element in the list. Here is a similar rule with no comma:

```
p blockquote {
font-size: medium;
}
```

Without the comma, it looks a whole lot like the preceding comma free #footer p rule, doesn't it? The selector p blockquote, with no comma, styles only a blockquote that's *part of* a paragraph, not every blockquote element.

The comma (or the lack of a comma) is an important distinction between grouped selectors and descendant selectors. Grouped selectors use commas. Descendant selectors do not.

TIP If you pay attention to the details such as whether you see a comma, a semicolon, a space, or a bracket and type carefully, you will have greater success with both the XHTML and the CSS examples in the book. If you do an exercise and it doesn't seem to work as I say it should, check carefully for typos. The syntax is exacting.

Quotation Marks

The last difference between the syntax rules for writing XHTML and writing CSS that you'll look at before moving on to Chapter 2 involves quotation marks.

You recall that in XHTML, all attribute values in a tag must be enclosed in quote marks. In CSS style declarations, however, property values do not appear in quotes. Most of the time, you don't see quotation marks in stylesheets, although you do use quotation marks in stylesheets when listing a font with two or three words and spaces in the name of the font.

For example, you looked at this style rule earlier, in which no quotes were used:

```
p {
font-family: Helvetica, Arial, sans-serif;
font-size: small;
color: blue;
}
```

The fonts listed here are one-word font names. Sans-serif is hyphenated and doesn't have a space, so it is considered one word. However, if you want to list a font name such as Times New Roman, which is more than one word and includes spaces, you wrap the name in quotation marks, like this:

```
p {
font-family: "Times New Roman", Times, Georgia, serif;
}
```

Notice that the comma separating Times New Roman from Times is *after* the ending quotation mark. Also note that although specific font-family names such as Times are capitalized, generic font names such as serif are not.

Real World Example

A strong thread emphasized throughout this book is that the use of the standard specifications recommended by the W3C by both web professionals and browser manufacturers makes writing XHTML and CSS easier, faster, and more universal.

There is a grassroots group working hard for the implementation of web standards called The Web Standards Project (WaSP) at www.webstandards.org (Figure 1.6).

The Web Standards Project site provides opportunities to take action in favor of web standards and offers information to help you learn to use those standards.

Be aware that any site given as a "Real World Example"—in fact, any site referred to in this book—is protected by copyright law from being copied. Copyright law protects both the images and the text in a website. I encourage you to look and learn, but not to take. There may be a few exceptions—for example, some CSS layout sites say in very clear terms that you have permission to take the material for your own use—but in general, it is best to assume that you do not have permission to "borrow" material from any website.

FIGURE 1.6
The Web Standards
Project home page
contains news in a
section called Recent
Buzz—listen to that
WaSP buzz!

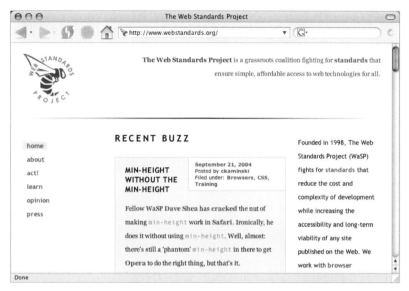

The Web Standards Project

Summary

XHTML helps you create web pages. You'll use it to format the headings, paragraphs, tables, images, and lists that logically organize your information so that you can convey your message with words, images, and information. XHTML pages, even without any CSS attached to them, are displayed by browsers. Without any CSS attached, your page might look plain and simple, but all your information and content is still displayed in a nicely organized way.

CSS is about presentation and is used by most web designers to style for the screen. CSS determines whether something is blue or green, on the left or on the right, large or small, visible or hidden, has bullets or doesn't have bullets. However, stylesheets have to be applied to something else, such as XHTML pages, to have any effect.

In Chapter 2, you will build your first XHTML document and your first stylesheet. While you're doing that, you'll learn where to write styles and how to link to styles. Chapter 2 will explain the meaning of the *Cascade* in Cascading Style Sheets.

Chapter 2

Location, Location: Where to Put a Style

There are some foundation concepts about the way Cascading Style Sheets work that we need to discuss before getting started with the specific details of building XHTML pages and stylesheets. There are several possible places where style rules can be located, and more than one set of style rules might be implemented in a particular XHTML page. The way these possible conflicts in style rules are resolved is referred to as the *Cascade*.

Chapter 2 is all about conflict resolution: you will learn the basics of how the location of a stylesheet places style rules in the Cascade and the rules for resolving conflicting styles.

Other basic concepts that are important to the way style rules are implemented in instances of conflict involve the factors of *inheritance* and *specificity*.

Inheritance is based on the fact that elements in an XHTML document are nested within one another in a relationship that is referred to as parent and child, or ancestral and descendant.

Specificity allows style rules to have *weight*, or importance, based on the specificity of any given rule. A more specific rule has more weight than a less specific rule and would therefore be used in preference to a less specific rule.

Taking the time to grasp the basic concepts of the Cascade, inheritance, and specificity will help you understand how, where, and when to add style rules in order to make your XHTML pages display as you want.

The Cascade

There are a number of complex rules regarding the Cascade, which, for the purpose of this book, can be boiled down to two simplified statements.

1. The closest rule wins.

2. The most specific rule wins.

TIP   When you are ready to move to more advanced levels of CSS implementation, *Cascading Style Sheets: The Definitive Guide*, by Eric A. Meyer will be a valuable resource.

We will walk through the Cascade using a paragraph on a very simple XHTML page as an example. We will take this paragraph through the various levels of the Cascade shown in Figure 2.1. Figure 2.1 is a bit complicated at first glance, but don't worry. The following sections walk you through each part of it step-by-step.

FIGURE 2.1
The Cascade and its effect on a paragraph

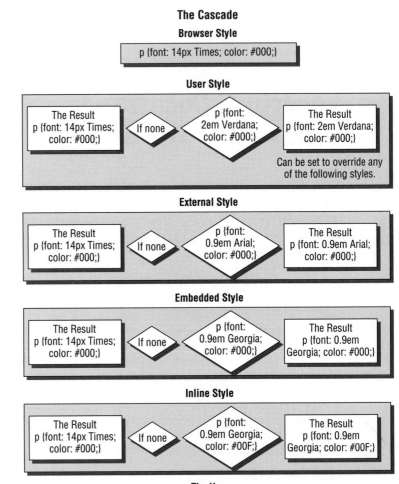

Begin with the Browser

Each browser has a set of style rules. These rules commonly set up basic display properties such as black text and font sizes for various elements.

The browser style rules are at the beginning of the Cascade. In terms of the two simple Cascade statements I listed, the browser style is the farthest away from any element, and the browser style rules are less specific than any rules placed subsequently in the Cascade.

Or, to put it another way, if no rules are written in user stylesheets, external stylesheets, or embedded stylesheets to change the styles set up by the browser, then the browser rules govern the appearance of a web page.

Figure 2.1 illustrates a paragraph displayed using a set of styles inherent in the browser with no additional style rules.

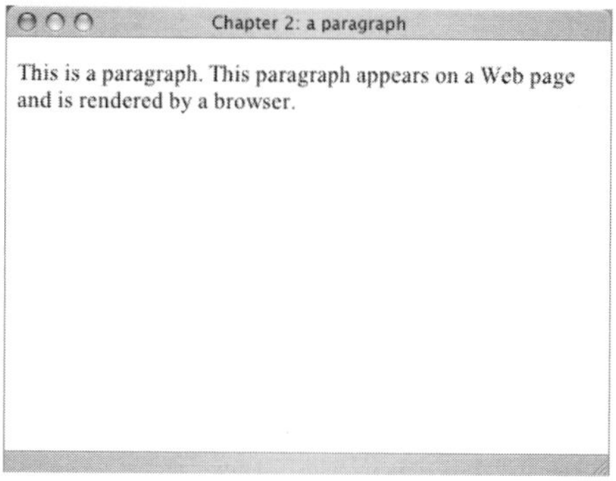

FIGURE 2.2
A paragraph displayed
with the browser's styles

This page is available on the CD in the folder for Chapter 2. If you copy it from the CD and save it on your computer, you can work along with the following examples. The file you want is `ch2_paragraph.html`.

NOTE   There will be many exercises in this book that you will want to save to your computer from the accompanying CD. Create a new folder on your computer named `Integrated HTML and CSS`. Inside this folder, you can add a subfolder for each chapter of the book. When you work on exercises for each chapter, save them to your computer in the appropriate folder.

If you work on the page as you go along, you will need to open it in a basic text editor such as Notepad, Simple Text, or Text Edit. (Do not use word processing software such as Word.) You can see what you are doing by opening the page in a browser using File ➢ Open File and browsing to the `ch2_paragraph.html` file on your computer. The page is shown in Listing 2.1.

There are several mysterious and as yet unexplained codes and symbols on this basic page. For the moment, you can ignore all of it except the particular sections I point out in discussing the location of style rules and the Cascade. In later chapters, you will learn everything there is to know about the other mysteries of this basic page.

LISTING 2.1:   A Basic XHTML Page

```
<!DOCTYPE html PUBLIC "-//W3C//DTD XHTML 1.0 Transitional//EN"
    "http://www.w3.org/TR/xhtml1/DTD/xhtml1-transitional.dtd">
<html xmlns="http://www.w3.org/1999/xhtml">
<head>
<title>Chapter 2: a paragraph</title>
</head>
<body>
    <p>This is a paragraph. This paragraph appears on a Web page
        and is rendered by a browser.</p>
</body>
</html>
```

User Styles

All browsers allow users the option of setting up style rules of their own. Many people who don't have any barriers to accessing the Web, such as poor eyesight, are not aware that these options exist. If a user chooses to do so, they can set their own rules to be more important than any style rules created by the web page designer.

Figure 2.3 shows one browser's preferences for web content. Notice the unselected option called Use My Style Sheet. Below it is a browse button that allows a user to locate on their computer a stylesheet written for their particular needs.

In the Languages/Fonts category in the browser preferences, the user may set a particular font size and font family for their default display, as shown in Figure 2.4.

TIP   Notice that this particular user has the preference for font size set to 16. In this book, we will deal extensively with stylesheets that use font sizes of 100 percent or 1 em (an em is a font size measurement relative to the user's preference). In this user's case, 100 percent or 1 em are equal to 16 as the font size. In every case, measurements in percents or ems are relative to the user's default font size, whatever it may be.

If you have the `ch2_paragraph.html` file open in your browser, you can experiment with your browser preferences for font size to see what difference it makes in the way the paragraph displays. After you change and save a preference, Reload (Refresh) your browser to see the change. When you finish, revert back to your normal settings.

External Styles

The browser and user stylesheets are out of your control. The first opportunity you as a designer have to enter the Cascade is with an external stylesheet.

NOTE   The fact that some things about the way a web page renders are out of your control is a hard concept for some beginners to grasp. Designers often want to achieve an exact appearance. This is difficult, if not impossible, to do with XHTML and CSS. You can create pages that work well and look wonderful in different browsers on different platforms or Internet-capable devices with various styles. But because of the rules of the Cascade and also because of differences in browsers and platforms, your page may not always have exactly the same appearance in every situation.

FIGURE 2.3

Internet Explorer (Mac) preferences for web content

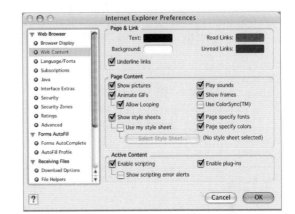

FIGURE 2.4
Internet Explorer (Mac)
preferences for
language/fonts

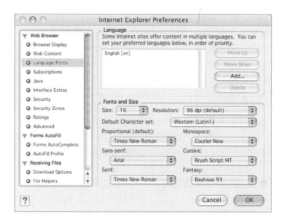

An external stylesheet is a text document created in Notepad or some similar text editor and saved with the file extension `.css`. There is one on the CD named `ch2external.css`; it is shown in Listing 2.2.

This stylesheet has a rule for the p element. It uses 0.9em as the font size, which makes the paragraph slightly smaller than the size the user has as their preference for font sizes, since 0.9em is slightly smaller than 1em. The rule also changes the font to Arial and sets a color code (#000) that represents black, which probably is the same as the browser's and user's default choice, so you won't notice a color change yet.

TIP   You don't really need the color code because the browser's stylesheet is already set for black. But later on you will change it to blue, so it is included here in anticipation of that.

You integrate that external style rule with your XHTML page by adding a `link` element to it.

The `link` element is inserted into the document head. It must be after the `title` element but before the closing `head` tag, like this:

```
<title>Chapter 2: a paragraph</title>
<link href="ch2external.css" rel="stylesheet" type="text/css" />
</head>
```

The `link` element links the XHTML page to a document whose relation (`rel`) to it is that of `"stylesheet"`. The stylesheet `type` is `text/css`. The `href` attribute is the URL of the stylesheet.

NOTE   There is one other method of integrating an external stylesheet with an XHTML page. It uses an `@import` directive, which, if used, affects the Cascade. However, I will wait to discuss this until you have the details of the Cascade well in mind.

LISTING 2.2:   A Simple Stylesheet

```
p {
font: 0.9em Arial;
color: #000;
}
```

With the link to the external stylesheet in place, save the XHTML page and refresh (reload) the browser page to render the paragraph with new style rule. Figure 2.5 shows the original page with no attached style rules behind a rendering of the page after the `ch2external.css` file was linked. You can clearly see the difference made by linking to the external stylesheet. The rule in the external stylesheet overrides the rule in the browser's default stylesheet, and the font displayed is now a slightly smaller-sized Arial.

The stylesheet `ch2external.css` could be linked to an unlimited number of XHTML pages. If the rule for `p` in `ch2external.css` was changed in any way, the rendering of every page linked to the stylesheet would instantly reflect that change. Talk about easy! Talk about powerful! One external stylesheet can change dozens, hundreds, or thousands of XHTML pages in a few seconds.

Embedded Styles

Style rules may be inserted in the head of the XHTML document itself. Such styles are referred to as *internal styles* or *embedded styles*. Embedded styles apply only to the document in which they are placed. If you are making a web page that will stand alone as a one-page document, embedded styles make sense.

Embedded styles also make sense when you have an external stylesheet linked to a page but you want to change something slightly on just one page.

TIP Embedded styles are sometimes used in the first stages of designing and building a new website. This helps with testing and approving a page design because everything needed to test or critique the page is in one file. When the first page is completed in the desired manner, the styles are moved to an external stylesheet so they can be used with other pages in the site.

The embedded style rules go in the XHTML document head, following the `title` but before the closing `head` tag. For example:

```
<title>Chapter 2: a paragraph</title>
<style type="text/css">
p {
font: 0.9em Georgia;
color: #000;
}
</style>
</head>
```

You will notice that this style rule is similar to the one used on the external stylesheet, except it is enclosed in a `style` element. The `style` element must have `type="text/css"` as an attribute for the browser to render the styles properly. The style changes the font family to `Georgia`.

To really understand what is happening with the Cascade, you need to keep the link to the external stylesheet, too. It will be listed *before* the style element in the document head. In Cascade terms, that means that the external stylesheet is farther away from the styled element than the embedded stylesheet. Or, to turn that explanation around backward, it means that the embedded style is closer in the Cascade than the external style. With both the linked stylesheet and the embedded stylesheet, the code looks like this:

```
<title>Chapter 2: a paragraph</title>
<link href="ch2external.css" rel="stylesheet" type="text/css" />
```

```
<style type="text/css">
p {
font: 0.9em Georgia;
color: #000;
}
</style>
</head>
```

With this new embedded rule added to the Cascade, you'll see a result similar to the browser window at the top of the stack in Figure 2.6. Note that the rule setting the font to Georgia in the embedded style overrides the rule setting the font to Arial in the external style.

FIGURE 2.5
An external stylesheet is linked to the page.

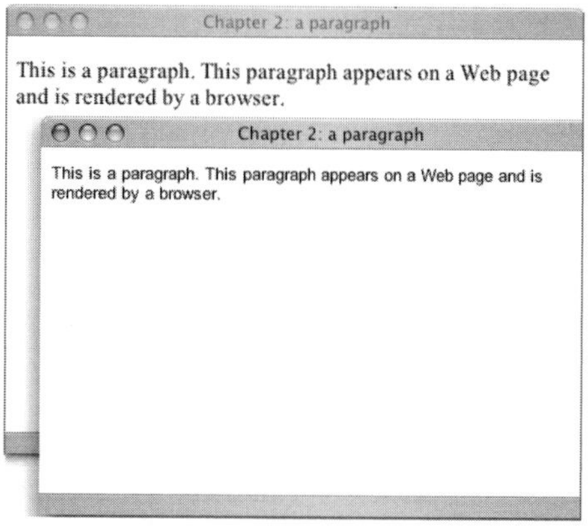

FIGURE 2.6
The embedded styles override the external styles.

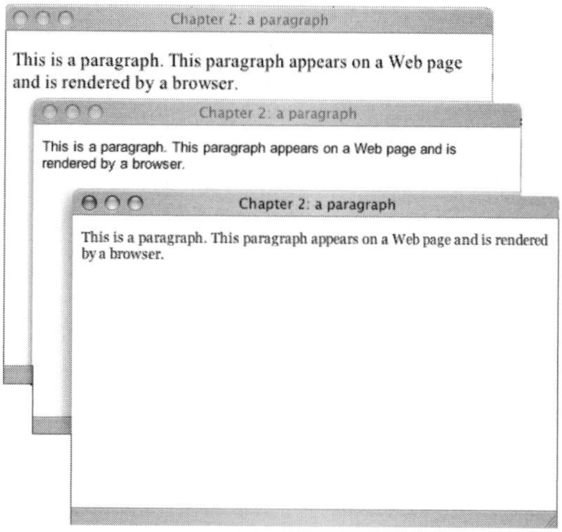

COMMENTS AND EMBEDDED STYLES

In older browsers, embedded styles were enclosed in XHTML comment marks. I'll explain what comment marks are in a moment. Here is an embedded style example, with comment marks:

```
<style type="text/css">

<!--

p {

font: 0.9em Georgia;

color: #000;

}

-->

</style>
```

Notice the symbols <!-- and --> surrounding the whole set of style declarations in the `style` element; these are comment markers. *Comments* are a way of telling the browser "don't display this." XHTML comments begin with an opening angle bracket, followed by an exclamation mark and two hyphens. The comment ends with two hyphens and a closing angle bracket.

```
<!--the comment goes here-->
```

Commenting is a time-honored programming convention for including annotations about what a program is doing at each stage. Most languages include symbols that tell a compiler (the software interpreting the program), "Whatever appears between these two marks is not an instruction for you to execute." A secondary purpose is to temporarily disable part of a program by enclosing it in comments, which can later be removed.

Why do you sometimes comment a style block? Some old browsers do not know what styles are, and the comments prevent them from adding the style rules to your page as if they were part of your text. These browsers can ignore your style instructions and display the page according to their default settings—which is not what you intended, but it's better than not displaying your page at all. Modern browsers, which do know what styles are, simply ignore the comment markers and read and follow the style rules as you intend.

Comments are extremely useful when mixed with the XHTML making up the body of the document because they are a way for you as the page designer to leave notes and pertinent information for future reference. The comments are not rendered visually in the browser, but they are visible to anyone reading the code.

Comments can be used within CSS style definitions, too. CSS comments begin with /* and end with */. As with XHTML comments, CSS comments tell the browser to ignore the material enclosed in the comment markers. You will see this in action in practice exercises later in the book.

An example of a CSS comment:

```
p {

font: 0.9em Georgia;

/*color: #000;*/

}
```

Because of the comment marks around the color declaration, the browser ignores that particular instruction.

Inline Styles

Inline (in the flow of the text) styles are a one-time-use affair. They are technically an embedded style, but people usually make a distinction between styles embedded in the document head and those embedded inline by calling the latter inline styles.

Inline styles are right in the XHTML as an attribute of the element you are styling. Therefore, in terms of the Cascade, they are the closest any style rule can possibly get to the element they are meant to style.

Making extensive use of inline styles defeats the purpose of controlling document display with one (or only a few) external documents. It also adds code to the page, which means extensive use of inline styles starts bumping up your download times. Because of this, using inline styles extensively is not the best practice, but you may find them useful from time to time.

Each time you want to use an inline style, you have to type it right into the specific element. The only element on the example page is a p element. With the inline style added, the p element would look like this:

```
<p style="color: #00F">This is a paragraph. This paragraph appears on a Web page
and is rendered by a browser.</p>
```

This style rule changes the `color` to #00F (blue) for this single paragraph element. It's not obvious from Figure 2.7, but the final example browser window displays blue text.

Notice one more thing about Figure 2.7. The font in the frontmost example browser window is still Georgia. Because nothing in the inline style changed the rule for the `font-family` style embedded in the document head, the value `Georgia` was inherited for the font family of this p element.

FIGURE 2.7
The inline style makes
the color blue.

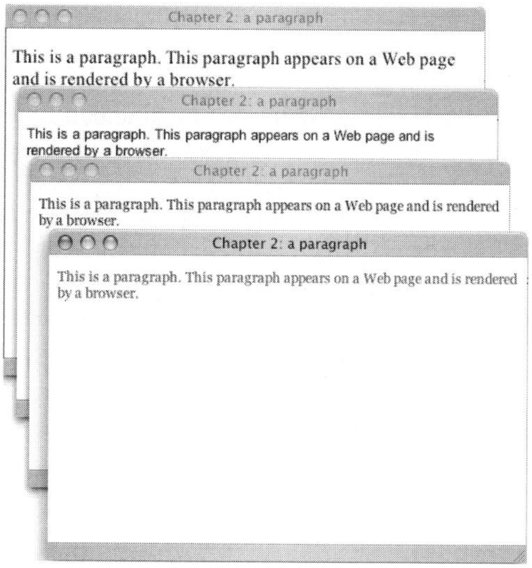

Inheritance

Inheritance affects the rendering of styles because styles are inherited from antecedent (or parent) elements. XHTML documents are rendered using a hierarchical system. Elements are nested one inside another in an ever-descending hierarchy. In Listing 2.1, there are two examples of this. The document hierarchy begins with the html element (seen in this line: `<html xmlns="http://www.w3.org/1999/xhtml">`) and terminates with `</html>`.

Everything in the document is a descendant of the `html` element. The next level in the hierarchy (or *document tree*) is the `body` element. The p element is a descendant of the `body` element. A stripped down view of these elements and their hierarchical relationship is

```
<html>
    <body>
        <p></p>
    </body>
</html>
```

Let's examine the relationship the Cascade and inheritance have in how a particular element might render. Suppose you have an external stylesheet that sets a `font-family: Arial` rule for the `body` selector, like this:

```
body {
font-family: Arial;
}
```

If there were no other style rules for the p element anywhere in the Cascade, the value `Arial` would be inherited by the p element as a descendant of the `body` element.

Specificity

The W3C has a set of complicated mathematical formulas to determine the *weight* (or importance) of any particular style rule. Selectors with higher specificity or more weight override styles with less weight.

Let's look at a much more complex XHTML page than Listing 2.1; take a look at Listing 2.3.

LISTING 2.3:   A More Complex XHTML Page with Numerous Elements

```
<!DOCTYPE html PUBLIC "-//W3C//DTD XHTML 1.0 Transitional//EN"
  "http://www.w3.org/TR/xhtml1/DTD/xhtml1-transitional.dtd">
<html xmlns="http://www.w3.org/1999/xhtml">
<head>
<meta http-equiv="Content-Type" content="text/html; charset=iso-8859-1"/>
<title>Chapter 2 Example</title>
<link rel="stylesheet" href="mystyles.css" type="text/css" />
</head>
<body>
<div id="masthead">
```

```
  <h1 id="siteName">My Daily Rant</h1>
  <div id="globalNav">
    <a href="#"> home </a> | <a href="#"> archives </a> |
    <a href="#"> about </a> | <a href="#"> contact </a> </div>
</div>

<div id="content">
  <h2 id="pageName">Recently...</h2>
  <div class="feature">
    <img src="specificity.gif" alt="library mural" width="280" height="200" />
    <h3>Art in Public Places </h3>
    <p>The Art in Public Places project has installed ...</p>
    <p>This mural has provoked ...</p>
  </div>
</div>

<div id="sidebar">
  <div id="hotnews">
    <h3>Today's News Quote</h3>
    <p class="newsbite">&#8220;This new bill will bring immediate relief
      to overburdened taxpayers.&#8221;<br />
      <span class="source">&ndash;The President </span></p>
    <p class="comment">To which I say, this doesn't help anyone in my tax
      bracket. How about a raise in the minimum wage instead?</p>
  </div>
</div>
</body>
</html>
```

There is a good bit of code in this listing that you haven't learned anything about yet. Once again, I encourage you to ignore the unexplained parts by trusting that by the end of the book all will be revealed and focus in on the bits and pieces needed to understand specificity as I point them out in the next few paragraphs.

In the browser, with a linked external stylesheet, Listing 2.3 renders something like Figure 2.8. There are several p elements in Listing 2.3, for example:

```
<p>The Art in Public Places project has installed a mural, a photo of which you see
on the left, on the library courtyard wall.</p>
```

A closer look at the document reveals that this particular paragraph is a descendant of an element identified with a class attribute, namely <div class="feature">. A class selector has more weight than a general selector. So in a conflict between these two rules,

```
p {
font-family: Georgia;
}
```

and

```
p.feature {
font-family: Arial;
}
```

The second rule would have a higher specificity and be used for the paragraph in question.

TIP   A div (for division) is a generic container element in XHTML. It can literally contain anything on a web page. By assigning a class or id selector to a div, you can structure the page to take advantage of the rules of specificity and inheritance.

ID selectors are also given more weight than general selectors. Look at this section of Listing 2.2 [2.3]: `<h2 id="pageName">Recently...</h2>`. In a conflict between these two rules,

```
h2 {
font-size: 1.6em;
}
```

and

```
#pageName h2 {
font-size: 1.4em;
}
```

the second rule has a higher specificity and would be used to style the particular h2 in question.

FIGURE 2.8
A styled rendering of the code in Listing 2.2 [2.3]

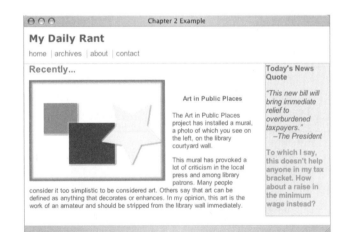

Using @*import*

There are two ways to link your XHTML page to an external stylesheet. One way is with a link element, which we discussed earlier in the chapter; the other is with an @import directive. Both link and @import can be used more than one time, which means it is possible to have several stylesheets affecting your document in various ways simultaneously. The Cascade, the rules of inheritance, and the rules of specificity will resolve any conflicts that arise when using more than one set of style rules.

TIP Whether you use the `link` element or the `@import` directive to link to an external stylesheet, the stylesheet is referred to as being "linked" to your document.

While both the `link` element and the `@import` directive do the same job, namely linking your XHTML page to a set of style rules, the `link` element is generally used unless there is a particular need for the unique attributes of `@import`. I'll explain those unique attributes.

The `@import` directive is popular among web designers who know that their target audience is still using that venerable old antique, Netscape Navigator 4.*x*. Netscape 4 does not know very many of the style specifications implemented in modern browsers. More importantly, it does not know what an `@import` directive is. To accommodate Netscape 4 in addition to the more current browsers, designers put styles Netscape 4 and other older browsers don't understand in an imported stylesheet because those browsers skip right over the `@import` directive while the more modern browsers obey the commands.

An external stylesheet can be imported *into another stylesheet* using an `@import` directive such as

```
@import url(http://www.example.com/styles.css)
```

As you can see from the URL value in the example, the imported stylesheet does not need to be part of your site, it can be on another site. That does not mean that you can link to just anyone's stylesheet without their permission, but in situations where there might be some requirement for a specific set of style rules, perhaps a standard corporate stylesheet for your company, using an `@import` directive in conjunction with your own stylesheet can be very efficient.

There is a unique drawback to using `@import`, however. If there is no `link` element in a document, a stylesheet using an `@import` directive will create an effect in Internet Explorer 6 known as a *flash of unstyled content (FOUC)*. The effect of FOUC is for the page to display completely unstyled and then redraw itself using the imported style rules. This is why the `link` element is the standard choice, with `@import` being used only in cases of specific need, or when a `link` element is also present.

TIP If you use both `link` and `@import` to link to stylesheets, the `@import` directive must be placed in the document head before the `link` element.

The `@import` looks like this in the document head:

```
<style type="text/css">
@import url(myotherstyles.css);
</style>
```

As you can see, the `@import` directive is contained in a `style` element, similar to what you saw in the previous example of an internal stylesheet. The statement gives the URL of the stylesheet to be imported.

Embedded styles, such as those you worked on previously, can be added to the `style` element that includes the `@import` statement. If you include some embedded style rules on an XHTML page that also contains an `@import` directive, the `@import` must come first. For example,

```
<style type="text/css">
@import url(myotherstyles.css);
p {font-size: medium;}
</style>
```

In the preceding example, you are importing a stylesheet called `myotherstyles.css`, and you are also adding an embedded style for the p element. Remember that the imported stylesheet can be linked to unlimited documents, but the embedded style will only affect this particular document.

You can combine `link` elements, `@import` directives, and embedded styles to create a connection between your XHTML page and any number of stylesheets, like this:

```
<link rel="stylesheet" type="text/css" href="mystyles.css" media="screen" />
<link rel="stylesheet" type="text/css" href="printstyle.css" media="print" />
<style type="text/css">
<!--
@import url(myotherstyles.css);
p {font-size: medium;}
-->
</style>
```

See the "Media Attributes" sidebar for an explanation of the `media` attributes used in the preceding style.

MEDIA ATTRIBUTES

Sometimes the `link` element or `@import` rule contains a `media` attribute. CSS allows you to write styles intended for specific devices, such as screen or print. Using a `media` attribute allows you to link to one stylesheet for screen display and a slightly different one for printers. For example:

```
<link rel="stylesheet" type="text/css" href="mystyles.css" media="screen" />

<link rel="stylesheet" type="text/css" href="printstyle.css" media="print" />
```

Most media types are not supported by web browsers yet. The complete list of media types includes all, aural, Braille, embossed, handheld, print, projection, screen, TTY, TV. Most modern browsers support all, screen, and print at this time. The Opera browser is ahead of the competition in that Opera 6.*x* and above supports the projection medium. Opera is likely to win the race to be the first CSS-capable browser in the handheld market, as well.

You will write a print stylesheet in Chapter 6.

Real World Example

Wired News was an early example of a complex three-column site design based on web standards and CSS layouts. If you look at the site at www.wired.com (Figure 2.9). you must view the source to appreciate how much of the heavy lifting for this site is accomplished with CSS.

To view the source, use the browsers View menu. Under View, select View Source or Page Source. You will see near the top of the page quite a few links to stylesheets for screen, print, and other media. You will also see several alternate stylesheets, which I did not explain in this chapter, but which you will get a chance to use if you work on the Style Me exercise on the accompanying CD. You will also note that there are no `@import` stylesheets linked to the page.

Wired News reports on technology and well as other topics. It is one of those sites with attitude, which is probably part of the reason it was willing to take the heat of being a pioneering example of a large, heavily trafficked site that follows web standards. Many busy sites have followed Wired's example with success.

FIGURE 2.9
Wired News was a
pioneering site in
adopting CSS for
layout and design.

Reprinted from Wired News, www.wired.com.
Copyright © 2004 Wired Digital Inc., a Lycos Network Company.
All rights reserved.

Summary

When the browser reads your XHTML page to render it, it reads (or cascades) from top to bottom and external to internal. Assuming there is no user stylesheet to consider, the browser first reads the style rules in linked external files. Next, it reads the rules in the embedded `style` element in the document head. Finally, it reads any inline style rules.

This rendering process, combined with rules governing specificity and inheritance, resolves any conflicts that might arise among various sets of style rules.

XHTML and CSS can be integrated with `link` elements, by `@import` declarations, and by styles embedded in the XHTML page itself. If the same element can be selected by two or more rules, then the Cascade determines which style will be displayed.

In order to achieve the effects you want with regard to the appearance of any web page, you must understand the Cascade, specificity, and inheritance. From time to time in the remaining chapters, special mention will be made of how the Cascade, specificity, and inheritance affect the styles you are writing.

In Chapter 3 you will start learning the basics of writing your own XHTML page and your own stylesheets.

Chapter 3

Page Basics: DOCTYPE, Head, Body, and Body Styles

When you look at a page on the Web, what you see is everything that's within the body element. But when you start creating a web page, there are some things you must do, even before you begin writing the content that will appear in the body. Yes, a web page is more than just a beautiful body.

In this chapter, you will learn about DOCTYPE declarations, which must be placed on the page before the document head. You will also learn about the document head itself, which is required to contain the document title and can contain all sorts of useful elements such as links to stylesheets.

These, then, are the basics of every page: the DOCTYPE declaration, the head element, and the body element. In every activity or exercise you do in the remainder of this book, you will begin and end every web page you make with the basic elements we will discuss in this chapter.

Learn the XHTML

You must take several steps before you write anything that actually appears in the browser window. You can decide on the color, background, and margins for your page even before you put content on it. In this chapter, you will:

- Learn what a DTD is and how to pick one for your page.
- Learn what you can put in the document head.
- Create a style for the body of your document.

The Goal

Listing 3.1 is the complete first page you will make as it will appear when you are finished. You will build it step-by-step in this chapter, and I will explain each part of the page as we move along.

LISTING 3.1: A Complete, Valid XHTML Page

```
<!DOCTYPE html PUBLIC "-//W3C//DTD XHTML 1.0 Transitional//EN"
    "http://www.w3.org/TR/xhtml1/DTD/xhtml1-transitional.dtd">
<html xmlns="http://www.w3.org/1999/xhtml">
<head>
<title>My First Practice Page</title>
</head>
```

```
<body>
<p>Hello, world</p>
</body>
</html>
```

Every page you make will include these elements. You will change the page title and the contents in the body, of course, but every page will begin and end just like this.

Now that you know what you are aiming for, let's look at it bit by bit.

DOCTYPES

The rules for different versions of HTML have been organized into *Document Type Definitions (DTDs)* and are declared using a declaration known as the *DOCTYPE declaration.* You need to be aware of the different versions of XHTML because the Document Type Definitions determine whether or not you are writing valid XHTML.

Valid simply means that you picked a DTD and wrote your HTML according to the rules in that DTD. You can write HTML without declaring a DTD, but in order to claim that your code is valid, there must be a DTD somewhere to check it against.

The theory behind writing valid code is that browsers know the same rules. If you use the standard rules, and the browsers use the standard rules, then everything should work the way you intend when you design a page. Reality doesn't match this theory perfectly yet, but the latest versions of the browsers are much closer to a dependable use of standards than they were during the nightmare years of web design when the browser makers were striving for leadership by creating techniques that only worked in their particular brand of browser.

Many repositories of DTDs exist, but the World Wide Web Consortium (W3C), found at www.w3.org, holds the one you will be most interested in. In addition to creating and keeping track of the various versions of HTML, the W3C provides a service that lets you check your code with a validator at http://validator.w3.org.

There are some older versions of HTML DTDs, but in this book we will only use the most recent version of HTML, namely XHTML. There are three possible DOCTYPE declarations for XHTML: *strict*, *transitional,* and *frameset.* These declarations look like this:

There are three possible DOCTYPE declarations for XHTML.

◆ strict:

```
<!DOCTYPE html PUBLIC "-//W3C//DTD XHTML 1.0 Strict//EN"
    "http://www.w3.org/TR/xhtml1/DTD/ xhtml1-strict.dtd">
```

◆ transitional:

```
<!DOCTYPE html PUBLIC "-//W3C//DTD XHTML 1.0 Transitional//EN"
    "http://www.w3.org/TR/xhtml1/DTD/xhtml1-transitional.dtd">
```

◆ frameset:

```
<!DOCTYPE html PUBLIC "-//W3C//DTD XHTML 1.0 Frameset//EN"
    "http://www.w3.org/TR/xhtml1/DTD/xhtml1-frameset.dtd">
```

To write valid XHTML, you pick one of these DTDs, declare it at the very beginning of your page, and then make sure you follow the rules for that DOCTYPE by running your page through a validator after you finish writing it.

Let's dissect a DOCTYPE piece by piece to see what it is saying. The first part simply means that you are declaring the DTD for your document, which is going to be written in XHTML, and this DTD is available to the public. Next you state that the DTD you are declaring is located at the W3C, is a particular DTD for XHTML, and is written in English. Finally, you give the URL for the particular DTD you picked.

NOTE   You can even write your own DTDs (though this is rare), which might or might not be shared with the public.

Using a strict DTD means that the only elements and attributes available are for structure, not presentation. With a transitional DTD, some presentation elements and attributes that are no longer part of the XHTML specifications can be used. A frameset DTD is used for the frameset document when using frames.

As I just mentioned, in a transitional DTD, some elements and attributes that are no longer part of the specifications can be used successfully. Such elements are termed *deprecated*. The W3C states that deprecated elements or attributes are those that have been replaced by newer constructs. Deprecated elements may become obsolete in future versions of HTML. Using a transitional DTD gives you the option of using presentational elements and attributes, since they do come in handy in certain situations.

TIP   The attribute `align="right"` that we used with a p element in Chapter 1 is an example of a deprecated attribute. The recommended method of achieving text alignment now is with CSS, but with a transitional DTD, presentational attributes such as this can still be used in the XHTML.

You will be using the transitional DTD in this book; that is, you will be using this DOCTYPE declaration:

```
<!DOCTYPE html PUBLIC "-//W3C//DTD XHTML 1.0 Transitional//EN"
    "http://www.w3.org/TR/xhtml1/DTD/xhtml1-transitional.dtd">
```

All the XHTML you will learn in this book will use the specifications set forth in the XHTML 1.0 Transitional DTD.

Using any XHTML DOCTYPE declaration ensures that a browser will render the page in a rendering mode that follows the W3C specifications as closely as possible. This is referred to as *standards mode*. If an incomplete DOCTYPE declaration is used, or if no DOCTYPE declaration is present at all, the browser uses a rendering mode referred to as *quirks mode*. The fact that a browser might switch from one rendering mode to another depending on the document's DOCTYPE declaration is known as *DOCTYPE switching*.

NOTE   Craig Saila has more information about DOCTYPES and quirks mode at www.saila.com/usage/tips/defn.shtml?doctype.

The XML Declaration

If you are using XHTML, the W3C suggests that you include an XML declaration before your DOCTYPE declaration. An XML declaration looks like this: `<?xml version="1.0" encoding="utf-8"?>` and tells the browser than a version of XML follows, and that the character encoding is utf-8, which includes character sets for most of the world's languages. Further, the W3C suggests that you combine the opening `html` element with the XML namespace (`xmlns`) after your DOCTYPE declaration. The XML namespace gives the URL of the specifications on the W3C site and looks like this: `xmlns="http://www.w3.org/1999/xhtml"`. The completed lines as recommended by the W3C look like this:

```
<?xml version="1.0" encoding="utf-8"?>
<!DOCTYPE html PUBLIC "-//W3C//DTD XHTML 1.0 Transitional//EN"
    "http://www.w3.org/TR/xhtml1/DTD/xhtml1-transitional.dtd">
<html xmlns="http://www.w3.org/1999/xhtml">
```

However, this is one of those situations where theory and reality bump heads. In this book, you are going to do only part of what the W3C suggests because the XML declaration causes an unexpected problem in Internet Explorer 6 on Windows: IE 6 goes into quirks mode when the XML prolog is present. To ensure IE 6 follows the standard rules set up in the W3C specifications—standards mode—simply leave out the XML declaration. According to XML specifications, the XML declaration is optional, so don't use it. You do need to include the opening html tag and XML namespace, however; that is, include this line:

```
<html xmlns="http://www.w3.org/1999/xhtml">
```

Let's Get Started

Now that you know what DOCTYPE declaration you will be using, you are ready to start typing. Open a text editor such as Notepad, Simple Text, Text Edit, or any other plain text editor. Every computer comes equipped with a basic text editing program, and that is all you need to get started. Type the DOCTYPE declaration and the opening `html` tag:

```
<!DOCTYPE html PUBLIC "-//W3C//DTD XHTML 1.0 Transitional//EN"
    "http://www.w3.org/TR/xhtml1/DTD/xhtml1-transitional.dtd">
<html xmlns="http://www.w3.org/1999/xhtml">
```

 TIP There are some free or very inexpensive text editors designed to help you write XHTML easily. They use color coding and indenting to help make your HTML more readable. Several are provided on the CD. You can also find many at www.tucows.com, including such popular choices as the Coffee Cup HTML Editor, Edit PLUS, BBEdit, and Ultra Edit.

The Head

The next part of the page is the head. The document `head` can contain many things including JavaScript, links to stylesheets, and information about the document itself such as the document title. The only thing that is *required* in the head is the `title`.

Type **<head>**, leave a couple of blank lines and type **</head>** to open and close the `head` element. With these additions, you should have:

```
<!DOCTYPE html PUBLIC "-//W3C//DTD XHTML 1.0 Transitional//EN"
    "http://www.w3.org/TR/xhtml1/DTD/xhtml1-transitional.dtd">
```

```
<html xmlns="http://www.w3.org/1999/xhtml">
<head>

</head>
```

THE TITLE

The `title` element goes inside the head. After the opening head tag, but before the closing head tag, type **<title>My First Practice Page</title>**.

```
<head>
<title>My First Practice Page</title>
</head>
```

The title must contain only text and character entities. (I will explain character entities in Chapter 6.) You may not use any XHTML in the title; for example, you cannot use italics or color.

So far you haven't typed anything that will appear in the browser window when you look at your page. The content of the head does not appear in the browser window, although the title does appear in the title bar at the top of the browser.

Even though the title does not appear on the browser page, a good title is incredibly important to your page's success. There are three reasons why titles are so important. The first is because the title is what is saved when a person adds your page to their Favorites or Bookmarks list.

The second is because search engines use the titles when they are indexing and cataloging the millions of web pages they search. Let's assume you have a craft site called Homemade Crafts, and one of your pages tells how to make homemade play dough. Let's also assume there is a mom out there frantically searching for a recipe for homemade play dough for her three kids who have been inside all day on a rainy day. If your page has a title like Homemade Crafts: How to Make Play Dough, that frantic mom will probably find it at the top of her search results. A good title results in success for you and for the mom in a hurry.

The third benefit of a good title is that it helps the user know exactly where they are when the page opens. A page title such as Homemade Crafts: How to Make Play Dough tells the user the name of the site and the name of the specific page within the site: two helpful orientation facts.

Saving

This is a good time to save your work. If you haven't already, start by making a new folder on your hard drive called `Integrated HTML and CSS`. Save everything you do in this book to that folder. When you save XHTML (or CSS) pages, the filenames you use should not have any spaces. Using all lowercase letters for filenames is preferred but not required. Save your document with an explanatory name like `ch3practice.html`. If you are not in the habit of typing the file extension (the `.html` in this case), you need to remember to type it when you save XHTML pages.

TIP   If your computer automatically adds a `.txt` file extension to your XHTML pages, you need to remove it so it will display properly in a browser.

Even though this is XHTML, the file extension when saving pages is `.html`. The root element in any XHTML page is actually `html` and it is saved as such. (There is an `.xhtml` file extension, but it is not used yet because of lack of browser support.)

You may have noticed web pages with the file extension `.htm`. This works too, and you can use it if you want. Just be consistent about whether you use `.htm` or `.html` so you don't end up with mistakes and broken links due to inconsistent filename extensions.

TIP As you travel the Internet, you may see web pages that have other filename extensions such as `.asp` and `.php`. This generally means that a scripting language, such as ASP (Active Server Pages), has been used to generate an HTML document.

The Body

The content of the body is what appears in the browser window. After the closing head tag, type **<body>**. Skip a line and type **</body>**. When the body ends, the page ends, so you also need to add a closing html tag.

```
</head>
<body>

</body>
</html>
```

Are you wondering where the opening html tag was? The html began at the very top of the page as part of your opening element. It was

```
<html xmlns="http://www.w3.org/1999/xhtml">
```

This element contained the opening html tag and the XML namespace. Everything on the page is contained within that opening html tag and the closing html tag at the end of the page. Thus, as I mentioned, html is the root element of any XHTML page.

Next, it's time to put a line of text in the body so there will be something to see on the page when you check it. Type **<p>Hello, world</p>** after the opening body tag.

```
<body>
<p>Hello, world</p>
</body>
```

Take a Look in a Browser

It is time for the magical moment known as a "browser check." Make sure the latest version of `ch3practice.html` has been saved. Open your browser of choice. Under the File menu there will be a command such as Open File that will allow you to browse through your hard drive to the `Integrated HTML and CSS` folder and open the page `ch3practice.html`.

You should see something similar to Figure 3.1 in the browser.

Learn the CSS

You have a real web page finished. Granted, it isn't very impressive yet, but it does have an element that must be styled for every page you write in the future. That element is the body. Every page has a body, every body needs a style. It seems a fitting element to use to begin your CSS learning.

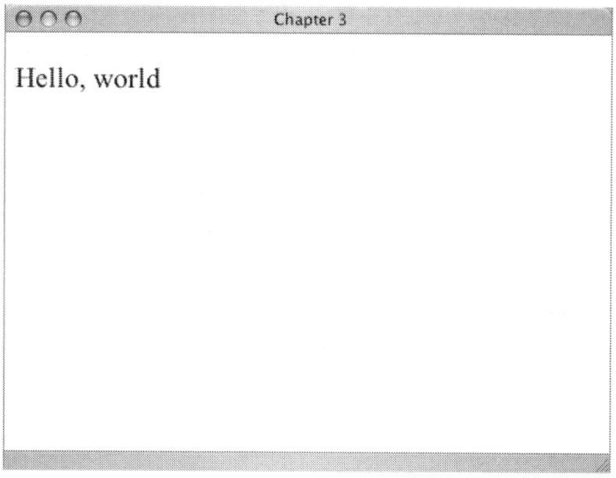

FIGURE 3.1

The XHTML page before any CSS is added

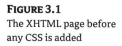

As there is for every element in HTML, there is an array of choices with CSS for the body element. In this chapter, you will learn about background color and background image options for the body. You will also learn about setting margins for the body. What you learn about backgrounds and margins will serve you throughout the rest of this book, because CSS can determine background colors, background images, and margins for any XHTML element!

Create the Stylesheet

Let's start with an external stylesheet. This gives you the flexibility to link the stylesheet to more than one XHTML page.

Open a new blank document in your text editor. Leave your ch3practice.html page open, too, because you need to work on both pages. Type **body** on the first line. Type the opening and closing curly braces now, as well.

```
body {
}
```

That is all you need to begin a stylesheet—nothing but the beginnings of a style rule. You don't need DOCTYPES or opening and closing tags: just the style rule. Save the page. Give it the filename ch3practice.css and save it in the folder you made called Integrated HTML and CSS. Each time you make a change to the stylesheet, save it again.

The Background

First, you will add a background color to the page. On a new line after the opening curly brace, type **background-color: #9CC;**. This is a light blue color. Refer to the Color Chart in the book's color insert for other color options if you don't want to use light blue. Be sure to pick a light color because your text ("Hello, world") is going to be the default black and you want to be able to read it.

```
body {
background-color: #9CC;
}
```

You made a change, so save the page. Before you do any more with the CSS for the body, let's talk more about color codes.

Specifying Colors for Web Pages

Devices displaying web pages create colors by mixing various combinations of red, green, and blue, or *RGB colors*. There are three ways to indicate exactly how much of each component is in a color. One is with hexadecimal notation, which expresses color values with numbers and letters such as #FF3366 (a shade of pink) or #A1A1A1 (a shade of gray). The opening hash mark is required with hexadecimal color notation. The first two characters (FF) represent the red, the middle two (33) the green, and the last two (66) the blue. If all three components are the same, the color is black (#000000), white (#FFFFFF), or a shade of gray (as in #A1A1A1).

When a hexadecimal number has three pairs of matched letters or numbers for the RGB values, the color can be expressed in shorthand by using just one character each; #FF3366 is the same as #F36. However, in #A1A1A1, where there are no matching pairs, the value cannot be expressed in shorthand.

A color value created with any combination of pairs of 00, 33, 66, 99, CC, or FF is considered a *web-safe color*. Some examples are #003399 (a dark purple), #CCFF99 (a light green), and #FF0000 (red). Most computer monitors can display millions of colors, but only 216 colors are considered web safe, which means that they should display in a similar shade on any device, platform, or operating system. Because the color #A1A1A1 is not any combination of the pairs I just mentioned, it is not considered a web-safe color.

The second method of expressing RGB values is with percentages. In this method, instead of giving a code for the amount of red, green, or blue, you give a percentage for how much red, green or blue is needed in a color. In a style rule it would look like this: `color: rgb(100%,100%,100%);` (the value for white). As you would expect with percentages, values can range between 0 percent and 100 percent.

The third way to express color values is the numeric form using numbers between 0 and 255. A rule in a stylesheet would look like this: `color: rgb(255,255,255);` (the value for white).

Whether you use any of the following lines:

```
color: #FFF;
color: rgb(100%,100%,100%);
color: rgb(255,255,255);
```

you end up with white.

You may recall some examples in Chapters 1 and 2 that expressed colors by name. There are 16 color names that are considered *predefined colors* and can be declared by name. These include colors such as white, black, red, blue, green, gray, purple, teal, and aqua. In a style rule they would be used like this: `color: white;`.

Most of the time this book will use hexadecimal notation, but don't be afraid to try out the other types of color notation on your own.

Along with the Color Chart in this book, other color resources include the following websites:

◆   Palette Man:

    www.wire-man.com/paletteman

◆   Web Whirlers:

    www.webwhirlers.com/colors/wizard.asp

♦ Developer Zone's Color Chooser:

```
http://archive.devx.com/projectcool/developer/reference/color-chart.html
```

♦ Lynda.com:

```
www.lynda.com/hex.html
```

♦ Color Schemer Online:

```
www.colorschemer.com/online.html
```

These websites have various resources including the web-safe color charts, many additional colors that are not considered web safe, color scheme choosers for sets of several colors and more.

Link to the Stylesheet

Go back to the page of XHTML, ch3practice.html. Add a link to connect your new stylesheet to the XHTML page. The link to the stylesheet goes in the head. Type this:

```
<link href="ch3practice.css" rel="stylesheet" type="text/css" />
```

after the closing title tag but before the closing head tag, like so:

```
<title>My First Practice Page</title>
<link href="ch3practice.css" rel="stylesheet" type="text/css" />
</head>
```

Let's take a look at that link element to see what you did. The link element links the stylesheet to this XHTML page. You can use the same link element on other XHTML pages and they will be linked to the same stylesheet. A change in the stylesheet will be instantly reflected on any page that is linked to it.

The href attribute gives the hypertext reference (href) to the filename and location of the stylesheet you linked. The rel stands for relation: in this case, the linked document is a stylesheet for the linking document. The type expresses the type of data to be loaded, which is a text file of CSS rules.

Take a Look

Time for another browser check. Make sure the latest version of both the ch3practice.html and the ch3practice.css are saved. In the browser, click Refresh (Reload) and the changed page will be displayed by the browser. You should see something similar to Figure 3.2.

The Margins

Notice that the text in the body of your document is offset a few pixels from the top and the left of the browser window. That is because there is a default browser margin for the body element. That margin can be increased or decreased on the top, right, bottom, or left sides of the body with a stylesheet rule.

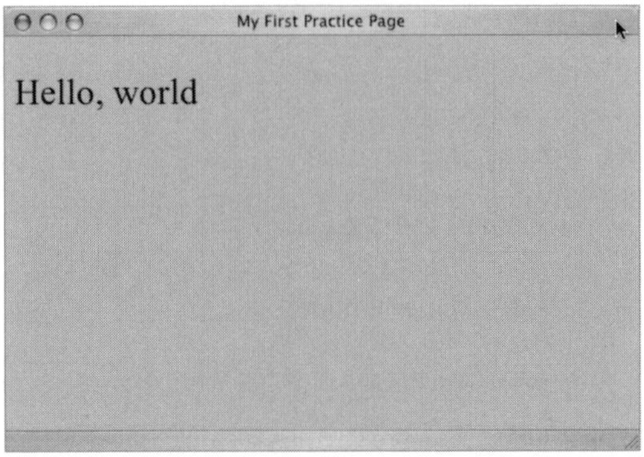

FIGURE 3.2
Reloading the page in the browser shows changes you have saved.

Leave this page open in the browser. Switch back to your text editor and bring forward the ch3practice.css page.

Many times designers place artistic images near the top and left of the browser page, and they want to make them snuggle right up to the edge of the browser window with no gap (or margin) on the top and left. To accommodate this, you will set the top and the left margin to 0. On the page ch3practice.css, type **margin-top: 0;**. Press Return (Enter) and type **margin-left: 0;**. With these changes, this is the body rule.

```
body {
background-color: #9CC;
margin-top: 0;
margin-left: 0;
}
```

TIP   When listing margin values in a stylesheet, begin at the top, then give the right, bottom, and left sides in clockwise order. If you don't specifically mention a margin value, it remains at its default setting. CSS rules for giving values for padding and border also follow this practice of listing values for top, right, bottom, and left sides of an element in clockwise order.

Save the stylesheet. Switch back to the browser. Your page has not changed, but the style rule for how it will be displayed has changed. To see that change, click Refresh (Reload) and you will see the effect of the 0 margin rule, as in Figure 3.3.

NOTE   To clearly demonstrate the margin setting of 0, I had to use the browser's default size for the paragraph text. In the other figures, the text was enlarged for easier viewing using the browser's View settings for text size. Therefore, Figure 3.3 has smaller looking text, when, in fact, it is the same text as in the other figures.

At this point, your page doesn't have an artistic image in the upper-left corner, and that text looks pretty crowded where it is. Before you give it some breathing room, let's take an excursion into measurement on the Web.

FIGURE 3.3
Your page with
margins set to 0

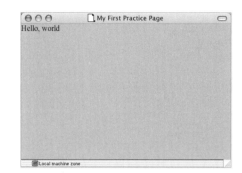

HOW FAR IS THAT?

A computer screen displays tiny dots of colored light arranged in a grid. Dots in this grid are called *pixels (px)*. Any spot on the screen can be mapped by figuring out how many pixels that spot is from the left and from the top. The measurements stating distance from the left and the top are referred to, respectively, as the *x-* and *y-coordinates*, a concept your may recall from math class. The *x*-coordinates run from left to right horizontally across the screen; the *y*-coordinates run from top to bottom vertically across the screen.

You just set the body exactly 0 pixels from the left and 0 pixels from the top margin. An inch is about 72 pixels. Normally, inches are not used at all in web measurement, but that familiar measurement does give you some idea of the space that an element measuring 72 pixels in width might occupy.

Move Your Body

Let's give the scrunched up text some air by changing the margin rule in your stylesheet. Change the `margin-top` to 10% and the `margin-left` to 15%. Save the stylesheet and refresh the browser page to see the change.

```
body {
background-color: #9CC;
margin-top: 10%;
margin-left: 15%;
}
```

You body content should now be placed something like Figure 3.4.

Color Isn't Everything

In addition to color, images can also be used as backgrounds. Background images can be used with any element, including body, paragraphs, headings, divisions, and tables. Background images can be fixed in place, repeated on one or both axes, given a set horizontal or vertical position, and even changed to something different when the element is in the hover state. Many of the exciting and beautiful designs you see based on CSS take excellent advantage of the ability to use background images to achieve stunning visual effects.

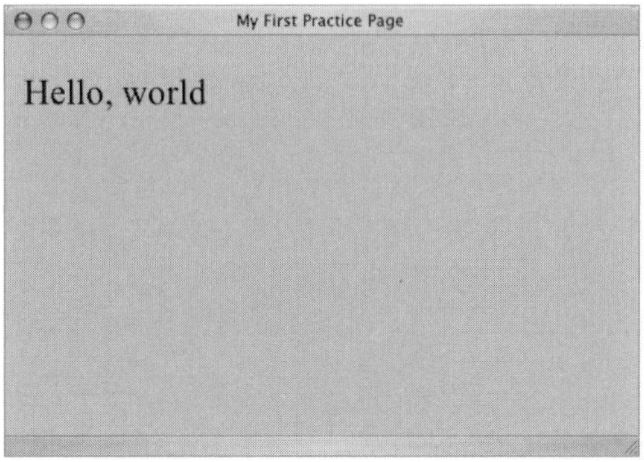

FIGURE 3.4
The body moves over
and down when the
margins change

NOTE Before CSS, the only elements that could have background images were the body and the `table` elements.

In the Chapter 3 folder on the CD accompanying this book, find the file `ch3bg_sm.gif`. Copy it to the same folder on your computer in which you are saving the `ch3practice.html` file.

Even with a background image in the body, it is a good practice to give the background a color as well. So keep the blue background color and add this graphic to the page as a background image. Because this image is a GIF, it has a transparent background, which allows the blue background of the body to shine through.

TIP Graphics on the Web are generally in GIF, JPEG, or PNG format. Only GIF and PNG files can have transparent backgrounds. JPEG is often used for images and photographs with thousands of colors. The GIF format is often used for buttons and other images with fewer colors. PNG files are not well supported yet and, as a result, are not used often.

The location of the background image is given as `url(filename);`. In this case, `background-image: url(ch3bg_sm.gif);` is what you need to include. Instructions for the `background-repeat` property should be set to `repeat` to make the image repeat over and over across and down the page. Type the following for the complete background-image rule:

```
background-image: url(ch3bg_sm.gif);
background-repeat: repeat;
```

Your document should look like this:

```
body {
background-color: #9CC;
background-image: url(ch3bg_sm.gif);
background-repeat: repeat;
margin-top: 10px;
margin-left: 15px;
}
```

Save the stylesheet and then switch to the browser and Refresh (Reload) the page to see what happens. You should see something similar to Figure 3.5.

FIGURE 3.5

The page with a repeating background image

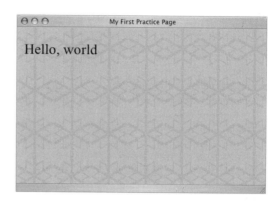

TIP The background declarations could be combined using CSS shorthand to just `background: #9CC url(ch3bg_sm.gif) repeat;`. When using CSS shorthand, the background property can have the following values stated, in this order: `background-color`, `background-image`, `background-repeat`, `background-attachment`, `background-position`. You will have an opportunity to try out each of these background properties as you procede through the book.

Using the same image, change the style so that the background image repeats only on the *x*-axis.

```
body {
background-color: #9CC;
background-image: url(ch3bg_sm.gif);
background-repeat: repeat-x;
margin-top: 10%;
margin-left: 15%;
}
```

As you can see in Figure 3.6, the background image repeats only across the x-axis for only one row.

FIGURE 3.6

The background image set to `repeat-x`

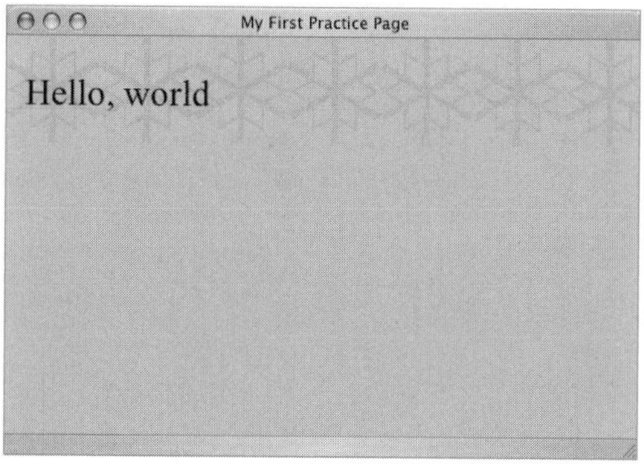

With keywords such as left, center, right or values such as percentages, pixels, or ems, you can use background images in even more ways. For example, to make the background image appear in the center of the page, add background-position: center; to your rule.

```
body {
background-color: #9CC;
background-image: url(ch3bg_sm.gif);
background-repeat: repeat-x;
background-position: center;
margin-top: 10%;
margin-left: 15%;
}
```

Instead of the keywords left, right, top, bottom, and center for the position of a background image, you can use a percentage measurement to position the image. If you use one percentage value it will apply to both the x- and y-axes. If you use two percentage values, the first will apply to the x-axis position, and the second will apply to the y-axis position. In the following example, the background-position is set to 100 percent of the x-axis (which is the same as using the keyword right) and 50 percent of the y-axis (which is the same as using the keyword center). Of course, you can use any percent value you need, such as 21% or 83%, to achieve a particular appearance when placing background images this way.

```
body {
background-color: #9CC;
background-image: url(ch3bg_sm.gif); background-repeat: repeat-x;
background-position: 100% 50%;
margin-top: 10%;
margin-left: 15%;
}
```

This style would look like Figure 3.7 in the browser.

Length is expressed in pixels or ems. Again, one value applies to both x- and y-axes, and two values apply to first the x-axis and then the y-axis.

NOTE *Cascading Style Sheets: The Designer's Edge* by Molly E. Holzschlag (Sybex, 2003) has a complete explanation, with graphics, for all of the background-position options.

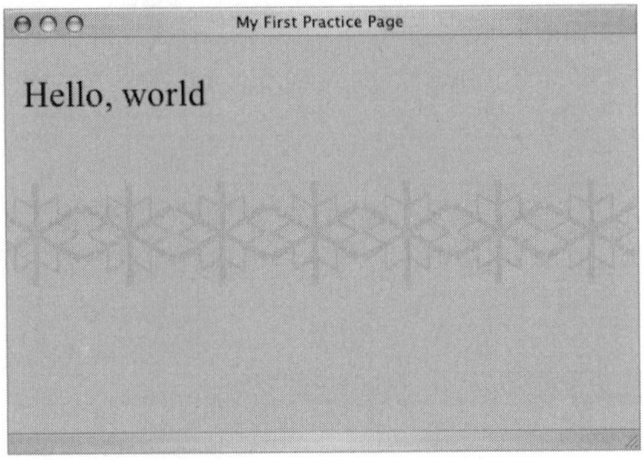

FIGURE 3.7
Background-position and background-repeat create this effect.

Real World Example

Many web designers support the idea of standards-based design and creative presentation with CSS. Such designers have incorporated these ideas into their own sites, as well as into the sites that they design for clients.

Jonny Blair Design at `www.jonnyblair.co.uk` (Figure 3.8) is an example of a designer's personal site that uses interesting styles for the body element—as well as other page elements—involving `background-color`, `background-position`, and `background-image` variations.

FIGURE 3.8

Jonny Blair Design offers more than one design for this page. The various choices rely heavily on background properties.

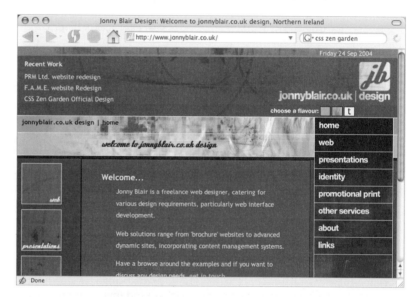

 When you complete this book, you will have the opportunity to use your new knowledge and skills to create two styles in a manner similar to what you see on the Jonny Blair Design page when you style the Style Me HTML page on the accompanying CD.

CSS Properties for the *body* Element

Table 3.1 lists the CSS properties discussed in this chapter that apply to the body element. Remember that other elements on the page, in addition to body, can have styled backgrounds and margins. The body element can also have other styles such as font styles that you will learn about in future chapters.

TABLE 3.1:   Properties for the *body* Selector

PROPERTY	POSSIBLE VALUES
background-color	`<RGB color>`, `<color name>`
background-image	`url(imagename.gif)`
background-repeat	`repeat`, `no-repeat`, `repeat-x`, `repeat-y`

TABLE 3.1: Properties for the *body* Selector *(CONTINUED)*

PROPERTY	POSSIBLE VALUES
background-position	top, center, bottom, left, right, *<percentage>*, *<length>*
background-attachment	scroll, fixed
margin	*<percentage>*, *<length>*
margin-top	*<percentage>*, *<length>*
margin-right	*<percentage>*, *<length>*
margin-bottom	*<percentage>*, *<length>*
margin-left	*<percentage>*, *<length>*

Challenge Yourself

For additional practice, make these changes in your stylesheet and then view the results in the browser.

1. Change the background color to #93C.

2. Try it with it the background-repeat set to repeat-y. Then try it set to no-repeat.

3. In an image editing program, resize ch3bg_sm.gif so that it is 100 × 100 pixels in size and save it with the filename ch3bg100.gif. Then change the name of the image in the url value to the new name.

4. Make or find a different background image and use it instead of ch3bg_sm.gif.

5. Change the margin-top and margin-left measurements to 5 percent.

Summary

A Document Type Definition (DTD) is the set of rules for the particular type of XHTML your page uses, and is referred to as the DOCTYPE declaration. It's placed first in the document, before the head element. The head contains the page title, links to stylesheets, and meta elements and can also contain other material such as JavaScripts.

Information in the document head does not appear on the browser page; therefore head elements cannot be styled for presentation. The body element contains everything that appears in the browser window. The body is the basic container for everything on your page and can be styled with CSS presentation rules.

The style for the body of your document can determine (among other things) background color, background image, and margins.

In Chapter 4 you will add headings to your page and learn how to style them.

Chapter 4

Headings and Heading Styles

In Chapter 4 you will explore the structural role that headings play on an XHTML page, and you will learn how style rules can determine the appearance of headings.

Headings organize information into meaningful chunks, thereby adding structure and clarity to your content. A well written `heading` at the beginning of a web page serves you in two ways: it helps your visitor quickly grasp the topic of your page, and it provides meaningful keywords to the search engines.

You will use CSS rules for color, font, background, and border to create distinctive headings. You will use a `class` selector to style the headings in this chapter.

In this chapter you will take a look at the box model, which governs the way CSS rules are applied to elements. You have been using the box model prior to this chapter, but it wasn't identified by name or described formally. The box model is another basic concept that will help you understand what you can accomplish with any CSS property.

Learn the XHTML

If this book were a web page, the chapter title would be an `h1` and the subtitle of the section you are reading ("Learn the XHTML") would be an `h2`. There are six levels of headings in XHTML, represented by the `h` tag followed by a number: `h1`, `h2`, `h3`, `h4`, `h5`, `h6`.

On a web page, the title of this chapter would be marked up like this:

```
<h1>Chapter 4: Headings and Heading Styles</h1>
```

The subtitle of this section, as you can probably guess, would be

```
<h2>Learn the XHTML</h2>
```

Without applying any CSS rules to headings, they have certain default features. They are *block-level* elements. Block-level elements are displayed on their own line, and any element following a block-level element is automatically placed on the next line. Headings are bold by default. The h1 is considered the most important heading on the page and is the largest by default. An h2, like the second level of an outline, is meant to be a subheading related to the main heading on the page. The default appearance is slightly smaller than that of an h1. A level three heading, or h3, is slightly smaller, and so on down to h6, as shown in Figure 4.1.

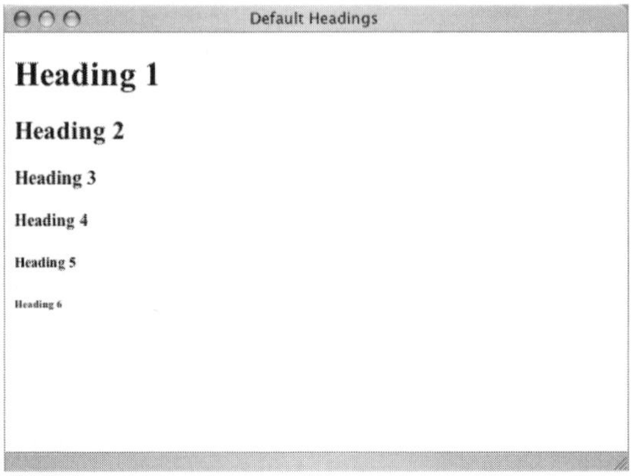

FIGURE 4.1
Default heading
display

Building Structure with Headings

Headings are used to identify page names and to title subsections of a page. The heading elements by themselves *do* give structure to a page, but in order to take full advantage of the CSS rules of specificity, it is good practice to augment the structure of the heading elements. Here's how:

- Place the heading element in a `div` element identified with an `id` attribute.
- Use `class` or `id` attributes to distinguish heading elements.

NOTE You can review the concept of specificity in Chapter 2.

We will explore using *divisions* (divs) on the page in depth in Chapter 8, but you'll get a glimpse of them in this chapter, where several `div` elements are used to give structural names to page components.

We will use `class` and `id` to style several headings.

THE LOGIC OF XHTML

In structural and accessibility terms, heading elements should only be used for text that is, in fact, a heading. In other words, heading elements should not be used to make text look large or bold if the text is not actually a heading. Conversely, text that has been made to look large and bold but is not marked up as a heading element should not be placed at the top of a page or page section *as if* it were a heading.

In essence, XHTML gives your content logical structure. There is a certain logic conveyed by creating an h1 element that this is the main heading on the page. Any device that can access the Internet, whether it is a computer, a cell phone, a screen reader, or a personal digital assistant, will understand that h1 element as the main heading on the page and display it accordingly.

Using XHTML logically ensures that your content can be accessed successfully by any Internet-capable device.

TIP Heading elements are indexed by some of the search engines. They look for h1 elements to decide what the page is about. Having important keywords describing the contents of the page in the headings can help your placement in the search results users get from such search engines.

How to Work through the Chapter

There are some images, a partially completed HTML page, and a partially completed CSS page in the Chapter 4 folder on the companion CD. Copy these files to the Integrated HTML and CSS folder on your computer (you can put them in a subfolder for Chapter 4 if you want). The files you need are

```
360bridge.jpg
delusions.jpg
headings_start.css
headings_start.html
star.gif
yellowgradient.gif
```

Start by opening the headings_start.html file in your text editor of choice. Look at the page in the browser; you should see something like Figure 4.2.

As you can see, the page includes a few headings, a list of links (that don't go anywhere for now), a couple of paragraphs, and an image I'll refer to as the deluded little bridge.

It is a bit disconcerting to see two headings one after another with no content between them, as you see here with "Keep Austin Weird" and "Delusions of Grandeur." Normally, this would not be a good practice. Eventually, the first of the two headings ("Keep Austin Weird") will become the page title and move to a location that separates it visually from the heading that follows it, but the page was built this way to give you more headings with which to practice your CSS.

FIGURE 4.2
The original headings page

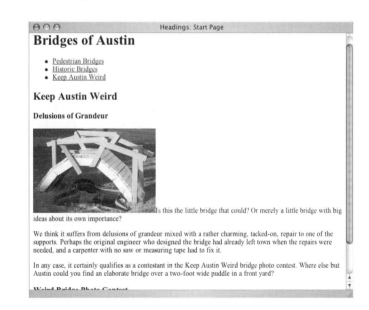

Another design decision that I made in order to give you additional practice styling headings was to use an h1 as a site name in a banner. As you will see as you proceed, the site name appears in front of a bridge photograph (the 360 bridge, so named because it is on Highway 360) as part of the banner. We will add the 360 bridge photo to the banner later. The text in the h1 could be added to the bridge graphic and display as part of the image. While it is perfectly acceptable to have a graphical banner that includes the site name, it would deprive you of an opportunity to style a text heading, so I went with styling the site name as text.

In your text editor, you should see the XHTML markup for the page, as shown in Listing 4.1.

LISTING 4.1:　　The XHTML Headings Start Page

```
<!DOCTYPE html PUBLIC "-//W3C//DTD XHTML 1.0 Transitional//EN"
  "http://www.w3.org/TR/xhtml1/DTD/xhtml1-transitional.dtd">
<html xmlns="http://www.w3.org/1999/xhtml">
<head>
  <title>Headings: Start Page</title>
</head>
<body>
  <div id="container">
    <div id="siteName">
      <h1>Bridges of Austin</h1>
    </div>
    <div id="nav">
      <ul>
        <li><a href="#">Pedestrian Bridges</a></li>
        <li><a href="#">Historic Bridges</a></li>
        <li><a href="#">Keep Austin Weird</a></li>
      </ul>
    </div>
    <div id="content">
      <h2>Keep Austin Weird</h2>
      <h3>Delusions of Grandeur</h3>
      <p><img src="delusions.jpg" alt="Delusions of Grandeur" width="250"
          height="167" /> Is this the little bridge that could?...</p>
      <h3>Weird Bridge Photo Contest</h3>
      <p> Send your entries for the best Keep Austin Weird bridge...</p>
    </div>
  </div>
</body>
</html>
```

The structure of the start page has some div elements already in place to allow for a CSS layout. They include a container div, which holds all the content. Nested in the container div is a div called siteName, where you see an h1 element. There is also a div called nav, which has a list of links.

Finally, there is a `div` called `content`, which contains the main content of the page, including a couple of `h3` elements, an image, and some paragraphs.

TIP   Remember that XHTML is case sensitive, so `sitename` is not the same as `siteName`. Be sure to match the case exactly when you write the selector rule in the stylesheet.

Some style rules have already been written for you that control layout and some of the colors. Those style rules are in `headings_start.css`. Add a link to the `heading_start.css` file in the `head` of `headings_start.html`:

```
<link href="headings_start.css" rel="stylesheet" type="text/css" />
```

Save the page and check in a browser to see layout, color, and font choices in the pre-made stylesheet; it should look something like Figure 4.3.

You can open the CSS page in your text editor and examine the style rules that were prepared in advance. By the time you have finished the book, you will recognize everything you see, but for now take note that the `body` background color and the fonts have been set. Notice that the container `div`, which contains everything in the body, has a background color of white (#FFF). The `body` element has a dark background color (#3C4138), which completely surrounds the white background of the `#container` element.

Adding to the XHTML

The first heading on the page, `<h1>Bridges of Austin</h1>`, is already in a `div` with the `id="siteName"`. (Notice the capital N in *siteName*.) Since there is only one `h1` element on the page, this is structurally specific enough for our needs.

FIGURE 4.3
Start page with the starting CSS file attached

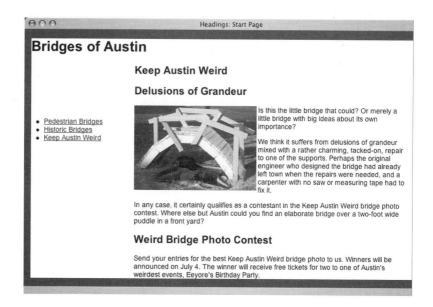

In the content area, there is one h2 and two h3 elements. You want to make all three of these appear differently, so you use classes to distinguish them. Add these class attributes to the three h2 elements on the page:

```
<h2 class="pageName">Keep Austin Weird</h2>
<h3 class="feature">Delusions of Grandeur</h3>
<h3 class="extra">Weird Bridge Photo Contest</h3>
```

Be careful to copy the spaces, quotation marks, and capitalizations exactly as they are here.

TIP   You could use a contextual selector for the h2 element in the div id="content" section of the page. The h2 would not be assigned to a class but would be styled with the selector #content h2. In a real-world situation, the contextual selector would be preferred because it results in a cleaner, faster XHTML page. In this chapter I wanted to give you some opportunities to use classes, hence the h2 is styled with a class.

Now the heading elements have some specific CSS attributes that you can grab onto and use in your stylesheet. Save the page, and let's move on to the styles.

Learn the CSS

If you haven't already, open headings_start.css in your text editor; it's presented here in Listing 4.2. Each time you make a change in the style rules, save the CSS page. If you have headings_start.html open in the browser, you will be able to view the effect of your change by selecting Refresh (Reload). The style rules already written for you and two comments make up the stylesheet at this point.

LISTING 4.2:   The Original Headings CSS Stylesheet

```
/*the following prepared style rules determine colors, fonts, layout,
  list appearance, and text wrap around the image in the content area*/

body {
  font-family: Arial, Helvetica, sans-serif;
  font-size: 100%;
  margin: 0;
  background-color: #3C4138;
}
h1 {
  font-size: 2em;
}

#container {
  width: 800px;
  background: #FFF;
  margin: 0 0 0 1em;
}
#content {
```

```
     margin: 0 2em 2em 15em;
     background-color: #FFF;
  }
  #content img {
    float: left;
    margin-right: 3px;
    margin-bottom: 3px;
  }
  #nav {
    position: absolute; top: 160px; left: 0px;
    width: 150px;
  }
  #nav ul {
    width: 150px;
  }

  /*start writing the new style rules below this comment*/
```

Notice that the body declaration of `margin: 0;` does not have a unit such as px or em added. You don't need to specify the unit because the value is 0.

Also note the use of contextual selectors in the stylesheet: `#content img` and `#nav ul` are examples of contextual selectors.

Start with *siteName*

Notice that the container `div` is already set for 800px in width. That is because the `360bridge.jpg` image that will become the background of the `h1` element is 800px in width. The entire image is 150×800, and you want to see it all. At the bottom of the existing CSS page, add this rule:

```
#siteName {
  width: 800px;
}
```

TIP A page width of about 800 pixels is currently considered the maximum size for a design. If you subtract space to use for browser borders and scroll bars, you are limited to about 768 pixels in width. Many monitors cannot display pages that are wider than this without horizontal scrolling. As monitor sizes and screen resolutions continue to increase, that number may change. See Chapter 12 for information on how to get statistics about who is using your website and what screen resolution they use.

The 360 bridge image that will be in the `siteName` `div` *could* be added as a background to the preceding siteName rule, but this chapter is about headings, so you will add the image to the background of the h1 element. A contextual selector will target the h1 in the `siteName` `div` like this:

```
#siteName h1 {
  background-image: url(360bridge.jpg);
}
```

Save the stylesheet and refresh (reload) the browser view. You should see something like Figure 4.4. The bridge image is 150 pixels in height, as noted previously, but right now you only see as much of it as is revealed behind the h1 element, which had a preassigned font-size value of 2em. Adding padding to the h1 element should allow more of the background to shine through. Add a new line to your rule:

```
#siteName h1 {
   background-image: url(360bridge.jpg);
   padding: 120px 0 0 0;
}
```

Like margin values, padding values are listed in clockwise order: top, right, bottom, left. To use padding to expand the #siteName h1 element, all you need is padding: 120px 0 0 0;. Since padding values are read clockwise, this CSS shorthand rule adds 120 pixels of padding to the top and allows zero room for padding on the right, bottom, and left. Padding at the top makes the text appear at the bottom of the image, as shown in Figure 4.5. You have to look carefully to see it because of the lack of contrast in the color of the text and the colors in the image. You will change the color of the text later, so don't worry about that for the moment. If you wanted to make the text appear at the top of the image, you'd add padding to the bottom.

There are two important concepts involved in the style rule just created. First, background images can display partially or completely, depending on what your design goals are. Creative use of the ability to hide and reveal bits and pieces of background images can create what appear to be image rollovers, translucency, and other interesting visual effects.

TIP One advanced technique, known as "sliding doors," creates a tab-like menu with interesting effects from background image placement. It is described in an article in the online magazine A List Apart at http://www.alistapart.com/articles/slidingdoors/.

FIGURE 4.4
Only part of the
bridge appears.

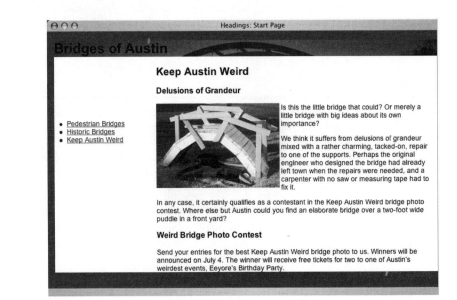

Second, elements can have padding. Padding can be placed around content in any combination on the top, right, bottom, and left sides as needed. Padding can be measured in pixels, ems, or percentages. If there is a background color or background image, the background shows through the padding.

Now, about that "Bridges of Austin" text sitting above the dark image. It is hard to see. You will use text-align: right; to move it to the right. You will use color: #D0B26F; (which was picked from the bridge image) to lighten up the text, and you will make it italics with font-style: italic;. Add these three declarations to the existing rule:

```
#siteName h1 {
   font-style: italic;
   color: #D0B26F;
   text-align: right;
   background-image: url(360bridge.jpg);
   padding: 120px;
}
```

TIP Image editing software programs such as Adobe Photoshop, Macromedia Fireworks, or Paint Shop Pro have tools that give you hexadecimal and RGB values for colors. There are also inexpensive software packages such as The Art Directors Toolkit at http://www.code-line.com/software /artdirectorstoolkit.html that help you find colors and color codes.

When you save the stylesheet and refresh the browser, you should see something similar to Figure 4.6.

FIGURE 4.5
Padding the h1 reveals the entire background image.

FIGURE 4.6
The lighter text
on the right

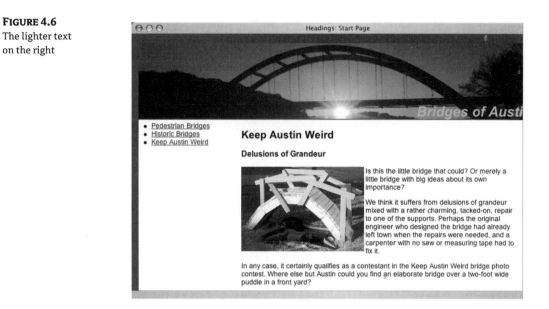

Headings with Class

Moving on to the h2 and h3 elements, you begin with a rule that will apply to every h2 on the page, regardless of class value.

```
h2 {
    font-size: 1.7em;
}
```

Since the h1 had a `font-size: 2em;` declaration, this rule will make the h2 slightly smaller in appearance than the h1.

To make the h3 elements slightly smaller, use this:

```
h3 {
    font-size: 1.5em;
}
```

The h2 and h3 elements are identified in the XHTML with three different class names because the design goal is to make them all look different. First is `pageName`. Since this is the title of the page, you will make it appear in small caps using `font-variant: small-caps;`. A value of `color: #3C4138;` will make it match the background color of the body. (You may have noticed that the background color of the body was selected to match a color in the bridge image.) Finally, you will use a 3-pixel-thick dotted border across the bottom as a visual separator. Type all this as a new rule:

```
.pageName {
  font-variant: small-caps;
  color: #3C4138;
  border-bottom: 3px dotted #3C4138;
}
```

NOTE   You could use h2.pageName as the selector for this rule, but since there is only one element on this particular page using class="pageName", there is no need to get that specific. A class can be used more than once, so if you wanted to do so, you could assign the class="pageName" attribute to other elements on the page.

Your browser should reveal the styled h2 looking similar to Figure 4.7.

New concepts in the style you just created include the fact that you can alter text to display as small caps with font-variant and, even more useful, elements can have border values. Borders go around the outer edge of the padding.

Like margin and padding, border can be added to elements on the top, right, bottom, or left. There are a number of border styles in addition to dotted, including solid, groove, ridge, and inset. Border widths can be expressed in pixels, ems, percentages, or with the keywords thin, medium, and thick.

Not all border styles are rendered properly by all the browsers yet. See Figure 4.8 for examples of several of the border styles with heading examples as interpreted by the Safari browser.

In fact, borders are so much fun, you will use one with the style rule for the feature heading. You will use a yellow accent image in the background, add a solid border on the right and bottom, and use a bit of padding to move the text away from the left edge.

The yellow background accent needs to repeat on the *y*-axis (vertically), and it needs to be moved completely over to the right side of the h2 box. Here is the complete rule:

```
.feature {
  background: url(yellowgradient.gif) repeat-y right;
  border-right: 1px solid #666;
  border-bottom: 1px solid #666;
  padding-left: 1em;
}
```

FIGURE 4.7
The h2 font size rule and
pageName class effect

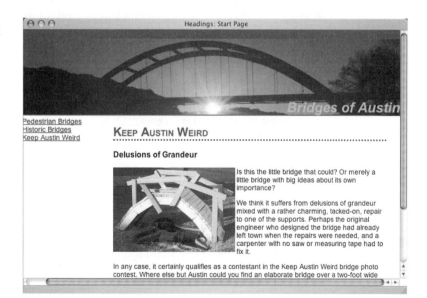

FIGURE 4.8
Some borders in 3px
black as examples of
border styles

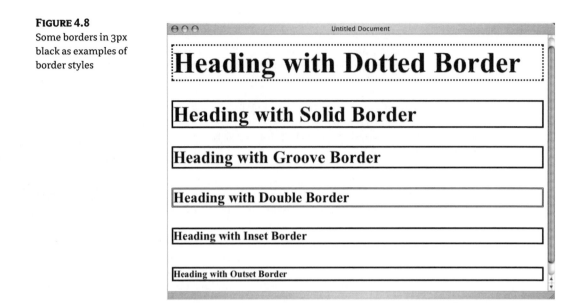

Type the new rule in the stylesheet, save it, and refresh (reload) to see something similar to Figure 4.9.

The last heading to style is h2 class="extra" element. You will use a background-image as an accent again, but this time it will be on the left. You need to align it horizontally in the center (this could be expressed as 50 percent). You do not want it to repeat. You also need 1em of padding on the left again, to move the text to make room for the accent graphic and to make this h2 element align nicely with the one above it. Here is the final class rule:

```
.extra {
  background: url(star.gif) no-repeat left center; padding-left: 1em;
}
```

Taken out of CSS shorthand, the rule would look like this:

```
.extra {
  background-image: url(star.gif);
  background-repeat: no-repeat;
  background-position: left center;
  padding-left: 1em;
}
```

The results, in either format, should look similar to Figure 4.10.

Compare Results

On the CD accompanying this book, the Chapter 4 folder contains two files showing how the completed XHTML page and CSS page should look: headings_finish.css and headings_finish.html. You can compare the changes you made to the starting versions with these finished versions.

TIP Typos are a problem when writing XHTML and CSS by hand. If something doesn't look the way you expect, check your typing for spacing, colons, semicolons, curly braces, and other syntax issues. If you are sure the part that doesn't seem to work is correct, work backward through the code looking for an error, perhaps a forgotten semicolon or a missing bracket. Often the error is somewhere before the place where things seemed to break down.

FIGURE 4.9

The feature class effect with a border only on the right and bottom

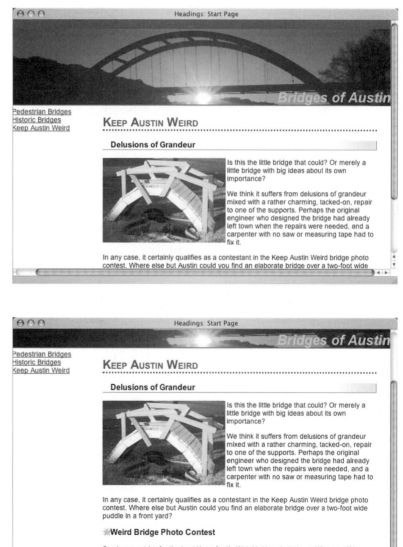

FIGURE 4.10

The extra class effect uses a star in the background with this header

The Box Model

In Chapters 3 and 4 we touched on `margin`, `padding`, and `border` properties. Let's take a look at the way these properties work together visually.

The W3C specification for how elements in a document display is referred to as a *visual formatting model*. Using this model, every element on the page generates a rectangular box. This box, called *the box model*, is represented in the diagram of Figure 4.11.

Each box has a content area (e.g., text, an image, etc.) and optional surrounding padding, border, and margin areas. Padding and margin are transparent, allowing the background or background image of the element (or parent elements) to show through. Values for each of these properties can be defined collectively or individually for top, right, bottom and left.

NOTE   A more in-depth discussion of the box model is available at `http://www.w3.org/TR/ REC-CSS2/box.html`. A 3-D version that also demonstrates the cascade is at `http://www.hicks-design.co.uk/journal/2004/05/3d_css_box_model/index.php`.

According to the W3C specifications, "The box width is given by the sum of the left and right margins, border, padding, and the content width. The height is given by the sum of the top and bottom margins, border, padding, and the content height." Understanding the box model will help you calculate how much space the various elements in your page design will fill.

FIGURE 4.11
The box model

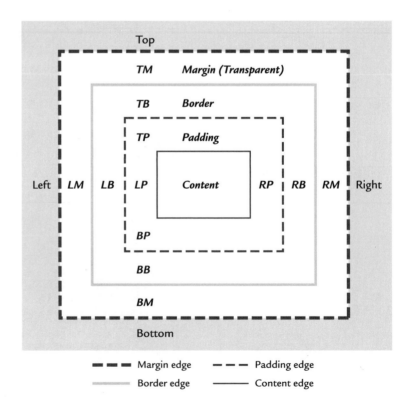

TIP   Internet Explorer for Windows (IE) does not calculate the size of the box according to the W3C specification mentioned here. A solution that lets you design for both IE6 and standards-compliant browsers, known as "the box model hack," is described at `http://www.positioniseverything.net/articles/box-model.html`. The box model hack allows you to write a style rule using two sets of measurements: one for standards-compliant browsers and one for Internet Explorer. If you use a correct DOCTYPE declaration, IE6 will interpret the box model according to the W3C specifications.

Real World Example

A List Apart (`www.alistapart.com`) is an online publication "for people who make websites." It is a real-world example of good use of headers to structure the information on a page. See Figure 4.12 for a look at Issue 185.

The page begins with a graphical banner. A menu bar is beneath the banner. The content area on the left is organized with h2 and h3 elements and paragraphs, giving it a simple and effective presentation that is intelligently marked up and easy to use. On the right, there are links to departments and items of particular interest.

Several years ago, A List Apart was one of the first websites to appear with a CSS-based layout. It is known for publishing articles that explore the cutting edge of what is possible with HTML, CSS, JavaScript, and PHP. It is owned by Jeffrey Zeldman, who was an early contributor to the Web Standards Project (`www.webstandards.org`) and is the author of *Designing with Web Standards*.

FIGURE 4.12
The main page of Issue 185 of A List Apart

© Copyright 1998–2004 A List Apart, "For People Who Make Websites" (alistapart.com)

CSS Properties for Headings

Table 4.1 summarizes the properties described in this chapter. Keep in mind that border and padding can be applied to all elements, not only to heading elements. Similarly, font-style, font-variant, and text-align values can be applied to any text, not only to heading elements.

TABLE 4.1:   Some Properties for the Heading Selectors: *h1, h2, h3, h4, h5, h6*

PROPERTIES	POSSIBLE VALUES
`border-width`, `border-top-width`, `border-right-width`, `border-bottom-width`, `border-left-width`	`thin`, `medium`, `thick`, *`<percentage>`*, *`<length>`*, `inherit`
`border-style`, `border-style-top`, `border-style-right`, `border-style-bottom`, `border-style-left`	`none`, `hidden`, `dotted`, `dashed`, `solid`, `double`, `groove`, `ridge`, `inset`, `outset`, `inherit`
`border-color`, `border-top-color`, `border-right-color`, `border-bottom-color`, `border-left-color`	*`<color>`*, `transparent`, `inherit`
`border`, `border-top`, `border-right`, `border-bottom`, `border-left`	Accepts shorthand declarations of width, style and color
`padding`, `padding-top`, `padding-right`, `padding-bottom`, `padding-left`	*`<percentage>`*, *`<length>`*, `inherit`
`font-style`	`italic`, `oblique`, `normal`, `inherit`
`font-variant`	`small-caps`, `normal`, `inherit`
`text-align`	`left`, `right`, `center`, `justify`, `inherit`

Challenge Yourself

Modify your work from Chapter 4 to achieve the following:

1. Add an h4 element to the XHTML page and write a style rule for it.

2. Change the position of the `star.gif` in the `.extra` rule.

3. Change the size of the h1 to 20px and the h2 to 18px.

4. Use padding or margin to move the words "Bridges of Austin" away from the right margin just a little bit.

5. Instead of `background-image` in the `.feature` class, try using `background-color` and different `border` styles.

Summary

In Chapter 4 you learned how to use previously discussed properties for `background` and new CSS properties for `border`, `padding`, `font-style`, `font-variant`, and `text-align` to create heading styles. You learned how to structure content using `id` and `class` attributes in the XHTML to create specific elements that could be styled with CSS.

In Chapter 5 you will learn more about using the `div` element and how it creates structure and allows you powerful options with contextual selectors.

Chapter 5

Page Divisions: *Div* for Structure and Layout

In terms of what you are learning in this book, structure is the XHTML and presentation is the CSS. The distinction between structure and presentation is basic to the successful integration of XHTML and CSS. If you take the raw text that will become the content of your website and mark it up with XHTML elements such as headings, paragraphs, lists, and block quotes, you are structuring your document. The XHTML elements carry structural logic with them. Well-structured pages can be displayed (or presented) in various ways in various Internet-capable devices and still be structurally sensible as headings, lists, or other content.

One element in particular, the div (for division), is what the W3C calls a generic mechanism for adding structure. A div, with a class or unique id attribute assigned to it, can assume a structural role on the page according to your particular needs. If you need a banner, a content area, a sidebar, and a footer, you can create that structure with div elements. Using id labels like "banner", "content", "sidebar", and "footer" with the div element gives you the ability to create page components that Jeffrey Zeldman refers to as "meta-structural" in his book, *Designing with Web Standards*.

Cleanly structured XHTML with well-planned meta-structural elements generate the power of CSS contextual selectors to create a multitude of presentation styles. First, write well-structured XHTML. Later, you can do anything you want to your page with CSS because the structural elements you need for your CSS selectors are built into the markup.

Learn the XHTML

XHTML is the successful result of the drive to remove presentational elements from the structure of a web page. You probably noted in previous chapters that XHTML by itself provides only a simple roster of headings, paragraphs, lists, and other very elemental building blocks. That simplicity of structure is what is needed to make content flow without stumbling blocks between devices such as web browsers, cell phones, and personal digital assistants.

You must first build your page with logical, structural XHTML markup. Standards expert Dan Cederholm sometimes refers to this concept as semantic markup, emphasizing the fact that tags should only be used for their logical, semantic purpose.

TIP   Dan Cederholm writes an informative site at www.simplebits.com and published a helpful handbook for web designers, *Web Standards Solutions: The Markup and Style Handbook.*

To make CSS really capable of meeting the demand for beautiful presentation, certain elements and attributes are needed in XHTML to allow the specificity of selectors and the inheritance of the cascade to shine in all its glory. You will use four of these markup elements and attributes to pry structure and presentation apart: `div`, `span`, `id`, and `class`. (You saw evidence of these in previous chapters.) First you will learn to use these elements and attributes to structure a page into CSS-readiness. Then you'll learn to position and lay out these elements.

div   Pages fall into logical divisions (divs), such as banners, navigation, subnavigation, search boxes, ads, content, and footers. By enclosing these page divisions in a generic container with a named `id`, e.g., `<div id="search">search content here</div>`, you create a unique structural element on the page that can be presented to the viewer using specific CSS rules. The `div` is a block-level element.

span   When the element you wish to style is inline, for example, just a few words in a sentence, the `span` element creates boundaries for the styling to apply to. Consider this example:

```
<p>Author <span class="author">Alice Walker</span> is our greatest living
writer. She is closely rivaled by the wonderful <span class="author">Elizabeth
Berg</span>.</p>
```

In that paragraph, only the words "Alice Walker" and "Elizabeth Berg" are styled according to whatever rules were specified for the `class` `"author"`. The two names have the same presentation values since they share the same `class` rule.

id   The `id` attribute, which *identifies* the element it's assigned to, does more than merely serve as a stylesheet selector, although that is certainly an important job. The `id` attribute can also be a target for a hypertext link or a referenced object in a script.

Remember that any `id` can only be used one time on a page; it must be unique. An `id` attribute must begin with a letter or an underscore and cannot contain blank spaces.

class   For elements that are not unique on the page—that is, styles you plan to use more than one time per page—there is the `class` attribute. A `class` attribute can be assigned to any element, either block or inline. The `class` attribute creates context on the page, so that the element can be presented to the viewer using specific CSS rules.

A `div` can be assigned to a `class`, a `span` can be assigned to a `class`, and any XHTML element, such a `p` or an `h3`, can be assigned to a `class`.

A `class` attribute must not contain any spaces, nor can it begin with an underscore. Both `class` and `id` values are case-sensitive. That is, in terms of case, there is a difference between "siteName" and "sitename" as an `id` or `class` name.

NOTE   While the ability to create classes is indeed a wonderful tool in CSS, don't get carried away with the notion and apply `class` attributes to every element. Remember, part of what you are hoping to accomplish is lean and clean XHTML. If you structure the page with appropriate and logical markup and use well-named `div` elements, you generally have sufficient context for most CSS selectors you will need.

Organizing Content Structurally

Let's revisit the page used in Chapter 4. It was presented to you with some prebuilt structure in the form of `div` elements. Let's look at each `div` to see what structural need it fills. Listing 5.1 is the complete page you saw before, with some added comments to note where `div` elements are closed.

LISTING 5.1: The Bridges of Austin Page with Some Comments Added

```
<!DOCTYPE html PUBLIC "-//W3C//DTD XHTML 1.0 Transitional//EN"
   "http://www.w3.org/TR/xhtml1/DTD/xhtml1-transitional.dtd">
<html xmlns="http://www.w3.org/1999/xhtml">
<head>
  <meta http-equiv="Content-Type" content="text/html; charset=iso-8859-1" />
  <title>Headings: Start Page</title>
</head>
<body>
<div id="container">
  <div id="siteName">
    <h1>Bridges of Austin</h1>
  <!--close siteName div-->
  </div>
  <div id="nav">
    <ul>
      <li><a href="#">Pedestrian Bridges</a></li>
      <li><a href="#">Historic Bridges</a></li>
      <li><a href="#">Keep Austin Weird</a></li>
    </ul>
  <!--close nav div-->
  </div>
  <div id="content">
    <h2>Keep Austin Weird</h2>
    <h3>Delusions of Grandeur</h3>
    <p><img src="delusions.jpg" alt="Delusions of Grandeur" width="250" height="167"
/>Is this the little bridge that could? Or merely a little bridge with big ideas
about its own importance?</p>
    <p>We think it suffers from delusions of grandeur mixed with a rather charming,
tacked-on, repair to one of the supports. Perhaps the original engineer who designed
the bridge had already left town when the repairs were needed, and a carpenter with
no saw or measuring tape had to fix it.</p>
    <p>In any case, it certainly qualifies as a contestant in the Keep Austin Weird
bridge photo contest. Where else but Austin could you find an elaborate bridge over
a two-foot wide puddle in a front yard?</p>
    <h3>Weird Bridge Photo Contest</h3>
    <p>Send your entries for the best Keep Austin Weird bridge photo to us. Winners
will be announced on July 4. The winner will receive free tickets for two to one of
Austin's weirdest events, Eeyore's Birthday Party.</p>
  <!--close content div-->
  </div>
<!--close container div-->
</div>
</body>
</html>
```

The first div you see is `<div id="container">`, which encloses everything on the page. This div was styled with a white background color. If the page had a different body background color, or if the text on the page was a different color, this structural device might not be needed. Notice that the value given to the id attribute for this div is a reflection of its purpose in the overall structure of the page.

TIP   Naming elements with descriptive id attribute values that reflect structural purpose is a good practice. Pick names that will hold up over time or as your site changes. If you come back to a site weeks or months after designing it and want to update or change the style rules, well-named id attributes can be very helpful. Names such as banner, header, siteName, mainnav, subnav, search, contact, footer, ad, content, and blogdate are examples of IDs that would be meaningful later.

Next you see `<div id="siteName">`. In Chapter 4, you wrote a style rule for the h1 element in the div siteName. You didn't make use of this element in any other way, but I wanted it there as an example of good structure. You could have used it; as noted in Chapter 4, the background image of the bridge that you used in the h1 element could have been used in the div siteName instead. In addition to the h1 element in the siteName div, there might also be other relevant information such as contact information or "About Us" links.

Moving on through the preceding example page, you see `<div id="nav">`. This div encloses a list of links for navigating the site. (In Chapter 4, the prebuilt CSS placed the nav on the left side of the page below the siteName.) By creating an element on the page called nav, you can take advantage of the CSS rules of specificity to write style rules especially for this unique element.

TIP   When you reach Chapter 7 and Chapter 9 you are going to write more style rules for the list of links in the div id="nav" section of this page.

The final div on the page is `<div id="content">`, which is well named because it holds the page's main content.

To *div* or Not to *div*

The div, class, and span elements should not replace logically structured XHTML elements.

Look at `<div id="content">` again:

```
<div id="content">
  <h2>Keep Austin Weird </h2>
  <h3>Delusions of Grandeur</h3>
  <p><img src="delusions.jpg" alt="Delusions of Grandeur" width="250" height="167"
/> Is this the little bridge that could? Or merely a little bridge with big ideas
about its own importance?</p>
  [...]
  <h3>Weird Bridge Photo Contest</h3>
  <p>Send your entries for the best Keep Austin Weird bridge photo to us. Winners
will be announced on July 4. The winner will receive free tickets for two to one of
Austin's weirdest events, Eeyore's Birthday Party.</p>
</div>
```

There are h2, h3, and p elements in content that structure the information. Additionally, the elements are contained in a div structure with the specific id "content". The XHTML structure is apparent in Figure 5.1.

CSS-Readiness

An example of a CSS-ready page can be found in the XHTML file for the CSS Zen Garden at www.csszen-garden.com. CSS Zen Garden is a web site that invites users to submit stylesheets which may be used to present the page in various designs. Look for the Download the Sample html File link. After you have the HTML page open in the browser, use the browser's View menu to view the source of the page. You will see the "Swiss army knife" of XHTML pages, ready for multiple uses by many different stylesheets and allowing for rules of many degrees of specificity. People who submit to CSS Zen Garden are not allowed to change the XHTML file in any way; they can only submit a stylesheet. Therefore CSS Zen Garden creator Dave Shea has created markup that allows for maximum flexibility. In doing that, he had to make some concessions to lean and clean structural markup.

For your own designs, you don't need to add redundancy like that at CSS Zen Garden. Plan your design, determine the needed elements to structure your page, and build your XHTML for that. Keep in mind that one of the reasons for using CSS is to keep XHTML files lean and mean so they download quickly.

Based on the resounding success of CSS Zen Garden in proving that CSS can create beautiful design, I was inspired to create a similar (but less complex) type of page for readers of this book. It is on the accompanying CD in a folder called styleme. When you finish the book, be sure to give yourself the challenge and fun of designing a stylesheet for the styleme.html page.

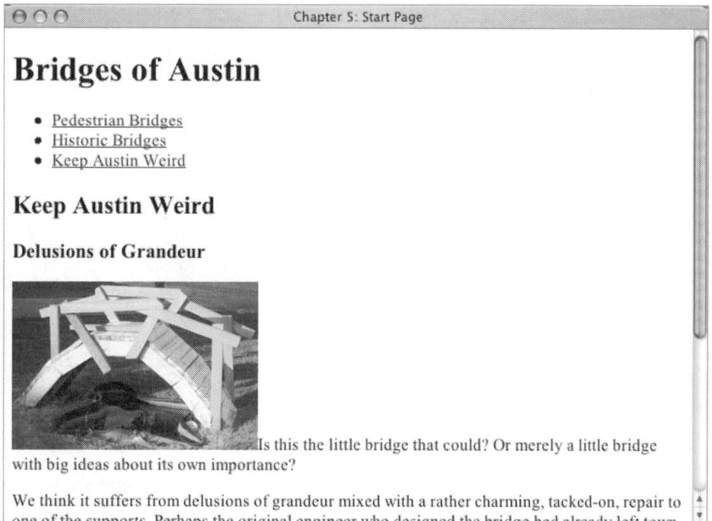

FIGURE 5.1
Page structure revealed

As you can see in Figure 5.1, the generic div that groups these structural elements in a container called "content" does not appear as an element. You may be wondering why it is needed if it isn't a visible part of the document structure. It is needed because it is part of the markup that makes the page ready for CSS. Building pages with div, span, id and class involves finding related elements that serve a "structural purpose" on your page (such as a list of links) and wrapping them into a unit with a div and/or span element. This adds a level of context to the possible CSS selectors that might be used to style this page. For example, while you could write a CSS rule for the selector p, you can use the element `"content"` to write a different CSS rule for the selector `#content p`. While the first selector, p, would style every paragraph on the page, the second selector, `#content p`, would style only the paragraphs that were descendants of the "content" div. The ability to target selectors that appear only in a specific context is the benefit of using carefully planned `div`, `span`, `id`, and `class` elements and attributes.

Learn the CSS

One of the most important ways CSS is used with `div` elements involves positioning. You need to move the following files from the Chapter 5 folder on the CD to the `Integrated HTML and CSS` folder on your computer to get ready to do some work with positioning:

```
360bridge.jpg
ch5_start.css
ch5_start.html
delusions.jpg
```

You should recognize these files from Chapter 4, but there are some differences. In the XHTML page, two of the headings were changed to `h3` elements to improve the structure. Now the site name is an `h1`, the page name is an `h2` in its own `div`, and the two subheads on the page are `h3` elements.

In the CSS file, the bridge image in the site name is now a background for `div id="siteName"` rather than for the `h1`. The rules for the `h1` have changed just a bit, as well. Backgrounds and borders have been removed from the heading styles because they will detract from what you will be doing with positioning in this chapter. To begin, the page looks something like Figure 5.2.

Open `ch5_start.css` in your text editor and let the positioning begin! You will use absolute positioning, relative positioning, and layouts based on float, margin, and z-index in the following pages.

FIGURE 5.2
The Chapter 5 Start Page

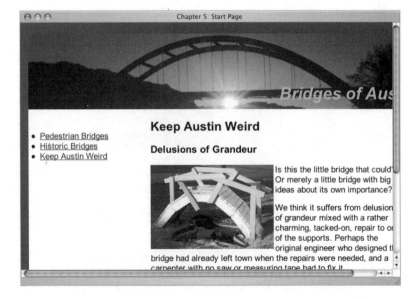

Absolute Positioning

The normal behavior of the browser (for English) is to read the document from left to right and top to bottom. This is referred to as *document flow*. An element can be removed from that normal flow with the CSS properties position or float.

There are several concepts to understand regarding *absolute positioning*. An absolutely positioned element is removed from the document flow and positioned with regard to the element's *containing block*. I will get to the concept of a containing block in just a bit, but first let's see how to write the CSS position rule.

The only element with absolute positioning in your document is <div id="nav">. The CSS rule positioning this element is

```
#nav {
    position: absolute; top: 200px; left: 0px;
    width: 150px;
}
```

In this rule, the position property is given the value absolute. That means that no matter what else is happening on the page, this element will go in the specified exact position within its containing block. You specify the position with a measurement from the top and left of the containing block. In this rule, the nav element is placed exactly 200 pixels from the top and 0 pixels from the left.

TIP The measurement of distance from the top and left could also be expressed in ems or percentages.

The containing block could be another element in the document or the *initial containing block*, which in most browsers is the html element.

The div element with an ID of nav is not nested in any other element on the page, other than the initial containing block. By positioning it absolutely, you have removed it for presentation from the normal document flow, or the order the elements appear in the XHTML. To get a true understanding of the fact that absolute positioning removes the element from the document flow, move the entire nav element somewhere else in the document flow and see what happens.

Open ch5_start.html in your text editor. The complete body element is shown in Listing 5.2.

LISTING 5.2: The *ch5_start.html* Page *body* Element

```
<body>
  <div id="container">
    <div id="siteName">
      <h1>Bridges of Austin</h1>
    </div>

    <div id="nav">
      <ul>
        <li><a href="#">Pedestrian Bridges</a></li>
        <li><a href="#">Historic Bridges</a></li>
        <li><a href="#">Keep Austin Weird</a></li>
      </ul>
```

```
      </div>

      <div id="pageName">
        <h2>Keep Austin Weird</h2>
      </div>

      <div id="content">
        <h3>Delusions of Grandeur</h3>
        <p><img src="delusions.jpg" alt="Delusions of Grandeur" width="250"
height="167" /> Is this the little bridge that could? Or merely a little bridge
with big ideas about its own importance? </p>
        <p>We think it suffers from delusions of grandeur mixed with a rather
charming, tacked-on, repair to one of the supports. Perhaps the original engineer
who designed the bridge had already left town when the repairs were needed, and a
carpenter with no saw or measuring tape had to fix it. </p>
        <p>In any case, it certainly qualifies as a contestant in the Keep Austin
Weird bridge photo contest. Where else but Austin could you find an elaborate
bridge over a two-foot wide puddle in a front yard? </p>
        <h3>Weird Bridge Photo Contest</h3>
        <p>Send your entries for the best Keep Austin Weird bridge photo to us.
Winners will be announced on July 4. The winner will receive free tickets for two
to one of Austin's weirdest events, Eeyore's Birthday Party. </p>

      </div>
    </div>
</body>
```

Grab the entire nav element and cut and paste it just before the last closing div tag, so that it appears in the document *after* the close of the `<div id="content">` element. Now the last part of the page should look like this (some of the text has been snipped for brevity):

```
      <div id="content">
        <h3>Delusions of Grandeur</h3>
        <p><img src="delusions.jpg" alt="Delusions of Grandeur" width="250"
height="167" /> Is this the little bridge ... </p>
        <h3>Weird Bridge Photo Contest</h3>
        <p>Send your entries ... </p>
      </div>

      <div id="nav">
        <ul>
          <li><a href="#">Pedestrian Bridges</a></li>
          <li><a href="#">Historic Bridges</a></li>
          <li><a href="#">Keep Austin Weird</a></li>
        </ul>
      </div>

    </div>
```

Save the page and look at it in the browser. Since the absolute positioning of the nav element placed it 200px from the top and 0px from the left of its containing block, you should see no difference whatever from when the nav element was higher up in the document flow, because position: absolute; removed this element from the document flow, as shown in Figure 5.3.

However, if you remove the link to the stylesheet and look at this document without any style rules attached, the nav element appears at the end of the document, just as it is now in the document flow, as shown in Figure 5.4.

FIGURE 5.3
Effect of moving the nav element in the document flow

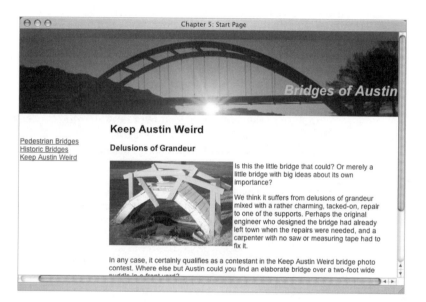

FIGURE 5.4
The document with no style rules attached

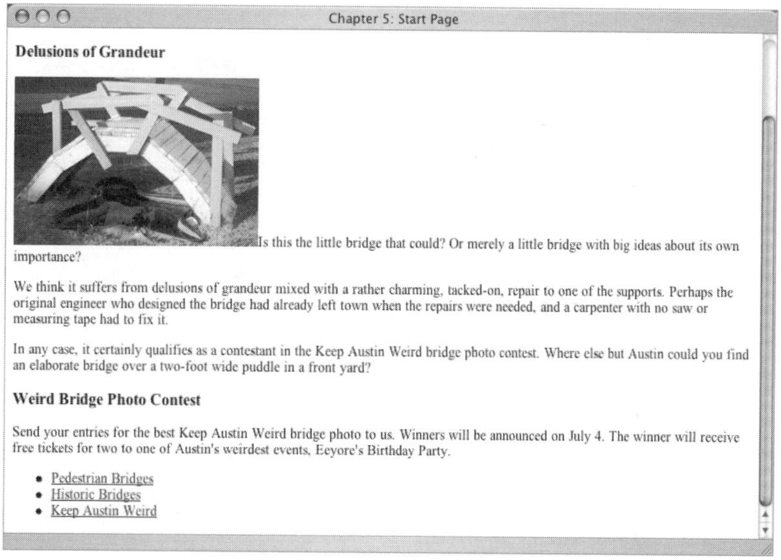

There might be situations where presenting the links at the end of the content, as in Figure 5.4, would be desirable in terms of usability and accessibility. With absolute positioning, the links can appear visually anywhere you want while fitting into the document flow in the most accessible position as well.

Relative Positioning

The chief distinction between absolute and relative position is that an element with `position: relative;` is positioned in the normal document flow and then offset by whatever value is specified from that normal position. Change the CSS rule for #nav to this:

```
#nav {
    position: relative; top: 15px; left: 10px;
    width: 150px;
}
```

With the nav element in the document flow after the content element, nav is now 15 pixels down from its normal position after content, and it's 10 pixels to the left of its normal position. It is in danger of disappearing completely! See Figure 5.5, which zooms in on the position of the nav element.

NOTE   If you increased the offset to top: 50px; for the #nav rule, the element would be outside of the normal viewing area, although it would still be in the document itself. This is not a good idea for the page navigation, but it is an illustration of the fact that elements can be hidden outside of viewing range in this way.

Since you don't really want the nav element there, change the stylesheet rule back to the original values:

```
#nav {
    position: absolute; top: 200px; left: 0px;
    width: 150px;
}
```

FIGURE 5.5
Relative positioning of
the nav element

bridge had already
carpenter with no

In any case, it cer
Weird bridge phot
elaborate bridge o

Weird Bridge

Send your entries
Winners will be ar
tickets for two to
Party.

- Pedestrian Bridges
- Historic Bridges
- Keep Austin Weird

Fixed Positioning

With `position: fixed;` the element stays fixed in place, even if you scroll down the page. It is fixed in relation to the user's *viewport*, or the view in the browser window. You are going to abuse the poor nav element again, but first you need to add more length to the XHTML page so you can scroll down. Just copy some of the text on the page and paste it back in to make a few more paragraphs of text and create a longer page.

Then change the style rule for #nav to:

```
#nav {
    position: fixed; top: 200px; left: 0px;
    width: 150px;
}
```

Remember, you need to save the `ch5_start.html` page as well as the CSS page, because you made changes to both of them. When the page is reloaded in the browser, you won't see any change until you start to scroll down the page. The nav element stays fixed in position in relation to the viewport window, no matter how far you scroll down the page. See the sidebar "`position: fixed` and Internet Explorer 6" for information about Internet Explorer 6 and fixed positioning. See Figure 5.6 for an example of the nav element when using `position: fixed`.

NOTE Page and element background images can also be given `position: fixed;` so that the view scrolls over an unmoving background.

With fixed positioning, if you move the scroll bar up and down really fast, the browser may struggle to keep up with you, and you might see a bit of jumping around. However, if you were actually reading down this page in a normal fashion and scrolling at a more sedate speed, the nav element would stay in place without any unpleasant effect.

FIGURE 5.6
The nav in
`position: fixed;`

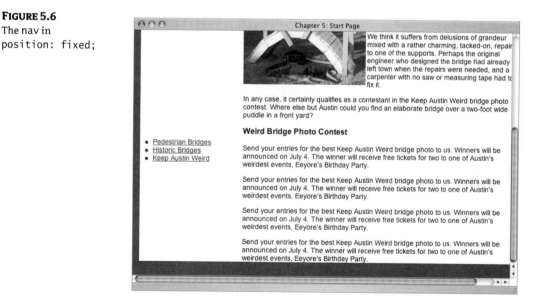

***POSITION: FIXED* AND INTERNET EXPLORER 6**

Fixed positioning does not work in Internet Explorer 6, but there are ways to make it behave. Several are mentioned here:

    css-discuss.incutio.com/?page=FixedLayouts

The simplest solution involves using what is called the "star html hack." A style rule is written for a selector such as `* html .fixed`. This selector is only used by Internet Explorer. In a stylesheet it could look something like this:

    * html .fixed {

    position: fixed;

    }

This rule would be written in addition to the normal style rules discussed previously for the element using fixed positioning. Since this example uses a class called `fixed`, that class would have to be assigned to the element using fixed positioning so that it would work in IE 6.

There is also a `position` value called `static`. Since using `static` amounts to the normal positioning in the normal document flow, you aren't going to spend any time working with it in this book. You might have need for `position: static` if an element you wanted to present in the normal document flow was inheriting some other positioning scheme from the element containing it. In such a case, you might need to explicitly set the `position` attribute back to the default `static` value.

Using Margins to Arrange Content

You are already working with an element that uses margin for layout. Do you know which one it is? If you said either content or pageName, you were right. Look at the #content selector first. Here's the rule:

```
#content {
  margin: 0 2em 2em 15em;
  background-color: #FFFFFF;
}
```

As you recall, values are set top, right, bottom, left, so this rule is putting 15 ems of margin on the left side of the content element (as well as 2 ems each at the right and bottom). This explains why there is such an expanse of unused white space in which to place the nav element and why the page appears to have two columns.

Let's change it around so that 15 ems are on the right and only 2 ems are on the left, like this:

```
#content {
    margin: 0 15em 2em 2em;
}
```

Save that and look in the browser. Oops, you have a problem. The page now looks like Figure 5.7.

Once again, you need to go back to your #nav selector. The rule puts it in a specific position, even if there is other text there, too. There are very good design reasons to sometimes stack the contents of one element right on top of the contents of another element (see the section on z-index below), but not in this case. In this case, you need to move the two elements apart. Keep in mind that the "container" div is set to 800px in width, so a position 600px from the left should be about right for this page. To move the nav element to the right side of the page, change the rule to this:

```
#nav {
    position: absolute; top: 200px; left: 600px;
    width: 150px;
}
```

The layout becomes usable once again. You should see something like Figure 5.8 in your browser.

For now, leave the page positioned as it is. You will take a side trip to style the #pageName h2 selector and come back to positioning in a bit.

FIGURE 5.7
content and
nav collide

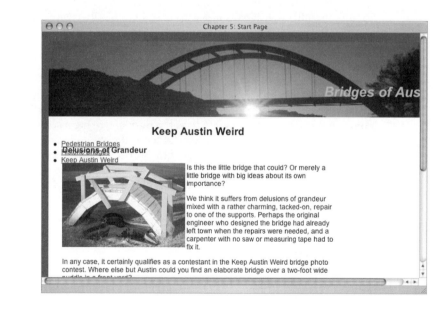

FIGURE 5.8
nav moves to the right

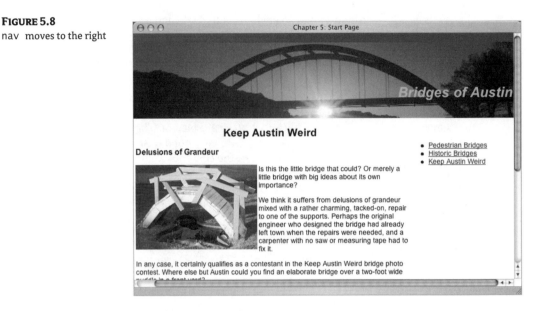

Using Classes to Style Headings

That h2 element that gives the page name looks a little lost with the page in this arrangement, so let's give it some attention. First, remove the margin values that were presenting pageName in line with the position the content element used to have. The new rule should be:

```
#pageName {
    margin: 0;
}
```

Now write a rule specifically selecting this h2 element. I thought it would be pretty to match the colors in the siteName text, align it on the right above the navigation, use small-caps, and create a 1-pixel solid border across the bottom. Of these, the only rule that you haven't seen before is letter-spacing: 0.4em;. The normal amount of letter-spacing is 0, so any value larger than 0 adds space between the letters. This letter-spacing value could be expressed in ems, pixels, or various lengths much more suited to print such as points, picas, and in (inches). Here is the complete new rule to add to your stylesheet:

```
#pageName h2 {
    font-size: 1.2em;
    font-variant: small-caps;
    color: #D0B26F;
    letter-spacing: 0.4em;
    text-align: right;
    border-bottom: 1px solid #D0B26F;
}
```

TIP   Remember that using relative measures, such as ems or percentages, means that if the user increases the text size using the browser controls, everything with a relative measure will increase. If letter-spacing is measured in ems, as in this example, increasing the browser's text size will also increase the letter-spacing. Therefore, you need to consider using letter-spacing with absolute measures such as pixels when designing your pages.

With these two changes to pageName saved, the result should look like Figure 5.9 in your browser.

Using *float* to Arrange Content

You may have noticed that the example CSS file has been using float since Chapter 4. Here is the relevant selector with the float attribute:

```
#content img {
  float: left;
  margin-right: 3px;
  margin-bottom: 3px;
}
```

This rule makes any image in the content element float to the left. What does that mean? Well, when an element is floated, other content flows or wraps around it. If an element is floated to the left, then other content flows around it on the right. In order to fully understand that statement, let's examine how the image and text display without floating.

TIP   There are many online resources to help you understand floats. Two excellent resources are Containing Floats by Eric Meyer at http://www.complexspiral.com/publications /containing-floats and Floatutorial at http://css.maxdesign.com.au/floatutorial/.

FIGURE 5.9
The h2 gets a much-needed makeover.

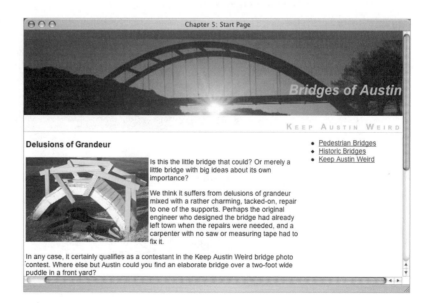

Use CSS comments to hide the float attribute briefly, like this:

```
#content img {
  /*float: left;*/
  margin-right: 3px;
  margin-bottom: 3px;
}
```

By enclosing the float attribute and value in CSS comments, the browser will ignore that rule, and the image will not be floated. If you look at the page in the browser, you should see the arrangement shown in Figure 5.10.

The image element is inserted on the page at the beginning of a paragraph element, like this:

```
<p><img src="delusions.jpg" alt="Delusions of Grandeur" width="250" height="167"
/>Is this the little bridge...
```

NOTE   Some attributes used here haven't been explained yet, but all will be revealed in Chapter 8.

Essentially, in Figure 5.10, the image and the text in the paragraph are sitting on the same baseline. (If you comment out the margin-bottom: 3px; rule, you can see this relationship even more clearly.) The browser is doing as instructed, since the image is *in* the paragraph, but it looks like some sort of mistake.

For comparison purposes and to further clarify how the image would look without any float, move the image element out of the paragraph like this:

```
<h3>Delusions of Grandeur</h3>
<img src="delusions.jpg" alt="Delusions of Grandeur" width="250" height="167" />
<p>Is this the little bridge...
```

Your results should look similar to Figure 5.11.

FIGURE 5.10
The image with no float value applied

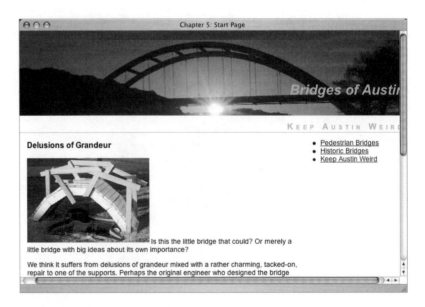

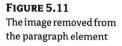

FIGURE 5.11
The image removed from the paragraph element

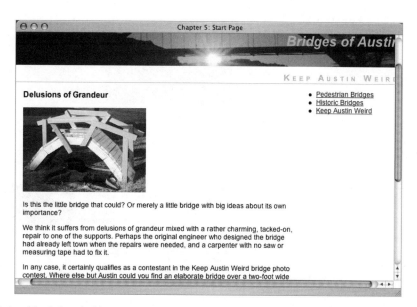

Since a paragraph is a block-level element, it automatically begins on a new line under the image element. While it no longer looks like a mistake, it isn't doing what you want, which is for the text to flow around the image.

Leave the image element where it is now, and go back to the stylesheet. You will make some changes to the `#content img` selector. Let's try out `float: right;`, and change the margins just a little so the text isn't bumping into the image on the left side. The new rule is

```
#content img {
    float: right;
    margin-right: 0px;
    margin-bottom: 3px;
    margin-left: 3px;
}
```

Now the image should be on the right, with the text flowing all around it on the left, as shown in Figure 5.12.

Leave the stylesheet as it is now, and move the image one more time, in order to see what happens when you float it midpage. Cut and paste to place the `img` element just under the second h3, like this:

```
<h3>Weird Bridge Photo Contest</h3>
<img src="delusions.jpg" alt="Delusions of Grandeur" width="250" height="167" />
<p> Send your entries...
```

Your browser view should look something like Figure 5.13.

FIGURE 5.12
Using float:right

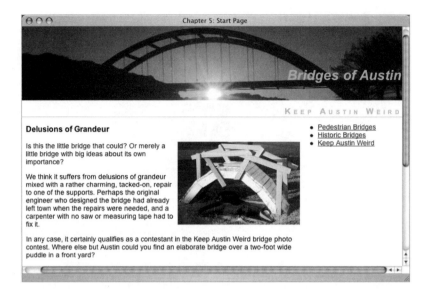

FIGURE 5.13
Image in midpage

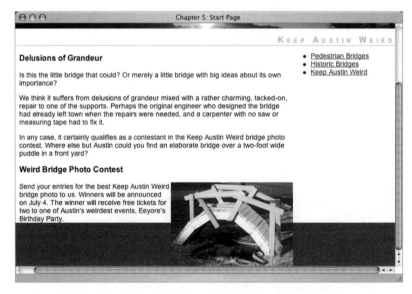

You can see in Figure 5.13 that there is a problem. Before you finish up with the img element, take a look at a solution to the problem with the image appearing to extend beyond the content as in Figure 5.13.

***CLEAR* TO THE RESCUE**

Sometimes when using float, elements and attributes such as background-color, content, and other elements do not extend beyond the floated element but instead stop short. Your page is having this problem. Should you experience this problem with floated elements, the solution is the clear property.

The possible declarations for the `clear` property are `clear: left;`, `clear: right;`, or `clear: both;`. Using `clear:left;` or `clear: right;` forces your content past anything floating on the left or on the right, respectively. Using `clear: both;` forces material past anything floating on *either* side.

The `clear` property can be assigned to elements such as `img`, `h3`, and `div`. In a situation where you are forcing the background color to extend past the floated element, a common solution involves creating a `class` declaration and using it in a `div`. First create the new `class` in the stylesheet. Use an explanatory name, such as `clearer`.

```
.clearer {
  clear: both;
}
```

To do this on the example page, you can add an element (using the `class` `.clearer`) at the end of the `content` element. Add `<div class="clearer"></div>` to the XHTML like this:

```
<p>Send your entries for the best Keep Austin Weird bridge photo to us. Winners
will be announced on July 4. The winner will receive free tickets for two to one of
Austin's weirdest events, Eeyore's Birthday Party.</p>
  <div class="clearer"></div>
<!--close the content div-->
</div>
```

With the `div` in place, even though it contains no content, the `clear` property will be applied, and you should see a result similar to Figure 5.14. With no content, this element is not an example of good XHTML structure, however.

NOTE An explanation of a way to clear floats without structural markup is at `http://position-iseverything.net/easyclearing.html`. It uses a technique beyond the basics described in this book that involves using the pseudo element `:after` and `visibility: hidden`.

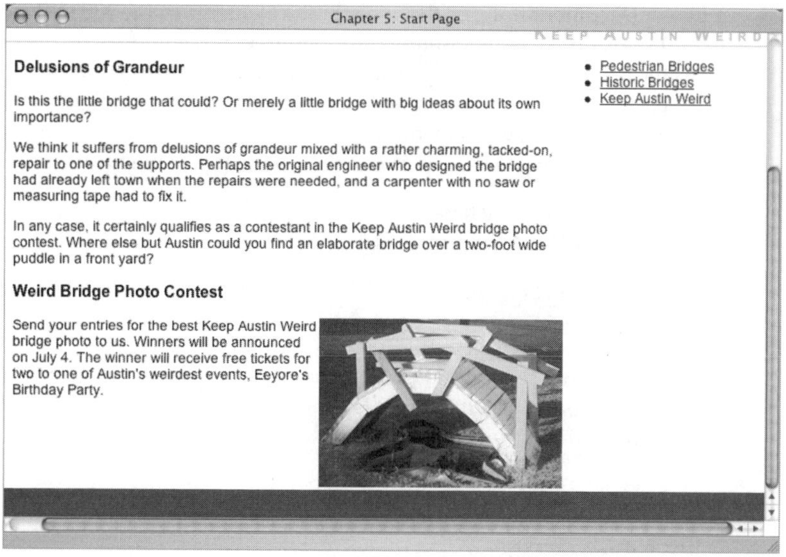

FIGURE 5.14
The effect of the `clear` property

FINISHING UP WITH THE *IMG* ELEMENT

The text wrap with the image on the right looks a bit messy because of the ragged right alignment of the text in the paragraph, so before you move on to floating elements other than img elements, let's restore the image to its original float: left; stylesheet rule:

```
#content img {
  float: left;
  margin-right: 3px;
  margin-bottom: 3px;
}
```

Also, restore the img element to its place in the document flow immediately following the first h3 element:

```
<h3>Delusions of Grandeur</h3>
<img src="delusions.jpg" alt="Delusions of Grandeur" width="250" height="167" />
<p> Is this the little bridge...
```

What Else Floats?

In versions of HTML before CSS came along, the *only* thing that could be floated were images. This was accomplished by using the align attribute to wrap the text on the right or the left of the img element:

```
<img src="delusions.jpg" align="left">
<img src="delusions.jpg" align="right">
```

But with CSS, oh my, you can float anything!

Many popular sites have layouts based on float. Let's try it. Get rid of the layout based on position: absolute; and switch to a float layout.

Document flow, or the order of the elements in the XHTML source, does make a difference with float, unlike with absolute positioning. When you float any element, the accompanying portions of the document flow wrap around it. Therefore, the first thing you need to do is move the nav element back up before the "content" element in the document flow so that the material in "content" wraps around the "nav" element.

Cut and paste the "nav" element to the top of the file, immediately following the pageName div:

```
<div id="pageName">
  <h2>Keep Austin Weird</h2>
</div>
<div id="nav">
  <ul> [...]
```

There are several stages involved in getting the layout to have the look you want, and some of the in-between steps will present layout problems. Learning to solve those problems will help you understand float.

Look at the existing #nav selector:

```
#nav {
  position: absolute; top: 200px; left: 600px;
  width: 150px;
}
```

To lay this out on the right using float, remove the position, top, and left declarations. Add a float: right; declaration, like this:

```
#nav {
  width: 150px;
  float: right;
}
```

The nav element already had a width declaration, which is needed. When using float, always include a width declaration as well. If you do not give a width value, the browser may assume it has a value of zero, which is not what you want.

The result should put the nav element on the right side of the page, but it is extending partially out of the container. A zoomed-in view of the top right corner would look something like Figure 5.15.

You now know several ways you could nudge the nav element a bit, including with padding and margin. Let's use a little margin-right:

```
#nav {
  width: 150px;
  float: right;
  margin-right: 3em;
}
```

A zoomed-in view of the top right corner of the page shows the margin-right had the desired effect, as in Figure 5.16.

FIGURE 5.15
The nav with
float: right;

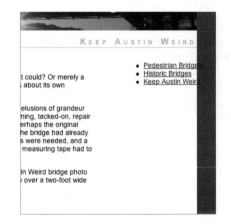

FIGURE 5.16
Nudge with
`margin-right`

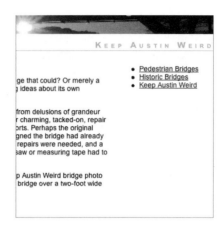

Why Not Left?

Floating the nav element on the right was easy enough. Try it on the left, too. Change the #nav selector rule:

```
#nav {
  width: 150px;
  float: left;
  margin-right: 3em;
}
```

Keep in mind where the `content` element is positioned right now. The last time you touched it, it had a large `margin` on the right like this.

```
#content {
  margin: 0 15em 2em 2em;
}
```

With these two rules in place, the `content` should flow around the nav in a manner exactly like you saw early in this discussion of `float` when you were floating the image of the deluded little bridge, as in Figure 5.17.

That makes the text hard to read because it is hard for the eye to follow, and there is all that silly looking white space on the right. The way it looked in the beginning (Figure 5.3) would be easier to read and more balanced, because the content had a nicely defined left edge. If you recall, that effect was created with this CSS rule:

```
#content {
  margin: 0 2em 2em 15em;
}
```

If you change the #content selector back to that earlier style, you should see something like Figure 5.18.

FIGURE 5.17
nav at `float: left;`

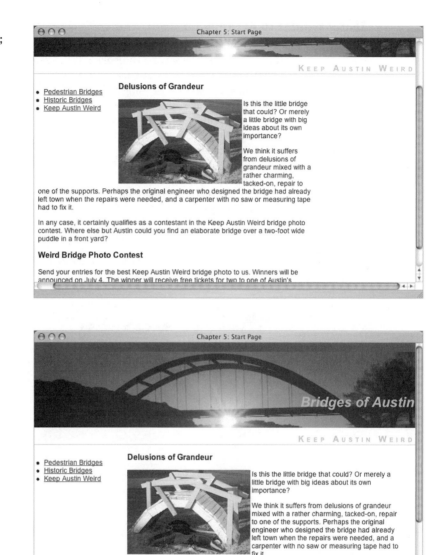

FIGURE 5.18
Layout combining
float and margin

The layout in Figure 5.17 uses a combination of `float: left;` for the nav element and `margin-left: 15em;` for the content element to create a layout that you are going to give a much deserved rest. The final layout scheme you will use is `z-index`.

Using *z-index* to Arrange Content

Basically, z-index is the third dimension of a web page. One dimension is the x-axis, which places elements on the horizontal axis. The second dimension is the y-axis, which places elements on the vertical axis. The final dimension is front-to-back, or z-index.

Some of the most interesting reasons for using z-index rely on JavaScript (or some similar scripting language) to do things such as make one element visible and another hidden when the user clicks a link or rolls over an element with a pointing device or mouse. Since explaining scripting languages is beyond the scope of this book, I will not do anything like that here, but you will take a look at a simple page that will help you understand z-index.

You need to move two files from the CD into your Integrated HTML and CSS folder: Ch5_z-index.html and z-index.css.

Open them both in your text editor, and open Ch5_z-index.html in the browser. In the browser, you should see something like Figure 5.19.

The XHTML page is very simple (Listing 5.3).

FIGURE 5.19
The starting Ch5_
z-index.html file

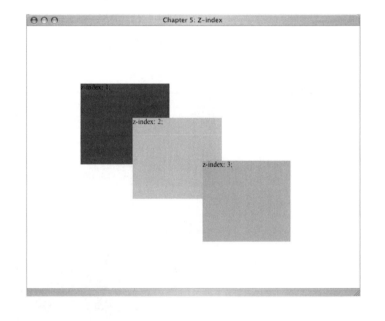

LISTING 5.3:   A Simple Page Demonstrating *z-index* for Layout

```
<!DOCTYPE html PUBLIC "-//W3C//DTD XHTML 1.0 Transitional//EN"
    "http://www.w3.org/TR/xhtml1/DTD/xhtml1-transitional.dtd">
<html xmlns="http://www.w3.org/1999/xhtml">
<head>
<meta http-equiv="Content-Type" content="text/html; charset=iso-8859-1" />
<title>Chapter 5: Z-index</title>
<link href="z-index.css" rel="stylesheet" type="text/css" />
</head>
```

```
<body>
<div id="one">z-index: 1; </div>
<div id="two">z-index: 2; </div>
<div id="three">z-index: 3; </div>
</body>
</html>
```

The XHTML page contains three div elements, each with a bit of text giving you a visual clue as to the z-index value of the div. The page is already linked to a stylesheet. The stylesheet contains the rules shown in Listing 5.4.

LISTING 5.4:   The Stylesheet Rules Used with *Ch5_z-index.html*

```
#one {
position:absolute; left:111px; top:114px;
width:180px; height:160px;
z-index:1;
background: #F00;
}

#two {
position:absolute; left:217px; top:182px;
width:180px; height:160px;
z-index:2;
background: #FC0;
}

#three {
position:absolute; left:358px; top:267px;
width:180px; height:160px;
z-index:3;
background: #6CC;
}
```

You already understand most of these terms; the only new CSS property for you to learn here is z-index. An element with a higher z-index is closer to the viewer. So the element with z-index: 1 is the furthest back, the element with z-index: 2 overlaps that and is closer to the viewer, and the element with z-index: 3 is the closest of the three. This concept is often referred to as *stacking order*, with the highest z-index value being on the top of the stack.

In the stylesheet, change the values for the position of all three elements to be exactly the same:

```
position: absolute; left: 111px; top: 114px;
```

With all three elements in the same position on the page, which one should you see? The answer is element three, the one with the highest z-index, as shown in Figure 5.20.

Move elements two and three a few pixels, as shown here:

```
#two {
position:absolute; left:116px; top:118px; [...]

#three {
position:absolute; left:120px; top:122px; [...]
```

With this shift of a few pixels down and to the right, you get a visual appearance similar to what you see in Figure 5.21.

FIGURE 5.20
Three elements in the same absolute position

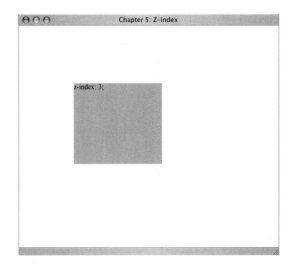

FIGURE 5.21
Elements shifted down and to the right

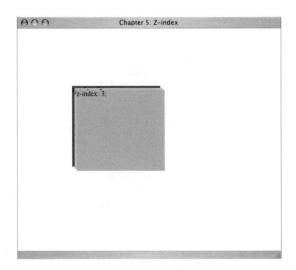

JavaScript and the Visibility Property

Visibility is a CSS property often used with stacked elements. Its possible values are `visibility: visible;` or `visibility: hidden;`. As you would guess, when the declaration is `visible`, the element can be seen, and when it's `hidden`, the element cannot be seen.

On the example page, if selectors #two and #three were set to `visibility: hidden;` you would see element `div id="one"`, even if all three elements were stacked in the same position, as in Figure 5.11.

Without JavaScript to switch visibility from `visible` to `hidden` or from `hidden` to `visible` based on some user action such as clicking a link, there isn't much use for this property at this point in your learning.

When you are ready to learn JavaScript, there is a site called JavaScript Source (`http://java-script.internet.com/`) that offers hundreds of free scripts with instructions about how to add them to the page. There are also many excellent books on the topic, including *JavaScript for the World Wide Web: Visual QuickStart Guide* by Tom Negrino and Dori Smith and *Mastering JavaScript: Premium Edition* by James Jaworski (Sybex, 2001).

By using `z-index` to overlap part or all of an element you can create interesting visual effects. Adjusting the position a few pixels in a different direction could create a look like a drop shadow. As I mention in the sidebar "JavaScript and the Visibility Property," `z-index` is seldom used, but when it is, it's usually with a JavaScript to hide or reveal elements stacked in the same position on a page.

Values with `z-index` don't have to start from 1 and progress in unbroken order. The elements in this example could have had `z-index` values of 10, 20, and 30, or 3, 7, 9, and the results would have been the same. If you have several stacked elements on a page and want to add a new one that you are sure will be at the very top of the stacking order, you can give it some high `z-index` value like 100.

TIP   Websites offering free CSS layouts using various positioning schemes include `http://www.glish.com/css`, `www.positioniseverything.net`, `http://www.inknoise.com/experimental/layoutomatic.php`, and `http://www.csscreator.com/version2/page-layout.php`.

Real World Example

One of the first real-world sites to use XHTML and a CSS layout is *Fast Company* magazine at `www.fastcompany.com`. The site was designed by Dan Cederholm whose book *Web Standards Solutions: The Markup and Style Handbook* was mentioned earlier.

A version of the site's home page is shown in Figure 5.22.

An interesting feature of this site is that the XHTML structure of the page works as either a two-column or three-column layout. One structure, two layouts—how did they do it? The technique is the assignment of a `class` attribute to the `body` element. That allows styles to be written for specific selectors, such as

```
body.index h1 {
  ...
}
```

FIGURE 5.22
The main page of *Fast Company* magazine

Assigning a class attribute to the body also means that all the styles for both the two-column and three-column pages can be in the same stylesheet. This demonstrates the power of contextual selectors used with well-structured XHTML and gives *Fast Company* magazine pages that are easy to use and easy to maintain.

Use your browser's View Source option to study the structure of this site.

CSS Properties

The CSS properties that were used to position or arrange content in this chapter include position, float, clear, and z-index. You used letter-spacing to change the presentation of "pageName".

CSS *integers* are whole numbers. Integers can be either positive or negative numbers for many properties, including z-index.

TABLE 5.1: CSS Properties for Arranging Content

SELECTOR	PROPERTY	POSSIBLE VALUES
all block level elements	position	static, relative, absolute, fixed, inherit
	float	left, right, none, inherit
	clear	left, right, both, none
	z-index	<integer>, auto, inherit
	visibility	visible, hidden, collapse, inherit
all elements	letter-spacing	<length>, normal, inherit

Challenge Yourself

For some extra practice with your new skills, try out these exercises.

1. Use position: absolute; to place the div id="content" element in a precise location.

2. For the #content img selector, change the float value to none. Then try adding clear: left; or clear: both; to the #content img declarations to see what happens.

3. Add letter-spacing to the #siteName h1 selector. For comparison, try adding first 2em and then 2px.

4. On z-index.css, change the z-index value of the selector #two to a value such as 10. What happens? Now change the z-index value of the selector #two to –2. What happens?

Summary

When you look at a web page, you may react to the way it "looks." But before you begin to think about designing the presentation of the page, you need to think about structuring the markup with logical use of XHTML elements so that the CSS will be easy to apply later. In Chapter 5, you learned how to use the div element to create page divisions with assigned id or class names. These page divisions can be placed in page layouts using various methods. You arranged layouts based on positioning with position and by arranging content on the page using float, margin, and z-index.

In Chapter 6 you will learn the XHTML and CSS to format text elements such as paragraphs, headings, and block quotes.

Integrated HTML
and CSS in Color

This full-color section augments and expands the XHTML and CSS techniques taught throughout the book. The first portion is a reference to help you select colors for your web pages. (There are 16 preset color names in CSS 2.0, in addition to the color codes shown: black, white, silver, gray, maroon, red, purple, fuchsia, green, lime, olive, yellow, navy, blue, teal, and aqua; CSS version 2.1 added a seventeenth color, orange.) Next, compare your work in various chapters with these color examples of how the finished pages look. The accompanying CD contains an HTML page to be styled. Two examples of styles for the Style Me page are shown. Finally, I've collected some examples of real websites to demonstrate the common characteristics of web pages that are user friendly, clear in purpose, and easy to navigate.

Web-Safe Colors

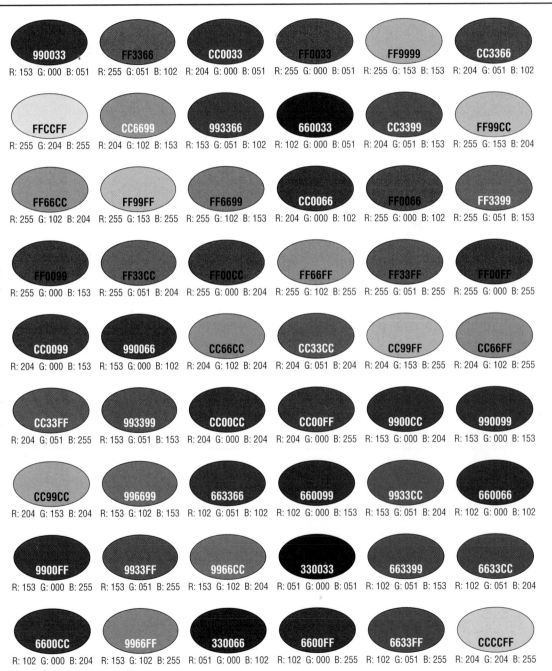

990033	**FF3366**	**CC0033**	**FF0033**	**FF9999**	**CC3366**
R: 153 G: 000 B: 051	R: 255 G: 051 B: 102	R: 204 G: 000 B: 051	R: 255 G: 000 B: 051	R: 255 G: 153 B: 153	R: 204 G: 051 B: 102
FFCCFF	**CC6699**	**993366**	**660033**	**CC3399**	**FF99CC**
R: 255 G: 204 B: 255	R: 204 G: 102 B: 153	R: 153 G: 051 B: 102	R: 102 G: 000 B: 051	R: 204 G: 051 B: 153	R: 255 G: 153 B: 204
FF66CC	**FF99FF**	**FF6699**	**CC0066**	**FF0066**	**FF3399**
R: 255 G: 102 B: 204	R: 255 G: 153 B: 255	R: 255 G: 102 B: 153	R: 204 G: 000 B: 102	R: 255 G: 000 B: 102	R: 255 G: 051 B: 153
FF0099	**FF33CC**	**FF00CC**	**FF66FF**	**FF33FF**	**FF00FF**
R: 255 G: 000 B: 153	R: 255 G: 051 B: 204	R: 255 G: 000 B: 204	R: 255 G: 102 B: 255	R: 255 G: 051 B: 255	R: 255 G: 000 B: 255
CC0099	**990066**	**CC66CC**	**CC33CC**	**CC99FF**	**CC66FF**
R: 204 G: 000 B: 153	R: 153 G: 000 B: 102	R: 204 G: 102 B: 204	R: 204 G: 051 B: 204	R: 204 G: 153 B: 255	R: 204 G: 102 B: 255
CC33FF	**993399**	**CC00CC**	**CC00FF**	**9900CC**	**990099**
R: 204 G: 051 B: 255	R: 153 G: 051 B: 153	R: 204 G: 000 B: 204	R: 204 G: 000 B: 255	R: 153 G: 000 B: 204	R: 153 G: 000 B: 153
CC99CC	**996699**	**663366**	**660099**	**9933CC**	**660066**
R: 204 G: 153 B: 204	R: 153 G: 102 B: 153	R: 102 G: 051 B: 102	R: 102 G: 000 B: 153	R: 153 G: 051 B: 204	R: 102 G: 000 B: 102
9900FF	**9933FF**	**9966CC**	**330033**	**663399**	**6633CC**
R: 153 G: 000 B: 255	R: 153 G: 051 B: 255	R: 153 G: 102 B: 204	R: 051 G: 000 B: 051	R: 102 G: 051 B: 153	R: 102 G: 051 B: 204
6600CC	**9966FF**	**330066**	**6600FF**	**6633FF**	**CCCCFF**
R: 102 G: 000 B: 204	R: 153 G: 102 B: 255	R: 051 G: 000 B: 102	R: 102 G: 000 B: 255	R: 102 G: 051 B: 255	R: 204 G: 204 B: 255

Web-Safe Colors

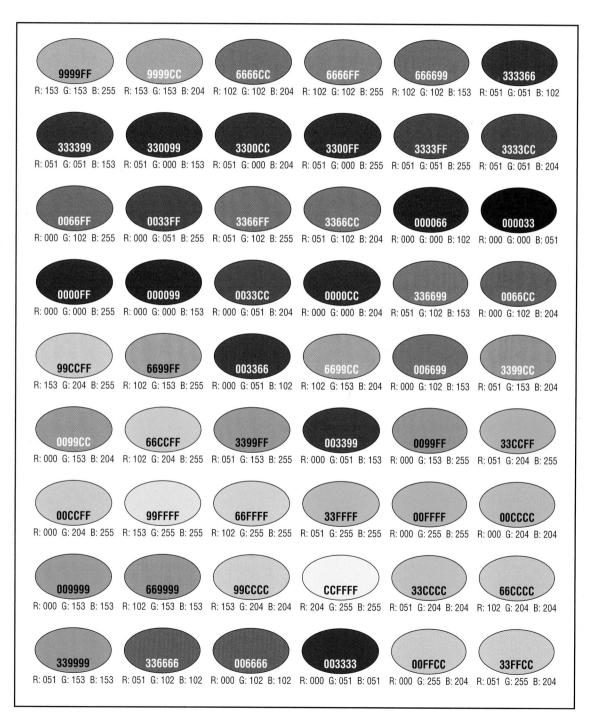

9999FF	**9999CC**	**6666CC**	**6666FF**	**666699**	**333366**
R: 153 G: 153 B: 255	R: 153 G: 153 B: 204	R: 102 G: 102 B: 204	R: 102 G: 102 B: 255	R: 102 G: 102 B: 153	R: 051 G: 051 B: 102
333399	**330099**	**3300CC**	**3300FF**	**3333FF**	**3333CC**
R: 051 G: 051 B: 153	R: 051 G: 000 B: 153	R: 051 G: 000 B: 204	R: 051 G: 000 B: 255	R: 051 G: 051 B: 255	R: 051 G: 051 B: 204
0066FF	**0033FF**	**3366FF**	**3366CC**	**000066**	**000033**
R: 000 G: 102 B: 255	R: 000 G: 051 B: 255	R: 051 G: 102 B: 255	R: 051 G: 102 B: 204	R: 000 G: 000 B: 102	R: 000 G: 000 B: 051
0000FF	**000099**	**0033CC**	**0000CC**	**336699**	**0066CC**
R: 000 G: 000 B: 255	R: 000 G: 000 B: 153	R: 000 G: 051 B: 204	R: 000 G: 000 B: 204	R: 051 G: 102 B: 153	R: 000 G: 102 B: 204
99CCFF	**6699FF**	**003366**	**6699CC**	**006699**	**3399CC**
R: 153 G: 204 B: 255	R: 102 G: 153 B: 255	R: 000 G: 051 B: 102	R: 102 G: 153 B: 204	R: 000 G: 102 B: 153	R: 051 G: 153 B: 204
0099CC	**66CCFF**	**3399FF**	**003399**	**0099FF**	**33CCFF**
R: 000 G: 153 B: 204	R: 102 G: 204 B: 255	R: 051 G: 153 B: 255	R: 000 G: 051 B: 153	R: 000 G: 153 B: 255	R: 051 G: 204 B: 255
00CCFF	**99FFFF**	**66FFFF**	**33FFFF**	**00FFFF**	**00CCCC**
R: 000 G: 204 B: 255	R: 153 G: 255 B: 255	R: 102 G: 255 B: 255	R: 051 G: 255 B: 255	R: 000 G: 255 B: 255	R: 000 G: 204 B: 204
009999	**669999**	**99CCCC**	**CCFFFF**	**33CCCC**	**66CCCC**
R: 000 G: 153 B: 153	R: 102 G: 153 B: 153	R: 153 G: 204 B: 204	R: 204 G: 255 B: 255	R: 051 G: 204 B: 204	R: 102 G: 204 B: 204
339999	**336666**	**006666**	**003333**	**00FFCC**	**33FFCC**
R: 051 G: 153 B: 153	R: 051 G: 102 B: 102	R: 000 G: 102 B: 102	R: 000 G: 051 B: 051	R: 000 G: 255 B: 204	R: 051 G: 255 B: 204

Web-Safe Colors

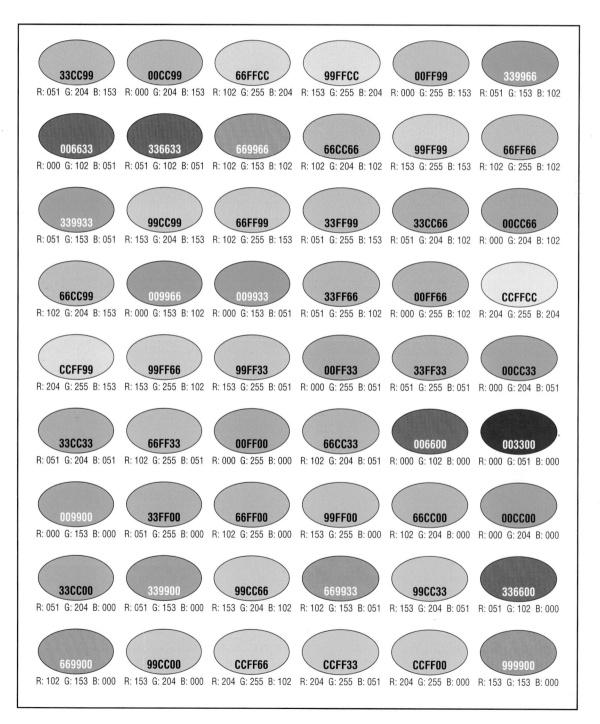

33CC99	**00CC99**	**66FFCC**	**99FFCC**	**00FF99**	**339966**
R: 051 G: 204 B: 153	R: 000 G: 204 B: 153	R: 102 G: 255 B: 204	R: 153 G: 255 B: 204	R: 000 G: 255 B: 153	R: 051 G: 153 B: 102
006633	**336633**	**669966**	**66CC66**	**99FF99**	**66FF66**
R: 000 G: 102 B: 051	R: 051 G: 102 B: 051	R: 102 G: 153 B: 102	R: 102 G: 204 B: 102	R: 153 G: 255 B: 153	R: 102 G: 255 B: 102
339933	**99CC99**	**66FF99**	**33FF99**	**33CC66**	**00CC66**
R: 051 G: 153 B: 051	R: 153 G: 204 B: 153	R: 102 G: 255 B: 153	R: 051 G: 255 B: 153	R: 051 G: 204 B: 102	R: 000 G: 204 B: 102
66CC99	**009966**	**009933**	**33FF66**	**00FF66**	**CCFFCC**
R: 102 G: 204 B: 153	R: 000 G: 153 B: 102	R: 000 G: 153 B: 051	R: 051 G: 255 B: 102	R: 000 G: 255 B: 102	R: 204 G: 255 B: 204
CCFF99	**99FF66**	**99FF33**	**00FF33**	**33FF33**	**00CC33**
R: 204 G: 255 B: 153	R: 153 G: 255 B: 102	R: 153 G: 255 B: 051	R: 000 G: 255 B: 051	R: 051 G: 255 B: 051	R: 000 G: 204 B: 051
33CC33	**66FF33**	**00FF00**	**66CC33**	**006600**	**003300**
R: 051 G: 204 B: 051	R: 102 G: 255 B: 051	R: 000 G: 255 B: 000	R: 102 G: 204 B: 051	R: 000 G: 102 B: 000	R: 000 G: 051 B: 000
009900	**33FF00**	**66FF00**	**99FF00**	**66CC00**	**00CC00**
R: 000 G: 153 B: 000	R: 051 G: 255 B: 000	R: 102 G: 255 B: 000	R: 153 G: 255 B: 000	R: 102 G: 204 B: 000	R: 000 G: 204 B: 000
33CC00	**339900**	**99CC66**	**669933**	**99CC33**	**336600**
R: 051 G: 204 B: 000	R: 051 G: 153 B: 000	R: 153 G: 204 B: 102	R: 102 G: 153 B: 051	R: 153 G: 204 B: 051	R: 051 G: 102 B: 000
669900	**99CC00**	**CCFF66**	**CCFF33**	**CCFF00**	**999900**
R: 102 G: 153 B: 000	R: 153 G: 204 B: 000	R: 204 G: 255 B: 102	R: 204 G: 255 B: 051	R: 204 G: 255 B: 000	R: 153 G: 153 B: 000

Web-Safe Colors

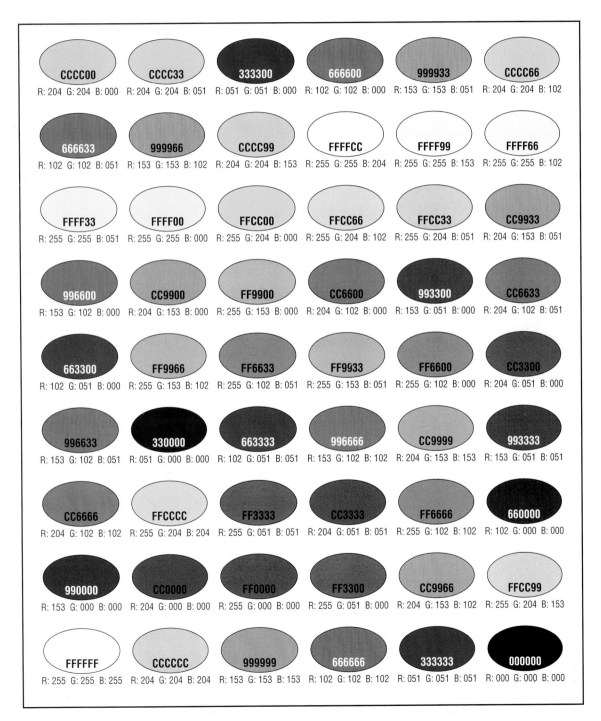

CCCC00 — R: 204 G: 204 B: 000
CCCC33 — R: 204 G: 204 B: 051
333300 — R: 051 G: 051 B: 000
666600 — R: 102 G: 102 B: 000
999933 — R: 153 G: 153 B: 051
CCCC66 — R: 204 G: 204 B: 102

666633 — R: 102 G: 102 B: 051
999966 — R: 153 G: 153 B: 102
CCCC99 — R: 204 G: 204 B: 153
FFFFCC — R: 255 G: 255 B: 204
FFFF99 — R: 255 G: 255 B: 153
FFFF66 — R: 255 G: 255 B: 102

FFFF33 — R: 255 G: 255 B: 051
FFFF00 — R: 255 G: 255 B: 000
FFCC00 — R: 255 G: 204 B: 000
FFCC66 — R: 255 G: 204 B: 102
FFCC33 — R: 255 G: 204 B: 051
CC9933 — R: 204 G: 153 B: 051

996600 — R: 153 G: 102 B: 000
CC9900 — R: 204 G: 153 B: 000
FF9900 — R: 255 G: 153 B: 000
CC6600 — R: 204 G: 102 B: 000
993300 — R: 153 G: 051 B: 000
CC6633 — R: 204 G: 102 B: 051

663300 — R: 102 G: 051 B: 000
FF9966 — R: 255 G: 153 B: 102
FF6633 — R: 255 G: 102 B: 051
FF9933 — R: 255 G: 153 B: 051
FF6600 — R: 255 G: 102 B: 000
CC3300 — R: 204 G: 051 B: 000

996633 — R: 153 G: 102 B: 051
330000 — R: 051 G: 000 B: 000
663333 — R: 102 G: 051 B: 051
996666 — R: 153 G: 102 B: 102
CC9999 — R: 204 G: 153 B: 153
993333 — R: 153 G: 051 B: 051

CC6666 — R: 204 G: 102 B: 102
FFCCCC — R: 255 G: 204 B: 204
FF3333 — R: 255 G: 051 B: 051
CC3333 — R: 204 G: 051 B: 051
FF6666 — R: 255 G: 102 B: 102
660000 — R: 102 G: 000 B: 000

990000 — R: 153 G: 000 B: 000
CC0000 — R: 204 G: 000 B: 000
FF0000 — R: 255 G: 000 B: 000
FF3300 — R: 255 G: 051 B: 000
CC9966 — R: 204 G: 153 B: 102
FFCC99 — R: 255 G: 204 B: 153

FFFFFF — R: 255 G: 255 B: 255
CCCCCC — R: 204 G: 204 B: 204
999999 — R: 153 G: 153 B: 153
666666 — R: 102 G: 102 B: 102
333333 — R: 051 G: 051 B: 051
000000 — R: 000 G: 000 B: 000

Pages from the Chapters

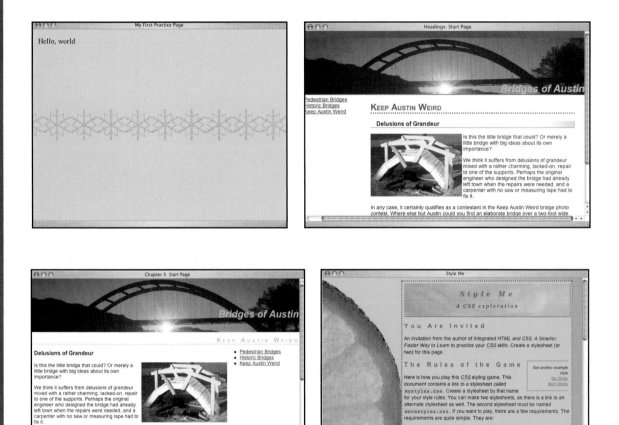

TOP LEFT: In Chapter 3, you practice placing a background image in a particular position and making it repeat (or not repeat). This background is vertically positioned halfway down the page and set to repeat horizontally. **TOP RIGHT:** Headings (Chapter 4) can be presented in different colors and styles, with borders or background images in various positions. **BOTTOM LEFT:** In Chapter 5, you learn to structure a web page for easy manipulation of a layout using div elements. **BOTTOM RIGHT:** The Style Me page on the CD, shown here in one example style, gives you an opportunity to try out your own CSS ideas with a structured web page.

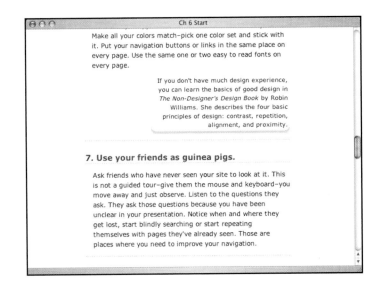

Make all your colors match–pick one color set and stick with it. Put your navigation buttons or links in the same place on every page. Use the same one or two easy to read fonts on every page.

If you don't have much design experience, you can learn the basics of good design in *The Non-Designer's Design Book* by Robin Williams. She describes the four basic principles of design: contrast, repetition, alignment, and proximity.

7. Use your friends as guinea pigs.

Ask friends who have never seen your site to look at it. This is not a guided tour–give them the mouse and keyboard–you move away and just observe. Listen to the questions they ask. They ask those questions because you have been unclear in your presentation. Notice when and where they get lost, start blindly searching or start repeating themselves with pages they've already seen. Those are places where you need to improve your navigation.

Yellow

Yellow is in sub_b folder

Home | Blue | Green | Yellow

Some junk text follows with a link to the Home page, and maybe the Blue page, and oh, well, why not the Green page. More junk text and even more would not be enough. More junk text and even more would not be enough. More junk text and even more would not be enough. More junk text and even more would not be enough. More junk text and even more would not be enough.

External Links: Google | Yahoo | Alta Vista

TOP: In Chapter 6 you work with a long page of text and use rules—such as wide margins for short line lengths and line-height adjustments—to improve the readability of the text. In this section of the page is an area accented for attention with both a line length change and a graphic image. **BOTTOM:** In Chapter 7 you link several pages together into a small site. You learn to change link colors based on background colors and to make links look like buttons by using CSS rules. Here, links in different divisions of the page are styled with different CSS rules to create both underlined and nonunderlined links. Other pages in the site teach you how to add background colors and borders to links to give them a button-like appearance.

In Chapter 8 you add images to web pages in several layouts, and you learn to make an image into a link to a web page or to a larger version of the image. **TOP:** This page shows images with description text in a simple page layout. **BOTTOM:** This version shows a different arrangement of images. The images on the left are links in a menu; the words in the headings are images as well.

TOP LEFT: Chapter 9 is about lists. Here you see lists used to create navigation with button-like menus. **TOP RIGHT:** You learn how to make accessible forms in Chapter 11. **BOTTOM LEFT:** Chapter 10 deals with creating accessible tables for the display of tabular data. This page shows a table with styled areas and background images. **BOTTOM RIGHT:** This page shows a styled form with a background image, a technique you learn in Chapter 11.

Making Your Web Pages Easy to Use

To keep visitors coming back to your site again and again, it must be easy to use. If information is hard to find, visitors just won't bother with your site. Ease-of-use requires *transparent navigation*—navigation so obvious and clear that no time has to be spent trying to puzzle out how to use the site. What makes a page easy to use has been studied by experts such as Jakob Nielsen (www.useit.com), Steve Krug (www.sensible.com), Keith Instone (www.user-experience.org), and many others. Their testing reveals that there is a basic set of features that a website must have in order to be easy to navigate.

All sites need site name identification, consistent main site navigation, and page name identification on every page. Large commercial sites also need subsection navigation, plus utility features such as search, shopping cart, and account view links. The inner pages of large sites need sectional navigation that relates to the particular page being viewed. Small sites (under about 50 pages) may not need search or utility features, but they need site name identification, consistent navigation, and page name identification every bit as much as the large sites. Three classic questions users have about navigation are: Where am I? What is this page about? and Where can I go from here? The example sites used here carefully answer those basic questions for the user on every page.

Lands' End (www.landsend.com) is a clothing retailer. It does a large catalog and phone order business but uses the Web very effectively, too. Their home page demonstrates good use of site name, main sections, subsections, utility features, and page identification.

© LANDS' END, INC. USED WITH PERMISSION.

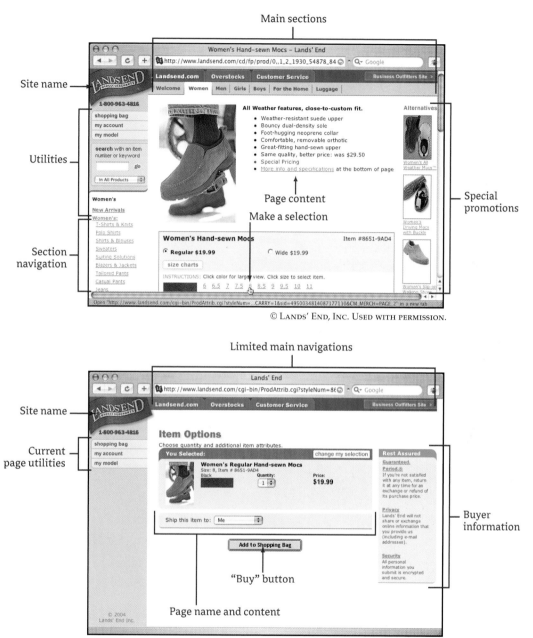

Main sections

Site name

Utilities

Page content
Make a selection

Section
navigation

Special
promotions

© Lands' End, Inc. Used with permission.

Limited main navigations

Site name

Current
page utilities

Buyer
information

"Buy" button

Page name and content

© Lands' End, Inc. Used with permission.

TOP: Clicking the link Hand Sewn Mocs for Women on the home page leads to this inner page. Note that the main section links and site name and utility sections are consistent with their appearance on the home page. Now you see added section navigation related to the Women subsection. Under the product description content is a noticeable box where the user selects a shoe size and color. **BOTTOM:** Selecting black and size 8 on the previous page leads you here. This inner Lands' End page focuses every bit of the user's attention on buying the shoe. The navigation choices are reduced. The utility features relate only to the purchase. The sectional navigation is to site pages reassuring the buyer about guarantees, online safety, and privacy. The Buy button is easy to spot.

Screenshots reproduced with permission of Abstracts Manager
(www.abstractsmanager.com, phone +61 3 9813 5333).

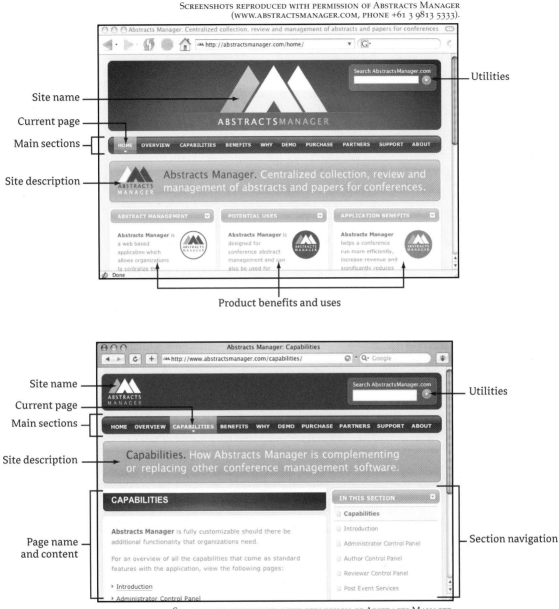

Screenshots reproduced with permission of Abstracts Manager
(www.abstractsmanager.com, phone +61 3 9813 5333).

Abstracts Manager (www.abstractsmanager.com) uses XHTML and CSS to clearly lay out the page and describe their product. **TOP:** The Abstracts Manager home page has a prominent site name and description of purpose (managing abstracts from conferences) as well as easy-to-use navigation. The prominent site description improves the site's usability and its accessibility. **BOTTOM:** On inner pages, Abstracts Manager uses a page description, similar to the site description on the home page, to clearly define what the page is about. The site name is reduced in size on the inner pages, while the navigation remains consistent with the home page.

Site name —

Main navigation —

Current page —

Page name —

Content —

SERCO TRANSARCTIC EXPEDITION
(HTTP://SERCOTRANSARCTIC.COM/); SITE DESIGNER DAMIEN DU TOIT (HTTP://CODA.CO.ZA/)

Current page —

Site name —

Main navigation —

Page name —

Content —

SERCO TRANSARCTIC EXPEDITION
(HTTP://SERCOTRANSARCTIC.COM/); SITE DESIGNER DAMIEN DU TOIT (HTTP://CODA.CO.ZA/)

The Serco Transarctic Expedition (www.sercotransarctic.com) provides information and many photos about Ben Saunders' lone ski trek across the Arctic. **TOP:** The home page uses a beautifully styled navigation system made from a list element and gives information explaining what the site is about. **BOTTOM:** The inner pages are consistent with the home page site name and main navigation. It is easy to tell which page you are on and to see what choices you have to explore in that area.

Main navigation

Site name

Current page

Selling
point
sidebar

Site
description

Content

Product highlight

Sarbox Solutions, Inc. (www.sarboxsolutions.com) is a company that helps people bring their business into compliance with a U.S. legislative act. It uses an arrangement of nested lists to create an easy-to-understand navigation system that features drop-down menu choices. The items in the menu are limited, and a large section of the home page is devoted to explaining what the site is about.

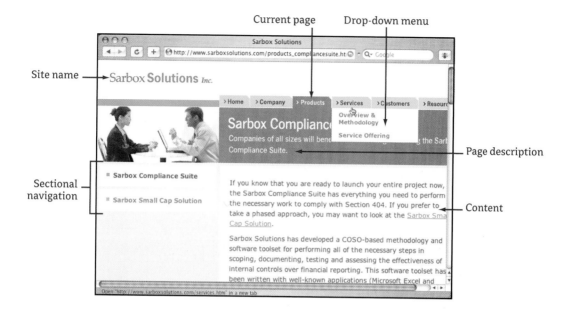

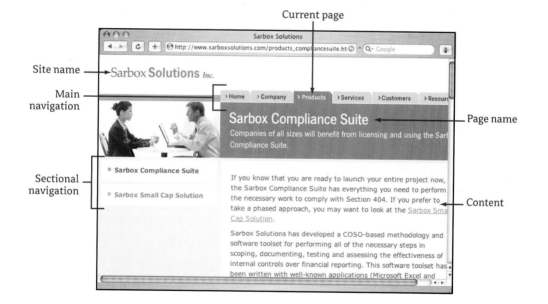

TOP: A view of the drop-down menu created with nested lists. The options in the drop-down menu correspond exactly with the items in the sectional navigation on each of the subpages under the main navigation tabs. **BOTTOM:** The same Sarbox Solutions page without the visible drop-down menu. Notice that the home page navigation and the inner page navigation is consistent and clearly indicates where you are and where you can go from that page.

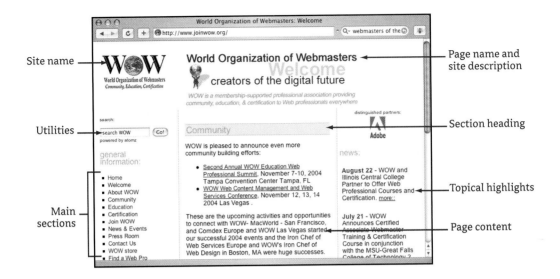

Site name

Utilities

Main sections

Page name and site description

Section heading

Topical highlights

Page content

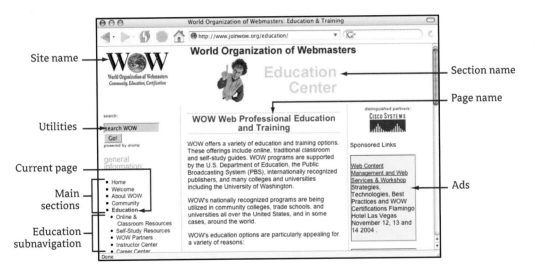

Site name

Utilities

Current page

Main sections

Education subnavigation

Section name

Page name

Ads

There are simple, text formatting tricks that can be used to create easy navigation. The World Organization of Webmasters (www.joinwow.org) has an easy-to-understand navigation plan using nested lists. In these examples, you know where you are, what the page is about, and where you can go next. **TOP:** The home page has the needed site name and page name. All the main navigation is in a list running down the left column. Notice that while the links in the content area are underlined for clarity, the underline is not needed in the list of links in the left column. **BOTTOM:** On the inner page for Education, notice that the word "Education" is presented in red in the navigation area to indicate the current page. Also note that the navigation within the subsection is a nested list under the Education item. This navigation scheme for subsection links is consistent throughout the site. In addition, note the subtle use of color and border in the Sponsored Links section on the right, which helps the user understand that these links do not lead to WOW pages.

Chapter 6

Paragraph and Text Styles

There are several XHTML elements that format text, including basic elements such as em and strong. In this chapter, you will work with such text-identification tools as acronyms, block quotes, and citations. You will also learn how to create codes for special characters such as copyright symbols. You'll see how to use CSS to style all these elements, and I'll walk you through creating your first print stylesheet.

Learn the XHTML

I will use an example file from the CD to demonstrate formatting text. In the Chapter 6 folder on the CD, find Ch6_start.html and copy it to your computer in the Integrated HTML and CSS folder.

If you look at this file in your browser, you see a long, all-text page. Figure 6.1 shows the browser view; the file is very long, so I won't include the entire thing, but Listing 6.1 shows a portion of the XHTML code.

FIGURE 6.1
The Ch6_start.html
text file in the browser

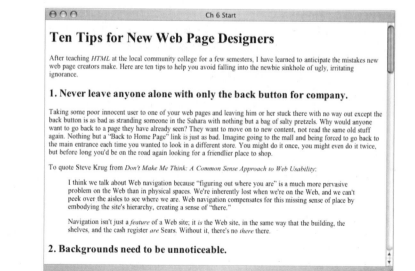

LISTING 6.1:   The Starting Text-Formatting Page

```
<!DOCTYPE html PUBLIC "-//W3C//DTD XHTML 1.0 Transitional//EN"
   "http://www.w3.org/TR/xhtml1/DTD/xhtml1-transitional.dtd">
<html xmlns="http://www.w3.org/1999/xhtml">
<head>
  <title>Ch 6 Start </title>
</head>
<body>
<h1>Ten Tips for New Web Page Designers</h1>
<p>After teaching <acronym title="Hypertext Markup Language">HTML</acronym>
   at the local community college for a few semesters, I have learned to
   anticipate the mistakes new web page creators make. Here are ten tips to
   help you avoid falling into the newbie sinkhole of ugly, irritating
   ignorance.</p>
<h2> 1. Never leave anyone alone with only the back button for company.</h2>
<p> Taking some poor innocent user to one of your web pages and leaving him
   or her stuck there with no way out except the back button is as bad as
   stranding someone in the Sahara with nothing but a bag of salty pretzels.
   Why would anyone want to go back to a page they have already seen? They
   want to move on to new content, not read the same old stuff again. Nothing
   but a &#8220;Back to Home Page&#8221; link is just as bad. Imagine going
   to the mall and being forced to go back to the main entrance each time you
   wanted to look in a different store. You might do it once, you might even
   do it twice, but before long you'd be on the road again looking for a
   friendlier place to shop.</p>
<p>To quote Steve Krug from <cite>Don't Make Me Think: A Common Sense
   Approach to Web Usability</cite>:</p>
<blockquote>
   <p>I think we talk about Web navigation because &#8220;figuring out where
      you are&#8221; is a much more pervasive problem on the Web than in
      physical spaces. We're inherently lost when we're on the Web, and we
      can't peek over the aisles to see where we are. Web navigation
      compensates for this missing sense of place by embodying the site's
      hierarchy, creating a sense of &#8220;there.&#8221;</p>
   <p>Navigation isn't just a <em>feature</em> of a Web site; it <em>is</em>
      the Web site, in the same way that the building, the shelves, and the
      cash register <em>are</em> Sears. Without it, there's no <em>there</em>
      there. </p>
</blockquote>
[...]
<div class="callout"><p>If you don't have much design experience, you can
   learn the basics of good design in <cite>The Non-Designer's Design
   Book</cite> by Robin Williams. She describes the four basic principles
```

```
  of design: contrast, repetition, alignment, and proximity.</p>
</div>
[...]
<div id="footer">
  <p>&#169; Virginia DeBolt<br />
  This article first appeared at www.vdebolt.com/ht/tentips.html. It has
  been modified slightly to add XHTML elements not present in the original
  version.</p>
</div>
</body>
</html>
```

This is a real article, something I wrote several years ago to help beginning HTML students. It still contains advice for beginning designers, so please take the time to actually read it while you are working with it.

Your design goal in this chapter is to make this long text article easy to read on the screen by improving the formatting of the text elements on the page. You also will make it easy to read in print.

However, before you can begin trying to change this page visually with CSS, there are several new XHTML elements to learn. Open `Ch6_start.html` in your text editor and examine the XHTML. Note that there is no stylesheet `link` element in the document `head`. You will add some style rules later.

First, you will work your way down the page and look at each new element in the XHTML.

Acronyms and Abbreviations

The first new element is `acronym`. Look for it here:

```
<h1>Ten Tips for New Web Page Designers</h1>
<p>After teaching <acronym title="Hypertext Markup Language">HTML</acronym>
```

The `acronym` element includes a `title` attribute. The `title` gives the actual meaning of the words that create the acronym. The default display of this element varies from browser to browser. In some browsers, the acronym will be displayed in italics, as in Figure 6.2. Other browsers may not show any visual clue that the `acronym` element is there.

All browsers should display the information in the `title` attribute if the user's cursor is held over the `acronym`. Most browsers show it as a tool tip, but some display the information at the bottom of the browser window in the status bar. See Figure 6.3.

FIGURE 6.2
This browser displays
the acronym in italics.

FIGURE 6.3
The title attribute
displays when the
cursor is held over the
acronym.

When using acronyms, it is considered adequate to identify the acronym with an acronym element including a title attribute the *first* time it is used. The acronym can be used after that without being identified as an acronym element in the XHTML. In the following example, *SPCA* is marked up as an acronym only when first used.

```
<p>Mr. Jones is a member of the <acronym title="Society for the Prevention of
Cruelty to Animals">SPCA</acronym> (Society for the Prevention of Cruelty to
Animals). The SPCA encourages the humane treatment of animals. The local SPCA meets
the second Monday of each month at the Community Center.</p>
```

THE *ABBR* ELEMENT

Related to acronym is abbr (for abbreviation). Like acronym elements, the abbr element needs a title attribute. For example,

```
<abbr title="Limited">Ltd.</abbr>
```

The abbr element is often rendered in italic type by the browser. Since browsers may vary in what the default style for abbr is, you can set it to your liking with a CSS rule. Like acronym, you only need to fully identify it on first use.

The use of acronym and abbr is subject to change, because the W3C is considering dropping acronym from the next version of XHTML and using only the abbr element for both acronyms and abbreviations. While the W3C is working on new specifications, they use the term *working draft*. A completed and adopted set of standards is identified as *recommended*. At the time of this writing, the W3C is still in the working draft stage with XHTML 2.0; the working draft states, "The abbr element indicates that a text fragment is an abbreviation (e.g., W3C, XML, Inc., Ltd., Mass., etc.); this includes acronyms." Keep an eye out for news from the W3C when the final recommendation for XHTML 2.0 is released so you can check on what actually happened with the acronym and abbr elements.

Special Characters

There are many symbols, marks, and characters needed in writing that are not among the letters and numbers on a keyboard. These are called *character entities* and *special characters*. A code number is assigned to each of these symbols or characters. Look at this example from Ch6_start.html in your text editor:

```
They want to move on to new content, not read the same old stuff again.
Nothing but a &#8220;Back to Home Page&#8221; link is just as bad.
```

MARKUP VS. WRITING WELL

Neither the acronym nor the abbr elements replace the need to be clear about what things mean in the plain text of your information. There are two ways of clarifying meaning when acronyms or abbreviations are first used in text.

◆ The first method is to give the full version of the text and immediately follow it with the acronym or abbreviation in parentheses. For example, "In this book you will learn about Cascading Style Sheets (CSS)."

◆ The second method is to give the acronym or abbreviation first, and immediately follow it with the full version in parentheses. For example, "In this book you will learn about CSS (Cascading Style Sheets)."

With an acronym or abbr element added to the XHTML, you get markup similar to what you saw in the example about Mr. Jones and the SPCA, or like this:

```
<p>In this book you will learn about <acronym title="Cascading Style Sheets">CSS</
acronym> (Cascading Style Sheets).</p>
```

This example of good writing plus appropriate markup provides the information to any reader and is carried over into print. (The information in an acronym or abbr element is not printed.) No particular browser is required, no hovering over an element with the pointing device is required—the only requirement is clear writing. Like using an acronym or abbr element in the markup, explaining what an acronym or abbreviation means in plain English in your text is only necessary when a term is first used. After that, you assume people understand what the term means.

Notice the “ and ”. These are special codes, which I'll tell you how to look up in a minute, for opening and closing double quotation marks, respectively. Special character codes must have the ampersand (&), the hash sign (#), a code number, and a semicolon (;). If you forget any of these, the symbol or character won't display properly. In the browser, you should see something like Figure 6.4 when using “ and ”.

But wait, you say! I can create a quotation mark using my computer keyboard. You have been using them in XHTML attributes, such as title="Hypertext Markup Language".

The important distinction here is that quotation marks produced by using the keyboard are *straight quotes*. Straight quotes are required in XHTML code. Straight quotes are the only type of quotation marks most simple text editing tools make, which is one reason basic text editing software is used to write XHTML code.

Straight quotes are often considered inch marks when viewed visually in the browser, however. For example:

```
<p>The photo is 8" by 10" in size.</p>
```

FIGURE 6.4
Quotation marks display
in the browser.

1. Never leave anyone alone with only the ba

Taking some poor innocent user to one of your web pages and leaving
back button is as bad as stranding someone in the Sahara with nothing
want to go back to a page they have already seen? They want to move
again. Nothing but a "Back to Home Page" link is just as bad. Imagin
the main entrance each time you wanted to look in a different store. Y
but before long you'd be on the road again looking for a friendlier pla

To quote Steve Krug from *Don't Make Me Think: A Common Sense A*

I think we talk about Web navigation because "figuring out wh
problem on the Web than in physical spaces. We're inherently l

For quotation marks in text, you want to be able to create quotes that curve, sometimes called *curly quotes*. Using the character codes “ and ”, you can create a genuine curvy quotation mark instead of a straight inch mark.

Web pages can be written in any language by using the multitude of special codes available. A complete list of XHTML Latin character entities can be found here:

```
http://www.w3.org/TR/2000/REC-xhtml1-20000126/DTD/xhtml-lat1.ent
```

Special characters, such as ampersands and angled brackets, are listed here:

```
http://www.w3.org/TR/2000/REC-xhtml1-20000126/DTD/xhtml-special.ent
```

When looking at this page or the previous URL to the W3C, you will see long lists of character entities and special characters written in a form like this:

```
<!ENTITY ldquo    "&#8220;"> <!-- left double quotation mark, U+201C ISOnum -->
```

I'll decipher that for you. You are looking at the listing for left double quotation mark, which is shown with the code “ mentioned previously. Note the `ldquo`. With an ampersand (&) and semicolon (;)—like this: `&ldquo;`—you also have a character entity that would be rendered in the browser as a left double quote. There are 252 *named* entity references similar to `&ldquo;`. These names can be used instead of the numeric code (in this case “) with what should be equivalent results in the browser. If you test in various browsers and see inconsistent results using named entity references, try it with the numeric code, as browser support for some of the named entity references is unreliable. For now, you don't need to worry about the meaning of the U+201C ISOnum part of the character entity listing.

Character entities for language types other than the Latin-based languages are at `www.unicode.org`.

En Dashes and Em Dashes

Another special character code in `Ch6_start.html` is the em dash. Look for it in Rule 4 in the example XHTML file:

```
Okay, sometimes the animated gifs are cute&#8212;for about three seconds&#8212;but
do they add meaning or significance to what you're saying?
```

An em dash is a dash the width of the character *M* for the font size in use; it's usually used to set off a phrase within a sentence. The code to create an em dash is —. In the browser, an em dash looks like the ones in Figure 6.5.

There is a slightly shorter dash called an en dash. An en dash is the width of the character *N* for the font size in use and is used to join words within a phrase, as in "the Canada–United States border." The code for an en dash is –. Table 6.1 provides a few additional codes.

An en or em dash for a font like Arial might be relatively shorter than an en or em dash for a font like Verdana, because Arial is a rather narrow font while Verdana is a rather wide font.

The em dash and the em unit that we have used for various measures of margin, padding, or font size are not the same measurement, although they are both related to the size of the font in use.

In CSS, an em is the value of a `font-size` for a given font. One em for a heading with a `font-size` of 18 pixels is different from one em for a paragraph with a `font-size` of 12 pixels. For that reason, ems are considered a relative measure. In terms of accessibility, relative measures are considered a very good thing indeed. This is because relative measures allow users to resize for better viewing with the browser controls.

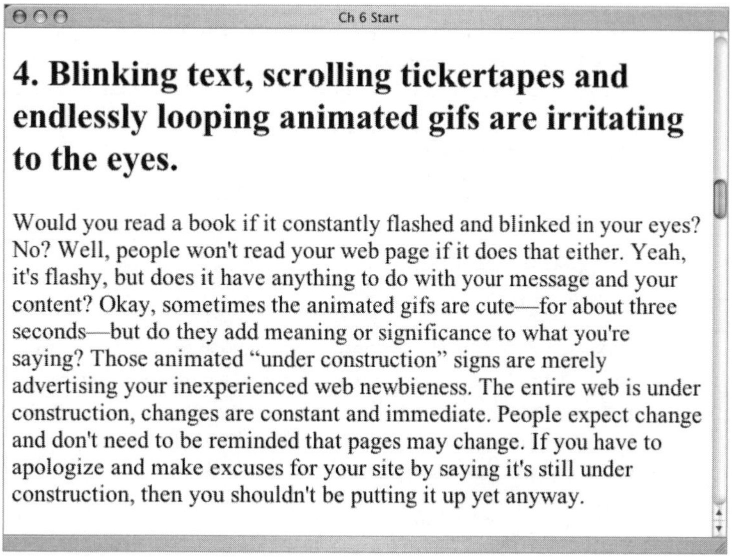

FIGURE 6.5
The em dash sets off the phrase "for about three seconds."

○ ○ ○   Ch 6 Start

4. Blinking text, scrolling tickertapes and endlessly looping animated gifs are irritating to the eyes.

Would you read a book if it constantly flashed and blinked in your eyes? No? Well, people won't read your web page if it does that either. Yeah, it's flashy, but does it have anything to do with your message and your content? Okay, sometimes the animated gifs are cute—for about three seconds—but do they add meaning or significance to what you're saying? Those animated "under construction" signs are merely advertising your inexperienced web newbieness. The entire web is under construction, changes are constant and immediate. People expect change and don't need to be reminded that pages may change. If you have to apologize and make excuses for your site by saying it's still under construction, then you shouldn't be putting it up yet anyway.

TABLE 6.1:   Selected Character and Symbol Codes

SAMPLE	CHARACTER	NUMERIC CODE	ALPHA CODE
–	En dash	–	–
—	Em dash	—	—
"	Left or opening double quote	“	“
"	Right or closing double quote	”	”
<	Less than or opening angle bracket	<	<
>	Greater than or opening angle bracket	>	>
&	Ampersand	&	&
¢	Cent	¢	¢
£	Pound	£	£
™	Trademark	™	™
©	Copyright	©	©

TIP More information about relative measurement of font sizes can be found at The Noodle Incident at `http://www.thenoodleincident.com/tutorials/box_lesson/font/index.html`, where you can see 264 screen shots of various font-size options in different browsers.

The *cite* Element

An XHTML element in `Ch6_start.html` that you haven't seen before is the `cite` element. You see an example here:

```
<p>To quote Steve Krug from <cite>Don't Make Me Think: A Common Sense Approach to
Web Usability</cite>: </p>
```

The `cite` element is intended to be used for citations such as book and magazine names. Sometimes `cite` elements contain a reference to another source, with a `cite` attribute giving the location of the original document. The example in `Ch6_start.html` is used to indicate that the words within the `cite` element tags are a book title. On the other hand, if something was quoted from the website that supports the book cited, the `cite` element might look like this instead:

```
<cite cite="http://www.sensible.com">Don't Make Me Think: A Common Sense Approach
to Web Usability</cite>
```

You are not seeing double. That is a `cite` element with a `cite` attribute. Most browsers render the `cite` element in italics, as in Figure 6.6.

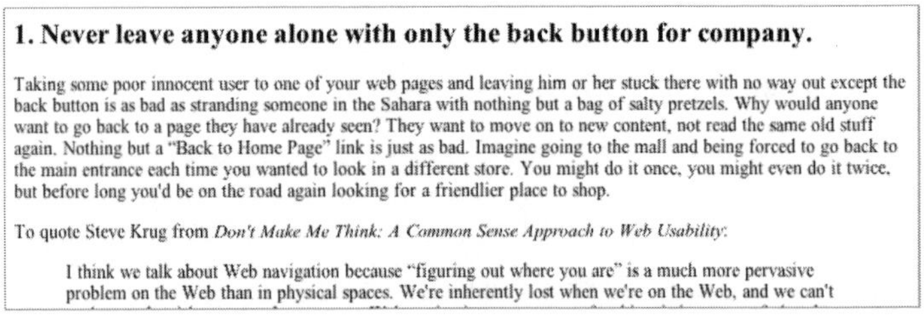

1. Never leave anyone alone with only the back button for company.

Taking some poor innocent user to one of your web pages and leaving him or her stuck there with no way out except the back button is as bad as stranding someone in the Sahara with nothing but a bag of salty pretzels. Why would anyone want to go back to a page they have already seen? They want to move on to new content, not read the same old stuff again. Nothing but a "Back to Home Page" link is just as bad. Imagine going to the mall and being forced to go back to the main entrance each time you wanted to look in a different store. You might do it once, you might even do it twice, but before long you'd be on the road again looking for a friendlier place to shop.

To quote Steve Krug from *Don't Make Me Think: A Common Sense Approach to Web Usability*:

I think we talk about Web navigation because "figuring out where you are" is a much more pervasive problem on the Web than in physical spaces. We're inherently lost when we're on the Web, and we can't

FIGURE 6.6
The `cite` element renders in italics.

As you are about to see in the following section, there are other ways to make a browser render text in italics. But keep in mind the accessibility requirement for logical formatting. None of the other ways to create italic text for a book or magazine title carry the logical element characteristics inherent in the `cite` element, which is expressly intended to be used for citations.

Block Quotes

If you experienced the agony of the term paper in high school, you know that when you quote more than a few words directly from a book or other resource in your writing, you ordinarily indent the quoted material to set it off as a *block quote.* The same rules are used in XHTML, where the `blockquote` element is used for this purpose. In `Ch6_start.html`, you see this example:

```
<blockquote>
  <p>I think we talk about Web navigation because &#8220;figuring out where
    you are&#8221; is a much more pervasive problem on the Web than in
    physical spaces. We're inherently lost when we're on the Web, and we
```

```
    can't peek over the aisles to see where we are. Web navigation
    compensates for this missing sense of place by embodying the site's
    hierarchy, creating a sense of &#8220;there.&#8221;</p>
  <p>Navigation isn't just a <em>feature</em> of a Web site; it <em>is</em>
    the Web site, in the same way that the building, the shelves, and the
    cash register <em>are</em> Sears. Without it, there's no <em>there</em>
    there.</p>
</blockquote>
```

Visually, all browsers indent the `blockquote` element on both the right and left margins and treat them as block-level elements, as shown in Figure 6.7.

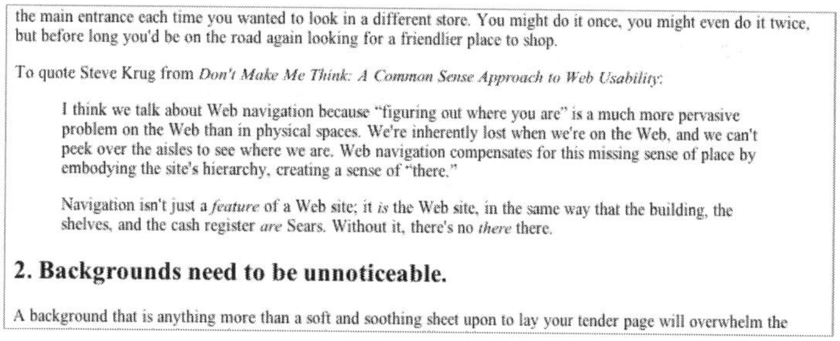

FIGURE 6.7
A block quote is indented
on the right and left.

By using CSS to set up margins, padding, or positioning, it is possible to create indented text. If what you want to do is indent text, use CSS rules. Do not use a `blockquote` element merely to indent text. The `blockquote` element should only be used for its logical purpose, namely to quote a block of material.

Formatting for Meaning: The *em* and *strong* Elements

The `blockquote` in the preceding section contains several em elements—for example, `<em>feature</em>` and `<em>there</em>`. The em (for *emphasis*) element is usually rendered in the browser as italics, as you can see in Figure 6.7. A few browsers render an em element in bold. Since em is a logical element, any browser (even an aural screen reader) will give some sort of emphasis to the em element.

If you want to be sure that an em element will appear visually as italics rather than bold, you can always write a CSS rule for em. You will do exactly that later in the chapter.

NOTE   The em (for emphasis) element is not the same em (for sizing) unit of measurement.

As you saw already, the `cite` element is often rendered in italics. You can also create italics using the i (for italic) element. So `<i>feature</i>` renders visually exactly like `<em>feature</em>` or `<cite>feature</cite>` does. However, the i element is strictly a visual rendering; it doesn't carry any logical underpinning that gives meta-meaning to an element, the way em or cite do.

Visually, it doesn't matter why the words appear as italics. When you first read the words in Figure 6.8, you didn't have any problem realizing that *Don't Make Me Think: A Common Sense Approach to Web Usability* was a book title, and that the words *feature, is, are,* and *there* were meant to be emphasized. As a reader, you have been trained in the visual conventions since first grade, and recognizing titles and emphasis are second nature.

The Web is not merely visual, however. For the approximately 10 percent of people who access the Web by some means other than visually, the distinction is clear between em and i or between cite and i, because aural screen readers give different voice inflections to the logical elements. In terms of structuring your XHTML for meaning, the logical element (em or cite) is a better choice than a visual element (i).

Of course, you might want a word to appear in italics strictly as a decorative design decision. In that case, it might be confusing to have the word rendered with emphasis in an aural screen reader. In a situation like that, the visual element (i) is a correct choice. Be wary, however, of too much italic type as a design choice because it is difficult to read, especially in large blocks.

THE *STRONG* ELEMENT

A related element can be seen in Rule 3 of Ch6_start.html: the strong element.

```
<strong>Click Here!</strong>
```

As you can see in Figure 6.8, the strong element usually renders as bold in the browser. If you want to be sure that all browsers render the strong element as bold, you can create a CSS rule for strong.

FIGURE 6.8

A strong example

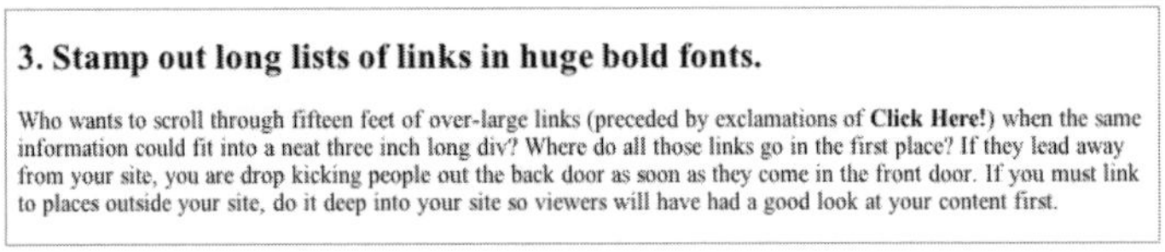

> **3. Stamp out long lists of links in huge bold fonts.**
>
> Who wants to scroll through fifteen feet of over-large links (preceded by exclamations of **Click Here!**) when the same information could fit into a neat three inch long div? Where do all those links go in the first place? If they lead away from your site, you are drop kicking people out the back door as soon as they come in the front door. If you must link to places outside your site, do it deep into your site so viewers will have had a good look at your content first.

The logical meaning of the strong element implies strong emphasis. It is often used to make words stand out as important, e.g.,

```
<p><strong>Do not</strong> light a match if you smell gas.</p>
```

The strong element is preferred over its purely visual counterpart, the b (for bold) element, for the same reasons that em is preferred over i. An aural screen reader will read strong in a different voice from normal text and in a different voice from that used for em. These contextual clues help users of assistive devices make sense of your content.

Like the i element, the b element can correctly achieve visual effects that are strictly for appearance's sake and do not carry any underlying logic or meaning of strong emphasis.

More Text Formatting Elements

There are several text formatting elements that I didn't use in Ch6_start.html but that you need to know exist.

Sometimes you may wish to display monospaced fonts (like those produced by old-fashioned typewriters) on your web page. Several elements display their contents, by default, in monospaced fonts:

◆ tt (for "typewriter text"), as in <tt>your text</tt>

◆ code (for "computer code"), as in <code>your code</code>

◆ kbd (for "keyboard"), as in <kbd>your text</kbd>

Each of these text formatting elements has a purpose, although their display results are usually the same. For example, kbd is used for formatting keyboard instructions. If you need to display computer code, use code. For general purpose monospaced text, use tt. These are all logical elements.

Normally, when you type more than one space or create a new line with the Return (Enter) key in your XHTML code, the browser ignores it. However, there is one element you can use that will maintain spaces and line breaks from an original document. This is the pre (for preformatted) element. It is often used for poems, ASCII art, and simple column construction, as in

```
<pre>some    preformatted    text</pre>
```

The pre element is sometimes used to display long code blocks on a page. The pre element is a block-level element, while kbd, tt, and code can be used inline.

In order to create street names or numbers like 1st, 2nd, and 3rd, use the sup (for superscript) element. The code would look like:

```
<p>I live at 1<sup>st</sup> and York.</p>
```

For chemical formulas such as H_2O, use the sub (for subscript) element: H₂0.

Making Your XHTML Text CSS-Ready

Most of the CSS rules needed to make this long text document (Ch6_start.html) easy to read will be applied to XHTML elements such as h2 and p.

Structurally, this is a simple page consisting of headings and paragraphs. When it is possible to style a page using only the XHTML elements themselves, such as p, h2, blockquote, and so on, then that is the best way to do the job. Don't add complexity to the markup or to the stylesheet unless it is needed. For this example, the majority of the CSS heavy lifting can be done with simple selectors.

There are exceptions to this general rule, however. You may have noticed that there are two divs in Ch6_start.html identified with the class name callout. The two div class="callout" elements contain a single paragraph. The class="callout" attribute *could* be used with the p element, so this seems to contradict what I just said about adding unnecessary complexity to the markup. However, when you get to the styling of the callout, you will see why it is necessary to have both a div and a p element for these two text items.

The final structural element on the page is one div element at the very end of the page with the id="footer" attribute.

There is no need to go beyond the added callout and footer elements with more named classes or IDs, because the XHTML elements that make up the page can be styled quite well without further structuring.

If this page were not a stand-alone document but were instead part of a larger site, you might need other elements such as navigation and site identification on the page that would require more structuring and more context building with additional id and class selectors.

Learn the CSS

You already know much of the CSS that will be used to style this document. You will use background, font, color, margin, and other style attributes you have already learned. The new CSS you will learn will be to make a print stylesheet.

First you will create a stylesheet for all media and link to it in the XHTML document head. Then you will create a print-media stylesheet and link to it after the all-media stylesheet in the XTHML document.

Think about the Cascade. Because of the Cascade, the *only* CSS rules the print stylesheet will need are rules that must be different from the declarations in the first all-media stylesheet.

Start Your Stylesheet

Open a blank document in your text editor of choice and save it in the same folder where Ch6_start.html is saved. Name the new document Ch6_allmedia.css.

One of the first rules for making text readable on the Web is to use short lines. Reading on a screen is difficult in comparison with reading on paper, and longer lines of text are harder for the eye to track. The easiest way to control line length in the Ch6_start.html document is by controlling the body element. On this page, everything in the body is main content, except for the footer. On a page with a more complex structure, the body might not serve so well as a way to control line length.

NOTE In Chapter 5, you used a div named "container" at a set pixel width. Nested in the "container" was a div named "content" with a wide margin to control line length and readability. See Figure 5.18 in Chapter 5 for a reminder of how you last laid out that page. The line length in the layout in Chapter 5 was further reduced by the use of floated images to cause the text to wrap around the images.

One way to accomplish the goal of narrowing the body element is to set a specific width for the body in pixels, perhaps 400 or 500 pixels. A more flexible way is to set wide margins on the left and right sides using percentages. An example using percentages is:

```
body {
  margin-right: 10%;
  margin-left: 10%;
}
```

If you use the same margin width on both the left and right sides, the document will be centered in the viewport. Using percentages for the margins allows more flexibility for users who might want to resize the text using the browser's View menu.

You'll use this method, but before you get to it, I want to point out another way to constrain the body element. You could set the body to a width in percent—say, perhaps 70% or 80%. If you didn't want the default left alignment for the body element, you could center it using margin-right: auto and margin-left: auto. Here's an example of this:

```
body {
  width: 70%;
  margin-right: auto;
  margin-left: auto;
}
```

Time to get that Ch6_allmedia.css page going! Begin with this rule for the body element:

```
body {
  margin-right: 20%;
  margin-left: 20%;
}
```

USING *MIN-WIDTH* AND *MAX-WIDTH*

Two CSS properties that can be helpful when you are constraining the size of page elements are `min-width` and `max-width`.

◆ Use `min-width` to set a minimum size for the element. In browsers that support `min-width` (Internet Explorer for Windows does not, while Firefox, Opera, Mozilla, Safari, and other more standards-compliant browsers do), the element can get no narrower than the `min-width` setting allows.

◆ Use `max-width` to set a maximum size for the element. In browsers that support `max-width` (you guessed it, IE does not), the element will get no wider than the `max-width` allows.

A free JavaScript that will fix IE's lack of implementation for `min-width` and `max-width`, including directions for how to use it, is here:

```
http://www.doxdesk.com/software/js/minmax.html
```

Save your `Ch6_allmedia.css` document again. If you look at `Ch6_start.html` in the browser now, nothing has changed. Eek! Why?

You have a stylesheet with a rule in it, but there is nothing to connect the stylesheet to the XHTML document. You must add a `link` to the stylesheet in the XHTML document. (Give yourself a pat on the back if you knew that.) You should include a `media` attribute in this `link` element because you are planning more than one stylesheet for different media. Your link element should follow the title and look like this:

```
<title>Ch 6 Start</title>
<link href="Ch6_allmedia.css" rel="stylesheet" type="text/css" media="all" />
</head>
```

In this situation, `media="screen"` would also be effective. A value of `screen` for the `media` attribute is for viewing on a computer monitor. See Table 6.2 for more `media` attributes. Be warned: most of these media types are not supported by any browsers yet, although there is good current support for `"all"`, `"screen"`, and `"print"`.

TABLE 6.2: *Media* Attributes for Stylesheets

ATTRIBUTE	USE
all	In all presentational media
aural	In speech synthesizers, screen readers, or any audio rendering
Braille	With Braille devices
embossed	When printing with a Braille device
handheld	With cell phones and personal digital assistants
print	When printing

TABLE 6.2:   *Media* Attributes for Stylesheets *(continued)*

ATTRIBUTE	USE
projection	When presenting a slide show with a projector
screen	For screen media such as desktop computers
tty	For teletype printers
tv	For television

Now that the link to the stylesheet is included, save the XHTML file and reload the browser. You should now see something similar to Figure 6.9.

Because you used percents rather than pixels to size the body element, when the browser window is resized (either larger or smaller) the lines of text reflow easily according to the user's window size. So, if one user actually wanted to read long lines of text in the browser, it would be possible to stretch the browser window to its full width and read that way. Conversely, if another user wanted to read shorter lines of text, the browser window could be made less wide and the text would reflow accordingly.

Had you instead set the body width to 500 pixels, it would never be any wider than that, no matter what the user did with the browser window. There are times when designing a web page when you must have a set pixel size to make something work. Most of the time when you need an exact pixel size it is because you have images arranged in a way that resizing the browser window would ruin, but exact measurements hold the images together in the desired proximity to one another.

In this case, it is better to stay loose and use percentages. Designs using percentages are often termed *fluid* and are considered more accessible than fixed pixel designs. The fact that fluid designs can be resized to suit the user's needs is a perfect example of accessible design.

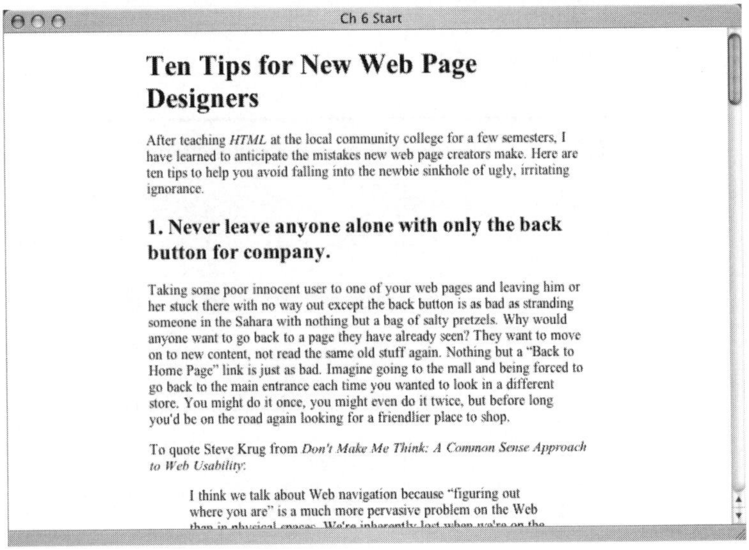

FIGURE 6.9
Margins narrow
the entire page.

When starting a new website and making early plans for your design, often one of the first decisions you make is whether to use a fluid or fixed plan for your layout. Such decisions are made on a case-by-case basis, depending on the site goals. As with a good many design decisions, there is no one right answer to the question of fluid versus fixed.

More Body Rules

You can do a lot more to your page while working with the body element selector. One declaration you always want to make sure you include in your body rule is background color. You are interested in ease of reading, so white (#fff) is a good choice for the background. You can also declare a font. Common wisdom is that sans-serif fonts are easier to read on a screen. Verdana is easy to read, and you haven't used it yet, so give it a whirl. As usual, you should add a couple of other common sans-serif fonts in case users don't have Verdana. Finally, you want to declare a font-size of 100% for accessibility reasons. Here is the new body rule:

```
body {
    margin-right: 20%;
    margin-left: 20%;
    background: #fff;
    font: 100% Verdana, Arial, Helvetica, sans-serif;
}
```

Save that change, then reload the page in the browser. The text should look like Figure 6.10, reflecting the change in the body font.

Black text on a white background provides the contrast needed for easy readability. There is no need to restrict yourself to this combination of colors, however. If you choose other colors for the background and the text, just be sure there is sufficient contrast between the colors to make the text readable for people with color perception problems.

FIGURE 6.10
Background and font settings appear.

CSS AND BROWSER SUPPORT

Setting the font-size for the body selector to 100% can cause an error in the way the Opera browser rounds numbers. Suggested ways to avoid this problem are to set the font-size to 100.01% or to 1em instead. In practical terms, 1em and 100% are equivalent measurements. The 100.01% size is a miniscule change, but it makes Opera behave without adversely affecting other browsers.

It is sad but true: browsers support the W3C recommended specifications for CSS in different ways depending on the platform and browser involved. There are many websites devoted entirely to helping CSS designers keep track of which CSS attributes and values work in any specific situation. One of the most complete browser support charts is from House of Style at

```
http://www.westciv.com/style_master/academy/browser_support/index.html
```

TIP   A free tool at `http://www.vischeck.com/vischeck/vischeckURL.php` will check a web page and show you how the page looks to various types of color-blind users. Checks like this will help you make sure there is enough contrast between the foreground and background colors of your page for good readability.

Heading Rules

The h1 is too large. In previous chapters, you got some experience setting font-size with ems, so in this chapter you will use percentages. Declare a font-size value of 130% for the h1. In addition, the h1 can be a dark gray (#333) instead of completely black. The h1 selector rule for this is

```
h1 {
   font-size: 130%;
   color: #333;
}
```

TIP   font-size: 130%; is equivalent to font-size: 1.3em;.

You have used margin before, but not negative margins. Well, it is time to get negative. Put –1.5em of negative margin on the h1. It might also look nice to add a 2-pixel dotted border on the right and bottom in a light gray (#ccc) color. The complete h1 rule for this is

```
h1 {
   font-size: 130%;
   color: #333;
   margin-left: -1.5em;
   border-right: 2px dotted #CCC;
   border-bottom: 2px dotted #CCC;
}
```

Save that and reload the browser to see something similar to Figure 6.11.

FIGURE 6.11
The styled h1 element

The h2 elements can be treated in a similar way. You can make them a little smaller than the h1—say, 120%. You can use a slightly less negative margin—say, –1em. You can match the color and border styles used on the h1 element but apply borders to the top and bottom to set off the numbered tips in a frame-like arrangement. And you can add some padding to the top of the h2, to push the heading into a more apparent proximity with the paragraph it heads. Here is the h2 selector, the results of which are shown in Figure 6.12:

```
h2 {
   font-size: 120%;
   color: #333;
   margin-left: -1em;
   border-top: 2px dotted #CCC;
   border-bottom: 2px dotted #CCC;
   padding-top: 1.5em;
}
```

Paragraph Rules

When there is a long page to read, it helps to put what I call "air" on the page. Air refers to white space or empty space, which helps the reader's eye separate and identify layout units and track from word to word while reading. You have added quite a bit of white space with your wide margins, but it would help to also have some white space *between* the lines of text.

White space is also called *negative space* in design terms. The empty space around parts of a design are often as important to the success of the design as the actual images or text used in the design. The negative space does more than increase readability; it adds contrast and emphasis to the items that *do* fill the space.

FIGURE 6.12
The styled h2 element

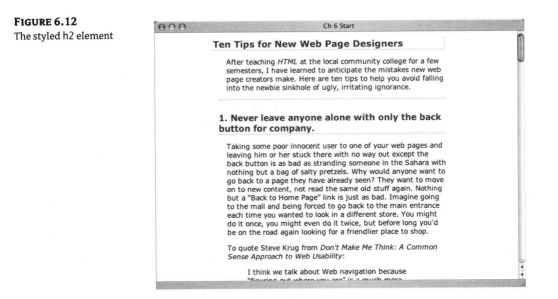

NOTE Apple Computer's website at www.apple.com frequently wins design awards, in no small measure due to the brilliant use of white space on its pages and in its ads.

Inserting space between lines of text is easy to accomplish with a line-height declaration. Since you are using percentages for the font-size, use percentages for the line-height as well. A line-height: 150%; rule should create a very nicely spaced paragraph. The rule would be:

```
p {
   line-height: 150%;
}
```

Viewed in the browser, this looks like Figure 6.13.

Block Quote Rules

The paragraphs in the block quote inherit all the body and paragraph rules already set up in the stylesheet, so it looks pretty good. You could leave the block quote alone, and it would be just fine. Write a style declaration for it anyway, just to give you more practice in styling XHTML elements.

Why not use the 2px dotted #CCC border again, but this time only on the left side?

```
blockquote {
   border-left: 2px dotted #CCC;
}
```

If you look at that in the browser, the text is too scrunched up next to the border. You want white space! A few pixels of padding-left will solve the problem:

```
blockquote {
   border-left: 2px dotted #CCC;
   padding-left: 2px;
}
```

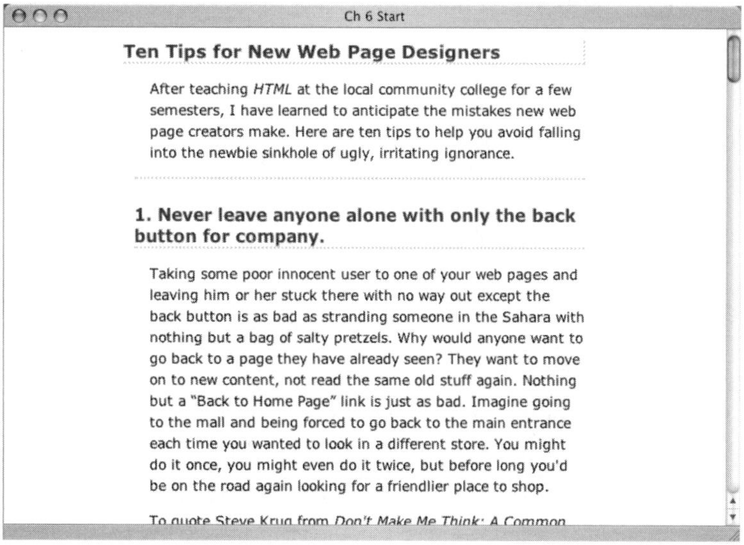

FIGURE 6.13
Paragraphs with line-height declared

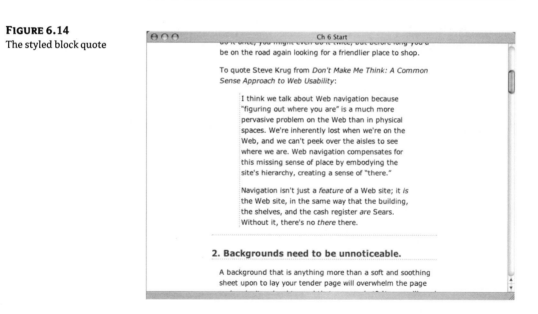

FIGURE 6.13
Paragraphs with line-height declared

FIGURE 6.14
The styled block quote

With the new rule in place, the block quote should look like Figure 6.14.

em and His Buddy *strong* Once Again

As previously mentioned, most browsers render em as italics and strong as bold, but some reverse these. You want to be sure that any browser will interpret these elements the way you want them.

Use `font-style` to declare italic fonts, like this:

```
em {
  font-style: italic;
}
```

Use `font-weight` to declare bold fonts, like this:

```
strong {
  font-weight: bold;
}
```

TIP   Headings are bold by default, so you don't need to declare a `font-weight: bold;` rule for headings.

Depending on the browser you are using to check your work, you may not see any difference in the appearance of the page with these two new rules in your stylesheet. But it will ensure consistent appearance across all browsers to have them among your CSS rules. If you were so inclined, you could add all sorts of CSS rules to your `em` and `strong` selectors, such as background colors and borders, but you don't need them for `Ch6_start.html`.

Acronym

There are two `acronym` elements in `Ch6_start.html`. Earlier you looked at this one:

```
<acronym title="Hypertext Markup Language">HTML</acronym>
```

In the section of the page about "image busting," you will find another:

```
<acronym title="dots per inch">dpi</acronym>
```

Because the visual appearance of an acronym may vary from browser to browser, add a rule to your stylesheet to call a little attention to the acronym and give it a consistent cross-browser appearance.

Although there is no iron-clad rule that says you must style an acronym in a particular way, so many web designers use italics and a dotted bottom border for acronyms that it has become one of those generally understood conventions: a dotted underline is a visual clue to a defined or expanded term, such as a glossary entry, and therefore to an `acronym` element. Since dotted border rules (as in `2px dotted #CCC;`) abound in your stylesheet already, it would be consistent with your design to continue in that tradition. You should already know how to write this rule:

```
acronym {
  font-style: italic;
  border-bottom: 2px dotted #CCC;
}
```

View the page in the browser; it will look like Figure 6.15. Hovering over the `acronym` should produce a visible rendering of the `title` attribute.

FIGURE 6.15
A styled acronym

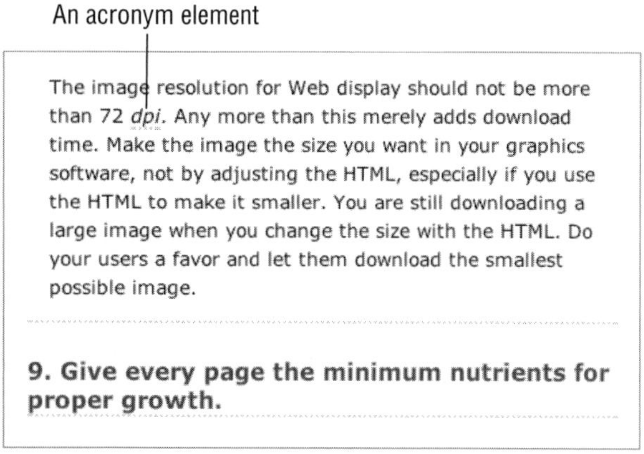

An acronym element

> The image resolution for Web display should not be more than 72 *dpi*. Any more than this merely adds download time. Make the image the size you want in your graphics software, not by adjusting the HTML, especially if you use the HTML to make it smaller. You are still downloading a large image when you change the size with the HTML. Do your users a favor and let them download the smallest possible image.

9. Give every page the minimum nutrients for proper growth.

Callout

In a magazine, a *callout* or *pull quote* is extracted from the text and set in display type. Sometimes this pull quote is displayed at quite a distance from the source of the material in the text.

In `Ch6_start.html` there are two divs identified with the `class="callout"` attribute. You won't attempt to create the effect you might see in a magazine, but you will set off the text in this class to make it visually distinct.

You will reduce the font size, move the callout to the right and right-align the text, and use background images to create a visual accent for the callout.

GENERAL CONVENTIONS

People who use the Internet and the Web frequently come to understand some of the unspoken conventions that help to navigate and interpret web pages. I mentioned the convention of using a dotted bottom border to offer a clue to the presence of an acronym, but there are many more. Here are a few others.

◆ When a word is underlined, it is understood to be a link.

◆ A small graphic with a word on it is usually a link.

◆ When a site logo in the upper-left corner of a web page is clicked, it usually leads to the home page.

◆ A phrase in large type is usually a heading.

◆ Lists of links are often displayed in a colored bar down the left or right side of a page.

◆ Main site navigation links will be consistent from page to page within a site.

◆ Most large sites have an easy-to-find search box.

◆ Some icons, such as those representing mailboxes and shopping carts, have an agreed-upon meaning. (There are not many icons that are immediately understood without textual help.)

Of course, people can and do break free from these conventional notions when designing websites. However, it pays to be careful when breaking conventions lest your visitors become confused or regard your site as unusable and go elsewhere.

Start by creating a `.callout` selector in the stylesheet. Add declarations for `font-size` and `text-align`. Move the text to the right and reduce the width of the callout by adding margin to the left. If you add a `margin-left: 30%;` declaration, the callout will be 70% of the width of the normal paragraphs. The rule so far:

```
.callout {
  font-size: 90%;
  text-align: right;
  margin-left: 30%;
}
```

You aren't there yet, however, because I intend to teach you a neat effect using two background images. On the CD in the Chapter 6 folder, you will find two GIF images: `callout_l.gif` and `callout_r.gif`. Copy these two images into the same folder on your computer where you have the HTML and CSS files for Chapter 6. The two GIFs are thin gray bars with a drop shadow and curved ends that will sit under the text of the callout like a tray.

The callouts are marked up like this:

```
<div class="callout"><p>If you don't have much design experience, you can learn the
basics of good design in <cite>The Non-Designer's Design Book</cite> by Robin
Williams. She describes the four basic principles of design: contrast, repetition,
alignment, and proximity.</p></div>
```

The `div` is assigned to a class and the paragraph is a descendant of the `div`. Since an XHTML element can only have one background image, you need two elements here to make this work: both the `div` and the p.

One GIF image will be used for the `.callout` class selector. After that, you will create an additional style for a `.callout p` descendant selector. The two graphic backgrounds will combine to create a single visual effect accenting the callout element.

You need to add the background image to the callout rules—use `callout_r.gif` first. The background image should not repeat, and it should be located horizontally at the right and vertically at the bottom of the `div`, like this:

```
.callout {
  font-size: 90%;
  background: url(callout_r.gif) no-repeat right bottom;
  text-align: right;
  margin-left: 30%;
}
```

You can look at it at this point, but it looks better with a little padding, so why not go ahead and add some? (You'll pad the bottom in just a minute, be patient.) The rule should be like this:

```
.callout {
  font-size: 90%;
  background: url(callout_r.gif) no-repeat right bottom;
  text-align: right;
  margin-left: 30%;
  padding-right: 4px;
}
```

Take a look in the browser after you save your stylesheet to see something like Figure 6.16.

The callout is almost finished. But the accent graphic on the bottom needs to curve up on the left side, too. If you had a fixed width for the callout, you could have easily made a single graphic in the exact width you wanted and just used that to do the job. But your callout is a percentage width and putting a fixed-size graphic under it just won't work.

You will use a technique that combines the effects of two backgrounds. This fluid technique allows the backgrounds to slide over each other and appear to grow or shrink to fit the size of the user's viewport.

TIP One of the first descriptions of multiple background designs was published by A List Apart by writer Douglas Bowman at `http://www.alistapart.com/articles/slidingdoors/` and is called the Sliding Doors technique.

I hinted at how this works earlier, but the complete process is like this. You already have a background on the class named `callout`. You have to find a place to add another background. Look at the XHTML:

```
<div class="callout"><p>If you don't ...</p></div>
```

In the `div` element there is a `p` element. You can create a selector in your CSS that will allow you to use a background for the `p` element descended from the `div class="callout"` element. The selector would be `.callout p`. You want to use the GIF with the left curve (`callout_l.gif`) as a background. You want the image not to repeat and to be horizontally on the left and vertically on the bottom. As noted about Figure 6.17, some padding at the bottom would be welcome, too. So your rule would be:

```
.callout p {
    background: url(callout_l.gif) no-repeat left bottom;
    padding-bottom: 8px;
}
```

FIGURE 6.16
The callout with right bottom background

Ch 6 Start

Make all your colors match–pick one color set and stick with it. Put your navigation buttons or links in the same place on every page. Use the same one or two easy to read fonts on every page.

If you don't have much design experience, you can learn the basics of good design in *The Non-Designer's Design Book* by Robin Williams. She describes the four basic principles of design: contrast, repetition, alignment, and proximity.

7. Use your friends as guinea pigs.

Ask friends who have never seen your site to look at it. This is not a guided tour–give them the mouse and keyboard–you move away and just observe. Listen to the questions they ask. They ask those questions because you have been unclear in your presentation. Notice when and where they get lost, start blindly searching or start repeating themselves with pages they've already seen. Those are places where you need to improve your navigation.

Save that and refresh the browser view. You'll see the page shown in Figure 6.17.

There are two `callout` elements like this on the page, and both should have the same style. Scroll down the entire page to see the second callout. Remember that a class can be used multiple times, so you can add as many callouts as you want to this page. If you used the `<div class="callout"><p>` structure to create them, they would all look the same.

NOTE   The text of a pull quote or callout can often be styled effectively using `float` to remove the quote from the normal document flow, move it to the left or right, and allow the remaining text to flow around it. It isn't particularly effective on this page, but keep `float` in mind for future reference.

Footer

The footer is another web page convention inherited from print. It holds information tucked away at the bottom (or foot) of the web page.

Most footer material is mean to be unobtrusive. Footers may contain legal information such as links to privacy policies or copyright notices. Footers often contain a link to the site designer's home page or a webmaster's e-mail link. Unless a user is specifically looking for such information, footers are generally not given much attention.

One way to make this information unobtrusive is to use a smaller font-size and make the text a light gray. Something like this:

```
#footer {
    font-size: 80%;
    color: #999;
}
```

Your view in the browser should be like Figure 6.18.

FIGURE 6.17
The callout with a finished curve under it

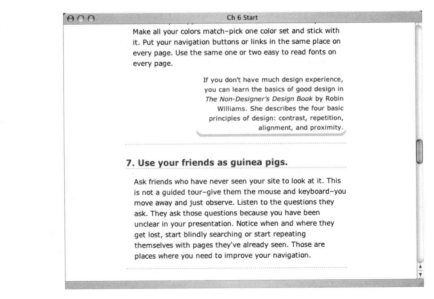

FIGURE 6.18

The styled footer

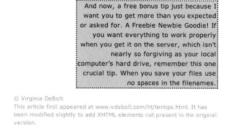

That helps, but there is a proximity issue with it snuggled up next to the last of the main content the way it is. Some visual separation is needed to clarify the distinction between the main content and footer content. In other situations on this page you have used `padding` to move things around, so move the footer down and away from the last paragraph with `padding-top`.

Use a `border-top` as well, to create a visual separator between the content and the footer. Why change your design now? Use a `2px dotted #CCC` border once again. The changed rule is:

```
#footer {
    font-size: 80%;
    color: #999;
    padding-top: 3em;
    border-top: 2px dotted #CCC;
}
```

Figure 6.19 shows the results of the additional change.

You have another proximity problem now, apparent in Figure 6.19. The `border-top` is too far away from the `footer` text. This is because `padding` comes between the content of your element and the `border`. (Please see the box model diagram in Figure 4.10 for a refresher on the box model.) You need a way to keep the `footer` content where it is but make the `border-top` appear closer to the content of the `footer`.

FIGURE 6.19

The changed footer

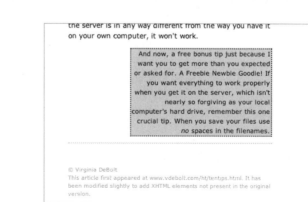

Have you figured out how yet? Understanding the box model is the key. You *don't* want `padding`, because `padding` comes between content and `border`. You *do* want `margin`, because `margin` is beyond the `border`.

Instead of using `padding-top`, you need to use `margin-top`, like this:

```
#footer {
  font-size: 80%;
  color: #999;
  border-top: 2px dotted #CCC;
  margin-top: 4em;
}
```

As you see in Figure 6.20, you finally have an unobtrusive and visually distinct footer.

FIGURE 6.20
The footer with
`margin-top`

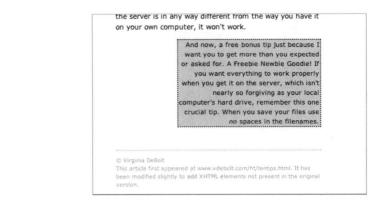

the server is in any way different from the way you have it
on your own computer, it won't work.

And now, a free bonus tip just because I
want you to get more than you expected
or asked for. A Freebie Newbie Goodie! If
you want everything to work properly
when you get it on the server, which isn't
nearly so forgiving as your local
computer's hard drive, remember this one
crucial tip. When you save your files use
no spaces in the filenames.

© Virginia DeBolt
This article first appeared at www.vdebolt.com/ht/tentips.html. It has
been modified slightly to add XHTML elements not present in the original
version.

This exercise with `padding` versus `margin` wasn't designed to be a trick. It is merely a way to point out that just because you used `padding` several times on this page to move content a bit, it doesn't mean that `padding` is the only tool at your disposal, or even the right tool for every situation.

The Whole Stylesheet

Before we get into the print stylesheet, look at your completed `Ch6_allmedia.css` file. A version named `Ch6_allmedia_finished.css`, which you can use for comparison with your `Ch6_allmedia.css` file, is in the Chapter 6 folder on the accompanying CD and is reproduced in Listing 6.2.

LISTING 6.2:   The All-Media Stylesheet

```
body {
  margin-right: 20%;
  margin-left: 20%;
  background: #FFF;
  font: 100%  Verdana, Arial, Helvetica, sans-serif;
}
h1 {
  font-size: 130%;
  color: #333;
```

```
    margin-left: -1.5em;
    border-right: 2px dotted #CCC;
    border-bottom: 2px dotted #CCC;


}
h2 {
    font-size: 120%;
    color: #333;
    margin-left: -1em;
    border-top: 2px dotted #CCC;
    border-bottom: 2px dotted #CCC;
    padding-top: 1.5em;
}
p {
    line-height: 150%;
}
blockquote {
    border-left: 2px dotted #CCC;
    padding-left: 2px;
}
em {
    font-style: italic;
}
strong {
    font-weight: bold;
}
.callout {
    font-size: 90%;
    background: url(callout_r.gif) no-repeat right bottom;
    text-align: right;
    margin-left: 30%;
    padding-right: 4px;
}
.callout p {
    background: url(callout_l.gif) no-repeat left bottom;
    padding-bottom: 8px;
}
acronym {
    font-style: italic;
    border-bottom: 2px dotted #CCC;
}
#footer {
    font-size: 80%;
    color: #999;
    border-top: 2px dotted #CCC;
    margin-top: 4em;
}
```

Print Preview

You have a brief stylesheet. It contains only the rules you need and nothing more. If you print the page as it is now, the rules you set will be used on the printed page. If no print media stylesheet is linked to a file, the all-media stylesheet will be used for, well, all media.

You should have an option in your browser's File menu that allows you to preview a printed page without using the paper and ink to actually print it. Use that to see how the page would print with only the current `Ch6_allmedia.css` stylesheet attached.

Feel free to make use of the browser's print preview in the next section.

Let's Go into Print

If you previewed the printed version of the current page as I suggested, you may have thought it looked readable enough and wondered why there was any need for a print stylesheet. A valid point; however, in a more realistic situation when you are posting an article such as this to a website, there would be more on the page than just this text. There would be images, navigation elements, maybe even ads, search boxes, and other elements.

Often there are elements on the page that you don't need or want in print. For example, what benefit is there in having a search form printed on a sheet of paper? It can't be used and merely eats into your ink budget to print. Therefore, one of the things you will learn to do with print stylesheets is how *not* to print selected elements on a page.

Start Your Stylesheet

Open a new blank document in your text editor. Save it in the same folder on your computer as `Ch6_start.html`. Name it `Ch6_print.css`.

Even though it is a blank document right now, go ahead and add a link to it in your `Ch6_start.html` document. Put the new link after the existing stylesheet link, like this:

```
<link href="Ch6_allmedia.css" rel="stylesheet" type="text/css" media="all" />
<link href="Ch6_print.css" rel="stylesheet" type="text/css" media="print" />
```

Notice that the `media` value is set to `print` in this case. Setting a `media` value of `print` means that this stylesheet will be ignored by devices other than printers. As mentioned earlier, putting the link to the print stylesheet after the all-media stylesheet means that the print rules come last in the Cascade.

The Cascade is affected by proximity. The last rule read is in the closest proximity to the element and is the rule applied. For example, if the `font-size: 130%;` rule in `Ch6_allmedia.css`, were followed by a `font-size: 16pt;` rule in `Ch6_print.css`, the 16pt rule would be the one used when printing.

Using the *display* Property to Remove Content

The `display` property is new to you. You will use it again in Chapter 9 to declare `display: block` or `display: inline` rules for lists. In this chapter, you will work with the value `none` for the `display` property.

Giving a selector a declaration of `display: none` completely removes the element from the visual display. The space closes up, and the page is shown as if the element did not exist. Using `display:`

none removes elements from the view of aural screen readers, too, so it cannot be used to hide things visually while still leaving them available to users with assistive devices.

TIP The visibility: hidden; property and value used to show or hide divs does not remove the element from the document. It merely hides it temporarily while holding open a position for it.

In the example just mentioned about not printing a search box, assume that the search box was contained like this: <div id="search">search form here</div>. The stylesheet selector #search could be used like this:

```
#search {
  display: none;
}
```

In a print stylesheet, this keeps the search div from displaying and printing.

There are not many elements in Ch6_start.html that you might use to try display: none;, because you want all the headings and paragraphs to display. But how about the footer? In your new Ch6_print.css document, add your first rule:

```
#footer {
  display: none;
}
```

Save that, reload the browser, and then use the browser's File menu to preview the print results. The page should look like Figure 6.21 (in the Safari browser's print preview) or Figure 6.22 (in Internet Explorer's print preview).

TIP Many people may not be familiar with Safari, a Mac-only browser. The Internet Explorer preview is included because it may be closer to what you are accustomed to seeing for this first print preview figure.

Remember, this rule only applies to print, so if you look for the footer in the normal browser window, you should still see it. To return the footer to the realm of the visible, see the sidebar, "Comment That."

FIGURE 6.21

The footer does not display in Safari's print preview.

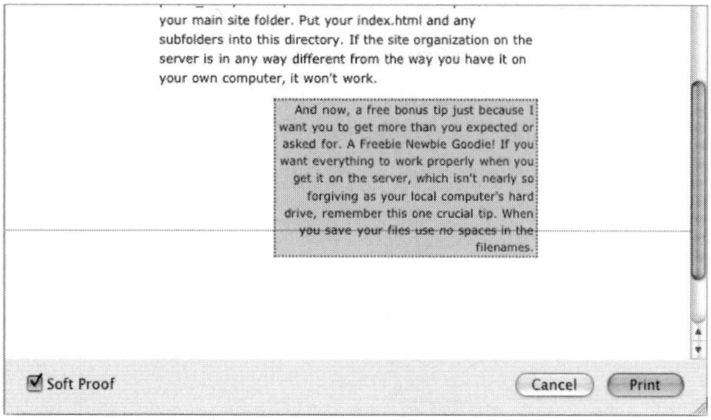

FIGURE 6.22

The footer does not display in Internet Explorer's print preview.

Setting Print Margins

The need for short line lengths is not so important in print. It is easier for the eye to track across a long line and then find its way back to the next line without getting lost when reading a printed page.

Ch6_allmedia.css has the body set with margins of 20% on both the left and right. You can change that rule in the Ch6_print.css stylesheet to allow the page to print the full width of a sheet of paper.

Printers understand measurement in inches (in) and points (pt), so use those units in your print styles. First, change the body margin to 0.5in to apply to top, right, bottom, and left:

```
body {
   margin: 0.5in;
}
```

If you use the browser's print preview to view this change, you'll see the layout shown in Figure 6.23.

Changing the Font Size for Print

Another change you should make for print is to set font-size values in points. You will need a rule for h1, h2, and p. A reasonable point size for most printed text is 12pt. You can make the headings slightly larger than that:

```
p {
   font-size: 12pt;
}
h1 {
   font-size: 18pt;
}
h2 {
   font-size: 16pt;
}
```

COMMENT THAT

The footer really should be there in print. I had you hide it temporarily to make a point. If you use comments around the rule in the CSS, it will still be there for your future reference, but it will not affect the display.

One of the nice things about using comments is that you can leave notes to yourself or to others with whom you might work. You could wrap the whole rule in a comment something like this:

```
/*this rule stops an element from displaying

#footer {

  display: none;

}*/
```

If you save that, the footer will indeed display when printing, but the rule will be saved to remind you at some later date how to stop elements from displaying.

Viewing the print preview now, you should not see a noticeable change from Figure 6.23.

NOTE A point is an actual physical measurement in print: it is 1/72 of an inch. Twelve points equal one pica in the print world. There is no corresponding physical measurement with pixels on a computer screen that can be guaranteed across platforms, screen resolutions, and browsers. Therefore, points are not a good choice for screen-media styles, but they are perfect for print-media styles.

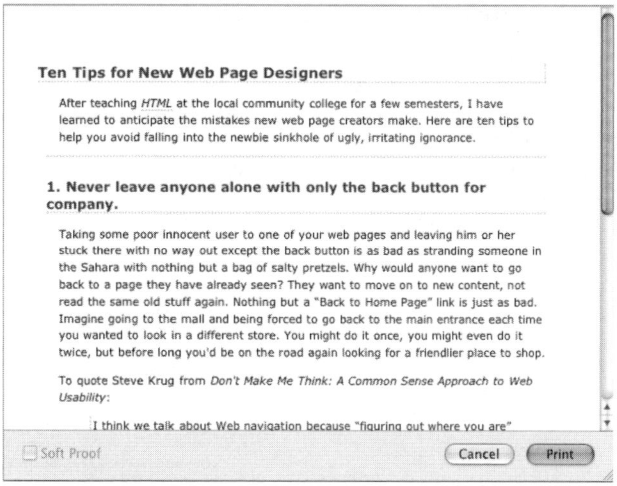

FIGURE 6.23
Half-inch margins in
a print preview

Ten Tips for New Web Page Designers

After teaching *HTML* at the local community college for a few semesters, I have learned to anticipate the mistakes new web page creators make. Here are ten tips to help you avoid falling into the newbie sinkhole of ugly, irritating ignorance.

1. Never leave anyone alone with only the back button for company.

Taking some poor innocent user to one of your web pages and leaving him or her stuck there with no way out except the back button is as bad as stranding someone in the Sahara with nothing but a bag of salty pretzels. Why would anyone want to go back to a page they have already seen? They want to move on to new content, not read the same old stuff again. Nothing but a "Back to Home Page" link is just as bad. Imagine going to the mall and being forced to go back to the main entrance each time you wanted to look in a different store. You might do it once, you might even do it twice, but before long you'd be on the road again looking for a friendlier place to shop.

To quote Steve Krug from *Don't Make Me Think: A Common Sense Approach to Web Usability*:

I think we talk about Web navigation because "figuring out where you are"

☐ Soft Proof   (Cancel) (Print)

PRINTING MEANS "USER'S CHOICE"

One thing to keep in mind with print is that the user has options that you have no control over. When setting up to print a page, the user decides whether or not to print background colors and images, whether or not to print URLs or page numbers in header or footer sections of the printed page, and sometimes what margins to use. Keep these things in mind when creating your print rules:

◆ It is safest to assume that the user will not print backgrounds. If you designed a page with a black background and white text, the user might get white text on a white page when printing.

◆ Not all users have color printers, so you may need to rethink all your color choices in your print style rules to ensure good contrast in black and white.

◆ If a background image is used, it may not appear on the printed page.

Changing the Font Family for Print

Serif fonts are generally considered more readable in print. You originally set the font in the body selector. Revisit the body selector and add a declaration changing to a serif font. Georgia is a readable serif font, so list it as first choice:

```
body {
   margin: 0.5in;
   font-family: Georgia, Times, serif;
}
```

Your print preview should reveal something similar to Figure 6.24.

Changing the Text Indent for Print

Although the first line of a paragraph may or may not be indented on the Web, a printed paragraph is expected to be indented. The property that will indent the first line of a given element is text-indent.

FIGURE 6.24
Print preview with serif fonts

> ### Ten Tips for New Web Page Designers
>
> After teaching *HTML* at the local community college for a few semesters, I have learned to anticipate the mistakes new web page creators make. Here are ten tips to help you avoid falling into the newbie sinkhole of ugly, irritating ignorance.
>
> ### 1. Never leave anyone alone with only the back button for company.
>
> Taking some poor innocent user to one of your web pages and leaving him or her stuck there with no way out except the back button is as bad as stranding someone in the Sahara with nothing but a bag of salty pretzels. Why would anyone want to go back to a page they have already seen? They want to move on to new content, not read the same old stuff again. Nothing but a "Back to Home Page" link is just as bad. Imagine going to the mall and being forced to go back to the main entrance each time you wanted to look in a different store. You might do it once, you might even do it twice, but before long you'd be on the road again looking for a friendlier place to shop.
>
> To quote Steve Krug from *Don't Make Me Think: A Common Sense Approach to Web...*
>
> ☐ Soft Proof   Cancel   Print

Revisit the p selector and add a couple of ems of indented space at the beginning of your paragraphs:

```
p {
  font-size: 12pt;
  text-indent: 2em;
}
```

A preview of the printed page reveals nicely indented paragraphs, as you see in Figure 6.25.

FIGURE 6.25
Indented paragraphs

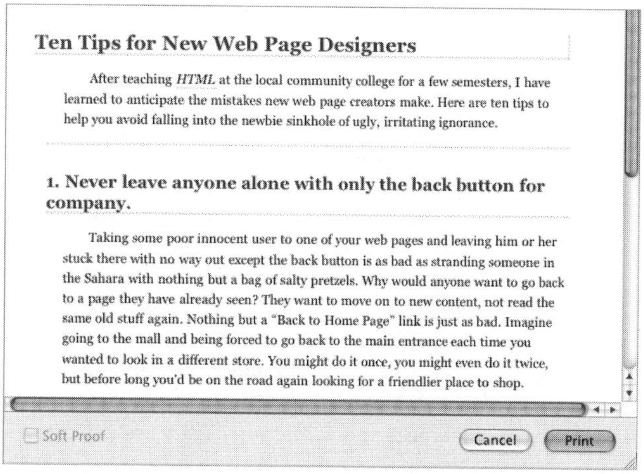

The Whole Stylesheet

That's it! You now have a readable document ready for reading on screen or in print. Your completed Ch6_print.css document includes only what you see in Listing 6.3.

LISTING 6.3:   The Print Stylesheet

```
body {
  margin: 0.5in;
  font-family: Georgia, Times, serif;
}
p {
  font-size: 12pt;
  text-indent: 2em;
}
h1 {
  font-size: 18pt;
}
h2 {
  font-size: 16pt;
}
```

You will also find a version of `Ch6_print.css` on the accompanying CD. It contains the four rules in Listing 6.3 and the `display: none` rule enclosed in comments.

The key concept to keep in mind for print stylesheets is that it is only necessary to include the selectors and rules that need a change from those in your main stylesheet. That statement is true, however, only if you take advantage of the Cascade by placing your print stylesheet link after your all-media stylesheet link.

Of course, most people don't print every web page they read. But if you think your content might be something people may want to print, you can see that it is not much more work for you to include a stylesheet that makes printing easy for your users.

Real World Example

Joe Gillespie's site Web Page Design for Designers, at `www.wpdfd.com`, has been a source of sound information on typography and web design for years. A recent view of the home page at Web Page Design for Designers (Figure 6.26) proclaims the eighth birthday of the site.

As you might imagine, the site began its days with a complex nested table design (you can still see some of those old pages in the reference section of the site) and has evolved to being marked up with standards-compliant XHTML and CSS. One of the most valuable pages on the site is the typography information at `www.wpdfd.com/wpdtypo.htm`. This page was written before the days of CSS, so some of the techniques he mentions are a bit dated and would be replaced by CSS now. But that does not detract from the valuable information on readability and typography contained in this article. I urge you to read it carefully.

Because of his interest in typography and readability, Joe Gillespie designed several tiny fonts. He calls them pixel fonts and mini fonts. They are designed so that they are readable at very small sizes, and you see them in use on the site. These fonts are great for navigation buttons or other places where you need to fit something into a small space and keep it readable. The fonts are not free, but they are inexpensive and worth keeping in mind in case you ever have a design problem that can only be solved by using a very small font size.

FIGURE 6.26
In August 2004, Web Page Design for Designers celebrated eight years on the Internet.

Written, designed, and produced by Joe Gillespie.

CSS Properties

Most of the CSS properties used in Chapter 6 were explained earlier in the book.

TABLE 6.3:   Properties for Element and Text Display

SELECTOR	PROPERTY	POSSIBLE VALUES
all elements	`display`	`none`, `inline`, `block`, `inline-block`, `list-item`, `run-in`, `table`, `inline-table`, `table-row-group`, `table-row`, `table-column-group`, `table-column`, `table-cell`, `table-caption`, `inherit`
all block-level elements	`text-indent`	*<length>*, *<percentage>*, `inherit`
all block-level elements except tables	`min-width`	*<length>*, *<percentage>*, `inherit`
all block-level elements except tables	`max-width`	*<length>*, *<percentage>*, `none`, `inherit`

Challenge Yourself

Take some time to experiment with the CSS that is used to display this page. Try out some ideas of your own, and see if you can make the changes suggested here.

1. The `border-top: 2px dotted #CCC;` used for the h2 elements is rather far away from the text of the h2. Can you move it closer to the h2 without giving up any of the white space between the h2 and the paragraph above it? (Hint: think about the `padding` versus `margin` discussion.)

2. Think of a different way to style the headings: perhaps using `background-color` or `background-image` rules or a different `font` color or size.

3. Change the print stylesheet so that the body selector `margin-top` is set to 0 while leaving the right, bottom, and left margins at 0.5in.

4. Instead of using a `background-image` for the callouts, try using a `background-color` or a `border` to distinguish them from the other text.

Summary

XHTML contains many elements to format text. You worked with a variety of elements, including headings, paragraphs, `blockquote`, `em`, `strong`, and `cite` in this chapter.

CSS allows effective techniques to make long articles on the Web more reader friendly. You used many CSS properties and rules to assist with readability and appearance.

Reading from a printed page makes different demands on a reader than reading from a computer screen. Adding a print-media stylesheet to your web design will help your users get the best results when printing your pages.

In Chapter 7 you will work with links, discovering how to incorporate them into your XHTML document and style them so readers of your page can easily use them.

Chapter 7

Links and Link Styles

The real Web doesn't work with individual pages completely detached from each other; it's composed of sets of multiple files and folders, organized and connected with each other through elements called *links*. You write links to allow navigation among all the files within a given site, to web pages outside the site, and to resources beyond just HTML pages: e-mail links, links to sound clips, and links to PDF documents.

CSS can help you to style links in various ways based on color and state (that is, whether a link has been visited or whether the pointer is hovering over the link).

Now that you're moving up to look at more than one page at a time, this chapter also introduces organizing and managing the various files that are assembled in the making of a website.

Organizing a Site

Before you get into writing the XHTML for links, you need to look at some of the basics of how a site is organized and stored. When you begin working on a new site, you should create a new folder (directory) on your computer where you will save every document that will be transferred to the server when the site is complete. This includes all the HTML files, all the images, and other material such as sound files, multimedia files, and any material that will eventually be transferred to a server as part of the site. You can add as many subfolders (subdirectories) to this folder as you need, so long as all your files are kept within the main site folder.

NOTE Although working with databases is not covered in this book, you need to be aware that databases are stored on computers and servers in different locations from the main site folder where you store documents related to your site.

I will discuss this again in Chapter 11 when you learn how to put a website on a server, but it is important enough to say here, too: the organization that you set up on your own computer for a website must be created in exactly the same way when you put your files on the server. That is because of the way links work. A link is like a path or a map to a file's location. If the file isn't in the exact location that you write in the link, then the computer returns one of those "File Not Found" errors that make users leave your site at warp speed.

TIP Absolute links, which you will learn about later in this chapter in the section "Relative and Absolute Links," will continue to work even if the site is not organized in exactly the same way on the server as on your computer.

On the CD, you will find a small sample site. In the Chapter 7 folder on the CD, find the folder called `link_exercises`. Copy this entire folder and everything in it. Save it on your computer in the folder with your other files for this book. You should see a folder named `link_exercises` when you are finished copying.

Taking an icon view of the folder, you should see something like Figure 7.1. Depending on whether you are using Windows, Linux, or Mac, there may be slight differences in your view and what you see in Figure 7.1, but the files and folders should have the names shown in Figure 7.1

In Figure 7.1, you see that there are two HTML files that are not in any subfolder and four subfolders: `assets`, `images`, `green`, and `yellow`.

Another way of looking at the `link_exercises` files is the list view of the folder, as in Figure 7.2. Again, your view may differ slightly from Figure 7.2 depending on your platform.

If the list is expanded to reveal the contents of all the subfolders, you see something like Figure 7.3.

FIGURE 7.1
`link_exercises`
icon view

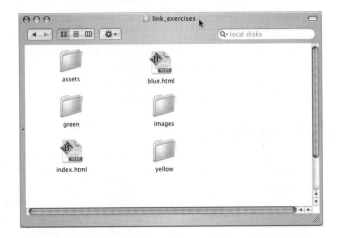

FIGURE 7.2
`link_exercises`
list view

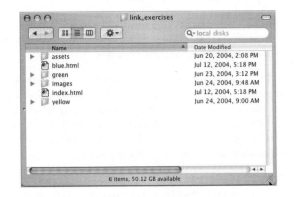

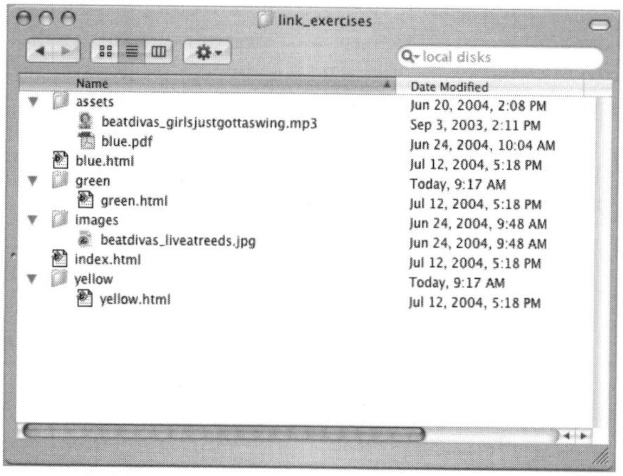

FIGURE 7.3
link_exercises
expanded list view

Anatomy of a URL

A *uniform resource locator* (URL) locates servers and files and is a mirror of your site organization. The first part of a URL is a *protocol* (or scheme) such as the Hypertext Transfer Protocol (http). Immediately after the protocol, you see the server name:

    http://www.aserver.com/

The URL might go deeper into a website, listing a path through folders and filenames to find an exact file to display:

    http://www.aserver.com/folder/file.html

Users can see your folder names and your filenames in the browser location (or address) bar as they navigate your site.

You will also see the acronym *URI,* for Uniform Resource Indicator. URL and URI perform the same function; that is, they point the way to the resource in question. URI is the umbrella term for URLs and other Uniform Resource Identifiers.

An important part of planning a site is to imagine all the files the completed site will contain so that a suitable organization plan can be put in place from the beginning.

ANNOUNCING SUBDIRECTORIES

I have recently noticed that several advertisers assume a certain level of Internet savvy from the general public and include subfolders in URLs that they use in ads. I've heard TV ads urging me to "Visit www.sbc.com/details for more information," or to "Visit www.bravotv.com/queereye for more information." At one time, the prevailing wisdom was to make everyone enter a site through the home page so as not to miss any advertising along the way. Now the idea seems to be to acknowledge that users are in a hurry and want the fastest route to the information, and to assume that users are so well-versed in using the Internet that a URL that includes a subfolder won't confuse them.

Getting well organized in the beginning is much easier than going back after a site has grown or expanded and moving files around or reorganizing the folder structure because the relative links (I'll explain relative links a little later) you already have built into your site will not work properly if files are moved. If you move files and folders after a site is already on a server, it will change URLs within your site, and bookmarked pages might not be found by users who were familiar with your site.

Folder Names

Websites frequently contain folders named `images`. The folder name `assets` is used for subfolders by some of the HTML-generating software tools, so it is often seen in a website. Depending on the size of the site, HTML documents might be organized into subfolders, as in the `green` and `yellow` example.

Subfolder names depend on the site. If a site has a large number of sound clips, it might be wise to organize them in a folder named `music` or `sound` or a similar name. If a site has a large number of PDF files, it might be wise to store them all in a folder named `pdf`.

The subfolder name should be short and reflect its purpose. Keep in mind that folder names might end up in a web address you want someone to remember and use. If the coach stood on the football field and announced, "Just go to the website at `xhs.edu/football` for our next game date," more people would remember and find the site than if he said, "Just go to the website at `xhs.edu/ph_f_c2`." (The information after the forward slash in this address is a subfolder on the `xhs.edu` server.)

If you organize a site for an elementary school, you might create subfolders named `calendar`, `grade1`, `grade2`, `staff`, and so on. If you organize a site for an ice skating rink, you might create folders named `classes`, `shop`, or `events`.

Do not use spaces in folder names. The hyphen (-) and the underscore (_) are allowed but should be avoided for folder names that might be released to the public in situations like the football example just mentioned. You can use numbers as long as the number is not the first character in the name. For example, a folder named `mp3` is acceptable. Capitals are allowed, but again, it pays to be careful. If the link is not capitalized in exactly the same way as the folder name and the server happens to be case sensitive (as some are), the link won't work. For example, `showdates/gigs.html` is different from `showDates/gigs.html` on case sensitive servers.

Home Page

Notice the file called `index.html`. This file is the site's home page. The site's home page must not be placed inside any of the subfolders.

TIP   The home page may be named `index.html`, `index.htm`, or `default.htm`, depending on the server. The browser will automatically open whichever of these is present on the server in any site or folder. See Chapter 11 for more information on publishing your site on a server and on finding help and information from the server company about whether the server is configured to use `index.html`, `index.htm`, or `default.htm`.

You probably know dozens of web addresses: `www.google.com`, `www.cnn.com`, `www.dell.com`, or any site you visit regularly. Most sites have a home page with the filename `index.html`. You don't have to remember or type in the name of this particular page in the website, such as `www.google.com/index.html` because the browser will automatically look for a file called `index.html` and open it. If the home page has a filename like `home.html`, it must be included in the URL when advertising the site or giving potential users the site address. A home page file named `home.html` will not be automatically opened by the browser unless there is a link specifically written that targets it.

More complex websites, such as large commercial sites, may use a database and some form of scripting to interact with the database. In sites like that—for example, Starbucks Coffee—when you type `www.starbucks.com` in the browser address bar, it quickly and automatically changes, to something like:

```
http://www.starbucks.com/Default.asp?cookie%5Ftest=1
```

From this, you can conclude that Starbucks is using Active Server Pages (ASP) technology and a database to produce web pages.

For the work you will be doing in this book, and for most small sites that aren't connected to a database, the home page will be named `index.html`.

This is true as you go deeper into a website as well. When the browser goes into a subfolder or directory, it looks for a file called `index.html` to open if no other filename is given in the link. If your `link_exercises` site had so many pages in the `green` folder that you wanted a main page for that folder, you could make an `index.html` page for the `yellow` folder. In `xhs.edu/football`, you know there is a folder named football on the server xhs.edu, and there is an index.html page in that folder that is the main page for the football section of the site.

Learn the XHTML

When you click a link on the Web, the link most likely uses the a (for anchor) tag with an `href` (for hypertext reference) attribute. An example:

```
<a href="somefile.html">Click me</a>
```

The default display for `<a href="somefile.html">Click me</a>` is for the words *Click me* to appear in blue and to be underlined. If you click the link and get whisked away to the page named `somefile.html`, then the next time you see `<a href="somefile.html">Click me</a>` rendered in the browser, the default display will be in the "visited" link color and still be underlined.

For years, all links were underlined, all unvisited links were blue, and all visited links were a reddish purple. With CSS, you can change those defaults. It is good to be careful when altering normal browser renderings, however, so your users don't get confused and not realize that a word is a link.

LINKS, ANCHORS, AND TERMINOLOGY

The a tag is one of the few tags that hindsight tells us could have been better named. One of its first purposes was to allow users to jump around to various points (anchors) on a single page. The word "anchor" makes sense there; calling a tag an anchor when it allows you to jump to another page in your site or to some completely different site does not make the same semantic sense. Some people resort to incorrectly calling the anchor tag "a link tag" although there is a real `link` tag that you have used to link your stylesheets to your XHTML pages in previous chapters. Still others call it an "an href" tag, even though the `href` is an attribute. You use a tags to *anchor* links to other documents or locations on a page, but a tags are not `link` tags.

You create a link to another web page using an a tag. You link to a stylesheet using a `link` tag. In everyday usage, the a tag used to link to another web page is often referred to as "a link," even though it is technically "an anchor."

TIP   Although you may be accustomed to underlining words in print for emphasis, it is not a good idea on the Web, because users think it indicates a link.

Linking from One Page to Another in the Same Directory

Open the index.html page both in your text editor and in the browser. You will add some links to this page. In the browser, the page looks like Figure 7.4.

FIGURE 7.4
The prebuilt
index.html page

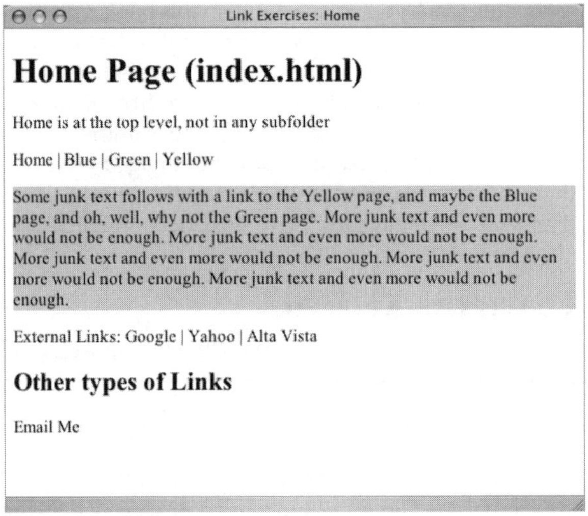

> **Link Exercises: Home**
>
> # Home Page (index.html)
>
> Home is at the top level, not in any subfolder
>
> Home | Blue | Green | Yellow
>
> Some junk text follows with a link to the Yellow page, and maybe the Blue page, and oh, well, why not the Green page. More junk text and even more would not be enough. More junk text and even more would not be enough. More junk text and even more would not be enough. More junk text and even more would not be enough. More junk text and even more would not be enough.
>
> External Links: Google | Yahoo | Alta Vista
>
> ## Other types of Links
>
> Email Me

The index.html page, as well as all the other pages in the link_exercises folder, is pretty ugly. The pages have an ever-changing color scheme. Just ignore the ugliness as best you can. You will see the reason for all the color changes as you get into the CSS for controlling how links appear, so be patient. Each page has a style section embedded in the head, which you will use to do the practice CSS exercises.

The first link you create will be from the index.html page, which you have open in your text editor, to the blue.html page. You do not need to have blue.html open to do this.

It is important to notice that index.html and blue.html are both in the same folder but neither is in any subfolder.

1. Let's begin with the menu. Find this line in index.html:

```
<div id="menu"><p>Home | Blue | Green | Yellow</p></div>
```

The word "Blue" will be the clickable part of your first link.

TIP   The vertical line (|) (sometimes called "the pipe") you see between the words that will become the clickable words in the menu is made with the key above the Enter (Return) key on the right side of your keyboard.

2. To create the link, add the highlighted text to the line:

```
<div id="menu"><p>Home | <a href="blue.html">Blue</a> | Green | Yellow</p></div>
```

3. Save that change and refresh (reload) the browser.

The results look like the close-up in Figure 7.5. Notice where the spaces in the XHTML are. There is a space before the a tag opens and after the a tag terminates. You don't want the spaces that separate the word "Blue" from its neighbors to be inside the a element, because they would be treated as part of the a element and underlined.

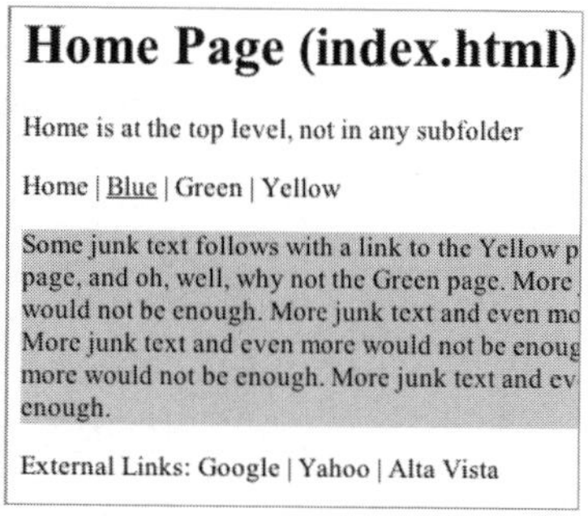

FIGURE 7.5
The word "Blue" is now clickable.

Home Page (index.html)

Home is at the top level, not in any subfolder

Home | <u>Blue</u> | Green | Yellow

Some junk text follows with a link to the Yellow p page, and oh, well, why not the Green page. More would not be enough. More junk text and even mo More junk text and even more would not be enoug more would not be enough. More junk text and ev enough.

External Links: Google | Yahoo | Alta Vista

If you click this word, you will indeed be taken to the blue.html page. (You can use the Back button to return to the index.html page, since you don't have any working links on the blue.html page yet.) There is another place where you can make a link to the blue.html page: in the thrillingly written text of the content division.

```
<p>Some junk text follows with a link to the Yellow page, and maybe the Blue page,
and oh, well, why not the Green page...</p>
```

Add this second link, exactly like the first one:

```
<p>Some junk text follows with a link to the Yellow page, and maybe the <a
href="blue.html">Blue</a> page, and oh, well, why not the Green page...</p>
```

Save and refresh (reload) the browser. You have made a link in the paragraph, but it is blue on blue because of the page's colors and a bit hard to see, as shown in Figure 7.6. As I mentioned earlier, with CSS you can change the link colors, so you will take care of the blue-on-blue visibility problem with a style in just a bit.

When you use the pointing device or mouse to hover over a link, the normal cursor changes to a pointing finger like the one in Figure 7.7.

It is possible to remove the underline from a link. If you do, be sure there is some other clue to the fact that the word is, in fact, a link. If a more obvious clue that clearly communicates clickability, such as an underline, fails to appear on a web page, users might start desperately running the mouse around a page searching for a clue to the existence of a link in the form of a pointing finger. Or even worse, visitors might just leave because the page seems unusable.

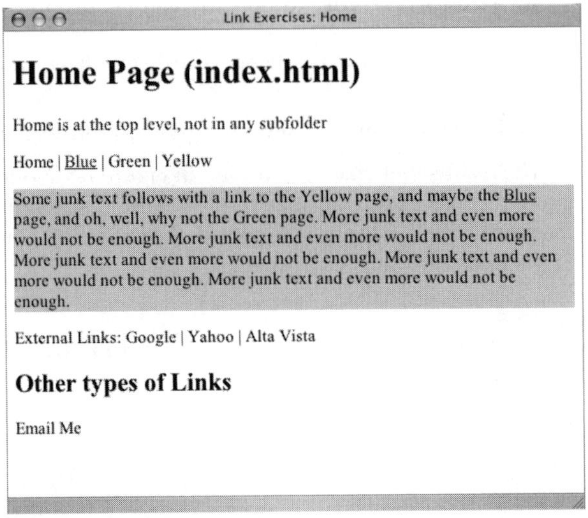

FIGURE 7.6
The blue link in a blue area is hard to see.

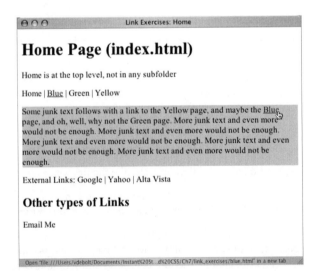

FIGURE 7.7
The cursor becomes a pointing finger over a link.

At this point, you have two links to `blue.html`. One is an obvious navigation area, and one is in some text. Otherwise, they are exactly alike. Before you move on to links to files that are not together in the same folder, you'll put some links on the `blue.html` page to connect it to `index.html`.

LINKING BACK TO HOME

Open `blue.html` in your text editor and in your browser. Other than color, the page is very like `index.html`. The `menu` is the same. You will start with the `menu`.

```
<div id="menu"><p>Home | Blue | Green | Yellow</p></div>
```

This time you want to make the word "Home" into a clickable link to the `index.html` page. It should be exactly like the link you wrote to `blue.html`, except the Home `href` value is `index.html`. Try to do it on your own before you look at the following.

Here's what you should have done:

```
<div id="menu"><p><a href="index.html">Home</a> | Blue | Green | Yellow</p></div>
```

While you are at it, also make the word "Home" in the paragraph of the `content` division a link, like this:

```
<p>Some junk text follows with a link to the <a href="index.html">Home</a> page,
and maybe the Yellow page, and oh, well, why not the Green page...</a>
```

Save those two changes and refresh (reload) the browser. I've zoomed in on the page, where you will see something like Figure 7.8.

It's party time! Now you can jump back and forth between Home and Blue as many times as you would like, because the two pages are linked.

The basics of the a element are simple, but there are some slightly more intricate things you need to know when the two files are not in the same folder. So before you can finish linking up all your site's pages, you need to learn about relative and absolute links.

FIGURE 7.8
Two links to Home
are working.

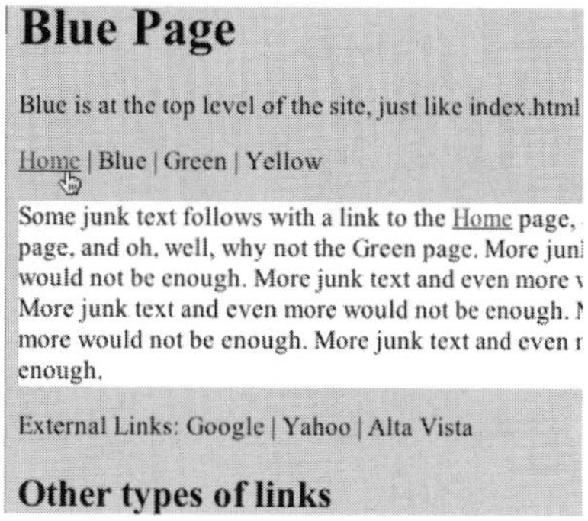

Blue Page

Blue is at the top level of the site, just like index.html

Home | Blue | Green | Yellow

Some junk text follows with a link to the Home page,
page, and oh, well, why not the Green page. More junk
would not be enough. More junk text and even more w
More junk text and even more would not be enough. N
more would not be enough. More junk text and even r
enough.

External Links: Google | Yahoo | Alta Vista

Other types of links

Relative and Absolute Links

Within your own website, in this case `link_exercises`, you generally write *relative* links. A relative link describes the path to a file in reference to the file where the link is located. It is a type of "you are here" map that describes the path from the file where the link is located to the destination file. The two links you just completed are relative links.

You can write a relative link to anything within the main site folder. A relative link to the home page of a site might be different on different pages of a site. To get to `index.html` from a page in the `green` folder, a different path is followed than to get to `index.html` from the `blue.html` page. Hold on to this thought about what a relative link is, and let's find out what an absolute link is.

If you write a link to a file outside your own site folder, you must write an *absolute* link. An absolute link gives the complete URL, or path, to a file. `http://www.google.com/` and `ftp://somesite.com/` are examples of absolute URLs. The absolute link must include the protocol, server, and possibly a folder or filename. An absolute URL with a scheme, server, folder, and file would look something like this:

```
http://www.example.com/folder/file.html
```

An absolute link will always be exactly the same, no matter where in a site it is located. You have a section requiring absolute links on your practice pages. You will write those links before we go back to relative links.

NOTE When writing an absolute link in XHTML that ends with a server or folder name, include the trailing slash: `http://www.example.com/`. When I give a URL to you, the reader, to visit, I sometimes provide an abbreviated version without the slash or even without the protocol, such as `google.com` or `www.sybex.com`. This is fine for readability in print, but be complete when writing code.

LINKING TO PAGES OUTSIDE YOUR SITE: WRITING ABSOLUTE LINKS

Each of your pages awaits links to Google, Yahoo, and Alta Vista (see Figure 7.9). These will be absolute URLs. Since you don't have Google, Yahoo!, or Alta Vista within your site folder, a relative link to these pages will not work.

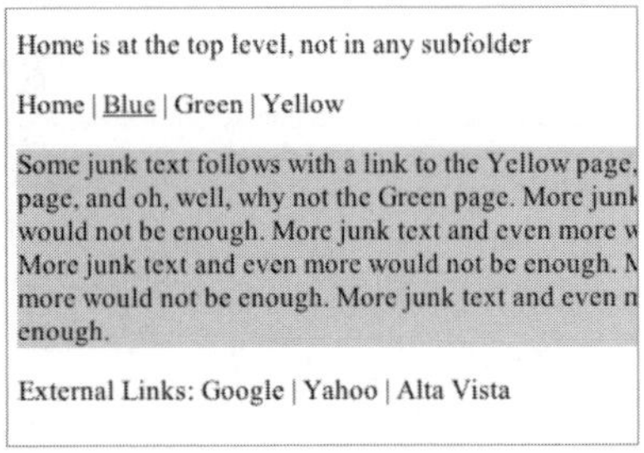

FIGURE 7.9
The External Links will be absolute links.

Home is at the top level, not in any subfolder

Home | Blue | Green | Yellow

Some junk text follows with a link to the Yellow page, page, and oh, well, why not the Green page. More junk would not be enough. More junk text and even more w More junk text and even more would not be enough. N more would not be enough. More junk text and even n enough.

External Links: Google | Yahoo | Alta Vista

The XHTML is here:

```
<div class="external">
    <p>External Links: Google | Yahoo | Alta Vista</p>
</div>
```

Normally it would be a bad idea to have links leading away from your site on every page. After all, you want people to stay on your site and sample your content.

However, one of the goals of this chapter is to learn to control link colors on various backgrounds, so these external links will become useful during the CSS exercises.

TIP Links to external sites are a plus when using weblogs. See Chapter 13 for more about weblogs.

Every one of the practice pages has the same lines of XHTML code for these links. If you complete the changes on one of the pages, you can copy it and paste it over the appropriate line on the remaining pages. That way you won't have to retype the same links four times.

You use the a element, just as with a relative link. The href attribute contains the absolute value for the URL. Here is a link to Google:

```
<a href="http://www.google.com/">Google</a>
```

The address of Yahoo is `http://www.yahoo.com/`, and the address of Alta Vista is `http://www.altavista.com/`. Try to complete those two links yourself before you look at the following code. Be aware that your lines may not wrap in exactly the same places as this example:

```
<div class="external">
  <p>External Links: <a href="http://www.google.com/">Google</a> | <a href="http://www.yahoo.com/">Yahoo</a> | <a href="http://www.altavista.com/">Alta Vista</a></p>
</div>
```

TIP You should write the link with a forward slash after the server name, as in `<a href="http://www.google.com/">Google</a>`. The page will open without the trailing forward slash, but using it is considered best practice. The new page will open faster with the forward slash in the URL, too.

The `index.html` page should look like Figure 7.10 in the browser when the external links are complete. If you click any of the new links to test them, you can use the Back button to return to your page. Notice that the color of the link changes after you visit a page.

Copy the completed set of links and paste it in the proper spot on each of your other HTML pages to replace the nonlinked text that is there.

Specifically, on every page you will replace this:

```
<div class="external">
   <p>External Links: Google | Yahoo | Alta Vista</p>
</div>
```

with this:

```
<div class="external">
  <p>External Links: <a href="http://www.google.com/">Google</a> | <a href="http://www.yahoo.com/">Yahoo</a> | <a href="http://www.altavista.com/">Alta Vista</a></p>
</div>
```

FIGURE 7.10
The home page with external links

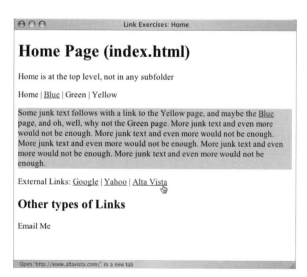

TIP In your browser's preferences, you can set preferences for history and cache. Sometimes these settings are under an Advanced heading, depending on the browser. You can select Clear History, which will give you a fresh start when you are testing pages and want to see a link color as it would be before a page was visited. You can select Empty Cache, which deletes all the saved versions of your page stored by the browser. Also under Cache, you can select Always Update Pages so that your changed pages will be displayed instead of a cached version of your page when you revisit a page.

Linking to Pages in Different Directories

As noted, a relative link gives a pathway from one place in your website to another place in your website. There has to be some code to use to explain this pathway to the computer, and there is: two periods (..) and the forward slash (/). The two periods are pronounced "dot dot." These two symbols, used separately, together, or in multiple combinations, give the computer the needed instructions to navigate your file and folder organization and find any file. Whether or not a relative link requires any, or one, or more ../ codes depends on where the files being linked together are *in relation to each other*. You are going to get some hands-on practice in a bit, which will help you understand relative links.

The two periods tell the computer to move up a level in the folder (directory) structure. The forward slash tells the computer to move into a folder (directory) or it separates a folder name from a filename.

Look at your folder setup again, and then you will write some specific examples. See Figure 7.11.

You already know that if two files are in the same folder, you merely have to name the file—e.g., a href="index.html" when the link is located on blue.html.

The next few subsections give you practice at linking documents in various places throughout a site's folder structure.

FIGURE 7.11
The site organization with path examples

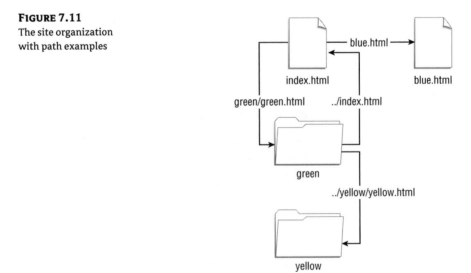

LINKING UP ONE LEVEL

The file green.html is located in the subdirectory green. To link to index.html from inside green, the path in the link must lead out of green and then give the filename. You use the ../ path to get from green.html to index.html, like this:

```
<a href="../index.html">Home</a>
```

Open green.html in your text editor and add the link. Find menu, which looks like this:

```
<div id="menu"><p><a href="../index.html">Home</a> | Blue | Green | Yellow</p></
div>
```

The same code is used in the paragraph to create a link to the home page.

```
<p>Some junk text follows with a link to the <a href="../index.html">Home</a> page,
and maybe the Blue page, and oh, well, why not the Yellow page...</p>
```

Your page should look similar to Figure 7.12. At this point, you still need to use the Back button to return to the Green page.

Your next link is to blue.html from green.html. A look back at Figure 7.11 reminds you that blue.html is located in the same place as index.html, so the same ../ works as the path to blue.html. In menu, you would add this:

```
<div id="menu"><p><a href="../index.html">Home</a> | <a href="../blue.html">Blue</
a> | Green | Yellow</p></div>
```

Write a link in the paragraph to make the word "Blue" in the paragraph a link. When finished, you should see something similar to Figure 7.13 in the browser.

FIGURE 7.12
The Home links on
the Green page

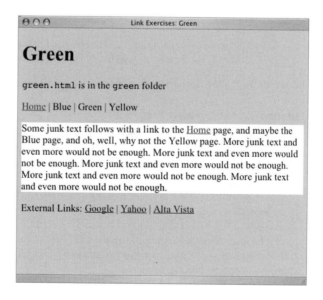

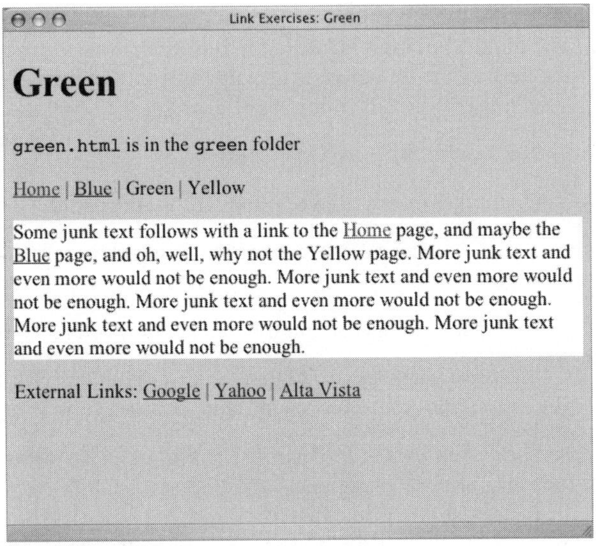

FIGURE 7.13
The Blue links on
the Green page

LINKING TO A PAGE IN A PARALLEL FOLDER

While you have `green.html` open, you should link to `yellow.html`, but `href="../yellow.html"` won't work. It would lead out of `green`, but there is no file called `yellow.html` to be found there.

Instead, you have to add the name of the folder where `yellow.html` is located to your pathway. The path must translate to "go out of `green`, then go into `yellow`, then look for a file called `yellow.html`." The path should be: `../yellow/yellow.html`.

Now `menu` looks like this:

```
<div id="menu"><p><a href="../index.html">Home</a> | <a href="../blue.html">Blue</
a> | Green | <a href="../yellow/yellow.html">Yellow</a></p></div>
```

With the Yellow link in the paragraph, you should see something similar to Figure 7.14.

INDICATING THE CURRENT PAGE

When writing links on `green.html`, you did not add a link in the menu area for Green. That is one way to indicate to the user that Green is the current page. There are other effective ways to give a visual clue in the menu area that the user is currently on a particular page. You will use CSS for this later in the chapter.

It is important not to remove the word "Green" from the main navigation, namely the `menu` division. New designers sometimes think, "Well, I'm on the green page where I don't need a link to the green page, so I'll just take that word out of the menu." Don't fall into this type of thinking. Once users have a look at your main navigation, they expect it to be the same from page to page within the site. If the words appear and disappear on different pages, or if the order of the words in the menu changes, users get lost.

FIGURE 7.14
The completed Green page

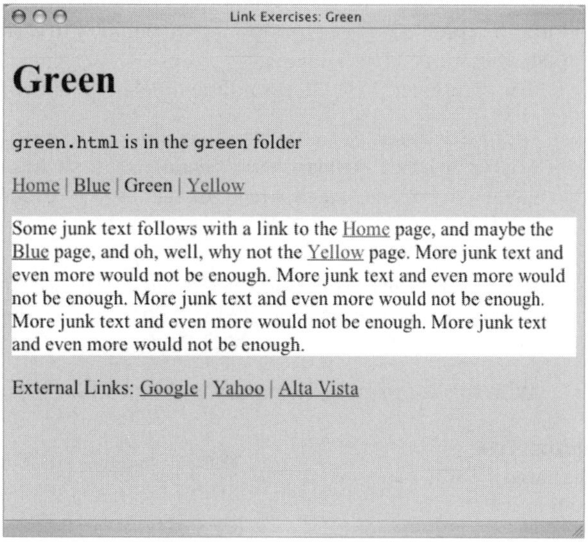

Link Exercises: Green
Green
green.html is in the green folder
Home | Blue | Green | Yellow
Some junk text follows with a link to the Home page, and maybe the Blue page, and oh, well, why not the Yellow page. More junk text and even more would not be enough. More junk text and even more would not be enough. More junk text and even more would not be enough. More junk text and even more would not be enough. More junk text and even more would not be enough.
External Links: Google | Yahoo | Alta Vista

LINKING FROM THE YELLOW PAGE

Open `yellow.html` in your text editor and in the browser. With the external links completed, the page looks similar to Figure 7.15 in a browser.

Like, `green.html`, `yellow.html` is in a subfolder. The subfolder is `yellow`. Other than the fact that the subfolder has a different name, the rules for navigating from within `yellow` to `index.html`, `blue.html` or into `green` and `green.html` are exactly the same as those you used for the links on `green.html`.

FIGURE 7.15
The opening Yellow page

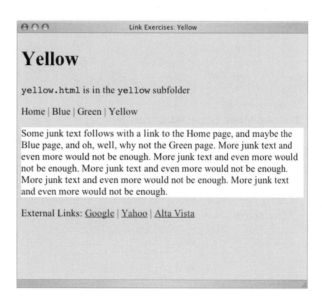

Link Exercises: Yellow
Yellow
yellow.html is in the yellow subfolder
Home | Blue | Green | Yellow
Some junk text follows with a link to the Home page, and maybe the Blue page, and oh, well, why not the Green page. More junk text and even more would not be enough. More junk text and even more would not be enough. More junk text and even more would not be enough. More junk text and even more would not be enough. More junk text and even more would not be enough.
External Links: Google | Yahoo | Alta Vista

Use `../` to indicate a path out of `yellow` to both `index.html` and `blue.html`. Use `../green` to indicate a path out of `yellow` and into `green`. Try to complete the links to all three of the other HTML pages before you check below.

The completed XHTML for all the links is as follows:

```
<div id="menu">
<p><a href="../index.html">Home</a> | <a href="../blue.html">Blue</a> | <a
href="../green/green.html">Green</a> | Yellow</p>
</div>
<div id="content">
   <p>Some junk text follows with a link to the <a href="../index.html">Home</a>
page, and maybe the <a href="../blue.html">Blue</a> page, and oh, well, why not the
<a href="../green/green.html">Green</a> page...</p>
```

With this completed, the page should look like Figure 7.16.

FIGURE 7.16
The linked
Yellow page

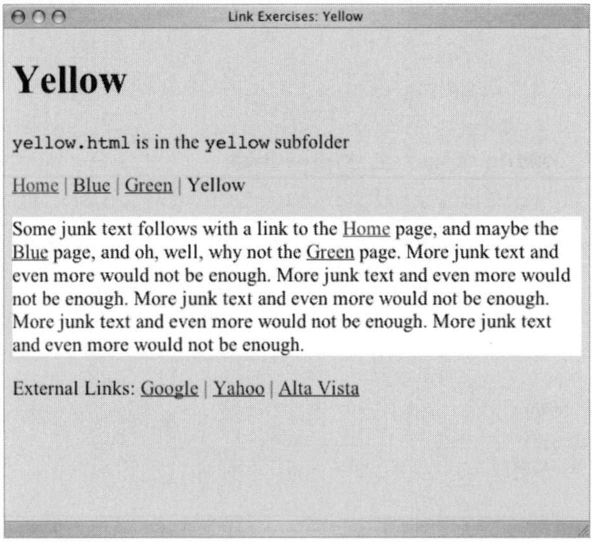

LINKING MORE THAN ONE LEVEL UP

You might have even more nested folders. What if inside `yellow` there was another subfolder: `subyel`? You could navigate from inside `subyel` through `yellow`, and then up to `index.html`. Your site organization would look like Figure 7.17.

The secret is `../../`. You can use the `../` construction as many times as you need it to move through the folder (directory) structure. In this example, the path `../../index.html` translates to "leave `subyel`, leave `yellow`, look for `index.html`."

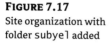

FIGURE 7.17
Site organization with
folder `subyel` added

COMPLETING YOUR SITE'S LINKS

Return to `index.html`. You need to add links to Green and Yellow there. Currently, `menu` on `index.html` is

```
<div id="menu"><p>Home | <a href="blue.html">Blue</a> | Green | Yellow</p></div>
```

To indicate a path to `green.html`, you do *not* need `../`, because you aren't moving *out* of a folder, you are moving *into* a folder. The path is `folder/file.html`.

For moving from `index.html` to `green.html`, then, the link is

```
<a href="green/green.html">Green</a>
```

The link from `index.html` to `yellow.html` follows the same plan, except that the name of the folder reflects the location of `yellow.html`.

Complete the links on `index.html`. The completed XHTML is

```
<div id="menu">
<p>Home | <a href="blue.html">Blue</a> | <a href="green/green.html">Green</a> | <a
href="yellow/yellow.html">Yellow</a></p>
</div>
<div id="content">
   <p>Some junk text follows with a link to the <a href="yellow/
yellow.html">Yellow</a> page, and maybe the <a href="blue_vd.html">Blue</a> page,
and oh, well, why not the <a href="green/green.html">Green</a> page...</p>
```

The navigation for `blue.html` is exactly like that used for `index.html`. Complete the links on `blue.html`. The completed XHTML is

```
<div id="menu"><p><a href="index.html">Home</a> | Blue | <a href="green/
green.html">Green</a> | <a href="yellow/yellow.html">Yellow</a></p>
```

```
    </div>
    <div id="content">
      <p>Some junk text follows with a link to the <a href="index.html">Home</a> page,
    and maybe the <a href="yellow/yellow.html">Yellow</a> page, and oh, well, why not
    the <a href="green/green.html">Green</a> page...</p>
```

Now you can click from any page on this site to any other. You are almost finished learning how to make links.

Linking to Non-HTML Files

Many types of files can be put on web servers for display in a browser or for download. In addition to MP3 and PDF documents, you might link to various sound formats besides MP3, QuickTime movies, Flash files, Microsoft Word or PowerPoint documents, executable files, or other types of files.

SERVER ABSOLUTE LINKS

There is one other type of absolute link that is slightly different from the absolute URL links such as `<a href="http://www.google.com/">Google</a>` described earlier.

The other absolute link is a *server absolute*. It can be used with Apache servers, if the server is configured for it. It uses a forward slash (with no dots) to force the path to start from the site's root level on the server, like this: `<a href="/index.html">Home</a>`. That link can be used in any directory or subdirectory, and when it is clicked the server will start the path to the file at the root level of the server, rather than relative to the location of the file where the link is anchored.

As another example, suppose you have a subfolder called `legal` and in it is a privacy policy page called `privacy.html`. Further, suppose you want this link to the privacy policy to be on every single footer on every single page in the site, no matter where the page is located in the site structure. With a server absolute link like this `<a href="/legal/privacy.html">Privacy Policy</a>`, you can use the same element on every page anywhere in the site. It works anywhere in your site, because the path to the file begins at the site root level on the server.

Server absolutes are often used with Server Side Includes (SSIs), which are beyond the scope of this book but are great time savers that I'll describe very briefly. SSIs are time savers because they use a single file to control any number of web pages. In that sense, they are like CSS files. You change one SSI file on the server, and every page in the site that uses that Include changes instantly. Includes are little snippets of HTML code. perhaps no more that this:

```
    <a href="/legal/privacy.html">Privacy Policy</a>
```

That snippet is saved on the server as an Include file, perhaps called `privacy.inc`. Instead of putting the actual a element on the page in places where you want a link to the privacy policy, you put an Include command, which says in plain English, "Put the HTML from `privacy.inc` in this spot." Because the snippet of HTML that makes up the `privacy.inc` file uses a server absolute link, the Include works anywhere in your site.

Within the scope of what you are learning in this book, you are most likely building and testing your pages on your local machine, not on a server. Therefore, relative links within a site will be what you write and use for now.

LINKING WITH PROTOCOLS OTHER THAN HTTP

A browser cannot open or display every type of document or file. For example, a browser cannot open a PowerPoint (PPT) file. Sometimes download sites for such documents are on FTP servers. The user downloads the file by the FTP protocol and opens it with the appropriate software. For links to FTP sites, use the FTP protocol in the href attribute, similar to this:

```
<a href="ftp://www.someserver.com/somefile.ppt">a PowerPoint file</a>
```

The MP3 and PDF examples are sufficient to teach you how to write links to any file that will open in a browser, because the technique is essentially the same in every case.

In the assets folder are an MP3 music clip and a PDF file (also known as an Acrobat file). The links to these items will be on blue.html. Open blue.html in your text editor. The page at this point looks like Figure 7.18.

When the user clicks the MP3 link, the sound could be played by one of many sound players, depending on the user's setup. It might play in Windows Media Player, Real Media Player, or Quick-Time Player. It is a good idea to offer a link to a download site for one of these players, although many computer users already have an MP3 player.

When the user clicks the PDF link, the file should open in Adobe Reader (Mac OS X might open it in Preview). Again, it is a good idea to provide a link to adobe.com so the user can download Reader, although many computer users already have it. The users who need the link to the sound player or Reader will appreciate it if you give them a way to download what they need to use your page.

FIGURE 7.18
The Blue page needs other links.

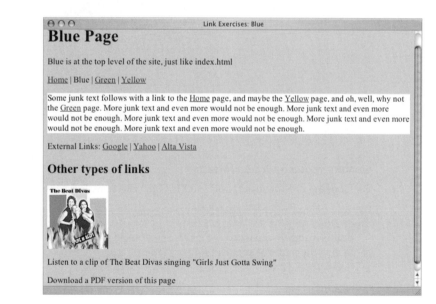

LINKING TO MP3 FILES

You can use a elements for both the MP3 file and the PDF file. First the sound clip. In `blue.html`, find this line in the XHTML:

```
<p>Listen to a clip of The Beat Divas singing "Girls Just Gotta Swing"</p>
```

The song title will be the clickable words. The file is in the subfolder called `assets`. The path from `blue.html` to the sound clip is `assets/beatdivas_gjgs.mp3`, which translates to "look in the folder `assets` and find the file `beatdivas_gjgs.mp3`." The complete p element would be:

```
<p>Listen to a clip of The Beat Divas singing "<a href="assets/beatdivas_
gjgs.mp3">Girls Just Gotta Swing</a>"</p>
```

When you click that link, your default audio player should open and play the clip. On my setup, it opens in a new page (like the one in Figure 7.19) to play the clip, and I must use the Back button to return to the HTML page. In some cases, the player launches in a separate window, leaving the page still open. When the clip finishes, the user closes the player to return to your page.

FIGURE 7.19
The sound player used for the MP3 depends on the user's setup. In my case, the file is played using QuickTime.

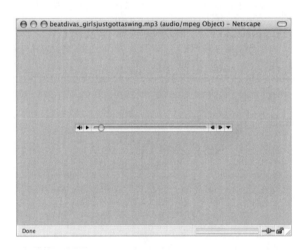

LINKING TO ACROBAT DOCUMENTS

Still looking at `blue.html`, find the XHTML where the link to the PDF file will be added.

```
<p>Download a PDF version of this page</p>
```

In this instance, the words "PDF version" seem like sensible link text, so write a link to the `blue.pdf` file in the `assets` subfolder there.

Ready? Here it is:

```
<p>Download a <a href="assets/blue.pdf">PDF version</a> of this page</p>
```

any links. If there were links present in the PDF version of the page, they would work just like links on a web page.

TIP   Web designers sometimes save web pages as PDF files during the design process and allow clients to view and approve design ideas on those documents. The PDF file looks and feels like a web page, includes the images, and can be e-mailed. To save XHTML files as PDF files, you need to own the full version of Adobe Acrobat (as opposed to the free Adobe Reader), or your computer must have built-in software that allows you to print pages as PDF files.

Images as Links

When creating an a element, you can insert more than words into the clickable area. You can also insert images. Make the image of The Beat Divas' album cover into a link to the sound clip. Find the img element:

```
<img src="images/beatdivas_liveatreeds.jpg" alt="The Beat Divas Live at Reeds"
width="125" height="125" border="0" />
```

TIP   Chapter 8 will deal with images in detail.

To make the image a link, the a element must enclose the img element. The img element then becomes the clickable portion of the link:

```
<a href="assets/beatdivas_gjgs.mp3"><img src="images/beatdivas_liveatreeds.jpg"
alt="The Beat Divas Live at Reeds" width="125" height="125" border="0" /></a>
```

Clicking the album cover image should do exactly what clicking the text link to the song did on your particular computer setup.

TIP   In many browsers, linked images have a blue line around them, like the blue underline on a text link. The attribute border="0" in the img element eliminates this blue line. Change the attribute to border="1" temporarily to see what happens. CSS styles can also be used to eliminate an image border. In a later exercise, you will use CSS to remove borders from the img element.

The album image could have instead been linked to The Beat Divas' own website instead of to the sound clip. An image can be used with either relative or absolute links. Linking to The Beat Divas' site is another example of an absolute link, but instead of linking to The Beat Divas' site through the image, in this case it makes sense to use the words "The Beat Divas" to link to their website (at http:// www.madykaye.com/divas/). The finished changes to this part of blue.html are

```
<a href="assets/beatdivas_gjgs.mp3"><img src="images/beatdivas_liveatreeds.jpg"
alt="The Beat Divas Live at Reeds" width="125" height="125" border="0" /></a>
<p>Listen to a clip of <a href="http://www.madykaye.com/divas/">The Beat Divas</a>
singing "<a href="assets/beatdivas_gjgs.mp3">Girls Just Gotta Swing</a>"</p>
```

In the browser, you see a page like Figure 7.20.

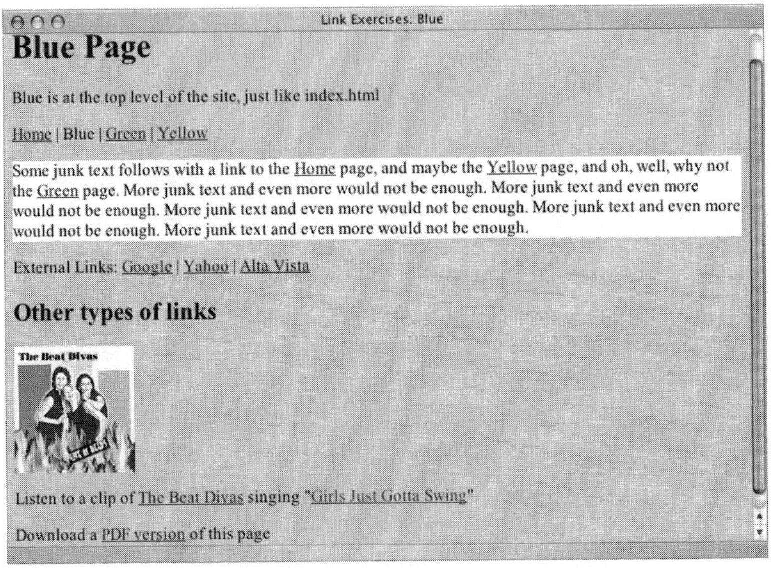

FIGURE 7.20

Links to the sound clip and The Beat Divas site

TIP   It is important to point out that there is nothing on this page that gives you any clue that the album image is a link to a sound file. It does not look clickable. If you do something like this on a real web page, it's a good idea to include some explanatory text, such as "Click the image to hear a sound clip." In Chapter 8 you will use images as links and add a text link under the image so that the purpose of the image will be absolutely clear.

E-mail Links

An e-mail link is an absolute link, but it doesn't use the `http` protocol; it uses the `mailto` protocol. Open `index.html` in your text editor and in your browser. Find this paragraph in the XHTML:

```
<p>Email Me</p>
```

To create the link, change the paragraph to this:

```
<p><a href="mailto:someone@somewhere.com">Email Me</a></p>
```

TIP   I suggest you use your own e-mail address instead of the fake `someone@somewhere.com`. That way you can test it out by sending yourself mail. Don't say I never let you have any fun!

Save that and reload the browser. Then click the e-mail link. A new mail document in your default e-mail program should open up with the TO: line filled in with the address you used. It should look like Figure 7.21.

You can add your own subject line to the blank e-mail by adding `?subject=some subject` to the end of the URL in your `mailto` attribute, like this:

```
<p><a href="mailto:someone@somewhere.com?subject=web site mail">Email Me</a></p>
```

Notice that there is no space either before or after the question mark. Save that and reload the browser. Try the link. You should see a subject line already in place in the blank e-mail document.

FIGURE 7.21

A blank e-mail document opens.

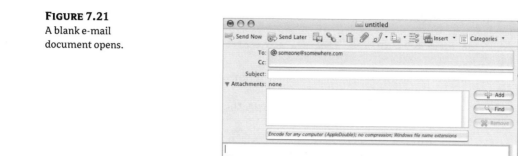

Linking to a Specific Location in a Page: Named Anchors

By giving an anchor tag a name, you can allow a browser to find that specific location in your document. A *named anchor* is simply an a element with a name attribute; it looks like this: `<a name="somename"></a>`. Don't type anything inside these a tags, because this is not something you click. It will actually be invisible on the page. You can use any name you want, but it must be unique. Names can be words or numbers.

To use a named anchor, you write an ordinary a tag elsewhere and, in the link `href` attribute, include a hash sign and the name of the anchor. Thus, `<a href="#somename">` is a link from one spot on a web page to another location on the same page where `name="somename"` occurs.

Practicing with named anchors requires a long page, so we will temporarily abandon your `link_exercises` pages. Look in the Chapter 7 folder on the CD for a page called `Ch7namedanchors.html` and copy it to your computer. Open it in your text editor and in the browser.

You're forgiven if you suddenly groan, "Oh, no! Not that again!" Unfortunately, you need a nice long page to help you understand named anchors.

A common practice on a long page of text is to put links near the top of the page that take you instantly down the page to the relevant sections. These links work using named anchors. You will make three.

1. In `Ch7namedanchors.html`, after the introductory paragraph but before the first tip, insert the paragraph highlighted here:

    ```
    <p>After teaching <acronym title="Hypertext Markup Language">HTML</acronym> at
    the local community college for a few semesters, I have learned to anticipate
    the mistakes new web page creators make. Here are ten tips to help you avoid
    falling into the newbie sinkhole of ugly, irritating ignorance.</p>
    <p>Quick Links: Tip 3 | Tip 6 | Tip 9</p>
    <h2>1. Never leave anyone alone with only the back button for company.</h2>
    ```

    You will use the Quick Links to navigate to Tip 3 or Tip 6 or Tip 9. First you have to insert something near those tips to navigate to: the named anchor.

2. Start with Tip 3 and name the anchor "3". Normally a word might make more sense than a number as a name; however, in this case, a number matching the number of the tip makes a clear connection that will hold up over time if you edit this page again at a later time. Put the anchor right before the beginning of Tip 3:

    ```
    <a name="3"></a><h2>3. Stamp out long lists of links in huge bold fonts.</h2>
    ```

3. Move on down to Tip 6. Name this anchor "6".

```
<a name="6"></a><h2>6. Create a sense of place.</h2>
```

4. Move down to Tip 9. Use "9" for a name for this one.

```
<a name="9"></a><h2>9. Give every page the minimum nutrients for proper
growth.</h2>
```

5. Look at the page in the browser. The named anchors are invisible elements. You see nothing added in front of Tips 3, 6, and 9.

6. Now write the links. Go back to the "Quick Links" paragraph you added at the top of the page and link the "Tip 3" text to the "3" named anchor. Remember, the link href attribute includes a hash sign and the name of the anchor. The link to Tip 3 is

```
<a href="#3">Tip 3</a>
```

7. Add similar links to the "Tip 6" and "Tip 9" text. The completed set is

```
<p>Quick Links: <a href="#3">Tip 3</a> | <a href="#6">Tip 6</a> | <a
href="#9">Tip 9</a></p>
```

NOTE   If you know that a named anchor is on a page, you can link directly to that spot even from another page. For example, `<a href="Ch7namedanchors.html#3">Tip Three</a>`. The page would open with Tip Three at the top of the browser window.

Links to named anchors don't have to always jump down a page: they can move up a page as well. If you place a named anchor such as `<a name="top"></a>` at the top of the page, you can link to it anywhere in the page with a link like `<a href="#top">Back to Top</a>`.

NAMED ANCHORS AND SKIP NAVIGATION LINKS

An often-used accessibility feature of a site is to put a "skip navigation" link at the beginning of a web page. Clicking this link allows the user to skip directly to a named anchor marking the beginning of the main content of the page.

One of many barriers to accessibility is lack of a pointing device or mouse. This is the case with certain types of Internet-capable devices and especially with aural screen readers that read a page aloud to the user. In such situations, the user must use the Tab key to navigate a page. With no skip navigation link, users may have to click Tab dozens of times to finally reach the part of the page they want. The skip navigation link provides a welcome opportunity to jump directly to the page content.

TIP   Accessibility expert Jim Thatcher has a tutorial on Skip Navigation at `http://www.jimthatcher`
`.com/skipnav.htm` that contains more information.

TAB INDEX

It is possible to navigate a web page using the Tab key. The user presses Tab to move from link to link (and also to move from one form field to the next). If the web designer does not explicitly set a tab index value (sometimes called tab order), it begins with the browser's location bar and moves through the page in the order that items appear in the XHTML source. If your browser has a search form in the address bar, the second Tab stop may be in the search form field.

If the page would be more usable or more accessible to Tab through the links in some order other than that of the XHTML source, a specific value can be set for `tabindex`. It is an attribute of the a element, like this:

```
<a href="index.html" tabindex="3">Home</a>
```

Tab index values must be whole number integers: 1, 2, 3, 4, and so on.

Tab index might be used in conjunction with a skip link to allow users to Tab immediately into the main content area.

As with any change you make in expected default browser behavior, you must be careful if you change tab order from its normal progression through the XHTML source order. Be careful to let users know what you are doing and what to expect when using the Tab key.

Transparent graphics are frequently used to create skip navigation links. The transparent graphic does not appear to the visual user but can be tabbed to or read aloud by an aural screen reader.

If you had one of these invisible Skip Links selected, you might see something like this graphic in the browser.

The XHTML for this is a link to a named anchor. If the transparent graphic used is `skip.gif` and the main content named anchor is marked a `name ="content"`, then the link is

```
<a href="#content"><img src="/images/skip.gif" width="1" height="1" alt="Skip to
main content" border="0" /></a>
```

In many cases, the link to allow you to skip the navigation is visible. Instead of a transparent graphic, text is used as the clickable part of the link—something like this:

```
<a href="#content">Skip to main content</a>
...some links go here...
<a name="#content"></a>Content goes here
```

TIP Accessibility expert Joe Clark outlines reasons why using visible text instead of transparent graphics is a good idea in this excerpt from his book *Building Accessible Websites* at `http://joeclark.org/book/sashay/serialization/Chapter08.html#h4-2020`. Note that this URL contains a link to a named anchor, thereby serving as a real-world example for you.

Learn the CSS

Turn your attention back to the files in the `link_exercises` folder. You will write some styles for the links on those pages.

CSS uses *pseudo class selectors* to style links based on their state. Links fall into pseudo classes because the state of a link is not written into the XHTML; it depends on the user's interaction. The four most common pseudo classes use these selectors:

```
a:link
a:visited
a:hover
a:active
```

The selectors need to be listed in link-visited-hover-active order (or L-V-H-A) in the style rules for most common uses. A link can actually be in more than one state at the same time—for example, both visited and hover. The Cascade requires the selectors to be in that order for the links to display reliably in normal use.

TIP   There are other pseudo selectors in CSS that are beyond the scope of this text. You can learn about them in *Cascading Style Sheets: The Designer's Edge* by Molly Holzschlag (Sybex, 2003).

You could write style rules for the previous selectors and they would apply globally to every link on our page.

The pages in the sample site are structured with some links in `div id="menu"`, some links in `div id="content"`, some links in `div class="external"`, and some links not in any structural element. Your brain may be shouting, "Hey, I can write some contextual selectors for the links!" about now. Here are some examples of what can be done with contextual selectors:

```
#menu a:link
#menu a:visited
#menu a:hover
#menu a:active
```

or

```
#content a:link
#content a:visited
#content a:hover
#content a:active
```

or

```
.external a:link
.external a:visited
.external a:hover
.external a:active
```

If that multiplicity of opportunities for link styles is not enough to fill your needs, you will also learn how to use `class` to indicate the current page.

Editing Embedded Link Styles

Normal practice for a website is to have one (or more) external style sheets linked to all the pages in the site.

The link_exercises made use of color to help distinguish the pages as you practiced with them. Those colors were in embedded style elements in the head of each page. As I show you how to write the CSS rules for links, you will continue to work in the individual style elements embedded in each page.

STYLING THE LINKS ON *BLUE.HTML*

Open blue.html in your text editor. The pre-existing style section of this page is

```
<style type="text/css">
<!--
body {
    background-color: #06C;
}
#content {
    background: #FFF;
}
-->
</style>
```

Make the a:link red-orange (the code is #F30). Add the rule that's highlighted here, making sure the new rule stays within the opening and closing style tags:

```
<style type="text/css">
  body {
    background-color: #06C;
  }
  #content {
    background: #FFF;
  }
  a:link {
    color: #F30;
  }
</style>
```

This rule applies globally to every a:link element on the page. Since you have been testing your pages, some of the links may appear as visited and not in red-orange. You can bring your browser back to an unviewed link state for all your links by selecting the Clear History option in the browser preferences. You should see something similar to Figure 7.22 in the browser after you clear history.

Of course, the moment you visit one of the linked pages, you are putting that link in a visited state again. The links need to be red-orange whether they are visited or not. You can write a style to take either possibility into account. Simply add another selector to the rule, like this:

```
a:link, a:visited {
  color: #CF0;
}
```

FIGURE 7.22

All links are red-orange
when unvisited.

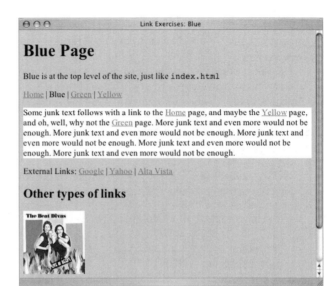

Notice the comma between the two selectors. Remember, with a comma between selectors, you are giving all the selectors listed the same style. Without the comma, you are creating a descendant selector.

The style attribute that removes the underline is `text-decoration: none;`. Remove the underline from these two types of links:

```
a:link, a:visited {
  color: #CF0;
  text-decoration: none;
}
```

Save that change and refresh (reload) the page, which now looks like Figure 7.23.

Make the `a:hover` and `a:active` links a lighter orange color (#F90) and use the underline. That rule is

```
a:hover, a:active {
  color: #F90;
  text-decoration: underline;
}
```

With that rule in place, you should see a change when hovering or actively clicking a link, similar to the "Yellow" link in Figure 7.24.

In the `content` division, the link color is a bit hard to see against the white background. You can write some contextual selector styles just for the links in `content`: make them a blue color like the page background color and make sure they are underlined. For good measure, make the `font-weight: bold`.

TIP   You can leave out the underline in something that is obviously a menu bar, but in the context of a paragraph, a link must have a visual clue, usually an underline, that the word is a link.

FIGURE 7.23
Links with the text-decoration removed

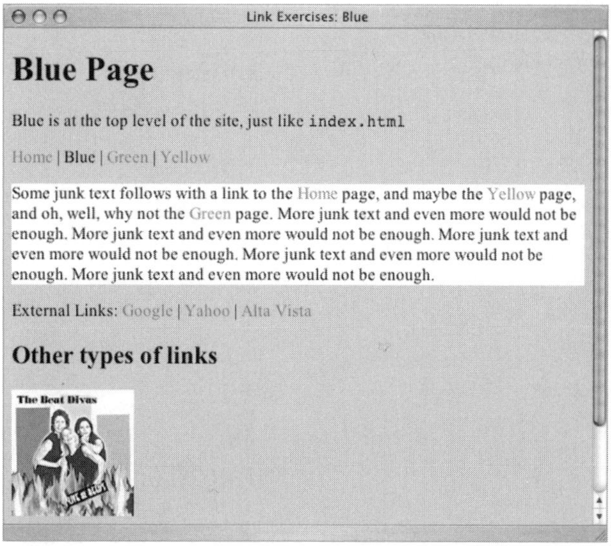

FIGURE 7.24
The link "Yellow" is a lighter orange and underlined when in hover state.

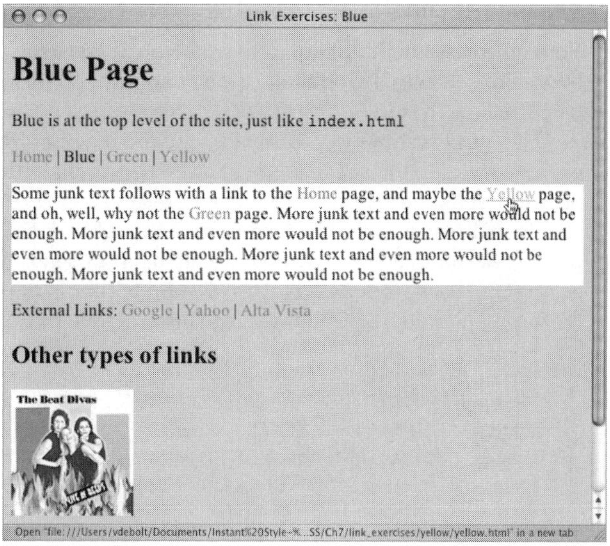

Use grouped selectors again, to save typing the same rule again and again for each selector. This time you can make all four states follow the same rule with one long comma-separated group selector:

```
#content a:link, #content a:visited, #content a:hover, #content a:active {
  color: #06C;
  font-weight: bold;
  text-decoration: underline;
}
```

In the browser, the resulting change should look similar to Figure 7.25.

FIGURE 7.25
The styled links in the
content division

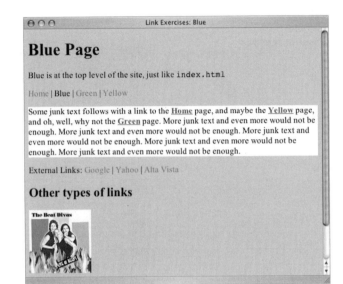

STYLING THE LINKS ON *YELLOW.HTML*

You could do something similar to what you did on `blue.html` to every page. Feel free to try out your own color schemes. I won't take time to go through those steps again. Instead, try some new styles using `yellow.html`.

Open `yellow.html` in your text editor and in your browser. Once again, you will add the practice exercise styles to the `style` element already present in the document head.

You can use `background-color` and `border` to make the `menu` links look like buttons instead of text. In this exercise, you don't care about the color of the link in its various states at the moment. You need a selector that will style all the a elements in `menu:`, namely, `#menu a`. Write a style create a light gray (#CCC) background and a 1-pixel solid border in dark gray (#333) on all four borders. Since this will look rather like a button, you can also remove the underline:

```
#menu a {
  background: #CCC;
  border: 1px solid #333;
  text-decoration: none;
}
```

If you look at `yellow.html` in the browser now, you see the page shown in Figure 7.26. The effect is in need of some white space, so how about adding some padding?

```
#menu a {
  background: #CCC;
  padding: 5px;
  border: 1px solid #333;
  text-decoration: none;
}
```

The padding adds to the button-like appearance, as you see in Figure 7.27.

FIGURE 7.26
The menu links look a bit like buttons now.

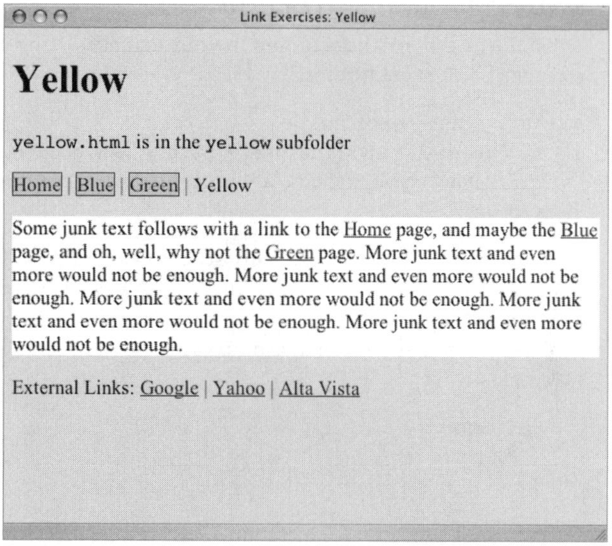

FIGURE 7.27
Padding is added around the links.

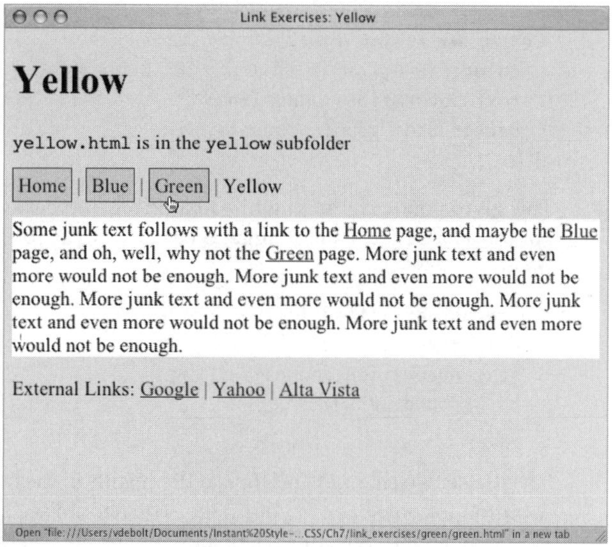

TIP The vertical pipe separators between the links looks silly with the links styled as in Figure 7.27, but leave them there anyway. It is much better to create an effect like this using a list. You will do just that in Chapter 9. For now, silly looking separators are not a worry.

To explore a few more of the possible CSS rules that could be used for links, you will write individual rules for each pseudo selector for the links in the `external` class.

STYLING THE LINKS ON *GREEN.HTML*

Open the green.html document in your text editor and the browser. The div assigned to the class external on green.html is

```
<div class="external">
<p>External Links: <a href="http://www.google.com/">Google</a> | <a href="http://
www.yahoo.com/">Yahoo</a> | <a href="http://www.altavista.com/">Alta Vista</a></p>
</div>
```

Once again, please add the new style rules to the existing style element in the head of green.html. You will write four rules, using L-V-H-A order. You will take advantage of the Cascade as you go along.

Class names, you recall, use a preceding period. A selector meant to style everything in the class external is

```
.external {
  rules here
}
```

You want a selector for a certain class (.external) for the a element in a certain link state. Such a selector is .external a:link.

Start with a rule such as:

```
.external a:link {
  color: #FFF;
  text-decoration: underline;
  background: #366;
}
```

This gives you underlined white text on a green background.

For the a:visited state, change to text-decoration: none and change the background to a different green (#399):

```
.external a:visited {
  color: #FFF;
  text-decoration: none;
  background: #399;
}
```

Save those two changes and look at the results in the browser. Click the link to Google and use the Back button to come back to your page. You should see something similar to Figure 7.28.

For the a:hover style, put a 1-pixel white border on the link:

```
.external a:hover {
  border: 1px solid #FFF;
}
```

Notice when you add this rule that the links are inheriting the previous style rules regarding color, text-decoration, and background since nothing in the .external a:hover rule has done anything to change them. You should see a link like Figure 7.29 when hovering over a link.

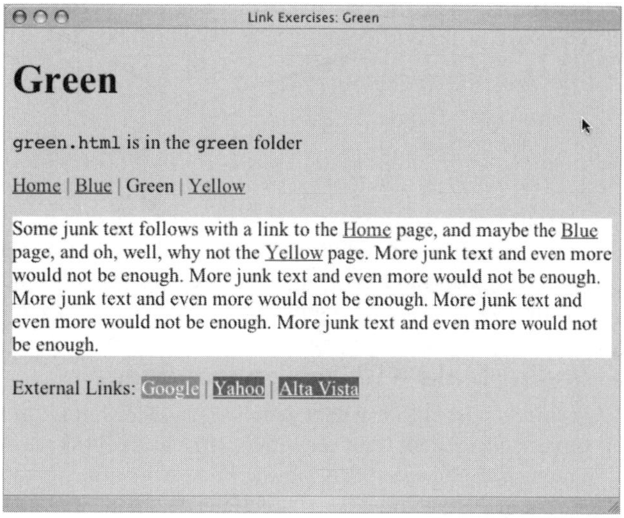

FIGURE 7.28
Styled a:link and
a:visited pseudo
states

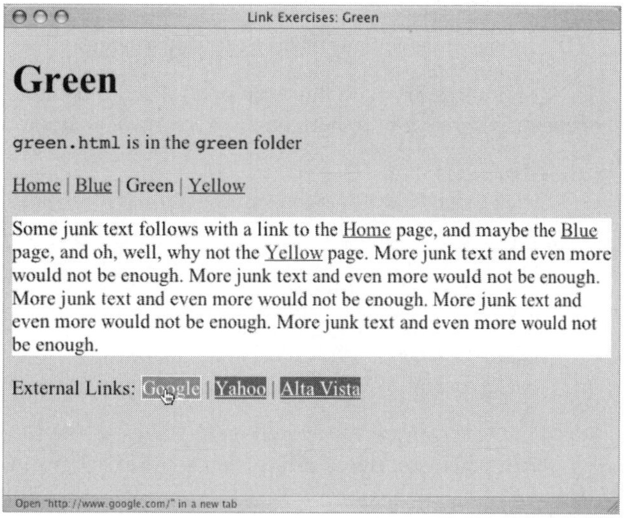

FIGURE 7.29
A border added to
the hover state

The final state is a:active. Make the link color red (#F00). You can only see the active state in the exact moment you click the link, so I can't capture a screen shot to illustrate it. Here is the rule:

```
.external a:active {
  color: #F00;
}
```

Remember that links can be in more than one pseudo state simultaneously. You have a border on the a element in the hover state. When you click the link to create the active state, you can see that the border is inherited. (You have `.external a:visited` in the Cascade following `.external a:hover`.) To get rid of the border in the `a:active` link, do this:

```
.external a:active {
  color: #F00;
  border: 0;
}
```

You know many CSS properties for `font`, `margin`, `padding`, `background`, `border` and `background-image`. All of those rules can be used with links. Here is one example of something you already know how to do that could apply to links. You could create a rollover using one `background-image` for `a:link` elements and changing to a different `background-image` for `a:hover`.

Styling Links with *background-image*

Use `index.html` to use `background-image` for links. On the accompanying CD, you will find `button-up.gif` and `button-hover.gif` in the `link_exercises/images` folder. Move those two graphics to your hard drive in the `link_exercises/images` folder.

You will style the links in the `div id="menu"` section of the page.

The first selector is `#menu a:link`. The style rule should give the URL of the background-image as `url(images/button-up.gif)`.

TIP Images use the same relative pathway scheme as links.

It isn't necessary with this very small link, but I suggest that you also set the `background` to `no-repeat` and give it both horizontal and vertical position set to center. Here is the rule in shorthand:

```
#menu a:link {
  background: url(images/button-up.gif) no-repeat center center;
}
```

Next, write a rule for the selector `#menu a:hover` and use the `button-hover.gif` for the `background-image`. Here's the rule:

```
#menu a:hover {
  background: url(images/button-hover.gif) no-repeat center center;
}
```

When you hover over the link, you see the background image change, similar to what you see in Figure 7.30.

NOTE Project Seven is a site that offers tutorials and code samples aimed mainly at Macromedia Dreamweaver users. However, many of their tutorials contain useful information for hand coders. Their tutorial on uberlinks at `http://projectseven.com/tutorials/css/uberlinks/` explains how to create a button rollover with CSS and doesn't require Dreamweaver.

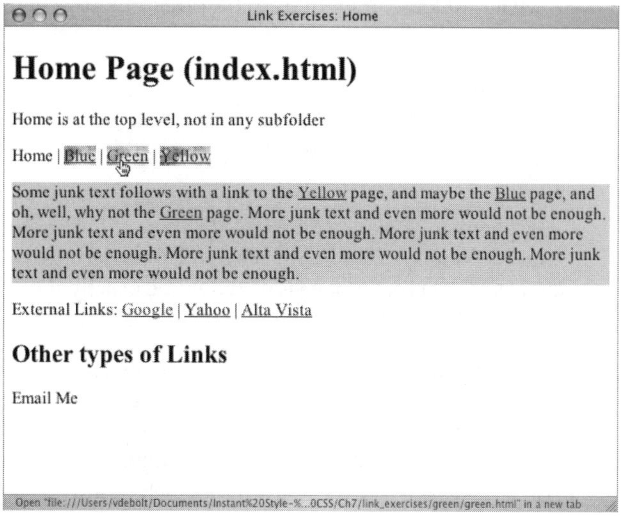

FIGURE 7.30
The background image is
slightly different in the
hover state, creating a
rollover effect.

Styling to Indicate the Current Page

Use the page `green.html` to work on current page indicators.

Earlier in this chapter there was a discussion about not including a link to the current page in the navigation. You will create a link to the current page and use a class to serve as a current page indicator.

1. First you need to write the link. Find this line:

```
<div id="menu"><p><a href="../index.html">Home</a> | <a href="../
blue.html">Blue</a> | Green | <a href="../sub_b/yellow.html">Yellow</a></p></
div>
```

Add a link to the current page for the Green link.

```
<a href="green.html">Green</a>
```

2. While you are in this spot, add a `class` name to the a attributes. You don't have a class rule yet, but you will name it `current`. The link becomes:

```
<a href="green.html" class="current">Green</a>
```

3. Write a CSS rule for the class. When applying a `class` to a specific element such as this a element, the selector needs to select an a element in the class `current` and give the pseudo state. There is no need to write a style for the selector `.current` before you write a style for your link, although you certainly could. The selector is `a.current:link`.

Make it look different from the other links by changing the color slightly (to #090) and removing the underline.

```
a.current:link {
color: #090;
text-decoration: none;
}
```

The page will look like Figure 7.31.

You could forge ahead with styles for the selectors a.current:visited, a.current:hover, and a.current:active, but the steps would be exactly the same as what you just did, so I won't detail them.

TIP Select Oracle at http://gallery.theopalgroup.com/selectoracle/ can help you distinguish between very similar selectors. For example, Select Oracle defines .current a:link as, "Selects any a element whose target has not been visited that is a descendant of any element with a class attribute that contains the word current." (In this situation, the a element is not a descendant.) It explains a.current:link as "Selects any a element with a class attribute that contains the word current and whose target has not been visited."

As current page indicators go, that one doesn't thrill me much. However, you could use background rules, color rules, or other CSS rules to make it more impressive. The important concept is that you can use a class indicator to provide a visual clue to the current page and at the same time have every item in your navigation a working link.

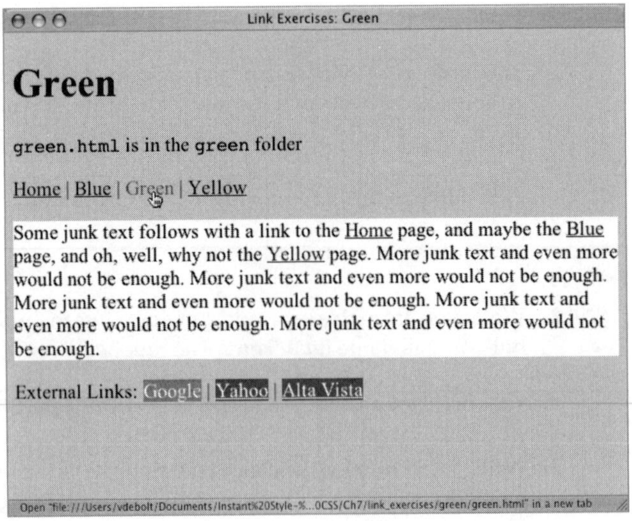

FIGURE 7.31
Green is a working link, but looks somewhat different to indicate that it is the current page.

Real World Example

As an example of intelligent linking, Accessify, at www.accessify.com, demonstrates a number of good practices. In Figure 7.32 you can see the skip navigation link with the content of the title attribute showing up as a tool tip.

Accessify is well-known for one of its free wizards, List O Matic, which helps users create both horizontal and vertical menus out of lists. But the main menu in the menu bar on the left does not use a list. Instead, the main menu is a single line of text like the Home | Yellow | Green | Blue menu in this chapter. However, Accessify uses clever CSS presentation rules to make the main menu appear in a vertical format with current page indicators and rollover effects. See Figure 7.33.

This site does double duty as an example of an attractive accessible site.

FIGURE 7.32
Accessify uses a skip navigation link and has two types of current page indicators. The first explicitly states "You are in: Home > Index page." The second is the small arrow pointing toward the word Home on the first link in the menu bar on the left.

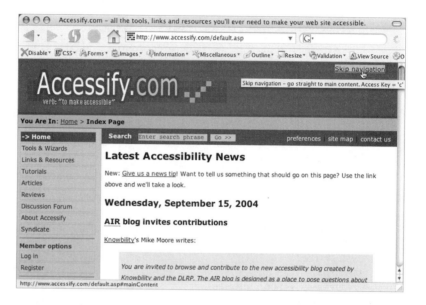

FIGURE 7.33
The main menu uses rollovers. Links are text with title attributes providing further accessibility information about the link.

CSS Properties

Most of the CSS properties used in Chapter 7 were explained earlier in the book. The new CSS properties used in Chapter 7 are shown in Table 7.1.

TABLE 7.1:   CSS Properties in Chapter 7 for the a Selector

PROPERTY	POSSIBLE VALUES
text-decoration	none, underline, overline, line-through, blink, inherit

Dynamic pseudo classes create styles that are dependent on the user's interaction with the page. Pseudo-class selectors are listed in Table 7.2.

TABLE 7.2:   Pseudo Class Selectors

CLASS	USE
LINK PSEUDO-CLASSES	
:link	Use with any anchor with an href attribute
:visited	Use with any anchor that has been visited
DYNAMIC PSEUDO-CLASSES	
:hover	Use with any anchor the mouse is hovering over
:active	Use with any anchor element while the mouse is held down

Challenge Yourself

For some extra practice with your new skills, try out these exercises.

1. There are many unstyled links on the pages of the practice site. Go through every page and add styles for each unstyled link on the page. Try different things with each page, such as font, font weight, background image, border styles, varied color schemes, and other ideas of your own.

2. Find skip.gif on the CD and use it to make an invisible skip navigation link at the beginning of Ch7namedanchors.html that skips to one of the named anchors down the page. Use the Tab key to navigate the page and find the link so you can test it.

3. Change the expected tab order on one of the practice pages using tabindex.

Summary

The concept of the Internet rests on the foundation of the hyperlink, which is created with the a element. You learned how to write relative and/or absolute links using HTTP, FTP, and MAILTO protocols. You learned how to write links to named anchors and how to set the tab index in links.

In a stylesheet, rules for links are most often written in L-V-H-A order. A `text-decoration` rule declaration is used to remove an underline from a link. Everything you've learned previously in this book about CSS rules for `font`, `background`, `padding`, `margin`, and `border` can be applied to a element style rules.

You will work further with links in Chapter 8 and in Chapter 9.

Chapter 8

Multimedia, Images, and Image Styles

Some of the exercises in previous chapters have included images. These images were already placed on the exercise pages for you. In this chapter, *you* will add images to pages. You will learn which attributes are necessary when using the img (for image) element, and you will build a horizontal and a vertical navigation bar that uses images. You will also work on practice pages for a photo gallery website.

The types of image formats that are displayed by browsers are limited. In this chapter, you will work with GIF (for Graphic Interchange Format) and JPEG or JPG (for Joint Photographic Experts Group) documents. There is growing support among browsers for another file type, PNG (for Portable Network Graphics), but they will not be used in these exercises. Any graphic you might have in some format other than GIF, JPEG, or PNG is not a web graphic. You will also learn some basic tips for using graphics software.

Using some prepared multimedia examples, you will learn how to add multimedia to your web pages. You will learn how to add Flash, QuickTime, Windows Media and Java applets to a web page.

TIP   Graphics software such as Photoshop and Fireworks can convert images in formats such as TIFF, PICT, and BMP into formats that are more usable on the Web. There are also very inexpensive tools designed just for this, such as Graphic Converter (www.graphic-converter.net).

Creating and Editing Images

Specialized software is required to create and edit web graphics. There is a definite learning curve involved in mastering graphic design tools, and this book is not going to address that issue at all. However, if you have such tools at hand, you can try basic tasks such as cropping and resizing images without much training in the software. A bit later in the chapter, I'll walk you through a few basic actions in graphics software programs.

In the Chapter 8 folder on the companion CD are two files named banner.png and button.png. These are the original Macromedia Fireworks PNG files that created the banner and button images with in the exercises. In the event that you have software that can open and work with PNG images, feel free to study these files as examples and change them to suit your own needs.

NOTE   It is a good idea to keep the original files used to create buttons or other web graphics. If you need to change or add to them later, you'll have the original information at hand.

In addition to Macromedia Fireworks, other software programs that can be used to create web graphics include Adobe Photoshop, Adobe Illustrator, Macromedia Freehand, Jasc Paint Shop Pro, and others. Some computers come with a basic graphics program, such as Paint, which makes simple web graphics.

Most monitors or viewing devices display at a resolution of 72 *dpi* (dots per inch). There is no reason to save a web graphic with a resolution of more than 72 dpi, because the vast majority of monitors cannot display the additional pixels of information. And even though the monitor cannot display the additional pixels, it takes time to download them, so images with a resolution higher than 72 dpi force your users to wait unnecessarily long for images to appear.

NOTE   Some Windows monitors display 96 dpi.

You may use your digital camera , or you may scan snapshots to use on the Web. The camera might take a photo at 300 dpi, which would be perfect for a printed photo. Your scanner might be set to scan photos at 150 dpi or 300 dpi. When processing these photos for web graphics, it is essential to reduce the image resolution to 72 dpi. In terms of download speed, a 72 dpi image download is like speedy jackrabbit in a race with a snail-like 300 dpi download. And once a user sits there for the agonizing seconds or minutes it takes a 300 dpi image to finally download, they'll only see 72 dpi in the monitor anyway!

NOTE   Keep a high-resolution original of your photos. You might need the additional pixels of information at some point. Save a low-resolution copy for any web work.

Any of the graphics software programs just mentioned allow you to make changes in resolution to a document's image size.

Reducing an image's resolution to 72 dpi is one facet in the process known as *image optimization*.

JPEG vs. GIF

Each image format has its unique virtues.

JPEG (pronounced "jay-peg"; JPEG stands for Joint Photographic Experts Group, the committee that defined the format) images are often used for photographs or art with many subtle color variations. A JPEG image can contain millions of colors. When many colors are required, most people are happier with the way a JPEG image looks in a browser than with a GIF image.

TIP   A JPEG cannot have a transparent background.

When saving a JPEG, you'll have options about setting the image quality to high, medium, or low. A low quality JPEG will download faster than a medium or high quality JPEG, and a medium quality JPEG will download faster than a high quality JPEG. Sometimes you have to play around with it a bit to determine which quality level will produce the best results and the smallest file size.

Selecting the lowest acceptable quality for a JPEG image is another facet in the process of image optimization.

Most people pronounce GIF with a hard *g*, as in "gift"; some use a soft *g* as in "giraffe." If there is a hard and fast rule about which way is correct, I have never heard it. At any rate, a GIF (Graphics Interchange Format) image can have a transparent background. The GIFs used in some of the practice exercises in this chapter have transparent backgrounds, so you will get a clear idea of what that means as the chapter progresses.

Although the GIF format can display as many as 256 colors, one of its virtues is that the number of colors used in the image can be reduced to only the essential colors. For example, a solid red button with a white triangle on it to indicate a link to the next page has only two colors: red and white. Saving that button as a GIF with the number of colors reduced to two makes for a very small file size and hence a very fast download. When solid colors for graphics such as buttons, banners, logos, and headings are required, a GIF can generally be used and will have a smaller file size than a JPEG would use.

Saving a GIF with the fewest acceptable number of colors is another image optimization technique.

The PNG (Portable Network Graphic) format allows transparent backgrounds, although this feature is not implemented in every browser. Specifically, Internet Explorer does not support transparency for PNG graphics. Text for buttons and headings may appear to have smoother edges than text made in other formats, and PNG files optimize well. Many modern browsers will display a PNG file, but with IE holding a dominant position in the browser market at this time, the PNG format has not come into common use yet. However, don't blow off the idea of ever using the PNG format, because if IE support does appear eventually, the PNG format could become widely used on web pages.

Basic Graphics Software Tips

If you are a beginner with graphics software tools such as Adobe Photoshop or Macromedia Fireworks, I can give you a few very basic tips that will help you get web pages of your own going.

CROPPING IMAGES

In both Photoshop and Fireworks, the icon for the Crop tool looks like a draftsman's square: ⧉ .

With the Crop tool selected, you simply draw a marquee around the area you want to keep and press Return (Enter), and the image is cropped. Figure 8.1 shows an example in Photoshop.

SIZING IMAGES

In the Image Size options for both Photoshop and Fireworks you can do two operations at one time: you can reduce the overall dimensions of the image in pixels, and you can reduce the resolution to 72 dpi.

In Figures 8.2 and 8.3, you see the Photoshop menu that allows you to select Image Size. The Image Size window shows Pixel Dimensions at the top and Resolution as pixels/inch under Document Size.

I find it easiest to change the resolution to 72 first, because the overall pixel dimensions of the image will change when the resolution is changed. With the Constrain Proportions option selected, you only need to change one of the pixel dimensions (either width or height) and the other will automatically change in proportion.

FIGURE 8.1
The Crop tool was used to create a marquee around the part of the image I wanted. Pressing Return crops the image to only that portion inside the marquee.

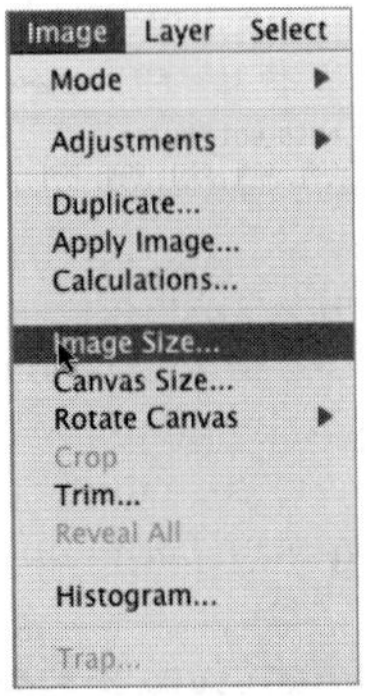

FIGURE 8.2

The Photoshop Image Size command is under the Image menu.

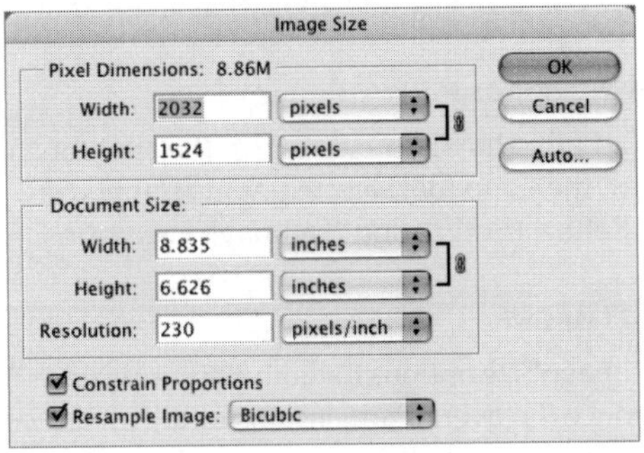

FIGURE 8.3

The Photoshop Image Size options let you re-size overall pixel dimensions and the resolution in pixels/inch.

In Fireworks, you must select Modify ➤ Canvas ➤ Image Size to get to the Image Size options (Figure 8.4). The Fireworks Image Size pop-up window is very similar to the one in Photoshop, as you can see in Figure 8.5.

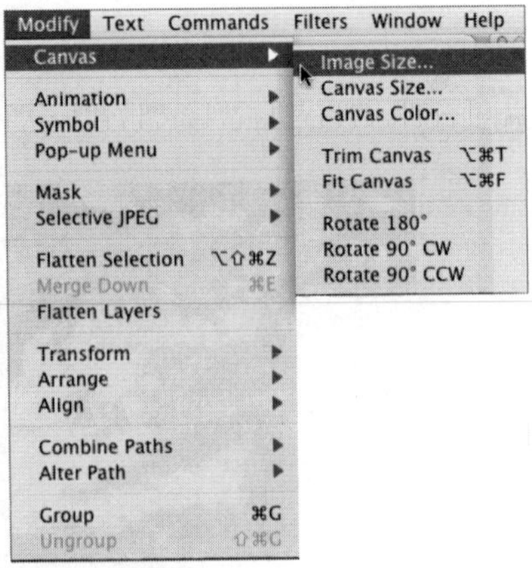

FIGURE 8.4

The Fireworks Image Size menu is under Modify ➤ Canvas ➤ Image Size.

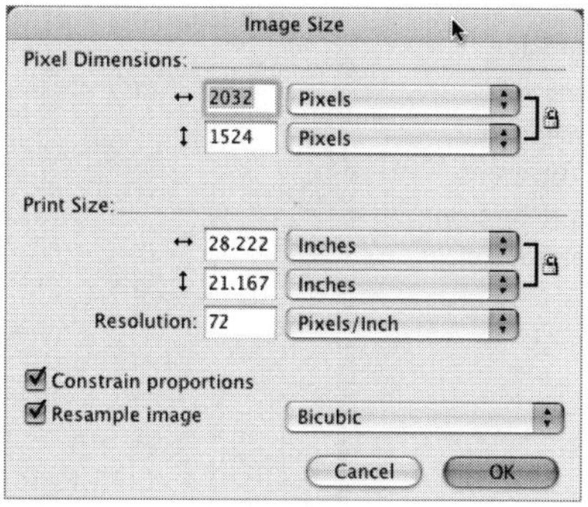

FIGURE 8.5

The Fireworks Image Size pop-up window works exactly like the one in Photoshop.

OPTIMIZING GIFS

To save an image in a web format in Photoshop, start with the File ➤ Save for Web menu command (Figure 8.6).

Photoshop opens a special Save for Web optimization palette that lets you see the image in either two or four views. Each view can be optimized individually to make the best choice. In Figure 8.7, you see the right panel selected, optimized as a GIF containing only eight colors. Clicking Save at that point saves it as a GIF, or you can change the number of colors, or see if you like it better as a JPEG.

FIGURE 8.6

The Photoshop Save for Web command

FIGURE 8.7

The Photoshop Save for Web options with the 2-Up view selected, allowing two different optimizations to be compared simultaneously

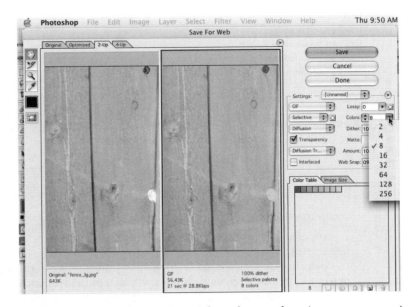

Fireworks keeps the web optimization palette options right at the top of any image, as you see in Figure 8.8. Once you have a 2-Up or 4-Up view open in Fireworks, as in Figure 8.9, you can compare optimizations at various settings for GIF to find the best options.

FIGURE 8.8

The Fireworks optimization options are always visible. Select either 2-Up or 4-Up to begin optimization.

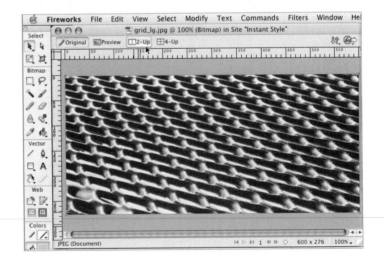

FIGURE 8.9

The Fireworks GIF optimizations options are similar to those in Photoshop.

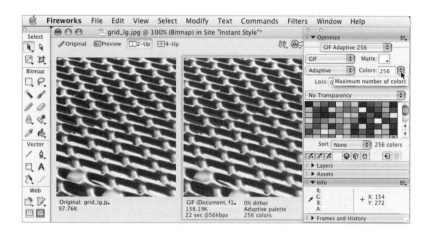

TIP   In Figure 8.9, the GIF is currently set for 256 colors, far more than are needed for an image such as this. Under the selected panel, image information shows the image at 138K. The number of colors should be reduced to bring this image to a size no larger than 10 to 20K.

OPTIMIZING JPEGS

JPEGs are optimized by quality, not by number of colors.

In Photoshop (Figure 8.10), you once again begin with File ➢ Save for Web. On a 2-Up Save for Web window, you view the options for JPEG. These options in Photoshop include a Low, Medium, or High quality setting and also a sliding scale for raising or lowering the quality of the JPEG in small increments.

In Fireworks (Figure 8.11), a 2-Up menu allows you to select JPEG with quality choices listed on a pull-down menu such as the JPEG – Better Quality you see displayed. There is also a sliding scale to allow small incremental adjustments in quality.

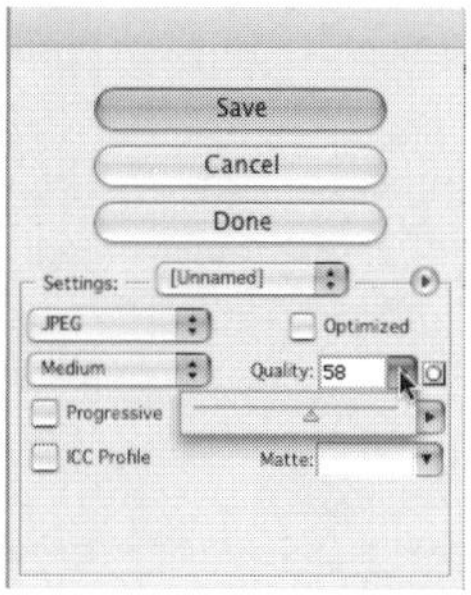

FIGURE 8.10

Photoshop's JPEG optimization choices

FIGURE 8.11
Firework's JPEG
optimization choices

As you can see, both tools have a similar way of doing things. Some of the menu choices to get to what you want are slightly different, but the basic chores you want to do are similar. This applies to Jasc Paint Shop Pro as well, although the jobs are accomplished perhaps by slightly different names or with slightly different menu options.

Because of these similarities, I'm only going to show you screen shots from Fireworks for the remainder of these graphics software tips. I trust that you realize that whichever tool you are using has similar options available somewhere in its menu choices.

MAKING BACKGROUND IMAGES

In order to tone down an image in a background, there are several techniques you can use. One is to adjust the image's hue and saturation.

In Figure 8.12, you can see a glimpse of the more saturated image behind the Hue/Saturation palette. Above the Hue/Saturation palette, you see the results of my adjustments in Preview mode. I not only reduced the saturation by quite a bit, but I also increased the brightness.

Another way to lighten an image so it can be used as a background is to reduce the opacity. To use the Opacity tool, select the layer holding the image and use the Opacity sliding scale to reduce the opacity. You see an example in Fireworks in Figure 8.13.

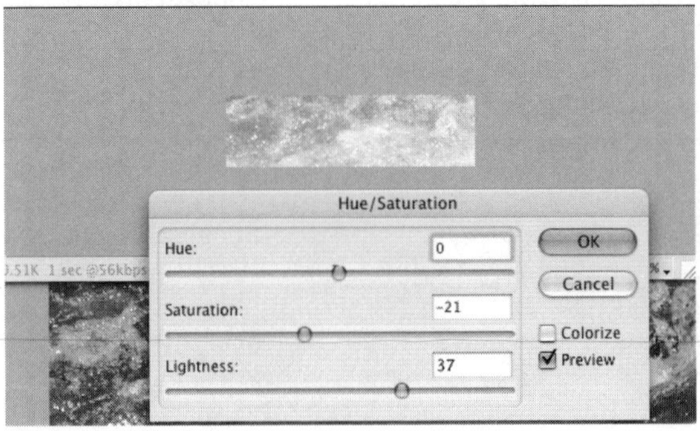

FIGURE 8.12
One way to lighten up
a background image is
with Hue/Saturation
settings.

FIGURE 8.13
Reducing the opacity makes the image much less intense when it's used as a background.

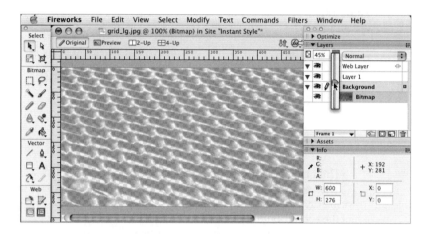

USING GRAPHICS SOFTWARE TO GET A COLOR CODE

Graphics software programs use an Eyedropper tool to select a color.

When you hover over a color with the Eyedropper tool, the Info panel gives you all sorts of information about the spot where you are hovering, including RGB values for the color. In Figure 8.14, you see that the color of a bit of the rope on the cover of this book is CC9933.

FIGURE 8.14
The Eyedropper tool selects a color. You can find the code for the color in the Info panel as separate RGB values, in this case CC9933.

Learn the XHTML

To begin learning how to incorporate images into your HTML pages, start by copying the `img_exercises` folder from the Chapter 8 folder on the CD to your computer. This folder includes several HTML files, a CSS file, and a subfolder with some images.

The *img* Element

You will need to know the size of each graphic in pixels. If you have software such as Fireworks or Photoshop, you can open an image in that software to get the image size. If you don't yet have any graphics software here's a trick that will work with Netscape, Mozilla, Firefox, or Safari browsers. Open the file `creek_sm.jpg` in one of the aforementioned browsers, as you see in Figure 8.15. You can jot down the image width and height shown the browser title bar.

FIGURE 8.15
Certain browsers
display the pixel
size of the image in
the title bar.

This image is 200 pixels in width and 109 pixels in height. Now, *that* is some information you can use.

The `img` element has several must-have attributes. The first is `src` (for source). A `src` attribute is a lot like an `href` attribute because it gives the path to the location of the image. Like `href`, the path used for the `src` attribute can be relative or absolute. If you are on one of the HTML pages in `img_exercises` writing a `src` value for the `creek_sm.jpg` image in the `images` subfolder, the `img` element is

```
<img src="images/creek_sm.jpg" />
```

TIP   The `img` element is an empty element. As I explained in Chapter 1, an empty element is one that doesn't include any text to be displayed on screen. In the case of `img`, you don't even need a second tag to close the element (the slash at the end of the `img` tag does the closing for you).

That tag will get the image to display in the browser, but it's not all you need. You also need width and height. Although width and height are not strictly required, I'm still going to insist that you need them, because it helps the browser render the page. If the browser knows how much width and height to allow on the page for images, it can render the text immediately instead of waiting for the images to download.

With the `width` and `height` added, the `img` element looks like this:

```
<img src="images/creek_sm.jpg" width="200" height="109" />
```

You aren't finished yet. The final requirement is `alt` (for alternative) text. This is the single most important thing you need to ensure accessible information, as well. The `alt` text describes the image. If the user is unable to see the image, the `alt` text will display. The use and purpose of the image is explained by the `alt` text.

NOTE   If you have never used any browser but Internet Explorer on Windows, you may think that the primary purpose of `alt` text is to display as a tool tip when you mouse over an image. This is not what `alt` text is supposed to do, and it doesn't appear as a tool tip in other browsers. `Alt` text is supposed to be visible when the image is not visible—that is, it is an alternative to the image.

For this image, suitable `alt` text might be something like "a color photograph of tree-lined creek."

```
<img src="images/creek_sm.jpg" width="200" height="109" alt="A color photograph of
a tree-lined creek" />
```

Figure 8.16 shows how the preceding `img` element would display in a browser if the image didn't appear. In the figure, the `alt` text is merely, "a tree-lined creek."

FIGURE 8.16

The `alt` text appears if the image does not.

If the `img` element is used as a button, the `alt` text should match the button text. In other words, if the button says Home, the `alt` text should say Home, too.

The `img` element as you have it in the last example has all the necessities: `src`, `width`, `height`, `alt`. There are other attributes that *might* be assigned to an `img` element, however: `name`, `id`, `title`, `longdesc`, `border`, `hspace`, `vspace`, `usemap`, and `ismap`. You don't need to worry about the `name` attribute because you would use `id` instead if a unique identifier were needed for the image. You don't need to worry about `border`, `hspace`, and `vspace` because you take care of those better with CSS. `usemap` and `ismap` relate to image maps, and you are not going to make an image map. That leaves `longdesc` and `title`.

THE *LONGDESC* ATTRIBUTE

Complex images such as charts and graphs often need a `longdesc` (for long description) attribute. If the image contains informational content that would make the page meaningless if the image were not seen, then `longdesc` is essential. The `longdesc` attribute points to a separate HTML file that gives a detailed description of the content of the image. It looks something like this:

```
<img src="images/chart.jpg" height="400" width="400" alt="monthly sales figures"
longdesc="sales.html" />
```

Browser support for `longdesc` is still somewhat problematic. Many web page designers are now using a workaround that involves putting a d after the element, which is made into a link to the long description. This practice is understood by people who need the long description information.

For the images you will use in `img_exercises`, `alt` text is adequate; there will be no need for `longdesc`.

THE *TITLE* ATTRIBUTE

The `title` attribute can be used with `img` elements. All browsers show the text of a `title` attribute visibly to all users if the element is hovered over; most browsers show it as a tool tip. The `title` attribute can include further description of an image or a link and often gives accessibility hints such as key combinations for access keys or tab index numbers or points to the location of long description (`longdesc`) files.

Again, there is no need for `title` attributes on the images in this chapter.

THE IMAGE STOCKPILE

Figure 8.17 shows the contents of the `images` subfolder in the `img_exercises` folder.

FIGURE 8.17
The images subfolder

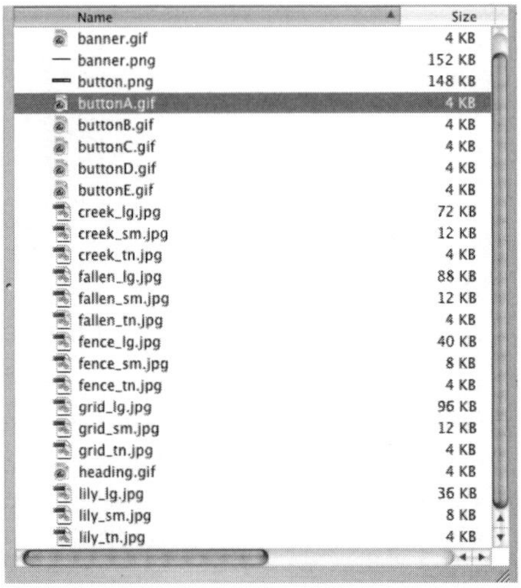

There are five button images that will be used in the basic navbars. There are also five main images saved at three different sizes each: lg (large), sm (small), and tn (thumbnail). There is a banner and a heading graphic. As I explained earlier, the two PNG files are examples for you but won't be used in an exercise.

The five images saved in various sizes are photos I took while out walking near my home. You are going to use them to create a small photo gallery. They aren't great art, but since I took them myself, we don't have to deal with copyright problems when using them, which makes them very attractive photos indeed.

TIP   Images on the Web are easy to copy and save. That does not mean that the image is copyright free and available for your use, however. Always check for copyright information and permission before using any graphic you obtain from a website.

Building Some Basic Navbars

Find the file Ch8_navbars.html. Open it in your text editor and in the browser. You will see that it is a partially completed page similar to Figure 8.18.

Look at the XHTML for the horiz division:

```
<div id="horiz">
  <h1>Insert images in horizontal line in this div</h1>
  <div><img src="images/buttonA.gif" width="100" height="18" alt="Button A" />
    <img src="images/buttonB.gif" alt="Button B" width="100" height="18" />
    more here... </div>
</div>
```

Each button is 100×18 pixels, and each is in the images subfolder. Notice that the img elements are separated only by a space. To finish the horiz navbar, remove the words "more here…" and insert img elements for buttonC.gif, buttonD.gif, and buttonE.gif. When you finish, the browser should look like Figure 8.19.

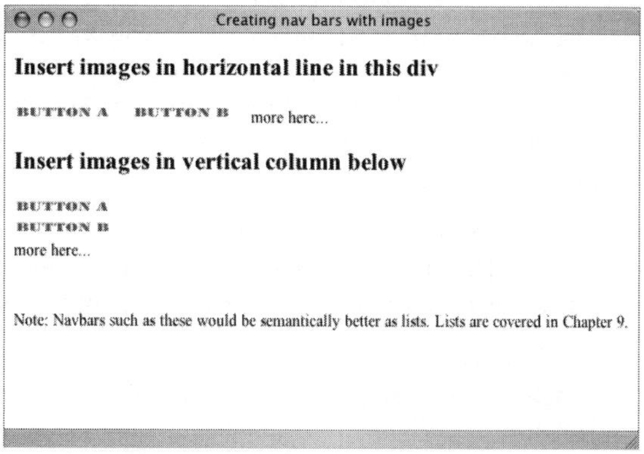

FIGURE 8.18
The beginning Ch8_ navbars.html page

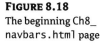

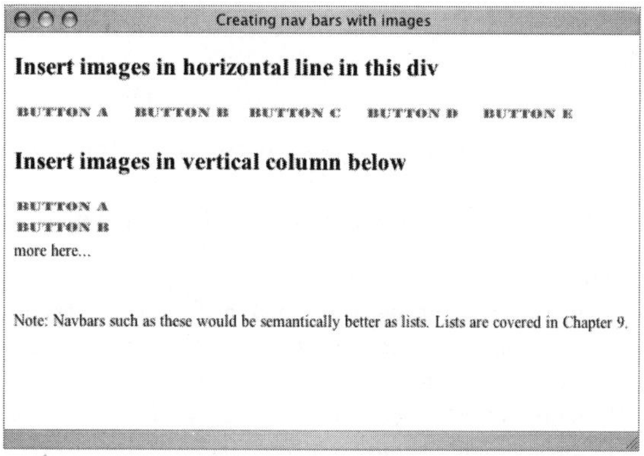

FIGURE 8.19
Completed horiz navbar

The completed div with the img elements in it is

```
<div><img src="images/buttonA.gif" width="100" height="18" alt="Button A" />
    <img src="images/buttonB.gif" alt="Button B" width="100" height="18" />
    <img src="images/buttonC.gif" alt="button C" width="100" height="18" />
    <img src="images/buttonD.gif" alt="button D" width="100" height="18" />
    <img src="images/buttonE.gif" alt="button E" width="100" height="18" />
</div>
```

With no styles attached to provide a set width for this navbar, the images will wrap just like words in a line of text if the user had a very narrow browser viewport, as shown in Figure 8.20.

A style for the selector #horiz specifying a width for the div of 525px would prevent the images from wrapping. With five images, each 100 pixels in width, and a space between each image, 525px is an adequate width to hold the navbar and prevent wrapping.

Of course, the whole notion of a button means that the image serves as a link. There are five HTML files in the folder that you can link to, or you can link these buttons to external sites such as Google. Here is one example of the buttons used as links:

```
<div><a href="fallen.html"><img src="images/buttonA.gif" alt="Button A"
    width="100" height="18" /></a> <a href="fence.html">
```

```
      <img src="images/buttonB.gif" alt="Button B" width="100" height="18" /></a>
      <a href="grid.html"><img src="images/buttonC.gif" alt="button C" width="100"
      height="18" /></a> <a href="index.html"><img src="images/buttonD.gif"
      alt="button D" width="100" height="18" /></a> <a href="lily.html">
      <img src="images/buttonE.gif" alt="button E" width="100" height="18" /></a>
    </div>
```

Turn your attention to the `<div id="vert">` element. It uses the same buttons but this time in a vertical arrangement. The markup is the same as in the horizontal navbar, except that instead of a single space between buttons, there is a `<br />` tag after each button image, which moves the next button down a line.

```
    <div id="vert">
      <h2>Insert images in vertical column below</h2>
      <div>
      <img src="images/buttonA.gif" alt="Button A" width="100" height="18" /><br />
      <img src="images/buttonB.gif" alt="Button B" width="100" height="18" /><br />
      more here...
      </div>
    </div>
```

Add the remaining images where it says "more here…" You should see a page like Figure 8.21 in the browser.

Before adding the a elements to the vertical display, the new XHTML is

```
    <div>
      <img src="images/buttonA.gif" alt="Button A" width="100" height="18" /><br />
      <img src="images/buttonB.gif" alt="Button B" width="100" height="18" /><br />
      <img src="images/buttonC.gif" alt="button C" width="100" height="18" /><br />
      <img src="images/buttonD.gif" alt="button D" width="100" height="18" /><br />
      <img src="images/buttonE.gif" alt="button E" width="100" height="18" />
    </div>
```

Add links to these button images in the same manner that you did for the horizontal navbar.

FIGURE 8.20
The images wrap if the
window is resized.

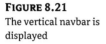

FIGURE 8.21
The vertical navbar is
displayed

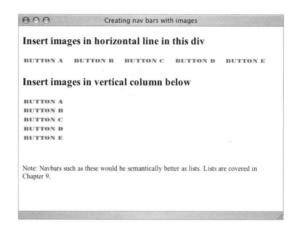

These simple graphic navbars illustrate two ways in which images can be strung together into a navigation structure. You will make some similar looking navbars with lists in the next chapter.

NOTE   In structural terms, building a navbar with a list creates a more logical page. A navbar made from a list can contain text or images. Combine what you are learning about links and images with the information on lists in Chapter 9 to get a complete understanding of navbars.

This section has given you some good practice getting images on a page and making them serve as buttons, but images are so important that you will benefit from learning several more ways to use them.

Designing a Photo Gallery

You will use these pages to create a small photo gallery:

```
creek.html
fallen.html
fence.html
grid.html
lily.html
```

Notice the similarity of the HTML page names and the image names. That's a clue as to which image goes with which page!

Some of the page basics have been prepared in advance for you. Open `creek.html` in your text editor and in the browser (Figure 8.22).

Notice that this page uses an imported style sheet, `layout.css`:

```
<style type="text/css">
<!--
@import url(layout.css);
-->
</style>
```

FIGURE 8.22
The beginning
`creek.html` page

Look at `layout.css` (Listing 8.1). It contains four rules to lay out the page and set some body properties. It does not contain a rule for the body background color, so depending on your browser's default background color setting, you may see a different color from the white in Figure 8.22.

LISTING 8.1:   *layout.css*

```
#navbar {
  float: left;
  width: 15%;
  top: 20px;
  position: relative;
  text-align: center;
}
#content {
  width: 80%;
  margin-left: 20%;
}
body {
  font: 100.01% Arial, Helvetica, sans-serif;
  color: #369;
  width: 95%;
}
#banner {
  text-align: center;
}
```

You will create a link to a new stylesheet and write new styles affecting the images as we proceed.

The pages also contain a working navbar using the thumbnail-sized images. This navbar is constructed in the same way as the one you built earlier using `buttonA.gif`, `buttonB.gif`, and so on. Under each thumbnail image there is also a text link. If an image or icon is not perfectly clear in meaning, it is good idea to provide a text equivalent as well. Look at the rules for the selector `#navbar` in `layout.css` to see what CSS rules are already determining the way the navbar displays.

Adding a Banner

Back in the `creek.html` page, find this in the XHTML:

```
<div id="banner">
  <h1>Insert banner.gif here</h1>
</div>
```

Replace the words "Insert banner.gif here" with an `img` element for `banner.gif`. Be sure to find out the width and height of this image.

The changed banner element should be:

```
<div id="banner">
<h1><img src="images/banner.gif" alt="Image Exercises" width="642" height="40" /></
h1>
</div>
```

With `banner.gif` in place, the page should look like Figure 8.23. Notice that the banner image is centered.

Notice that the `img` element is nested inside an `h1` element, making this graphic into the logical equivalent of the most important heading on the page.

FIGURE 8.23

The graphic in the banner division

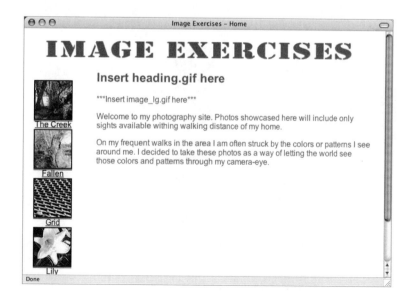

Adding a Heading

Look further down the page and find this:

```
<div id="content">
  <h2>Insert heading.gif here</h2>
```

Remove the words in the h2 element, and replace them with an img element for heading.gif. The new code is:

```
<div id="content">
<h2><img src="images/heading.gif" alt="same words as heading" width="156"
height="20" /></h2>
```

The alt text should reflect whatever the heading actually says. Like the buttonA, buttonB graphics, this graphic can be replaced by a graphic of a word that relates to the page content. On this page, an appropriate heading might be A Tree-Lined Creek. The alt text should be the same words: "a tree-lined creek."

TIP If a heading uses a font commonly found on most users' Internet-capable devices, there is no reason to create a graphic representing the heading. When an unusual font is wanted—such as this one called Stencil—a graphic may be the only way to ensure its appearance. The file heading.gif is 4K in size—not huge, but using graphics to create text could add up quickly.

With the very interesting heading graphic in place, the page should appear in the browser like Figure 8.24.

FIGURE 8.24
You add a heading to the page.

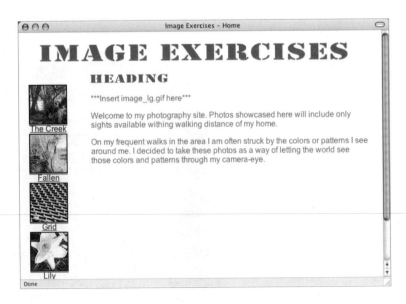

Inserting a Photo in Your Gallery

You are ready to add a large photo to the page. You will be replacing this text on the page with an image element:

```
***Insert image_lg.gif here***
```

On the page `creek.html`, the large image you want is `creek_lg.html`.

NOTE The large images are all 600px in width, but the height varies. Check each one for height before writing the code.

The `img` element for the `creek_lg.jpg` is:

```
<img src="images/creek_lg.jpg" alt="A tree-lined area of Gilleland Creek" width="600" height="328" />
```

Once you refresh, the browser will look like Figure 8.25.

Transparent GIFs

Earlier in the chapter, I promised to make transparency clear to you. Here's where I do that:

1. Open a blank text document and save it in the `img_exercises` folder as `ch8.css`.

2. Link `creek.html` to the new style sheet by adding this tag within the `head` element:

```
<link href="ch8.css" rel="stylesheet" type="text/css" />
```

FIGURE 8.25
The final image is added.

3. The first style will be a background color for the body. You can use any color you want. This style is for yellow:

```
body {
   background: #FF9;
}
```

4. Save everything and refresh (reload) the browser. The page should look like Figure 8.26: The two transparent GIFs, `banner.gif` and `heading.gif`, allow the yellow background to shine through between the letters. (If you are working along and have this image in your browser, you can see that the background is, indeed, yellow. Since the figures in the book are not in color, you'll have to trust me on this.)

5. Try a darker color:

```
body {
   background: #330;
}
```

In the browser you see the page shown in Figure 8.27.

Something is amiss in Figure 8.27. The background color does shine through. But a few white pixels appear in what is called a halo (or pixilation or jaggies) around the letters of the transparent GIF. They were there on the yellow background too but not noticeable. Here's why. When I made these transparent GIFs in Fireworks, I selected white as the matte color. That was because I intended these transparent graphics to end up on a white background. If I had intended to use #330 as the page background color, I would have made the matte color #330, too.

FIGURE 8.26
The background shines through the transparent GIFs.

FIGURE 8.27
A white "halo" shows around the letters when the dark background shows through the transparent GIF.

6. Get rid of those ugly, jagged halo effects by changing the body style once again:

```
body {
   background: #FFF;
}
```

Ahh, white. No jaggies.

The moral of this story is that even when you use transparency, you have to have some idea of your color scheme in advance. If you completely change your mind after the image is finished, you may have to go back into your graphics software and change the matte color.

Get to Work

You have some work to do before you can make any more progress on the ch8.css style rules. You need to insert the images into the other four pages in the same way that you just did for creek.html.

Repeat these steps on each page:

1. Within <div id="banner">, replace

```
<h1>Insert banner.gif here</h1>
```

with

```
<h1><img src="images/banner.gif" alt="Image Exercises" width="642" height="40" /></h1>
```

2. Replace

```
<h2>Insert heading.gif here</h2>
```

with

```
<h2><img src="images/heading.gif" alt="same words as heading" width="156"
height="20" /></h2>
```

3. Replace the large image on every page. The large image is different for every page:

- ◆ `fallen.html` gets `fallen_lg.jpg`
- ◆ `fence.html` gets `fence_lg.jpg`
- ◆ `grid.html` gets `grid_lg.jpg`
- ◆ `lily.html` gets `lily_lg.jpg`

Don't stop until every page has a banner, a heading, and a large image. Then take a moment to click around through the pages and enjoy your work.

TIP Our little site has only five images. With more images, you might have a whole page of thumbnails as your main page. Each thumbnail is linked, as in the example, to a page with more information about the image and a larger version of the image.

Learn the CSS

Use the `ch8.css` stylesheet you made earlier for all the new styles. The default display for an image used as a link in many browsers is for the image to have a blue line around it. You can see how this looks in Figure 8.28. If you change the default colors for the a elements, the image border reflects that color change.

As you learned earlier, one way to eliminate that border is to use the attribute `border="0"` in the `img` element. On these five pages, with five images used as links on each page, you would have to type that attribute 25 times. Why do all that and add to the size of every HTML page as it downloads in the process? You can write a style to eliminate the border across the whole site.

The thumbnail images are in this division:

```
<div id="navbar">
<a href="creek.html"><img src="images/creek_tn.jpg" alt="Creek" width="75"
  height="75" /><br />
Creek</a><br />
```

The CSS selector you need is `#navbar img`. You need to set a value of zero for the `border` property of that selector. Add this rule to `ch8.css`:

```
#navbar img {
  border: 0;
}
```

Poof, just like that the borders are gone for any `img` element within a `navbar` section, as shown in Figure 8.29.

FIGURE 8.28
Images as links often display a blue border.

FIGURE 8.29
No more borders on the images, although you still see underlines on the text links.

Sometimes you *want* borders. You could use a border around the large image like a frame for the great photographic art. The large images are in div id="content". Write a CSS selector like you did for the navbar: #content img. Add a 6px ridged border in the blue color you are using (#369), like this:

```
#content img {
    border: 6px ridge #369;
}
```

That style looks like Figure 8.30.

FIGURE 8.30
Do you really want all those borders?

Oops. That put a border on the heading img element, too. The selector #content img selects every image in the content division: not what you want. You need some class: apply it to the img for which you want to have a border. Call the class .photo. You can simply change the rule you wrote a moment ago to a class instead of the ID selector. Instead of using #content img as the selector, change the selector to .photo. Now the border will only be applied to elements in the class photo. The changed rule is

```
.photo {
  border: 6px ridge #369;
}
```

TIP   Remember that a class name in a stylesheet must be preceded by a period.

Now go into the XHTML and add the class attribute to the img element, like this:

```
<img src="images/creek_lg.jpg" alt="Creek" width="600" height="328"
  class="photo" />
```

The results in the browser should look similar to Figure 8.31.

If you want this effect on every large photo, you have to add the class attribute to each img element where you want it.

NOTE   Remember, the border-style values are dotted, dashed, solid, double, groove, ridge, inset, and outset. Play around with these to see if you can design a frame-like effect you like better than the one I suggested.

FIGURE 8.31
Only the image in the class photo has a border.

Link Color and Decoration

I think the navbar link text would look better if it were not underlined and had some white space around it. The font-size could be reduced a bit, to 85 percent (or .85em). The blue color could also be changed to match the other blue on the page (#369). A different color on hover would be nice for the link text.

Start with the #navbar img style you already have. Add some margin-top to the img. I think 8 pixels looks good, but you can try other amounts. The changed style is

```
#navbar img {
  border: 0px;
  margin-top: 8px;
}
```

You can use a comma-separated group selector for all the pseudo states of the a selector, except :hover, like this:

```
#navbar a:link, #navbar a:visited, #navbar a:active {
  font-size: 85%;
  color: #369;
  text-decoration: none;
}
```

If you write a style after this one for the a:hover pseudo state, it will inherit the font-size and text-decoration rules. You need only a new color value:

```
#navbar a:hover {
  color: #C36;
}
```

FIGURE 8.32
The navbar styles
are reflected.

With all these rules in place, the page looks similar to Figure 8.32.

NOTE Remember that `text-align: center` was applied to the navbar in `layout.css`.

Backgrounds

We discussed background images earlier in the book. In case you would like to use one in this chapter, an image named `banner_bg.jpg` is in the `img_exercises` folder and can be used as a background for the banner. (The original Fireworks file, `banner_bg.png`, is there for your inspection, also.)

This image is 1200 pixels in width. At this size it should be wide enough for almost any monitor. It gives a fluid quality to the banner at that width because the image seems to grow or shrink as the browser window is resized.

To add this background, use the `#banner` selector, with declarations to set the background for no-repeat and center the background both horizontally and vertically:

```
#banner {
  background: url(banner_bg.jpg) no-repeat center center;
}
```

The new banner should look like Figure 8.33.

On the CD, you will find a file named `ch8_finish.css`. It is the stylesheet for the Photo Gallery pages that you just completed.

Size Matters

Throughout this chapter I have stressed the importance of figuring out the correct size in width and height of an image before writing the `img` tag. Generally, it is a good practice to match the actual width and height of the image to the width and height attributes you use in the XHTML, but there are exceptions.

FIGURE 8.33
The banner back-
ground fits even
a wide browser
viewport.

You can use the `width` and `height` attributes of an `img` element to make an image any size you want. Sometimes it is a good idea to change the visual display of an image using `width` and `height` values. Sometimes it is terrible idea.

Sizing Images via HTML: The Good

In Chapter 7, you used a 1×1-pixel transparent GIF to create a skip link. You could use that tiny transparent GIF (which downloads very quickly) but change the width and height values in the XHTML code. Something like this, perhaps:

```
<img src="skip.gif" width="10" height="10" alt="skip to content" />
```

The effect of this would be to make the transparent graphic take up more space on the page. Try changing width and height values for images. Open the page you haven't touched yet: `Ch8_smallimage.html`, as shown in Figure 8.34.

You will also use `bluebar.gif`. This GIF is 5×1 pixels and less than 1K in file size. It is a solid bit of blue (color #369) and will download almost instantly. You will insert it immediately under the `banner.gif`, but instead of using the real dimensions of `width="5"` and `height="1"`, use `width="642"` (to match the banner above it) and `height="2"`. The solid blue color will stretch to fit these dimensions.

This `bluebar.gif` is strictly for decoration. It adds nothing to the content of the page. People using screen readers or people surfing with images off don't need `alt` text for this image. Leave the `alt` attribute in the `img` element, but put nothing (not even a space) between the quotation marks for the value. This is telling the user that the image is not part of the content and no `alt` text is needed.

The entire banner code is now:

```
<div id="banner">
  <img src="images/banner.gif" alt="Image Exercises" width="642"
    height="40" /><br />
  <img src="bluebar.gif" width="642" height="2" alt="" />
</div>
```

FIGURE 8.34
The beginning Ch8_
smallimage.html page

FIGURE 8.34
The beginning Ch8_
smallimage.html page

FIGURE 8.35
The tiny blue graphic be-
comes a horizontal rule
by changing the actual
image dimensions to
width and height values
in the XHTML.

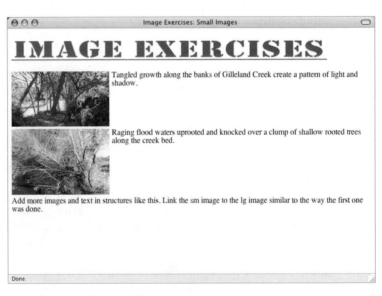

The effect in the browser is shown in Figure 8.35.

Enlarging graphics this way works fine for solid blocks of color and for tiny transparent images.

Sizing Images via HTML: The Bad

Unless you are actually trying to distort an image, any other kind of playing around with the true size of an image by changing width or height is probably a bad idea.

Find this in `Ch8_smallimages.html`:

```
<div class="images">
  <p><a href="images/creek_lg.jpg"><img src="images/creek_sm.jpg"
    alt="Creek" width="200" height="109" border="0" /></a></p>
```

Change the image size in the code to `width="400"`, `height="125"`. As you can see in Figure 8.36, the browser displays the image in the size specified. But if you look closely at the image, it has a bad case of the jaggies (also called pixilated) and looks bad, bad, bad. Quick, change those values back to 200×109.

As you might have guessed, this process can work to make images appear smaller as well. For example the 72K image, `creek_lg.jpg`, could be inserted in that position on the page. With the width and height values set to 200×109, the large image would look exactly like the small one on the page now. Except for one important thing: the user just waited through the download of a 72K image. The small image at 12K would have appeared exactly the same but would have downloaded much more quickly.

Now you understand why there are three different-sized versions of each image in the images folder for this set of exercises. Except for the few instances just mentioned, it is best for quality and download time to match the real image size to the display size on the page. It takes a bit more time to prepare the images, but it pays off.

Linking Directly to Images

`Ch8_smallimage.html` is an example of another way to lay out a photo album site.

Here the small image is linked directly to the large image. When the user clicks the link, the image opens in the browser with no HTML page holding it. Therefore, the web designer has no control over background colors or any other aspect of what the user sees. They simply see the image. There is no navigation on the image, so the user must use the Back button to come back to the HTML page. You may have noticed that the first image, The Creek, is already linked to the large version as an example.

FIGURE 8.36
The resized image gets pixilated and blurry looking.

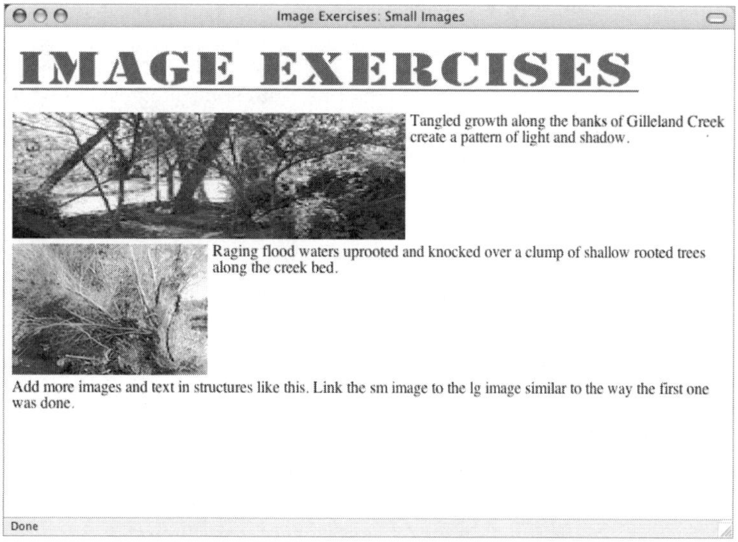

Displaying images in this simple fashion is fine for jobs such as quickly putting up photos from your nephew's birthday party so the other members of your family can see them. Sometimes a direct link to a high-resolution graphic is used to provide press or publicity images. This allows a user to download a print-quality image. For example, a direct link to a high resolution photo of Saturn from the Cassini space mission might be found at the NASA site.

Notice that each image and its accompanying text is in a `div` assigned to the class `images`. The prewritten style rules for this page are in the `head`. Be sure to take a look at them so you will understand what rules are already being applied to the images as you place them in the new `div` elements on the page.

Finish the page. You need five `<div class="images">` elements in all. One is already finished for you. Another has an image but no link to the large image yet. One more such `div` is already on the page but contains text telling you to replace the text with an image and the descriptive paragraph.

1. Start by copying the following `div` and pasting it on the page two more times so you have the needed five `div`s:

```
<div class="images">
<p>Add more images and text in structures like this. Link the sm image to the lg
image similar to the way the first one was done.</p>
```

2. In the second, partially completed `div`, add a link to the `fallen_lg.jpg` to this element:

```
<img src="images/fallen_sm.jpg" alt="Fallen" />
```

3. In the next three `div`s, insert the `img` element for each of the three remaining small images: `fence_sm.jpg`, `grid_sm.jpg`, and `lily_sm.jpg`.

4. In each of the three incomplete `div`s, add the paragraph text. The text for each of the paragraphs in Listing 8.2 is on the accompanying CD in a file called `image.txt`, if you would like to copy and paste the text sections.

5. Link each of the small images to its corresponding large image.

The four changed image links, with some suggested text to describe each image, are shown in Listing 8.2.

LISTING 8.2:   The Changes to the *Ch8_smallimage.html* Page

```
<div class="images">
  <p><a href="images/fallen_lg.jpg"><img src="images/fallen_sm.jpg" alt="Fallen"
border="0" /></a> Raging flood waters uprooted and knocked over a clump of shallow
rooted trees along the creek bed.</p>
</div>
<div class="images">
  <p><a href="images/fence_lg.jpg"><img src="images/fence_sm.jpg" alt="Fence"
width="200" height="122" border="0" /></a>This is a fence with a peculiar pattern of
```

markings. I always wonder how these marks appear. Are they from a weed cutter gone
amok? Insects? A kid banging the fence with a stick?</p>
</div>
<div class="images">
  <p><a href="images/grid_lg.jpg"><img src="images/grid_sm.jpg" alt="Grid"
width="200" height="92" border="0" /></a>Picnic tables in the park are constructed
of a reinforced metal gridwork and covered in some sort of rubberized coating to
prevent rusting. It makes for an interesting pattern.</p>
</div>
<div class="images">
  <p><a href="images/lily_lg.jpg"><img src="images/lily_sm.jpg" alt="Lily"
width="200" height="134" border="0" /></a> The Easter lily burst into bloom in June.
This is a two year old plant that was planted last spring.</p>
</div>
```

In the browser, you should see something like Figure 8.37.

## Body Talk

Dress up the appearance of the Ch8_smallimage.html file a bit. It could use a body style. Give the
body a set width of about 650 pixels; the banner.gif is 642px, so 650px is enough. I think a centered
body would look good; with margin-right and margin-left set to auto, the body will be centered
in most browsers (see the sidebar "Centering Issues" for more information about this). And don't forget a background-color.

**TIP**   A fixed width of 650px for the body is a potential barrier to anyone with accessibility issues
requiring extra large text sizes.

**FIGURE 8.37**
Ch8_smallimage.html
with all the images in
place

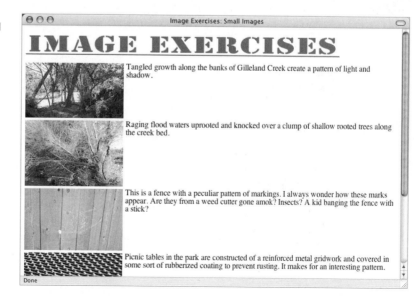
```

The body style is similar to this:

```
body {
  width: 650px;
  margin-right: auto; margin-left: auto;
  background: #FFF;
}
```

This also has the effect of reining in the lines of text that describe each image and preventing them from growing unreadably long. See Figure 8.38. The completed `creek.html` page is shown in Listing 8.3.

FIGURE 8.38

The centered body

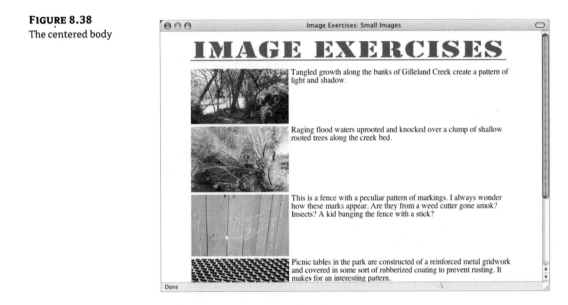

LISTING 8.3: The completed *creek.html* page

```
<!DOCTYPE html PUBLIC "-//W3C//DTD XHTML 1.0 Transitional//EN" "http://www.w3.org/
TR/xhtml1/DTD/xhtml1-transitional.dtd">
<html xmlns="http://www.w3.org/1999/xhtml">
<head>
<title>Image Exercises - Home</title>
<style type="text/css">
@import url("layout.css");
</style>
<link href="ch8.css" rel="stylesheet" type="text/css" />
</head>
<body>
<div id="banner">
```

```
  <h1><img src="images/banner.gif" alt="Image Exercises" width="642" height="40" /
></h1>
</div>

<div id="navbar"><a href="creek.html"><img src="images/creek_tn.jpg" alt="Creek"
width="75" height="75" /><br />
  Creek</a><br />
  <a href="fallen.html"><img src="images/fallen_tn.jpg" alt="Fallen" width="75"
height="75" /><br />
  Fallen</a><br />
  <a href="grid.html"><img src="images/grid_tn.jpg" alt="Grid" width="75"
height="75" /><br />
  Grid</a><br />
  <a href="lily.html"><img src="images/lily_tn.jpg" alt="Lily" width="75"
height="75" /><br />
  Lily</a><br />
  <a href="fence.html"><img src="images/fence_tn.jpg" alt="Fence" width="75"
height="75" /><br />
Fence</a></div>

<div id="content">
  <h2><img src="images/heading.gif" alt="same words as heading" width="156"
height="20" /></h2>
  <img src="images/creek_lg.jpg" alt="Creek" width="600" height="328" class="photo" /
>
  <p>Tangled growth along the banks of Gilleland Creek create a pattern of light and
shadow.</p>
</div>
</body>
</html>
```

CENTERING ISSUES

I mentioned that you center something horizontally on a page with a rule like:

```
#content {
    margin-left: auto;
    margin-right: auto;
}
```

This is what the W3C standards deem correct. However, browser support for this standard is not uniform. In some browsers you can center a div (as well as the text that is in the div) like this:

```
#content {
```

```
    text-align: center;

}
```

This doesn't work in all browsers, either. Plus, it centers your text, which you must overrule later in the Cascade if you don't want the text centered.

The solution is to use both rules at the same time. Browsers missed by one rule will be caught by the other. Like this:

```
#content {

  margin-left: auto;

  margin-right: auto;

  text-align: center;

}
```

Now, of course, if you don't want the centered text in your centered div, you come along after this rule with another rule to set the text-align to what you want. You probably want left alignment, so the rule would be:

```
#content p {

  text-align: left;

}
```

This would left-align paragraphs in the content div. But you might also have lists, block quotes, or other elements in the content div that you wanted left-aligned. In actual practice, you might want to put the content div in a container (#container) div. Center the container div in the way I described, and then left-align every element in the content div with a second rule.

```
#container {

  margin-left: auto;

  margin-right: auto;

  text-align: center;

}

#content {

  text-align: left;

}
```

Technically, this is a hack. It is called the Horizontal Centering Hack, but it will survive a trip through a CSS validator with no ill effects, since all the rules used are valid rules. It becomes a hack because the need to combine the rules in this fashion to achieve horizontal centering in all browsers is not the method the standard specifications stipulate.

Adding Multimedia to Your Page

If you love web pages that pop and sizzle with sound and motion, multimedia is where it's at. Multimedia involves images, but a multimedia file is much more than the static images you have worked with up to this point. Multimedia usually involves movement, possibly sound and user interaction. You will learn how to add Flash, QuickTime, Windows Media, and Java applets to your XHTML.

Creating the Flash, QuickTime, Windows Media file or Java applet is beyond the scope of this book. Creating files in any of these formats requires software and skills that that take time and study to master.

If you already have the needed skills, you can create your own multimedia files. If you haven't started down that particular learning path yet, you can find samples and examples of multimedia on numerous websites that you can use on your web pages to add a bit of that illusive coolness factor.

The `object` tag is the current recommendation from the W3C for adding multimedia objects to web pages. However, the `object` tag is often coupled with the older `embed` tag in a double-whammy approach needed to ensure that your multimedia element shows up in every browser. Eventually, all browsers will interpret the `object` tag correctly and the `embed` tag will no longer be needed.

The `object` element is recommended by the W3C as a replacement for the older `applet` element as well. This is another area of spotty implementation by the browsers, and the example you will see in this section uses `applet`.

There is limited support for CSS within Macromedia's most recent version of Flash. The other multimedia types discussed here do not make use of CSS.

The Plug-In Problem

An issue with the multimedia formats for some users is the fact that they must download and install a plug-in in order to play the files involved. The situation is improving, with many browsers automatically including certain plug-ins in their installation. Flash is widely supported because it is now installed with the browser. However, as you will see in the section on Flash, the web designer can specify a particular version of Flash, which might mean a new download and install for the user.

All new Windows operating system computers come with Windows Media Player installed, and most new computers with Mac operating systems have QuickTime installed. This means that in cases where WMP is the only option for playing a multimedia file, Mac users will have to download a plug-in; when QuickTime is the only option, Windows users will have to download a plug-in. And Linux users will have to download a plug-in to view any multimedia effects. Viewers may be so irritated by the fact that they need to download something in order to see your content that they may simply leave, or they may be quite willing to download and install a new plug-in to see your content. The timeworn but sage advice to "know your audience" will help you balance your desire for sound and motion with the goals your audience has when visiting your site.

Flash

An entire website can be done in Flash. There are several software programs that write Flash files, but the best known is from Macromedia. Macromedia Flash can be used to write applications, connect to a database, gather form data, play movies and music, or simply animate something small such as a banner ad or a button.

For years there was a raging debate over Flash. Flash designers loved it because they had complete control over appearance and it allowed them to generate a lot of razzle-dazzle on the Web. Accessibility gurus hated it because it was inaccessible. To Macromedia's credit, they have made many improvements in Flash to make it more accessible. Careful use of the latest versions of Macromedia Flash can create quite acceptably accessible uses for Flash.

A Flash file is saved with the file extension `.fla`. When it is exported for use on the Web, the file extension becomes `.swf`, which is pronounced "swiff."

Look in the Chapter 8 `multimedia` folder on the accompanying CD for `ch8_flash.html` and `abitofflash.swf`. Copy both these files to the same folder on your computer. The `ch8_flash.html` page is a finished page. You can look at it in the browser to see what the Flash will look like when you are finished adding it to your page.

Begin a new XHTML document and prepare it to be ready to add the Flash element. Save it with a filename such as `myflash.html`.

The `object` element has several attributes when using Flash. The first is `classid`. This is a long string of code numbers that must be typed correctly, so you might consider using copy and paste. The second attribute needed is `codebase`. This attribute sends people to Macromedia to download the Flash plug-in if they don't have it. In the following snippet, note `version=6`. This refers to the Flash 6 player. If the user doesn't have a Flash Player at version 6 or above, they will be prompted to download the latest version. At the time of this writing, the latest version of Flash is version 7. (See Figure 8.42 later in this chapter for an example of a message about a missing plug-in.)

A `width` and `height` are needed. The `title` is there for accessibility, since the object element does not use an `alt` attribute.

Before I explain the `param` elements, take a look at the complete `object` element:

```
<object classid="clsid:D27CDB6E-AE6D-11cf-96B8-444553540000" codebase="http://
download.macromedia.com/pub/shockwave/cabs/flash/swflash.cab#version=6,0,29,0"
width="350" height="350" title="A Bit of Flash">
  <param name="movie" value="abitofflash.swf" />
  <param name="quality" value="high" />
  <param name="LOOP" value="false" />
</object>
```

Each `param` (for parameter) element has a `name` and a `value`. The `param` elements give the source file location, set the quality, and set the `value` for loop to `false`. The `value="false"` is the same as "no" in plain English, meaning "No, the file will not loop but will only play once."

TIP A loop in a computer program means that the program plays, then goes back to the start and plays again. Loops can be set to play a specific number of times and then stop, or to repeat endlessly.

The `object` element by itself won't work in every possible browser, so you need to repeat the some of the same information using an embed element, like this:

```
<embed src="abitofflash.swf" width="350" height="350" loop="False" quality="high"
pluginspage="http://www.macromedia.com/go/getflashplayer" type="application/x-
shockwave-flash"></embed>
```

The `embed` element repeats the information about the source of the movie, the width and height, the loop value, and the quality value. Instead of `codebase`, it uses an attribute called `pluginspage` to point users who don't have the Flash Player to the download site. Finally, the `embed` element includes a `type` attribute.

The `embed` element is nested in the `object` element. The two together are shown in Listing 8.4.

LISTING 8.4:   The Completed *object* and *embed* Elements Needed to Add a Flash Movie to a Page

```
<object classid="clsid:D27CDB6E-AE6D-11cf-96B8-444553540000" codebase="http://
download.macromedia.com/pub/shockwave/cabs/flash/swflash.cab#version=6,0,29,0"
width="350" height="350" title="A Bit of Flash">
  <param name="movie" value="abitofflash.swf" />
  <param name="quality" value="high" />
  <param name="LOOP" value="false" />
  <embed src="abitofflash.swf" width="350" height="350" loop="False"
    pluginspage="http://www.macromedia.com/go/getflashplayer"
    quality="high" type="application/x-shockwave-flash">
  </embed>
</object>
```

With all that in place, take a look in the browser. You should see something similar to Figure 8.39.

QuickTime

Most recent computers include software for processing movies imported from the owner's camera. Once you have edited the movie into what you want, you have the option to export it in a format that can be played on a web page. One of those format choices is Windows Media, which comes loaded on any Windows computer. Another movie format option is QuickTime, which comes loaded on any Apple computer. Of course, with the proper plug-in, Windows computers can play QuickTime movies, and Apple computers can play Windows Media. The Real One Player, which is available on many computers, can play QuickTime movies, too.

FIGURE 8.39
The Flash movie
ends like this.

You can use a QuickTime movie provided on the accompanying CD to practice using QuickTime. QuickTime movies are saved with the file extension `.mov`. You need to copy these two files to your computer: `ch8_qt.html` and `newzealandQT.mov`.

The `ch8_qt.html` page is a finished page. When you have created your own page for the movie, it should work like this page.

TIP The Media Access Generator (MAGpie) tool can create captions for QuickTime, Flash, and other media. It is available at `http://ncam.wgbh.org/webaccess/magpie/`.

Begin a new XHTML page. Save it with a name such as `myqt.html`. You will add the movie to this page. The `object` element will hold the movie. Again you need to use an `embed` element also.

You will recognize some of the attributes needed for QuickTime objects. You need to include

```
classid="clsid:02BF25D5-8C17-4B23-BC80-D3488ABDDC6B"
```

Note that the `classid` is specific to QuickTime and is not the same set of numbers as those used for the Flash Player. You must give the codebase for the player version,

```
codebase="http://www.apple.com/qtactivex/qtplugin.cab"
```

and set the `width="320"` and `height="256"` size for this particular movie.

See Listing 8.5 for the complete snippet, including both the `object` and the `embed` elements. As you type it, see if you can figure out what the `param` values do. I'll explain the `param` values after you have it typed.

LISTING 8.5:   The Complete *object* and *embed* Elements for a QuickTime Movie

```
<object classid="clsid:02BF25D5-8C17-4B23-BC80-D3488ABDDC6B" width="320"
  height="256" codebase="http://www.apple.com/qtactivex/qtplugin.cab">
  <param name="autoplay" value="false" />
  <param name="controller" value="true" />
  <param name="pluginspage" value="http://www.apple.com/quicktime/download/
indext.html" />
  <param name="target" value="myself" />
  <param name="type" value="video/quicktime" />
  <param name="src" value="newzealandQT.mov" />
  <embed src="newzealandQT.mov" width="320" height="256" autoplay="false"
    pluginspage="http://www.apple.com/quicktime/download/indext.html"
    controller="true" border="0" target="myself" type="video/quicktime">
  </embed>
</object>
```

Your page may not have any text, but the *movie* should appear something like Figure 8.40 in the browser after you type the preceding snippet on your page.

FIGURE 8.40
The opening screen of
the QuickTime movie

You may have noticed that the movie does not begin to play until the user clicks the triangle play icon. That is because of the `param name="autoplay" value="false"` element in the `object` element. If that value were set to `true`, the movie would begin to play automatically.

The `param name="controller" value="true"` means that there will be controllers with the movie. Since the movie doesn't start playing automatically, it is unusable without the controller.

If the user does not have a QuickTime Player, this `param` points out the download site:

```
<param name="pluginspage" value="http://www.apple.com/quicktime/download/
indext.html" />
```

The QuickTime Player can launch as a separate application window or play right on the web page using `param name="target" value="myself"`.

The `param name="type"` tells the browser what type of object is being played (`value="video/quicktime"`).

The source file URL is given in `param name="src" value="newzealandQT.mov"`.

The attributes in the `embed` element provide the same information.

Windows Media

Windows Media Player plays all sorts of multimedia files: sound files, movies, radio channels, and various video formats. Windows Media Player can play files in all of these formats: `.avi, .asf, .asx, .rmi, .wav, .wma, .wax, . mpg, .mpeg, .m1v, .mp2, .mp3, .mpa, .mpe, .qt, .aif, .aifc, .aiff, .mov`, and others.

I couldn't find any free examples or create a sample file for you to try, but I can show you the code that is needed to add a Windows Media object to your web page. It is very similar to the other `object` and `embed` combinations used previously. Because there is no real file for you to use, the source is listed as `somefile.wma`. See Listing 8.6.

LISTING 8.6: The *object* and *embed* Elements Needed to Add a Windows Media File to a Web Page

```
<object width="320" height="290" id="mediaplayer1" classid="CLSID:22d6f312-b0f6-
11d0-94ab-0080c74c7e95">
  <param name="Filename" value="somefile.wma" />
  <param name="AutoStart" value="True" />
  <param name="ShowControls" value="True" />
  <param name="ShowStatusBar" value="False" />
  <param name="ShowDisplay" value="False" />
  <param name="AutoRewind" value="True" />
  <embed type="application/x-mplayer2" width="320" height="290"
    src="somefile.wma" filename="somefile.mpg" showcontrols="True"
    showstatusbar="False" showdisplay="False" autostart="True" autorewind="True"
    pluginspage="http://www.microsoft.com/Windows/Downloads/Contents/MediaPlayer/">
  </embed>
</object>
```

Even though `somefile.wma` is not a real file, if you open the page in the browser it will attempt to find the file. You may see something like Figure 8.41 indicating that the file is not there, or you may just see a blank space.

FIGURE 8.41

The little icon with the question mark in the 320×290 space reserved for the Windows Media object indicates a missing file.

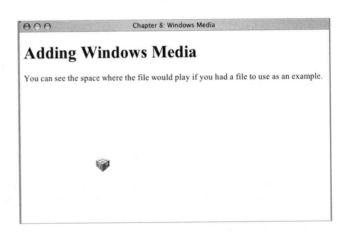

In the Safari browser, where I do not have a Windows Media Player plug-in, I also see a message telling me where to find the plug-in so I can install it, as shown in Figure 8.42.

Java Applets

Java is a programming language capable of building large web application programs and software. Java is not the same thing as JavaScript, which is a different programming language used extensively with websites.

When a Java programmer writes a very small application to do one small task, it is called an *applet*. Applets can be used on web pages, but they have never become very popular there because they may cause the browser to crash.

FIGURE 8.42
This message about the download site for Windows Media Player is similar to messages you would see for missing Flash and QuickTime plug-ins.

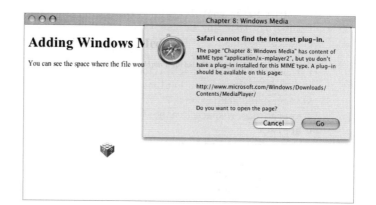

There are free applets available for use on websites. Some are provided by Sun Microsystems at `http://java.sun.com/applets/`. You will use one of Sun's freebie applets to create a rotating quote display.

Java code is saved in what are called *class* files. This is not the same thing as a class selector in CSS. The `JavaQuote.class` file on the accompanying CD is the code for the applet you will add. The instructions with the applets provided by Sun say that the `.class` file should be in the same directory as the HTML page where it will be used, so save it on your computer that way. The directions provided by Sun also give a URL for the `codebase` attribute that is on a Sun server, as in the finished example:

```
codebase="http://java.sun.com/openstudio/applets/classes"
```

Look at the `ch8_applet.html` page provided on the CD, which is a finished page showing how the applet should look and work after you have it on a new page.

Get a new XHTML page ready to insert this snippet. As I mentioned earlier, the W3C recommends using `object` rather than `applet` as the element for this, but it would not work for me using `object`, so you will note that the example element is `applet`. The entire element is shown in Listing 8.7.

LISTING 8.7:   The *JavaQuote* Applet Element

```
<applet codebase="http://java.sun.com/openstudio/applets/classes"
  code="JavaQuote.class" width="300" height="125" >
  <param name="bgcolor" value="ffffff" />
  <param name="bheight" value="10" />
  <param name="bwidth" value="10" />
  <param name="delay" value="1000" />
  <param name="fontname" value="Arial" />
  <param name="fontsize" value="14" />
  <param name="link" value="http://java.sun.com/events/jibe/index.html" />
  <param name="number" value="3" />
  <param name="quote0" value="In our 12 years of international application
development, in 42 different languages, we have found Java the easiest to implement
world spanning applications.|- MicroBurst Inc.|000000|ffffff|7" />
```

```
  <param name="quote1" value="Simplicity is key. Our customers need no special
technology to enjoy our services. Because of Java, just about the entire world can
come to PlayStar.|- PlayStar Corporation|000000|ffffff|7" />
  <param name="quote2" value="The ubiquity of the Internet is virtually wasted
without a platform which allows applications to utilize the reach of Internet to
write ubiquitous applications! That's where Java comes into the picture for us.|-
NetAccent|000000|ffffff|7" />
  <param name="space" value="20" />
</applet>
```

There are some `param name` attributes in the `applet` element that you have not seen in the other multimedia examples. Some, such as `fontsize`, are obvious. The less obvious ones include the following:

♦ `bheight`, for border height

♦ `delay`, the delay between frames in milliseconds

♦ `number`, the number of quotes

The `param` for `quote0`, `quote1`, and `quote2` is explained by Sun as follows:

A " | " delimited string where the first item is the quote, the second item is the company, the third item is the RGB hexadecimal text color, the fourth item is the RGB hexadecimal background color, and the last item is the length of time in seconds to display the quote. N represents a value between 0 and number –1.

Finally, `space` is the distance in pixels between the quote and the company.

You probably noticed that you didn't have to type that long string of numbers in the `classid` for the applet. That information is replaced in an applet by the more human readable `.class` file.

The applet running in your browser should look something like Figure 8.43.

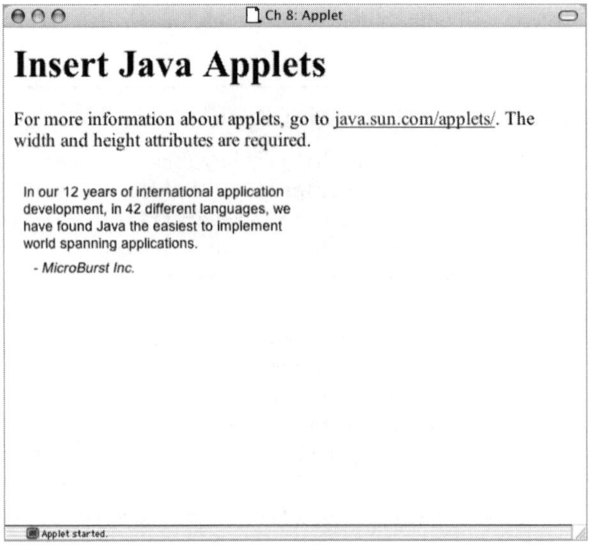

FIGURE 8.43

The applet as it appears in the browser

Real World Examples

Images do many jobs on a web page. They add interest, color, and information. On some sites that is all images are asked to do. On other sites, multimedia images create movement and interesting user interactions with the site.

Mozilla.org (Figure 8.44) uses images sparingly. The site is really an example of the old adage, "Content is king." Users go to this site looking for the latest browser and for information. The images used here are minimal decorative elements such as logos and icons and a few fund-raising product images. Huge images and multimedia bells and whistles on this site would be unwelcome.

With rocker David Bowie at `www.davidbowie.com`, however, coolness matters and glitz is a definite plus. In Figure 8.45, you see a page on his site with a Flash jukebox.

David Bowie is known for being one of the first musicians to understand and tap into the power of the Internet to build rapport with his fans. His site has been redesigned a number of times, always with an eye on the coolness factor.

The choice of Flash that you see in Figure 8.45 means that Bowie's aging baby boomer fans with declining eyesight will be unable to resize the text used in many places on the site, the way they would be able to do with XHTML. Will they leave the site because of that? Probably not. It is likely that his long-term and very loyal fans will keep coming back and will be willing to overlook such details in search of the latest in concert and album news.

Both sites demonstrate the importance of knowing your audience.

FIGURE 8.44

The Mozilla.org home page. Mozilla creates a free browser with useful web developer tools called Firefox and the Mozilla browser.

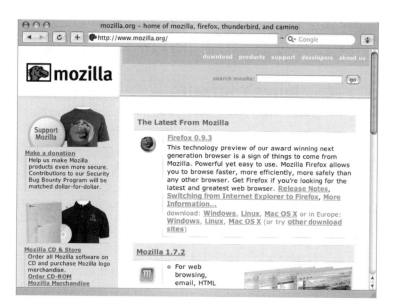

FIGURE 8.45
David Bowie's site uses
Flash extensively, in-
cluding a Flash jukebox.

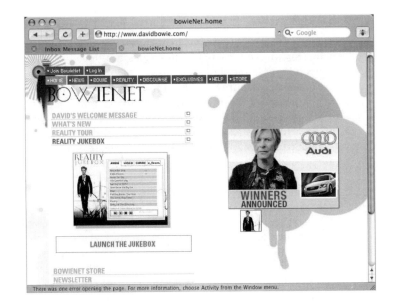

CSS Properties

No new CSS properties were harmed in the making of this chapter.

Challenge Yourself

To test-drive the CSS and multimedia you've learned in this chapter, try these additional webpage changes:

1. Consider `creek.html` to be the home page for the five photo gallery pages. Make the banner image on every page a link to the site home page.

2. If you have a way to create a new background graphic or to crop the 1200-pixel file provided on the CD, try using a background graphic of about 600 pixels for the background image of the banner (see Figure 8.33). Instead of using `no-repeat`, have it repeat on the horizontal axis only. Compare the results with what you did in Figure 8.33.

3. On the `Ch8_smallimage.html` page, reverse the position of the photo and the text. Put the text on the left and the image on the right in each `div`.

4. Instead of centering the body of `Ch_smallimage.html` using a fixed width, try centering with a body width set to a percentage value to create a more accessible body size.

5. Set the Flash file to `value="true"` for the loop `param` and see what happens.

6. Change the value for `number` in the applet to `"4"` and add a quote of your own as `quote3`. (The first quote is `quote0`.)

Summary

The image formats predominantly used in web pages number only three: GIF, JPEG, and PNG. The JPEG is often used for photos or images with thousands of colors. The GIF is often used for images with fewer colors or when a transparent background is needed.

No matter which image type you use, it is important to optimize the image to its smallest possible file size so that it downloads as quickly as possible. It is also important, in most cases, to create the image in the size you actually intend to display on the web page.

In this chapter you used images to create banners, headings, navbars, decorative lines, and a photo gallery. The `img` element requires several attributes, including `src`, `width`, `height`, and `alt`.

CSS properties for background, padding, margin, border, text-align, float, and position may all be used to style the display of the `img` element.

Multimedia files are not created with XHTML and are not readily styled with CSS. However, you do need XHTML to add multimedia elements to a page. You learned the XHTML required to add multimedia.

Coming up next: the super-useful list.

Chapter 9

Lists and List Styles

Lists are extremely useful on the Web. Users are often in a hurry and scan pages rapidly in search of a particular tidbit. Organizing important points in a bulleted or numbered list helps users find information quickly. Lists are easy to read because the lines are short and there is usually considerable white space.

There are three types of lists. Ordered lists (ol) are numbered with Arabic numerals, Roman numerals, and upper- and lowercase letters of the alphabet. Unordered lists (ul) use bullets or markers. Definition lists (dl) consist of a term and its definition.

With CSS, you can determine what type of bullet or number to use (if any!) with a list, whether the list will display horizontally or vertically, and how the list will be positioned with regard to the bullets or markers.

Using the structure of a list to create menus is both logical and accessible. With the addition of CSS to set background and hover rules, lists of links can be made to appear very much like buttons with rollovers.

Learn the XHTML

Both ordered and unordered lists use the li (for list item) tag. A simple unordered list would be constructed like this:

```
<ul>
  <li>Bread</li>
  <li>Milk</li>
  <li>Eggs</li>
</ul>
```

The browser displays something like Figure 9.1 for this list.

Lists can be nested. An outline is a good example of a nested list. If you want several types of bread, you can list them under the "Bread" list item. The nested list is a complete unordered list element, *nested within* the "Bread" list item. Look at this example:

```
<ul>
  <li>Bread
    <ul>
      <li>Whole wheat</li>
      <li>Hot dog buns</li>
      <li>Bagels</li>
    </ul>
  </li>
```

```
      <li>Milk</li>
      <li>Eggs</li>
  </ul>
```

Notice that the opening and closing ul tags fall within the opening and closing li tags for "Bread." Properly nested lists must follow this example. With the nested list of bread types, the list looks like Figure 9.2. Notice that the browser indents each list.

You can carry on nesting lists as deeply as you need to go, as long as you remember to keep the nested list inside the li element it is describing. For example, you can add an item for "2 pkg Foot Long" and a second item for "5 pkg Regular" as a nested list under the "Hot dog buns" item.

Here's the code:

```
<ul>
  <li>Bread
    <ul>
      <li>Whole wheat</li>
      <li>Hot dog buns
        <ul>
          <li>2 pkg Foot Long</li>
          <li>5 pkg Regular</li>
        </ul>
      </li>
      <li>Bagels</li>
    </ul>
  </li>
  <li>Milk</li>
  <li>Eggs</li>
</ul>
```

FIGURE 9.1

A simple unordered list

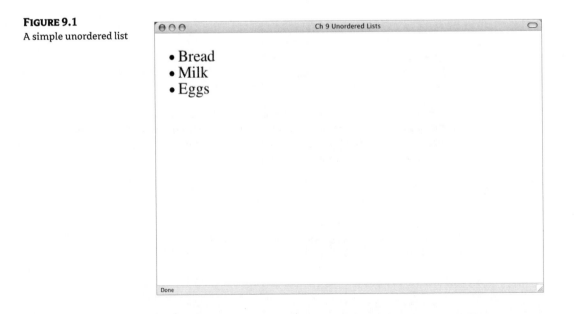

In the browser, you should see something like Figure 9.3. Notice that the browser makes a distinction in the type of bullet it uses to mark second and third level nested lists.

Ordered lists are exactly like unordered lists, except the opening list tag is <ol> and the closing list tag is </ol>.

FIGURE 9.2
The types of bread are a nested list.

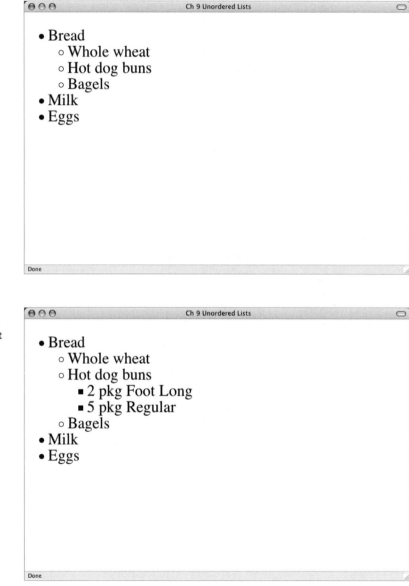

FIGURE 9.3
A third-level nested list. Note that the default list marker for each level is different.

Save a copy of your unordered list file with a new name. You will use it to make a quick and dirty ordered list. On your newly saved page, change all the lists to ordered lists. To accomplish that, simply change all the <ul></ul> tags in the shopping list to <ol></ol>. Suddenly you have ordered lists instead of unordered lists.

Here is the code:

```
<ol>
  <li>Bread
    <ol>
      <li>Whole wheat</li>
      <li>Hot dog buns
        <ol>
          <li>2 pkg Foot Long</li>
          <li>5 pkg Regular</li>
        </ol>
      </li>
      <li>Bagels</li>
    </ol>
  </li>
  <li>Milk</li>
  <li>Eggs</li>
</ol>
```

You should see something similar to Figure 9.4.

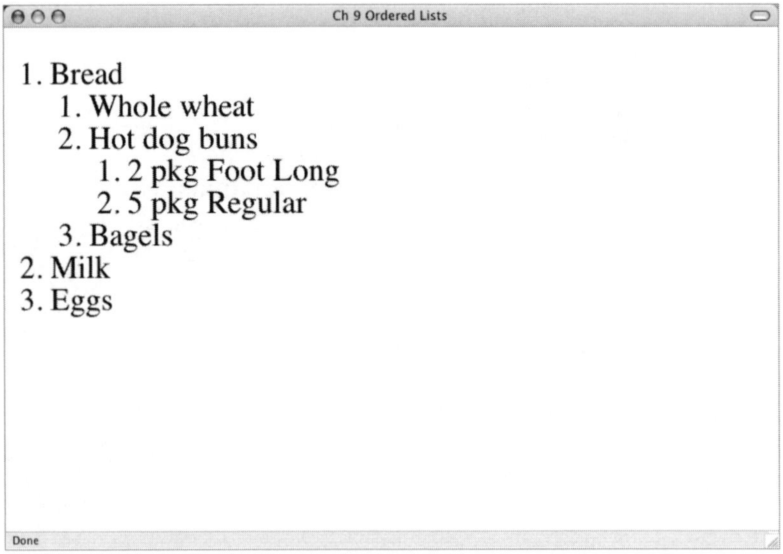

FIGURE 9.4
Nested ordered lists shown with the default decimal number markers.

You saved a lot of typing in this exercise by converting an unordered list to an ordered list, but perhaps you noticed something a bit odd about a numbered grocery list. There is no reason for a grocery list to be an ordered list, because there is no ordered series of steps. A true ordered list would list steps in chronological order or in a required sequence, for example:

```
<ol>
  <li>Turn off computer</li>
  <li>Remove battery</li>
  <li>Wash screen with damp, lint-free cloth</li>
</ol>
```

Definition Lists

Definition lists are different from ordered and unordered lists because they are meant to list terms and their definitions. The opening tag is dl (for definition list). The list contains terms, tagged with dt (for definition term). Each term is defined with a dd (for definition data) element.

The structure of a definition list (without any data) is the following:

```
<dl>
  <dt></dt>
  <dd></dd>
</dl>
```

If you have more than one term, you add more dt and dd elements to the list, like this:

```
<dl>
  <dt></dt>
  <dd></dd>
  <dt></dt>
  <dd></dd>
</dl>
```

Make a definition list defining the terms "Ordered Lists" and "Unordered Lists." When you finish, it should look like Figure 9.5.

Start a new page for this list. See if you can use Figure 9.5 and the preceding examples to write the code yourself.

Here it is:

```
<dl>
  <dt>Ordered Lists</dt>
    <dd>Ordered Lists use numerical or alphabetical markers to organize lists of
information by sequence or chronological order</dd>
  <dt>Unordered Lists</dt>
    <dd>Unordered Lists use bullets or markers to itemize items in a list</dd>
</dl>
```

If you study Figure 9.5, you will notice that the browser indents the dd by default.

FIGURE 9.5
A definition list

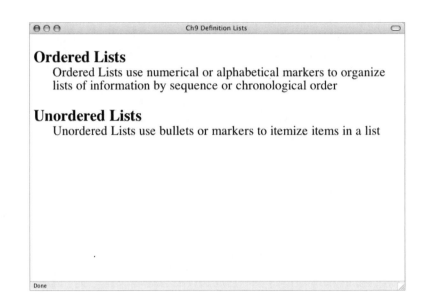

Initial Value in Ordered Lists

By default, an ordered list will start with number 1. You can change that to any other number you need with the start attribute.

Here is a more suitable ordered list than the grocery shopping example. It is a series of steps to get a new computer ready to use. In this example, if you ended a three-item list to insert a paragraph or heading, then wanted to continue numbering with item 4 in a new list, you would use a start="4" attribute in the second list. Type the example below and use it later when you learn the CSS.

For example, supposed you want organize your list in two sections: one for the setting up your computer and one for installing software. You might do this:

```
<p>Set up equipment </p>
<ol>
  <li>Computer
    <ol>
      <li>Cable modem</li>
      <li>Wireless base station
        <ol>
          <li>Check firewall</li>
          <li>Check reception strength</li>
        </ol>
      </li>
      <li>Check network connections</li>
    </ol>
  </li>
  <li>Printer</li>
  <li>Speakers</li>
</ol>
```

```
<p>Install software </p>
<ol start="4">
  <li>Install Photoshop from CD</li>
  <li>Download Firefox </li>
</ol>
```

Notice the `start="4"` attribute in the `ol` element after "Install Software." Even if you are using Roman numerals or alphabetical markers, you still express the start number with a standard Arabic numeral. For example, if you want an alphabetical list to start with the letter D, you use `start="4"`. To get a Roman numeral IV, you use `start="4"`.

In the browser, you will see something like Figure 9.6.

FIGURE 9.6

Setting a start value of 4 in a list

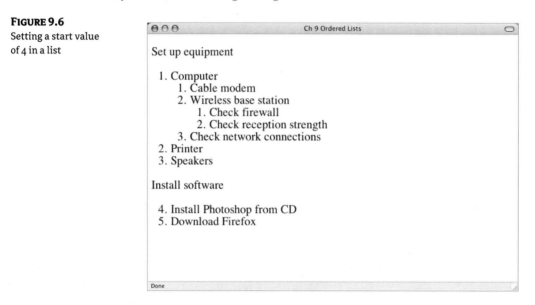

Learn the CSS

As you saw earlier, the default marker style for ordered lists is an Arabic numeral. The Arabic numerals—1, 2, 3, 4, and so on—in CSS terms are `decimal` values. The CSS property that is used to change the type of marker is `list-style-type`. (For CSS shorthand, use `list-style`.) For ordered lists, the `list-style-type` choices, other than the default `decimal` type, are `decimal-leading-zero`, `upper-alpha`, `lower-alpha`, `upper-roman`, `lower-roman`, and `none`.

If you haven't already typed the preceding ordered list example about setting up a computer, start a new XHTML page and type that list example. You will write CSS selectors for that page. The top-level list selector is `ol`. The second-level list selector (containing the items "Cable modem," "Wireless base station," and "Check network connections") is `ol ol`. The third-level list selector (containing the items "Check firewall" and "Check reception strength") is `ol ol ol`.

Armed with the proper selectors for your nested lists, make this list start with capitalized Roman numerals, change to capitalized alphabet letters at the second level, and then change to decimal numbers at the third level.

NOTE   As you know, decimal is the default marker. However, if the second-level list (ol ol) is set to upper-alpha, the third level list (ol ol ol) will inherit the upper-alpha value. Therefore, you must explicitly set it back to decimal.

You won't do anything to this page beyond write some CSS rules for lists, so embed the styles in the head. The complete style element to be added to the head is

```
<style type="text/css">
ol {
  list-style: upper-roman;
}
ol ol {
  list-style: upper-alpha;
}
ol ol ol {
  list-style: decimal;
}
</style>
```

The results of this change should look like Figure 9.7.

TIP   Of course, everything you know about CSS applies to lists. You can write styles for fonts, colors, line heights, margins and other style properties you already know about for ol, ul, and li elements.

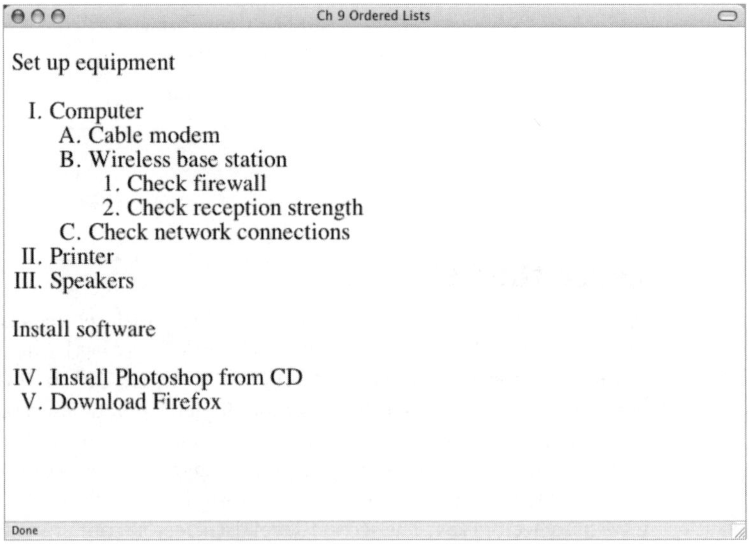

FIGURE 9.7

List-style-type set to upper-roman, upper-alpha, and decimal

Ch 9 Ordered Lists

Set up equipment

   I. Computer
      A. Cable modem
      B. Wireless base station
         1. Check firewall
         2. Check reception strength
      C. Check network connections
  II. Printer
 III. Speakers

Install software

 IV. Install Photoshop from CD
  V. Download Firefox

Done

Unordered List Markers

Not all browsers have the same defaults for nested unordered lists. In the browser used for Figure 9.3, the browser's built-in style is

```
ul {
list-style: disc;
}
ul ul {
list-style: circle;
}
ul ul ul {
list-style: square
}
```

These three—disc, circle, and square—are the only bullet types for unordered lists. You can change the default bullet by writing rules such as:

```
ul {
list-style: square;
}
ul ul {
list-style: disc;
}
```

For even more fun with an unordered list and CSS, use an image as a bullet. On the CD, find star.gif in the Ch 9 folder. Save it in the same folder where you have the practice list pages for this chapter.

The CSS property you want is list-style-image (in CSS shorthand, list-style). Here's how it works:

```
list-style-image: url(somegraphic.gif);
```

If the graphic happened to be in a subfolder named images, the url might be like this: url(images/somegraphic.gif).

TIP When writing a url value in a stylesheet, the path to the file is relative to the location of the stylesheet.

To make one rule that will be inherited by every unordered list on the page, embed this in the head:

```
<style type="text/css">
ul {
  list-style: url(star.gif);
}
</style>
```

Using the grocery store example of an unordered list, that change should look like Figure 9.8 in the browser.

FIGURE 9.8

Graphic list markers

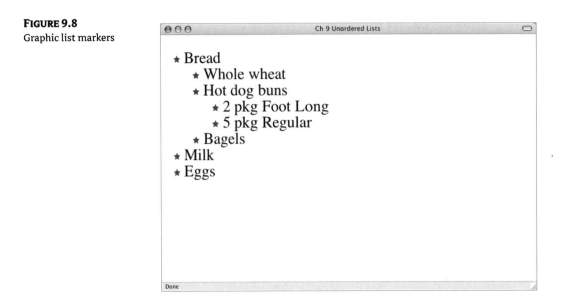

List-Marker Positions

Using the property `list-style-position`, you can alter the default `list-style-position` from `outside` to `inside`. What `list-style-position: inside;` does is move the marker into the list item content.

With some silly text added to make the change very obvious, you can see an example of a list marker positioned inside in Figure 9.9.

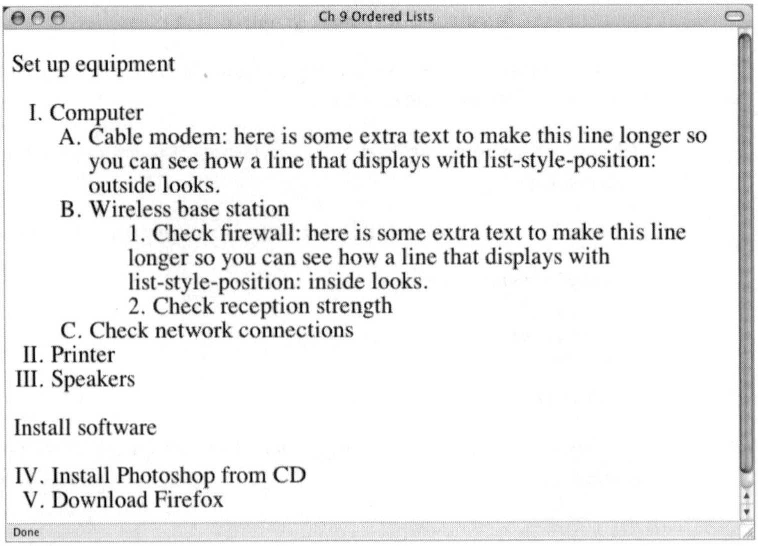

FIGURE 9.9

The third-level list is positioned inside

A second-level list item was made lengthier also. It uses `list-style-position: outside`, but there is no need to include the rule in your style element in this situation since `outside` is the default display value. This helps you see how an outside position marker hangs outside the list item's content.

The changed rule for the `ol ol ol` selector is

```
ol ol ol {
list-style: decimal inside;
}
```

NOTE   When using shorthand for list styles, the `list-style` possible values in order would be `list-style-type`, `list-style-image`, and `list-style-position`.

Back to Definition Lists

The CSS for definition lists is familiar to you. Font, color, padding, background, border, and other CSS properties you are familiar with can be applied to definition lists. For example, you might want the `dt` in bold with 1em of `margin-top` to give it air. You might want the `dd` to be a small font size. If you wrote style rules for that, it would look something like Figure 9.10.

Those two rules for your definition list are

```
dt {
   font-weight: bold;
   margin-top: 1em;
}
dd {
   font-size: small;
}
```

FIGURE 9.10
The styled definition list

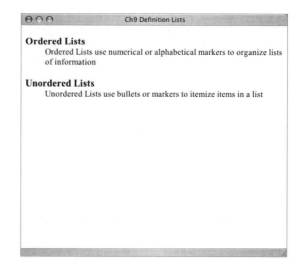

Lists as Links

A web page menu falls logically into the idea of lists. A menu is, in fact, a list of links. Lists as links satisfy accessibility concerns perfectly. For years, designers combined JavaScript with images to create links; today, most designers make them with lists and CSS.

A history lesson: Because the a element involves interactions such as clicking or hovering by the user, it was a prime spot for designers to add cool behaviors such as image rollovers to a page. Using JavaScript, the designer could swap one image for another when certain interactions such as mouseovers and clicking occurred. This meant that the user was downloading several image files for each link on the page to use in its various states. It also meant that users without JavaScript were not always able to use graphic menus. (JavaScript is considered a barrier to accessibility in many situations.) To compensate for the possible lost function if a user did not have JavaScript capability, designers often created elaborate scripted menu setups using graphic button rollovers and then added the exact same menu as text links at the bottom of the page for users without JavaScript or images.

Once designers figured out the secrets of doing something that looks and acts like a graphic rollover with CSS, the majority rushed into the technique with enthusiasm. It eliminates the need to create duplicate text menus at the bottom of the page because the links are text already. It also eliminates the need for the user to have JavaScript working in order to use the menu. However, it does not completely eliminate the need to download images, because designers often create effects with different background images that change in the a:hover pseudo state.

The *display* Property

The values for the display property were listed in Chapter 6. The two you need for making lists behave in fabulous new ways are display: inline and display: block.

There are some files in the Chapter 9 folder on the CD that you need to save to your Integrated HTML and CSS folder:

```
ch9_linkstyles.html
ch9_historic_linkstyles.html
ch9_ped_linkstyles.html
360bridge.jpg
delusions.jpg
historic.jpg
pedestrian.jpg
ch9_import.css
```

Open ch9_linkstyes.html in your text editor and in your browser. You are familiar with this page, but a few changes have been made in it for this exercise. The styles governing layout, colors, fonts, and other rules were imported to the page using ch9_import.css. You will make a new stylesheet just for the work with lists and will link to it. The menu now has working links, giving you a three-page site to practice with.

First a new stylesheet: open a blank text document and save it as ch9links.css. Add a link element to the ch9_linkstyles.html document head for the new stylesheet. Place it after the style element already in the head:

```
<link href="ch9links.css" rel="stylesheet" type="text/css" />
```

Eventually, you will need to add the stylesheet link to the other two HTML documents in this little site: ch9_historic_linkstyles.html and ch9_ped_linkstyles.html. Go ahead and do it now.

If you change the display of the a elements in the list to `display: block`, some interesting things happen. For one thing, the entire content area of the a element becomes clickable, not just the text.

On your new (still blank) stylesheet document, start a rule for #nav a, which will select all the a elements in the nav division:

```
#nav a {
    display: block;
}
```

Make sure both the HTML and CSS files are saved and look at the page in the browser. Notice that the pointing finger cursor signals a link, even when the cursor is not on the link text. You should see something similar to Figure 9.11.

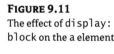

FIGURE 9.11

The effect of `display: block` on the a element

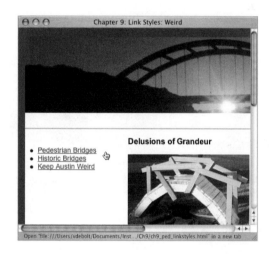

More Styling for Navigation Elements

You will get rid of the bullet marker in a moment. First, add a few styles to make the a element look more like a button.

You need a background color: #868366 is present in the banner image. You need to set an exact width: 170px is enough. A bit of `padding-top` would space the links out: perhaps 0.5em. A solid 1px border in the golden color of the sunset (#D0B26F) would be effective. You don't want the links to be underlined, so use `text-decoration: none`. Finally, make the link text black (#000). With all these rules added to the #nav a selector, you now have:

```
#nav a {
    background: #868366;
    display: block;
    width: 170px;
    padding-top: 0.5em;
    border: 1px solid #D0B26F;
    text-decoration: none;
    color: #000;
}
```

These new rules should make the page look something like Figure 9.12 in the browser.

Seeing the a elements styled with the li markers still visible makes you aware of the position of the markers in the li elements. This list uses the default list-style-position: outside; and you can see that the marker is indeed outside the content of the li.

Even after you remove the marker, you need to be aware of the space outside the li content when changing margins and padding for li elements.

The next step is to remove the markers from the #nav ul element. Set the list-style-type value to none:

```
#nav ul {
   list-style-type: none;
}
```

That gives you the sought-after button-like appearance, as you see in Figure 9.13.

FIGURE 9.12
The complete a
element styling

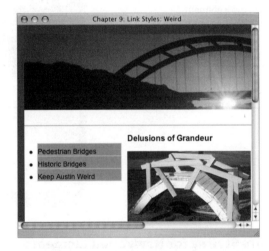

FIGURE 9.13
The markers no longer
appear if the list-
style-type is set
to none

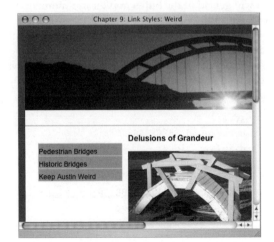

But Does It Roll Over?

You need one more style: `#nav a:hover`. This will give you the rollover effect you want. Use a different background color (`background-image` changes are also possible) for the `a:hover` pseudo state to achieve the effect. A color picked from the banner image might work one more time: #A48A4A. If you leave the text black, it will be hard to read when hovering over the link, so make it white instead.

The selector you need is `#nav a:hover`.

Here is the new rule:

```
#nav a:hover {
  background: #A48A4A;
  color: #FFF;
}
```

The vertical navbar with CSS rollovers is complete. You should see something like Figure 9.14 in the browser.

FIGURE 9.14

The rollover effect

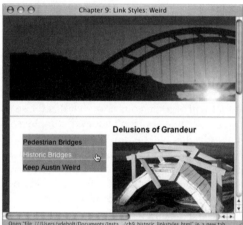

Horizontal Lists

The `display` property can make elements that are not normally block level elements behave as block level elements. Conversely, the `display` property can make elements that are not normally inline elements behave as inline elements. The magic bullet of horizontal list display is `display: inline;`.

You will use an example from a real website for the horizontal lists exercises. My geeky friend Taylor Carpenter has a small website at `www.codecafe.com`. See Figure 9.15.

Taylor can type Perl, C++, or Java faster than I can type English, but he stopped learning HTML after HTML 3.2 and doesn't know much about CSS. His web page used tables for layout and deprecated tags such as `font` to control appearance. The menu (Home, Services, About, and Contact Us) is in a row of table cells. I redid his page in a CSS layout so he could get some ideas about how it is done. Part of that effort was to make the menu a horizontal list with CSS rollovers. That's where you come in.

FIGURE 9.15

A screen shot of the
CodeCafe home page

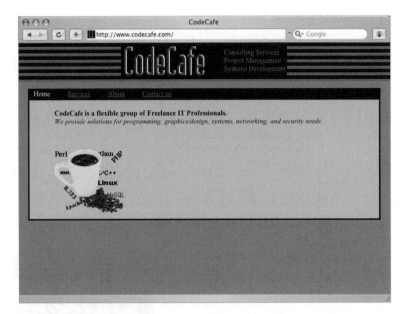

Copy `codecafe.html` and `cc_import.css` to your computer from the Chapter 9 folder on the CD. Open `codecafe.html` in your text editor. You will also need to open and save a blank text document that will become your new stylesheet. Use the filename `cc.css`.

You can see that you don't have the complete page in `codecafe.html`, only a partial bit containing a list of links that will become the horizontal menu bar.

Before you start, a few comments on `codecafe.html`. There are a few styles in an imported style sheet (`cc_import.css`) that establish background color and fonts. The XHTML page already has a link to the imported styles. You will add a second style sheet to the page for the work with the list.

The links use a hash sign, as in `<a href="#">Home</a>`, to create a fake link that doesn't go anywhere but will change on hover.

If you check `codecafe.html` in the browser, you will see something similar to Figure 9.16.

The new stylesheet that you will write for the links will be `cc.css`. Add the link element for the new stylesheet to the document. Remember, the `@import` directive should be first, then the `link` element, like so:

```
<style type="text/css">
@import url("cc_import.css");
</style>
<link href="cc.css" rel="stylesheet" type="text/css" />
```

Before you change the list to its horizontal arrangement, make a couple of general appearance changes. The `#nav` division needs a black background color:

```
#nav {
  background: #000;
}
```

The changes should look something like Figure 9.17.

FIGURE 9.16
The beginning page with an unstyled list element

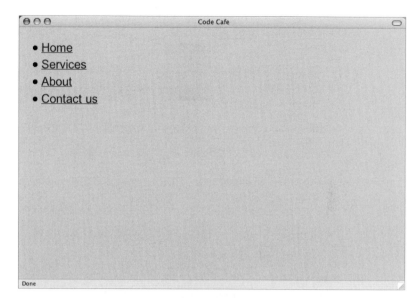

FIGURE 9.17
The list on a dark background

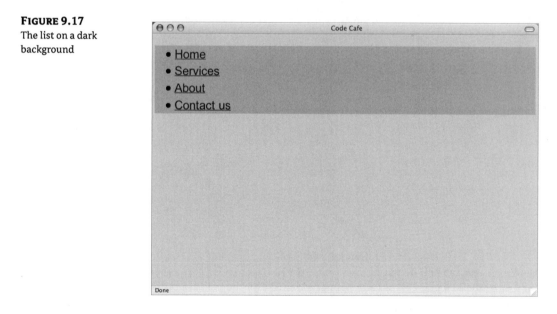

NOTE The blacks and grays used in the CodeCafe code examples from the CD are slightly darker than those used for the figures in the book, due to contrast limitations of the black-and-white illustrations in this book. The view in your browser will be darker.

Let's move on to the li rules. I keep saying this list is going to display in a horizontal line. How do you make that happen? To make the list appear in a horizontal arrangement, use display: inline.

TIP Since you don't have any other elements from the complete page, a general selector of li will style this set of list items. If you were working with a complete page, you might need a contextual selector with more specificity such as #nav li.

Go ahead and remove the list item markers. To remove the list markers, use list-style: none. Here is the li rule:

```
li {
  list-style: none;
  display: inline;
}
```

With those changes, the browser display should look like Figure 9.18.

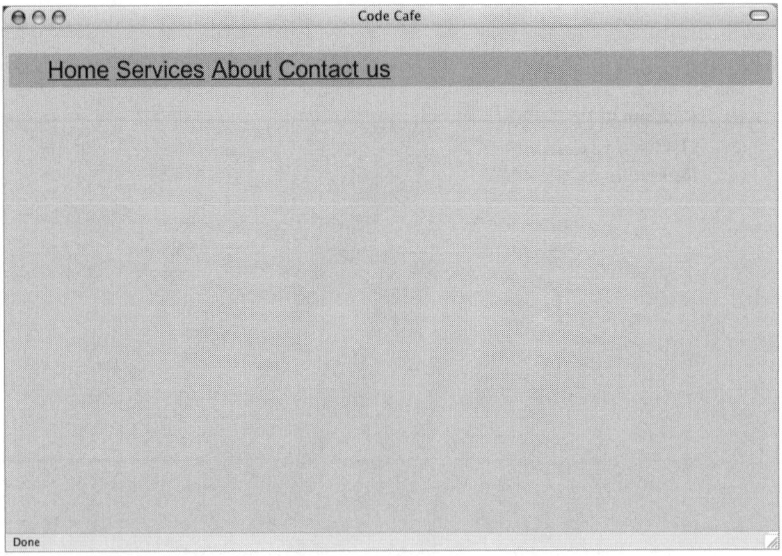

FIGURE 9.18
The list items styled with display: inline;

Well, it is horizontal, and the markers are gone, but it needs help! Start with spacing. You need to space the list items out. One way to do this would be to add some margin-right to the li rules. Give the li a good bit of "air" with at least 10px for the margin-right. The changed rule is

```
li {
  list-style: none;
  display: inline;
  margin-right: 10px;
}
```

With the changed rule in place, the page should look like Figure 9.19.

FIGURE 9.19
margin-right is used
to create space between
the list items

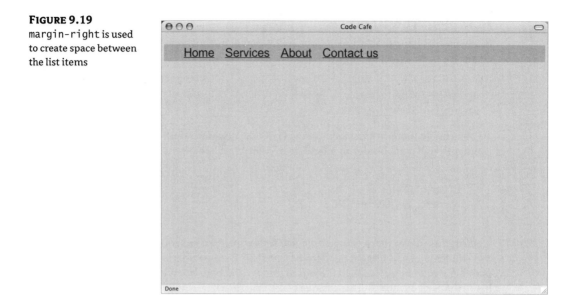

On Taylor's original page, he had the menu left aligned, but I thought it should be centered. You can use text-align to center the entire unordered list. The selector is ul. Here's the rule:

```
ul {
    text-align: center;
}
```

You can see the centered list in Figure 9.20.

Next you will work on the a elements to achieve the button-like look and the rollover effect.

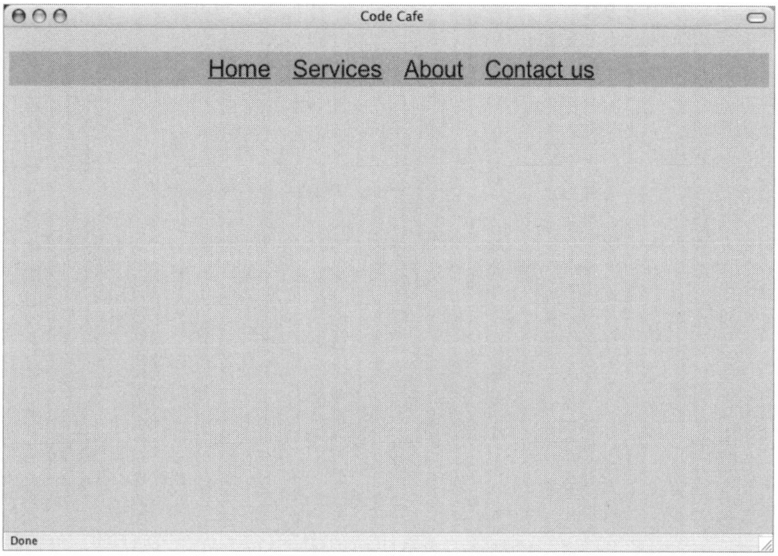

FIGURE 9.20
The list is centered

How 'Bout Those Links?

A few modifications to the a elements and you will be finished. The a elements are hard to read, so change the a to white; see Figure 9.21.

```
a {
   color: #FFF;
}
```

You can do more to create a button-like look. A border around each a element will help. How about a 1-pixel solid border in a light gray color? Use border: 1px solid #CCC.

```
a {
   color: #FFF;
   border: 1px solid #CCC;
}
```

With this rule in place, you should see something like Figure 9.22.

I still see a few things that need to change. Remove the underline from the a elements. I think some padding would help, too. Add 0.25em to the top and bottom and 0.5em to the right and left. In shorthand, that's padding: 0.25em 0.5em;.

The changed a selector is

```
a {
   color: #FFF;
   text-decoration: none;
   border: 1px solid #CCC;
   padding: 0.25em 0.5em;
}
```

As you can see in Figure 9.23, the padding both solves a problem and creates a new problem.

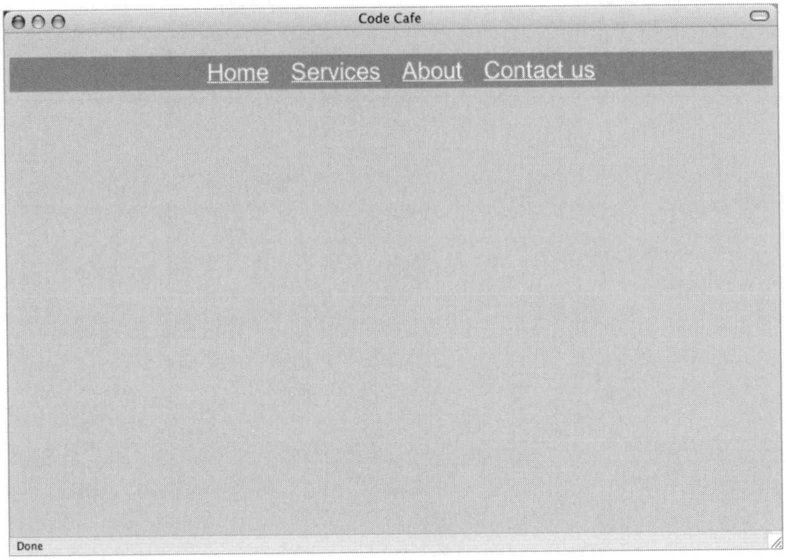

FIGURE 9.21
The white link color helps readability

FIGURE 9.22
The border on the a
elements

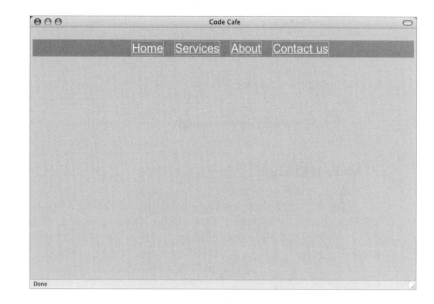

FIGURE 9.23
The link with no under-
line and some padding

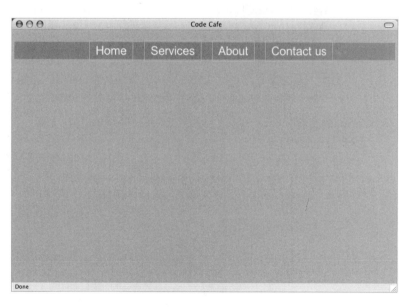

Back to the *nav*

The problem created by the padding is that the a element now appears larger than the nav element holding it: the bordered links appear to be spilling out of the dark area of the nav element.

One way to resolve this is to increase the padding in the #nav rule. About 0.5em on all four sides will take care of it. The changed #nav rule looks like this:

```
#nav {
  background: #000;
  padding: 0.5em;
}
```

With the nav element now taking up more space, you should see something like Figure 9.24 in the browser.

Make It Change

Finally, the rollover effect.

For a:hover you can use a new color for the link text. A yellow shade that might work is #F8DD47. Also, change the background color to the already present gray: #757575. The two new styles are

```
a:hover {
  color: #F8DD47;
  background: #757575;
}
```

Now you should get a rollover effect when hovering over a link, similar to that in Figure 9.25.

Another very popular way to achieve a different look for the a:hover pseudo element is to change a background-image. One background-image is used for the a:link, a:visited, and a:active states, with a different one for the a:hover state.

TIP Listamatic, at css.maxdesign.com.au/listamatic/, has helpful tools that allow you to generate code for lists of links with various CSS styling options.

FIGURE 9.24
Padding is added to the nav element

FIGURE 9.25
The background changes
when the user hovers
over the link

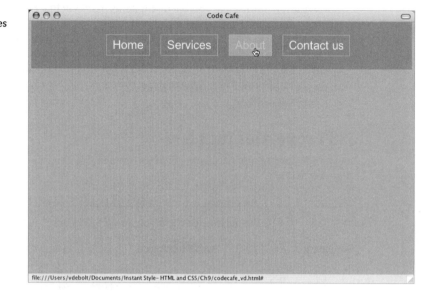

Real World Example

Digital Web Magazine is a publication for web designers that includes tutorials, articles, interviews, book reviews, and software reviews at www.digital-web.com. This nonprofit publication is created by a worldwide network of volunteers. A view of their home page is shown in Figure 9.26.

FIGURE 9.26
Digital Web Magazine is
an online magazine for
web designers

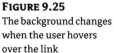

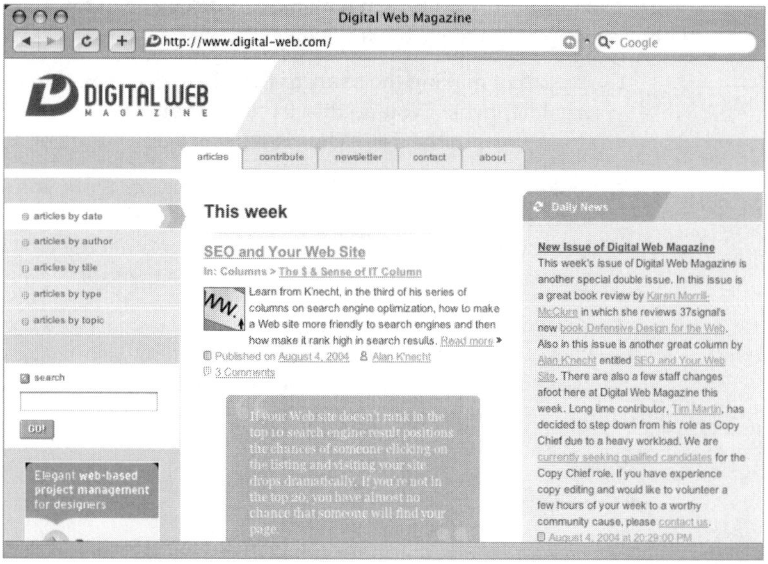

© Digital Web Magazine

Across the top of the page you see menu items that look like tabs with links to articles, contribute, newsletter, and so on. These links are actually a list.

On the left side, you see links that look like buttons with rollover effects that lead to articles by date, articles by author, and so on. Again, these links are actually a list.

In addition to serving as an example of attractive and functional use of lists in the real world, I can also recommend Digital Web Magazine as a source of good reading as you continue to develop your skills as a web designer.

CSS Properties for Lists

New CSS properties for list display were covered in this chapter. Table 9.1 shows the new CSS properties you learned.

TABLE 9.1:   CSS Properties for the *ul*, *ol*, and *li* Selectors

PROPERTY	POSSIBLE VALUE
list-style-type	disc, circle, square, decimal, decimal-leading-zero, upper-alpha, lower-alpha, upper-roman, lower-roman, none, inherit
list-style-image	uri, none, inherit
list-style-position	inside, outside, inherit

Challenge Yourself

Take some time to experiment with the CSS discussed in this chapter. Try out some ideas of your own and see if you can make the following changes.

1. Instead of making the star.gif apply to every marker on your page of unordered lists, see what happens if you do this: ul ul {list-style: url(star.gif);}. Where does the star first appear in the list? When is it inherited?

2. Make a two-level nested list with information about your friends, family, or pets. At the first level, give the name of the person or pet. Under each name in the list, nest a list of characteristics such as birthday, zodiac sign, or some other relevant fact. When you have the list the way you want it, write some CSS rules to style the lists.

3. Pick either the horizontal or the vertical list exercise and try using background images instead of background colors to create the rollover effect. Use background-image1.gif and background-image2.gif from the CD if you need images for this.

Summary

Lists are the workhorses of the Web. They are easy to read, make finding information go quickly, help you set up ordered steps or processes, and accommodate a myriad of marker types and numbering schemes. This versatility makes lists popular for many different situations.

There are three types of lists in use on the Web: ordered, unordered, and definition. Ordered and unordered lists are constructed of a simple series of list items. Definition lists contain terms and their accompanying definitions.

A list can contain any textual element, including links. Because navigation menus on web pages are often a list of links, the `list` element is often used to create menus and navbars. Using `display: block` or `display: inline`, lists can be styled with CSS rules that make them appear in a button-like vertical or horizontal display.

Coming up next in Chapter 10, you will learn how to create and style a table.

Chapter 10

Tables and Table Styles

In this chapter, you'll see why you shouldn't use a table for layout. However, you *will* build a table meant to display tabular data—the preferred use for a table based on web-accessibility recommendations. You will also learn how to make the table accessible to all users and how to write styles to control the presentation of a table.

A Tangled Table Tale

The topic of tables requires another history lesson. In versions of HTML prior to 1996, CSS was not available. Even when the first recommendation for CSS was released by the World Wide Web Consortium (W3C), there was very limited support for the standard in browsers available at that time. Without CSS to lay out a page, designers took what they knew about publishing in print and applied that to web page design. When laying out a magazine or newspaper page, the designer thinks in terms of a grid, an arrangement of columns and rows. Designers saw the table as the equivalent layout tool for web pages. For quite some time, tables were the only layout tool in town. There were tables nested within tables, tables beside tables: tables, tables everywhere.

About the same time that designers grew really masterful at creating complicated arrangements of myriad numbers of nested tables, it became apparent that nested table layouts were a serious barrier to users with accessibility needs because they were often rendered as senseless gibberish when not accessed visually. More and more people were using the Internet, and more and more people were finding barriers to accessing the Internet in the process.

Limited support for CSS appeared in Internet Explorer 3 (1996) and Netscape Navigator 4. Designers began using CSS in limited ways, while still mostly misusing tables to achieve page layouts. The W3C responded with improved versions of HTML and CSS. The W3C also responded with the Web Accessibility Initiative (WAI) that provided guidelines for content accessibility and authoring tool accessibility as well as other accessibility information. Designers, frustrated with the lack of browser support for these new technologies, raised their cries for browser support for the W3C standards to a fever pitch, and the Web Standards Project (www.webstandards.org) began aggressively urging standards support on the browser makers.

The U.S. government added Section 508 to the Americans with Disabilities Act, which required certain accessibility features to be integrated with the website of any federal agency or federal contractor.

The WAI and the Section 508 requirements cover a range of web-based technologies, including audible screen readers and Braille readers. They also address issues relating to site graphics, frames, animations, image maps, scripting languages, plug-ins, and forms. Try as they might, without proper implementation of the standards by the browser makers, it was very difficult for people making web pages to comply with these accessibility requirements.

In the flurry of activity around the notion of making web-based information accessible to all people, tables received a lot of attention. Most of that attention was negative. Finally, however, standards-compliant browsers began to appear on the scene, and a rush to lay out with CSS and remove table layouts from web pages began—a process that is still ongoing.

TIP Two excellent sources of accessibility information and training are WebAIM at www.webaim.org and Knowbility at www.knowbility.org.

The negative attention to tables gave some people the impression that they should never use a table, ever, for any reason. Since you are about to read the chapter in this book that teaches you how to build a table, you can probably guess that the idea that tables are nothing but bad is not correct. Tables have a real purpose on the Web. They do the job of displaying data in an organized grid better than any other structure. Such tables are called data tables, a convention that has arisen to distinguish them from layout tables. You will explore data tables in this chapter.

You could say that the `table` element is going through an adolescent phase and is suffering from growing pains. The uses for tables are changing and may evolve even more in the future because XML now has ways to make elements that are not actually tables behave as if they were using the `display` property. CSS 3—not yet a recommendation at the time of this writing—will provide a way to create tables with CSS.

Because CSS is taking over the job of laying out a page, people are moving away from using tables for layout. However, a knowledgeable designer can, in fact, design a page with a simple and accessible tables-based page layout. Standards guru Jeffrey Zeldman, author of *Designing with Web Standards* calls such layouts "hybrid" designs. Such designs are also referred to as "transitional" designs. To a great extent, the decision as to whether a completely CSS-based layout or a hybrid design of CSS with simple tables for layout is best for your particular needs depends on your audience and your understanding of who will be seeking your information.

Learn the XHTML

The `table` element is composed of a number of horizontal table rows (`tr`) that are filled with cells of table data (`td`). As rows are added to the table, the cells in each row create a vertical column. Both rows and columns in a table can contain table header elements (`th`) as row or column labels. Figure 10.1 illustrates a completed table element.

Begin a new XHTML document and type along as you go though the steps of building a table.

FIGURE 10.1
A diagram of a table's structural parts

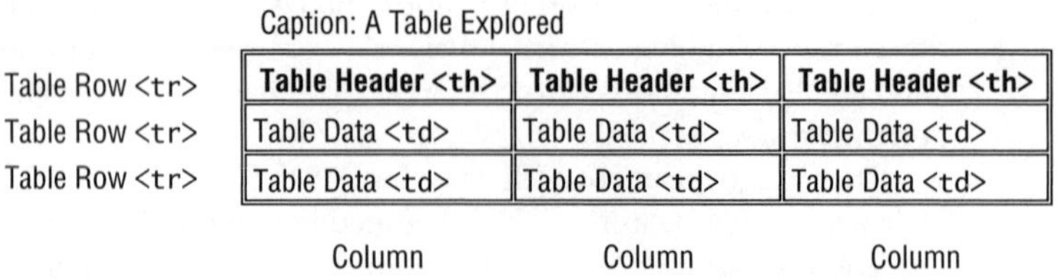

Caption: A Table Explored

Table Header <th>	Table Header <th>	Table Header <th>
Table Data <td>	Table Data <td>	Table Data <td>
Table Data <td>	Table Data <td>	Table Data <td>

Table Row <tr>
Table Row <tr>
Table Row <tr>

Column   Column   Column

Begin by typing **<table>**, press Return (Enter) a few times, then type **</table>**. This gives you both the opening and closing tags for the table, so you can view it row by row as you go along, and it will be properly terminated to display in the browser correctly.

```
<table>

</table>
```

For a while, ignore the idea of headings for the rows or columns and just make a row (tr) of td elements. The number of td elements you put in a row ultimately determines the number of columns your table will have. Let's use three. Type **<tr>** to begin the row, press Return (Enter) a few times and type the closing **</tr>**:

```
<table>
  <tr>

  </tr>
</table>
```

That gives you the row structure, but there is nothing in it. You need td elements for that. Since you want three data cells in your row, type **<td></td>** three times, like this:

```
<table>
 <tr>
  <td></td>
  <td></td>
  <td></td>
 </tr>
</table>
```

You don't have any content, of course, but that is basically the structure of a table. To add more data cells to a row, you add more td elements. To add more rows, you add more tr elements. Here is an example of the table with two rows:

```
<table>
 <tr>
  <td></td>
  <td></td>
  <td></td>
 </tr>
 <tr>
  <td></td>
  <td></td>
  <td></td>
 </tr>
</table>
```

Notice that the number of data cells in each row is the same. Look at Listing 10.1 for a completed table with some content in the th and td elements.

LISTING 10.1:   The XHTML to Create the *table* Element in Figure 10.1

```
<table width="90%" border="1" cellpadding="3">
  <caption align="top">
  A Table Explored
  </caption>
  <tr>
    <th>Table Header</th>
    <th>Table Header</th>
    <th>Table Header</th>
  </tr>
  <tr>
    <td>Table Data</td>
    <td>Table Data</td>
    <td>Table Data</td>
  </tr>
  <tr>
    <td>Table Data</td>
    <td>Table Data</td>
    <td>Table Data</td>
  </tr>
</table>
```

Table Attributes

Several attributes of a table element are shown in the opening table tag in Listing 10.1. Let's look at those.

The first is width="90%". This makes the table element occupy 90 percent of the width of its container, in this case the body element. If the user resized the browser window, a table with a width expressed in percentages would resize with the viewport. Width can also be expressed in pixels.

TIP   CSS can be used to set width for a table using the table property.

If you have been typing along, you have a table with two empty rows already built. If you haven't been typing along, you will find ch10_unfinished.html in the Chapter 10 folder on the CD. Open it in your text editor so you can add some width attributes. Start by adding width="80%" to the table element like this: <table width="80%">.

Let's add some content to the table cells so there will be something to see in the browser window. Something simple will do, like this:

```
<tr>
  <td>One</td>
  <td>Two</td>
```

```
      <td>Three</td>
    </tr>
    <tr>
      <td>Four</td>
      <td>Five</td>
      <td>Six</td>
    </tr>
```

Save that and do a browser check. Your table should look something like Figure 10.2.

In addition to assigning a value to the width of the entire table in the opening `table` tag, you can also use `width` attributes to set a value for each column.

TIP   If you don't give a specific `width` attribute, the columns will assume widths based on the content they hold.

Since the first row of a table establishes the width and number of columns that will be in the table, it is only necessary to add `width` attributes to the first row of the table. Before you add widths to the first row of `td` elements, add a border.

BORDER ATTRIBUTES

I want to do more with `width`, but first you need to have some borders showing. It helps you to visualize the table. As you know, `border` can be set with CSS rules, and you will do that later in the chapter. However, you may have noticed this attribute in Listing 10.1: `border="1"`.

NOTE   Various `table` attributes are allowed in XHTML Transitional, so you will use them for now. The same effects can be achieved with CSS, but since the Transitional DTD allows attributes, I thought you would benefit from using them while you learn the XHTML needed to build columns and rows.

Add `border="1"` to your opening table tag, like this:

```
<table width="80%" border="1">
```

With borders showing, your table should look like Figure 10.3. 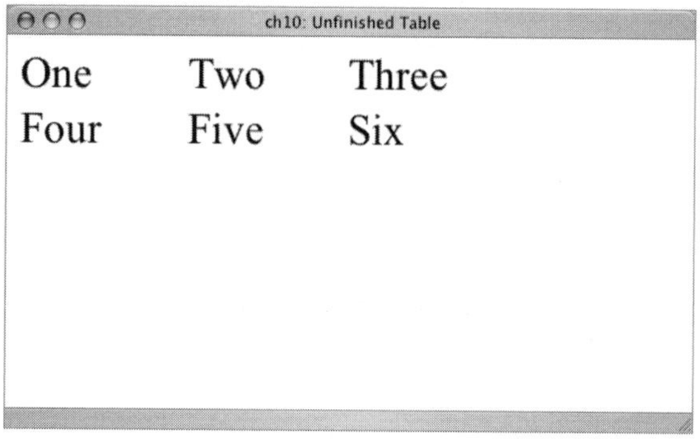

FIGURE 10.2
The beginnings of
your table

FIGURE 10.3
The table with borders

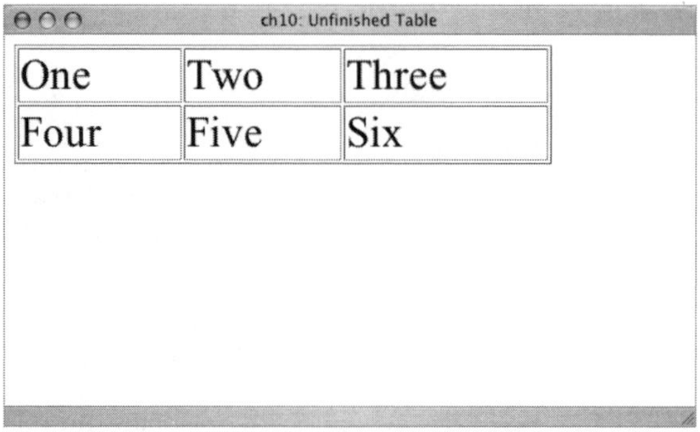

With the borders showing, you can see that the column with the longest word (Three) is slightly wider than the other columns. This takes you right back to the width attribute.

COLUMN WIDTH

As I just pointed out, whatever you set up for the first row of the table gets replicated in every row you add to the table, so you only need to add width attributes to the first row.

Since you currently have a "stretchy" table that is 80 percent of the browser viewport in width, use percent to specify the width of each column as well. Try resizing your browser window to watch the table shrink or grow to maintain that 80 percent size.

TIP Even with a fixed pixel width for the table element, individual column widths could be set with either percentages or pixels.

The percentages that you enter for the width attribute of each td element in the first row are percentages of the table element. Your column widths must add up to 100 percent, because you are talking about 100 percent of the table element, not 100 percent of the viewport. Since you have three columns, if you want them to be approximately the same width, you should use 33 percent, 33 percent, and 34 percent for a total of 100 percent of the width of the table element. So your first row looks like this:

```
<tr>
  <td width="33%">One</td>
  <td width="33%">Two</td>
  <td width="34%">Three</td>
  </tr>
  <tr>
```

Watch closely when you refresh (reload) the browser following that change—you should see the table border shift just slightly as the table is redrawn with widths in the size specified (see Figure 10.4).

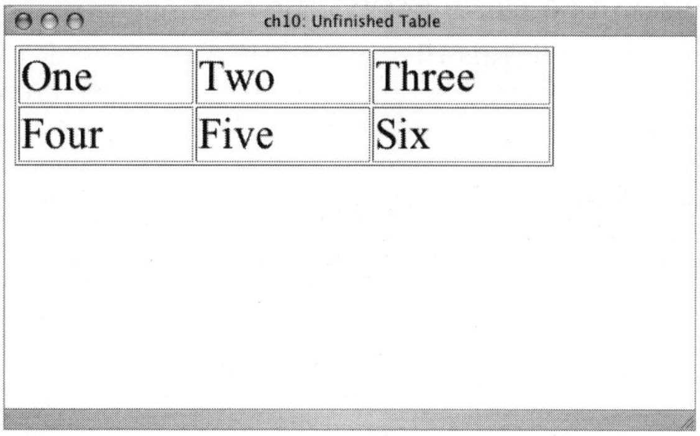

FIGURE 10.4

The table (which is 80 percent of the window) with approximately equal column widths

CELL PADDING AND CELL SPACING

The final remaining attribute you may have noticed in Listing 10.1 in the table element is `cellpadding`. When setting up a table using XHTML attributes, there are two related attributes: `cellpadding` and `cellspacing`.

In the case of `cellpadding`, space is added between the contents of the `td` element and the cell walls. In Listing 10.1, the added space is 3 pixels, like this: `cellpadding="3"`.

TIP　In CSS, `padding` can be set for the `td` or `th` element.

In the case of `cellspacing`, space is added between the table cells. It is easier to understand with a visual, so add some `cellpadding` to your table. In the table element, add the attribute `cellspacing="5"`. The changed `table` element will look like this:

```
<table width="80%" border="1" cellspacing="5">
```

The effect of that change should appear similar to Figure 10.5 in the browser. People who learn XHTML after already learning page layout software such as QuarkXPress or PageMaker often exclaim, "Oh, it's like the gutter!" when they see `cellspacing` in action. So, if gutters are a known quantity to you, perhaps the analogy is helpful. 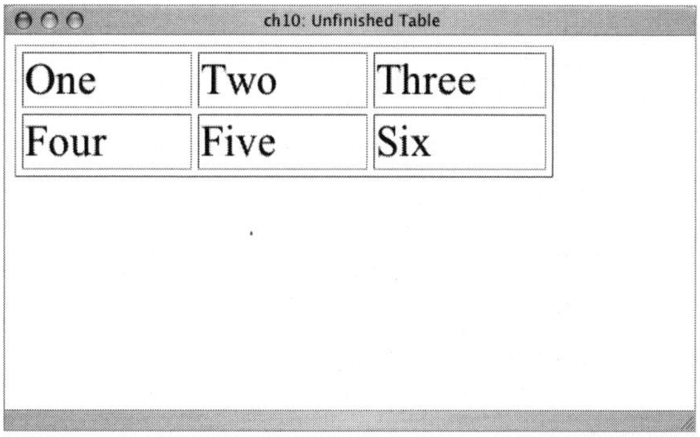

FIGURE 10.5

The table with 5 pixels of `cellspacing`

Making a Table Accessible

On the CD, there is a file named `ch10_table2.html`. You will use it to learn about making data tables accessible. Open it in your text editor and in your browser. The table should look like Figure 10.6 in the browser.

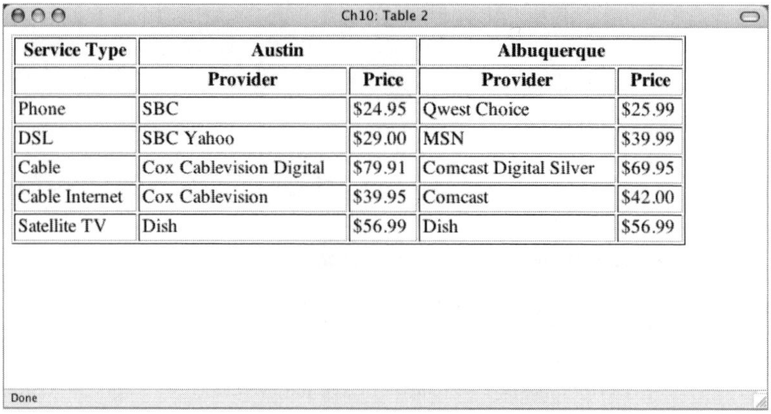

FIGURE 10.6

The beginning table information

Service Type	Austin		Albuquerque	
	Provider	Price	Provider	Price
Phone	SBC	$24.95	Qwest Choice	$25.99
DSL	SBC Yahoo	$29.00	MSN	$39.99
Cable	Cox Cablevision Digital	$79.91	Comcast Digital Silver	$69.95
Cable Internet	Cox Cablevision	$39.95	Comcast	$42.00
Satellite TV	Dish	$56.99	Dish	$56.99

(Window title: Ch10: Table 2)

The complete page for `ch10_table2.html` is shown in Listing 10.2.

LISTING 10.2:   The Beginning *ch10_table2.html* Page

```
<!DOCTYPE html PUBLIC "-//W3C//DTD XHTML 1.0 Transitional//EN"
   "http://www.w3.org/TR/xhtml1/DTD/xhtml1-transitional.dtd">
<html xmlns="http://www.w3.org/1999/xhtml">
<head>
<title>Ch10: Table 2</title>
</head>

<body>
<table width="90%" border="1" cellpadding="3" >
  <tr>
    <th> </th>
    <th colspan="2">Austin</th>
    <th colspan="2">Albuquerque</th>
  </tr>
  <tr>
    <th>Service Type</th>
    <th>Provider</th>
    <th>Price</th>
    <th>Provider</th>
    <th>Price</th>
  </tr>
```

```
  <tr>
    <td>Phone</td>
    <td>SBC</td>
    <td>$24.95</td>
    <td>Qwest Choice</td>
    <td>$25.99</td>
  </tr>
  <tr>
    <td>DSL</td>
    <td>SBC Yahoo</td>
    <td>$29.00</td>
    <td>MSN</td>
    <td>$39.99</td>
  </tr>
  <tr>
    <td>Cable</td>
    <td>Cox Cablevision Digital</td>
    <td>$79.91</td>
    <td>Comcast Digital Silver</td>
    <td>$69.95</td>
  </tr>
  <tr>
    <td>Cable Internet</td>
    <td>Cox Cablevision</td>
    <td>$39.95</td>
    <td>Comcast</td>
    <td>$42.00</td>
  </tr>
  <tr>
    <td>Satellite TV</td>
    <td>Dish</td>
    <td>$56.99</td>
    <td>Dish</td>
    <td>$56.99</td>
  </tr>
</table>
</body>
</html>
```

This table already has one of the accessibility requirements: it uses th elements as column headers. This is essential for accessibility and proper interpretation of the table. If headings are needed for the rows, th elements can also be used in the first cell of each row. The column headings are: Service Type, Austin, Albuquerque.

TIP   Notice in Figure 10.6 that the default display for the th element is bold and centered.

SPANNING ROWS AND COLUMNS

Note especially this table row:

```
<tr>
  <th>Service Type</th>
  <th colspan="2">Austin</th>
  <th colspan="2">Albuquerque</th>
</tr>
```

As you see in Figure 10.6, the column headings Austin and Albuquerque span two columns. The XHTML creating that is `colspan="2"`. A table cell can span any number of columns by specifying this attribute with the number of columns to be spanned, in a `th` or `td` element.

There is a similar attribute for spanning multiple rows: `rowspan`. Use `rowspan` as an attribute in the `th` or `td` that you wish to have span more than one row, in a similar fashion to using `colspan`. For example, `<td rowspan="3">` creates a table cell that spans three rows.

Although you have headers in your table, you need to make sure that the headers are associated with the proper data cells. The `headers` attribute is used for this.

KEEP IT SIMPLE

In general, a data table using a simple grid without any spanned rows or columns is more accessible. A table with only one level of row or column headers is better than a more complicated one. If the table needs more than one header element for each row or column, it might be better to divide it into two or more simpler tables.

HEADERS

The `headers` attribute is used to associate specific data cells with specific headers. An `id` is assigned to each `th` element. Find the two rows in your table that use the `th` element. Suggested `id` names if you need to add to each of the `th` elements are shown here:

```
<tr>
  <th id="service">Service Type</th>
  <th colspan="2" id="austin">Austin</th>
  <th colspan="2" id="albuquerque">Albuquerque</th>
</tr>
<tr>
  <th> </th>
  <th id="txprovider">Provider</th>
  <th id="txprice">Price</th>
  <th id="nmprovider">Provider</th>
  <th id="nmprice">Price</th>
</tr>
```

TIP For an empty table cell, use `<td> </td>`. Putting the nonbreaking space in the empty table cell makes the table render the rows, columns, and borders correctly.

Now that each th has an id, turn your attention to the td elements. Each td is associated with the relevant th using a headers attribute, like this:

```
<td headers="service">Phone</td>
```

More than one of the named IDs can be listed in the headers attribute, if more than one th applies to the particular data cell. A space is needed between the names when more than one ID name is listed. For example:

```
<td headers="austin txprovider">SBC</td>
```

Each td in the table needs these attributes. The code is shown in Listing 10.3.

LISTING 10.3: The *td* Elments with Headers Included

```
<tr>
  <td headers="service">Phone</td>
  <td headers="austin txprovider">SBC</td>
  <td headers="austin txprice">$24.95</td>
  <td headers="albuquerque nmprovider">Qwest Choice</td>
  <td headers="albuquerque nmprice">$25.99</td>
</tr>
<tr>
  <td headers="service">DSL</td>
  <td headers="austin txprovider">SBC Yahoo</td>
  <td headers="austin txprice">$29.00</td>
  <td headers="albuquerque nmprovider">MSN</td>
  <td headers="albuquerque nmprice">$39.99</td>
</tr>
<tr>
  <td headers="service">Cable</td>
  <td headers="austin txprovider">Cox Cablevision Digital</td>
  <td headers="austin txprice">$79.91</td>
  <td headers="albuquerque nmprovider">Comcast Digital Silver</td>
  <td headers="albuquerque nmprice">$69.95</td>
</tr>
<tr>
  <td headers="service">Cable Internet</td>
  <td headers="austin txprovider">Cox Cablevision</td>
  <td headers="austin txprice">$39.95</td>
  <td headers="albuquerque nmprovider">Comcast</td>
```

```
    <td headers="albuquerque nmprice">$42.00</td>
  </tr>
  <tr>
    <td headers="service">Satellite TV</td>
    <td headers="austin txprovider">Dish </td>
    <td headers="austin txprice">$56.99</td>
    <td headers="albuquerque nmprovider">Dish</td>
    <td headers="albuquerque nmprice">$56.99</td>
  </tr>
```

SCOPE

The scope attribute is used with simple data tables where there is no use of colspan or rowspan. It associates the td cells with the appropriate headers. In this table, the only headers are for columns, so the correct attribute is scope="col".

TIP   If you are also using th elements for each row, the correct scope attribute in each row th is scope="row".

If the table does not use colspan to divide the Austin and Albuquerque columns into two columns, then scope="col" is enough as an attribute for each of the th elements; it would look like this:

```
  <tr>
    <th scope="col">Service Type</th>
    <th scope="col">Austin</th>
    <th scope="col">Albuquerque</th>
  </tr>
```

The scope attribute tells a browser or screen reader that the contents of the data cells in each column are related to the heading at the top of the column.

Whether you use headers or scope to identify the td with its related th, when you view the table with a visual browser such as Internet Explorer or Safari, it will still look like Figure 10.6. Even though you don't "see" the information, it is there in the code, and a browser or screen reader that does present such information to the user can use it.

CAPTION

The caption is visible. It is placed immediately after the opening table tag, like this:

```
  <table width="90%" border="1" cellpadding="3">
    <caption align="top">
    Cost Comparison for Basic Services in Austin and Albuquerque
    </caption>
```

This caption is positioned at the top of the table using align="top". You can also position captions with align="bottom". Enter the caption in the XHTML code immediately after the opening table element, even when it is aligned at the bottom of the table. With the caption added, the table should appear like Figure 10.7 in the browser.

FIGURE 10.7
The caption adds information considered necessary for accessibility.

Cost Comparison for Basic Services in Austin and Albuquerque				
Service Type	**Austin**		**Albuquerque**	
	Provider	**Price**	**Provider**	**Price**
Phone	SBC	$24.95	Qwest Choice	$25.99
DSL	SBC Yahoo	$29.00	MSN	$39.99
Cable	Cox Cablevision Digital	$79.91	Comcast Digital Silver	$69.95
Cable Internet	Cox Cablevision	$39.95	Comcast	$42.00
Satellite TV	Dish	$56.99	Dish	$56.99

SUMMARY ATTRIBUTE

The `summary` attribute is part of the `table` element. `Summary` is another accessibility attribute that is not seen visually in browsers but can be used to provide information to users with screen readers. Add this to the table element:

```
<table width="90%" border="1" cellpadding="3" summary="The cost of services for
phone, TV, and Internet service in Austin is compared with the cost of similar
services in Albuquerque.">
```

In a visual browser, you'll still see something like Figure 10.7.

The `summary` attribute is used by designers who lay out a page with a table to inform the interested user that the table is being used for layout. A general summary such as `summary="layout table"` does the job in that situation.

Learn the CSS

On the CD, you will find `ch10_table3.html`. Open that in your text editor and in the browser. This is the same table you were using before, but the attributes regarding `width`, `border`, and `cellpadding` have been removed. In this section, you'll recreate the same effects with CSS.

The `headers`, `summary`, and `caption` elements are still there, so the table is already accessible. With no CSS rules and no table attributes, you are back to an appearance like Figure 10.8 in the browser.

Start a new stylesheet; name it `ch10_table3.css`. Add a link to the still-blank stylesheet to the document:

```
<link href="ch10_table3.css" rel="stylesheet" type="text/css" />
```

Begin with the `table` selector. If you give it a background color (a light yellow is shown below) and set the width for 80 percent, you will have this style:

```
table {
  background: #FFC;
  width: 80%;
}
```

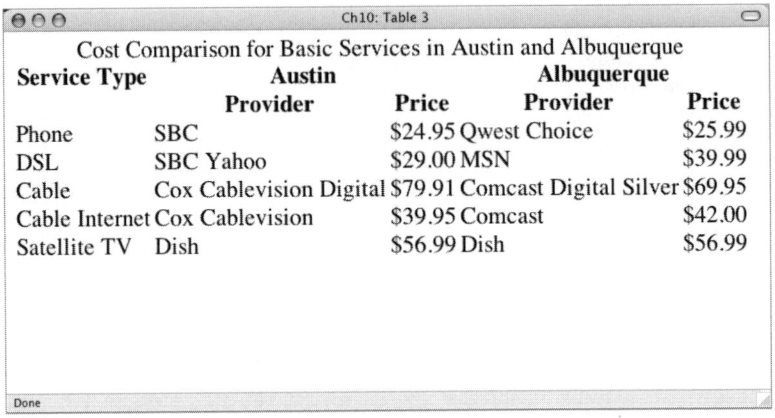

FIGURE 10.8
The unstyled table

FIGURE 10.8
The unstyled table

Look at Figure 10.9. You can see that the table is 80 percent of the width of the viewport, and you can see that the background color does not appear behind the caption.

Next, add the border. If you add a border to the `table` element, it will only go around the outside of the table element, not between the columns and rows as you want here. Add `border: solid 1px #333` to the `th` and `td` elements instead. In the previous exercise, the table had the attribute `cellpadding="3"`. To do that that with a CSS, give the `th` and `td` elements a `padding: 3px` declaration:

```
th, td {
    border: 1px solid #333;
    padding: 3px;
}
```

When you check the new style in the browser, you should see something similar to Figure 10.10.

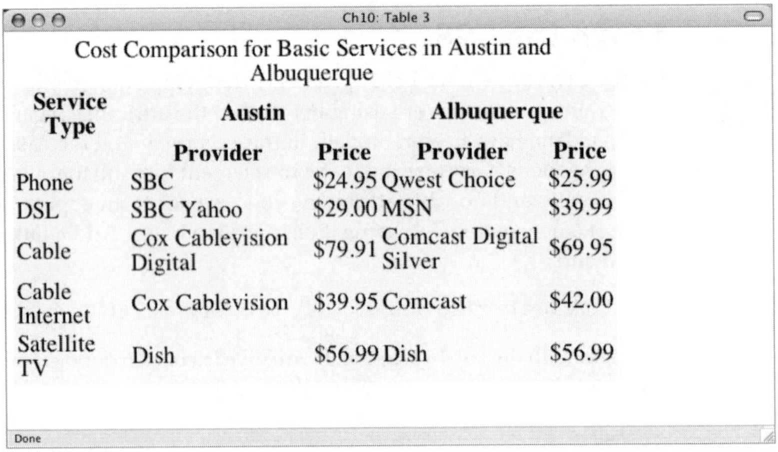

FIGURE 10.9
A size and background
style for the table

FIGURE 10.10

The table cells with border and padding values added

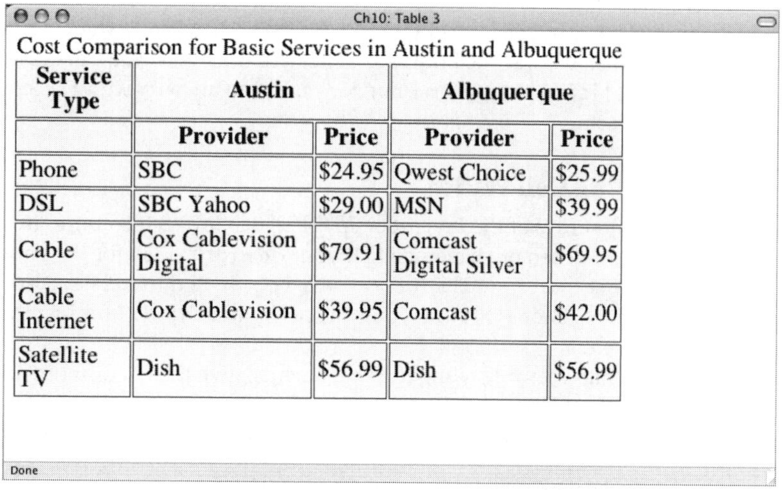

Cost Comparison for Basic Services in Austin and Albuquerque				
Service Type	**Austin**		**Albuquerque**	
	Provider	**Price**	**Provider**	**Price**
Phone	SBC	$24.95	Qwest Choice	$25.99
DSL	SBC Yahoo	$29.00	MSN	$39.99
Cable	Cox Cablevision Digital	$79.91	Comcast Digital Silver	$69.95
Cable Internet	Cox Cablevision	$39.95	Comcast	$42.00
Satellite TV	Dish	$56.99	Dish	$56.99

If you look closely at Figure 10.10, you will notice that there is not one border between the cells, but two. You can eliminate the extra border using the `border-collapse` property. Go back to the table selector to add the rule, like this:

```
table {
   background: #FFC;
   width: 80%;
   border-collapse: collapse;
}
```

You should see the effect of `border-collapse: collapse` as something similar to Figure 10.11.

FIGURE 10.11

The borders collapsed

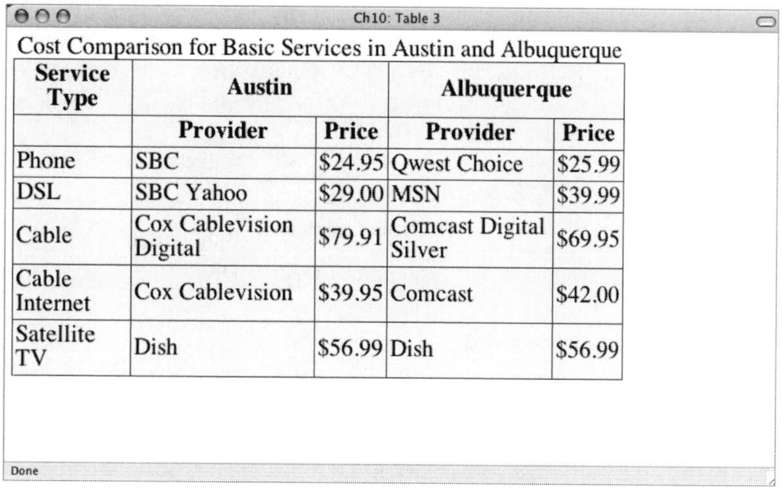

Cost Comparison for Basic Services in Austin and Albuquerque				
Service Type	**Austin**		**Albuquerque**	
	Provider	**Price**	**Provider**	**Price**
Phone	SBC	$24.95	Qwest Choice	$25.99
DSL	SBC Yahoo	$29.00	MSN	$39.99
Cable	Cox Cablevision Digital	$79.91	Comcast Digital Silver	$69.95
Cable Internet	Cox Cablevision	$39.95	Comcast	$42.00
Satellite TV	Dish	$56.99	Dish	$56.99

TIP Use border-collapse: separate when you *do* want borders separated by some distance. When border-collapse: separate is in force, you can determine the equivalent of XHTML cellspacing using the border-spacing property with a specified value as to the length of the spacing.

Setting Cell Width

The first row of the table sets up the width for each column. In your accessible table, the two rows are composed of th elements. If you use width: 33% for the th selector, you will run into problems in the second row. The first row can be assigned to a class. Add that to the first row, like this: <tr class="rowone">. Now you can specify width: 33% for just that row, as I'll show you in one moment.

While you are styling the th elements, give them a different background color, maybe a shade of orange (#FC3) that will contrast nicely with the pale yellow rows. The selector for a th that is descended from a tr with a class of rowone is tr.rowone th:

```
tr.rowone th {
   width: 33%;
   background: #FC3;
}
```

With this change in place, the table will look similar to Figure 10.12 in the browser. Notice that the background color change only applies to the th cells that are in the tr with the class rowone.

TIP You can use a class to alternate colors for every other row in a lengthy table. Assign the class attribute to the appropriate tr element to set the desired background-color.

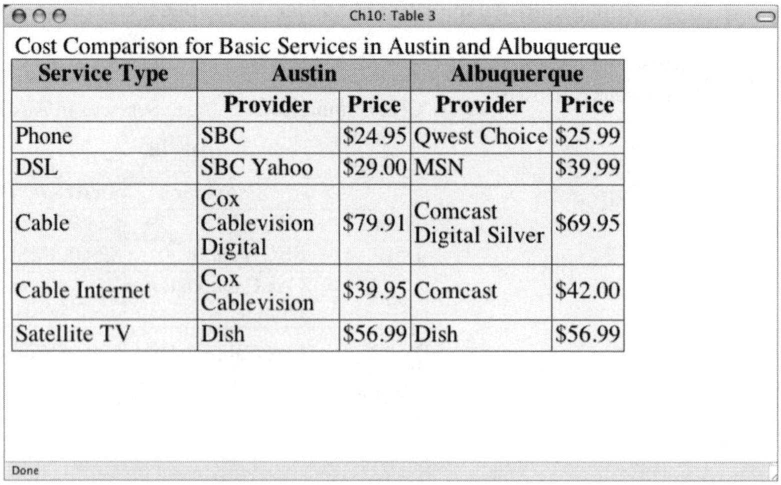

FIGURE 10.12

The styled first row of th elements

Cost Comparison for Basic Services in Austin and Albuquerque

Service Type	Austin		Albuquerque	
	Provider	Price	Provider	Price
Phone	SBC	$24.95	Qwest Choice	$25.99
DSL	SBC Yahoo	$29.00	MSN	$39.99
Cable	Cox Cablevision Digital	$79.91	Comcast Digital Silver	$69.95
Cable Internet	Cox Cablevision	$39.95	Comcast	$42.00
Satellite TV	Dish	$56.99	Dish	$56.99

Styling a Table Caption

The table is looking a little better. However, I think the caption would look better if it were in font-weight: bold. Make that change:

```
caption {
  font-weight: bold;
}
```

With that change in place, you should see something similar to Figure 10.13 in the browser.

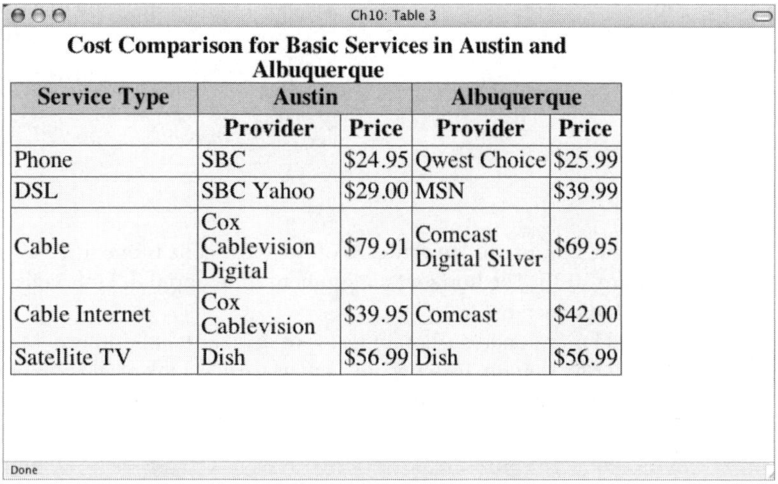

FIGURE 10.13

The styled caption element

	Ch10: Table 3			
Cost Comparison for Basic Services in Austin and Albuquerque				
Service Type	**Austin**		**Albuquerque**	
	Provider	**Price**	**Provider**	**Price**
Phone	SBC	$24.95	Qwest Choice	$25.99
DSL	SBC Yahoo	$29.00	MSN	$39.99
Cable	Cox Cablevision Digital	$79.91	Comcast Digital Silver	$69.95
Cable Internet	Cox Cablevision	$39.95	Comcast	$42.00
Satellite TV	Dish	$56.99	Dish	$56.99

Done

Cell Alignment

If you narrow the browser window so that the text in some of the table cell wraps, you will notice that the default vertical alignment for table cells is middle. The wrapping of content in the table cells is automatic (see Figure 10.14).

TIP   The caption did not wrap automatically. I placed a <br /> after the word "Services" so that the caption would fit the narrower window for this exercise. If I resize the browser window to a wider view, the caption will retain the line break unless I remove it.

The content of table cells can be aligned vertically with the values top, middle, or bottom.
The CSS to control the vertical alignment of the content of table cells is vertical-align. Change the rule for the th, td selector to include vertical-align: top and see what happens.

```
th, td {
  border: 1px solid #333;
  padding: 3px;
  vertical-align: top;
}
```

FIGURE 10.14

A narrow browser
window reveals the
vertical cell alignment

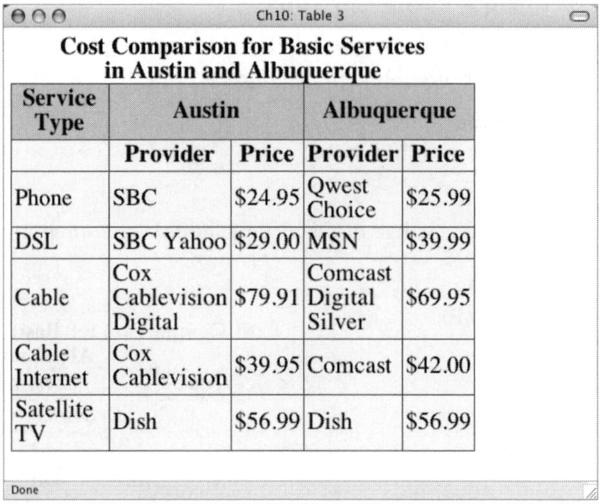

You should see the contents of the table cells move to be aligned with the top of the row, as in Figure 10.15. The horizontal alignment of material in table cells uses the `text-align` property that you have seen before.

As I mentioned earlier, in terms of horizontal alignment, `th` elements are set at `text-align: center` by default. Leave them as they are and look at the `td` elements. They are set at `text-align: left` by default. Change the `td` element to `text-align: right` so you can see a change. The new rule for the stylesheet is

```
td {
    text-align: right;
}
```

FIGURE 10.15

The `vertical-align: top` rule in effect

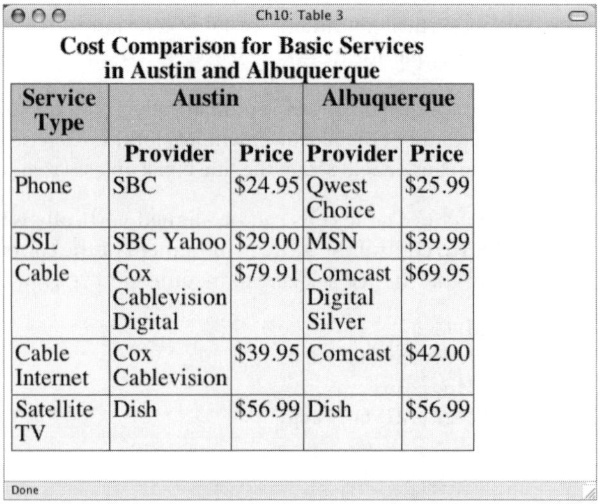

FIGURE 10.16
Text in the td cells is
right aligned

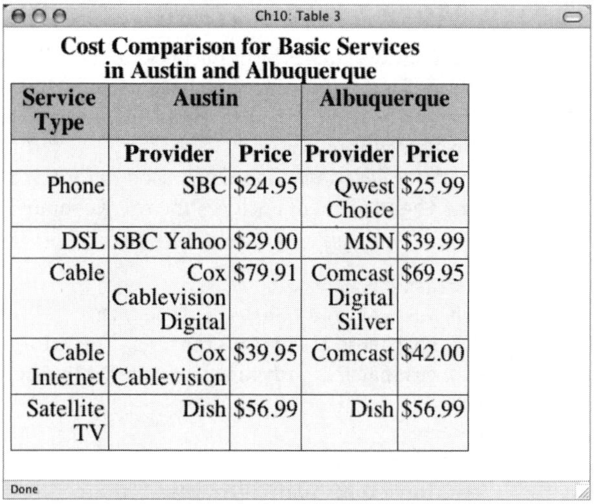

In the browser, you should see a change similar to Figure 10. 16.
See Listing 10.4 for the completed ch10_table3.css style rules.

LISTING 10.4:   The Complete *ch10_table3.css* Stylesheet

```css
table {
  background: #FFC;
  width: 80%;
  border-collapse: collapse;
}
th, td {
  border: 1px solid #333;
  padding: 3px;
  vertical-align: top;
}
tr.rowone th {
  width: 33%;
  background: #FC3;
}
td {
  text-align: right;
}
caption {
  font-weight: bold;
}
```

Learn More XHTML: *thead, tbody, tfoot*

Let's finish the study of tables by going back to XHTML for more table elements. Although it sounds like the instructions for a child's dance activity, thead, tbody, and tfoot are actually additional XHTML elements that can be used in a table. These elements are handy because they give you further structure that you can style within a table.

The thead (for *table head*) element is used to format a tr element. Using ch10_table3.html as an example, the thead element encloses the rows containing the th elements, like this:

```
<thead>
  <tr class="rowone">
    <th id="service">Service Type</th>
    <th colspan="2" id="austin">Austin</th>
    <th colspan="2" id="albuquerque">Albuquerque</th>
  </tr>
  <tr>
    <th> </th>
    <th id="txprovider">Provider</th>
    <th id="txprice">Price</th>
    <th id="nmprovider">Provider</th>
    <th id="nmprice">Price</th>
  </tr>
</thead>
```

There can only be one thead element in a table.

The tbody (for *table body*) element adds structure to the table rows that make up the body of the table. In the example table, Listing 10.5 shows how it can be used.

LISTING 10.5:   An Example Showing the *tbody* Element

```
<tbody>
  <tr>
    <td headers="service">Phone</td>
    <td headers="austin txprovider">SBC</td>
    <td headers="austin txprice">$24.95</td>
    <td headers="albuquerque nmprovider">Qwest Choice</td>
    <td headers="albuquerque nmprice">$25.99</td>
  </tr>
  <tr>
    <td headers="service">DSL</td>
    <td headers="austin txprovider">SBC Yahoo</td>
    <td headers="austin txprice">$29.00</td>
    <td headers="albuquerque nmprovider">MSN</td>
```

```
        <td headers="albuquerque nmprice">$39.99</td>
      </tr>
      <tr>
        <td headers="service">Cable</td>
        <td headers="austin txprovider">Cox Cablevision Digital</td>
        <td headers="austin txprice">$79.91</td>
        <td headers="albuquerque nmprovider">Comcast Digital Silver</td>
        <td headers="albuquerque nmprice">$69.95</td>
      </tr>
      <tr>
        <td headers="service">Cable Internet</td>
        <td headers="austin txprovider">Cox Cablevision</td>
        <td headers="austin txprice">$39.95</td>
        <td headers="albuquerque nmprovider">Comcast</td>
        <td headers="albuquerque nmprice">$42.00</td>
      </tr>
      <tr>
        <td headers="service">Satellite TV</td>
        <td headers="austin txprovider">Dish </td>
        <td headers="austin txprice">$56.99</td>
        <td headers="albuquerque nmprovider">Dish</td>
        <td headers="albuquerque nmprice">$56.99</td>
      </tr>
    </tbody>
```

The tfoot (for table footer) formats the table row containing the table footer. The example table does not have a footer; however, the element is used in exactly the same way as thead and tbody. There can only be one tfoot element in a table.

Browsers are very literal in their interpretation of thead, tbody, and tfoot. If you mark up the first row in this table as tfoot, the browser will display it at the foot of the table.

If you add the thead and tbody elements to your ch10_table3.html page, you can add a style for the tbody element. Table elements can be styled with background-image, so try that.

You will find background-image.gif in the Chapter 10 folder on the CD. Make sure you have the graphic in the same folder as your current stylesheet. Add this rule to the stylesheet:

```
tbody {
  background: url(background-image.gif) repeat;
}
```

In most browsers, the background image should repeat to fill the entire tbody element. The background color set for the td elements is still there, but the background-image value overrides it in the Cascade. The result is similar to Figure 10.17.

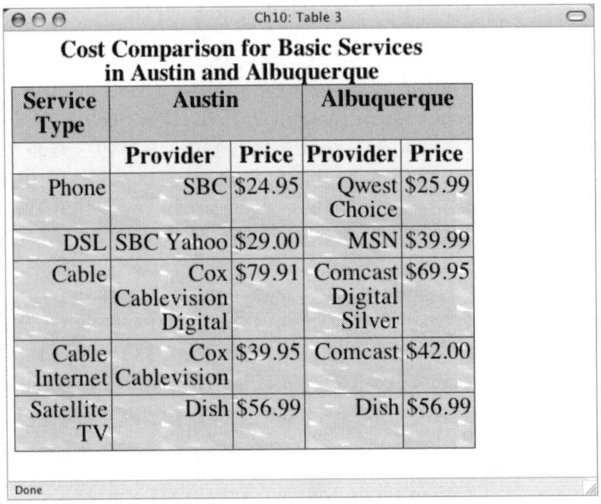

FIGURE 10.17
A style added to the tbody element

Real World Example

Quik n Simple Trade Manager is software meant to track and manage stock trades. I've never used the software, but I've admired the data table designed to compare the features of two versions of the software. This data table is accessible as well as functional; you can see it at

`http://www.quiknsimple.com/features/compare.html`

You can understand how it was built by viewing the source code. The table includes `summary`, `caption`, `thead`, `tbody`, and `scope` elements and attributes.

CSS Properties

All the CSS properties you have learned in previous chapters can be applied to tables, table cells, and the content of tables. Classes and IDs can be used with tables to increase specificity when writing style rules. New CSS properties learned in Chapter 10 are shown in Table 10.1.

TABLE 10.1:   Properties for Tables

PROPERTY	POSSIBLE VALUES
border-collapse	collapse, separate, inherit
border-spacing	`<length>`, inherit
vertical-align	top, middle, bottom

Challenge Yourself

For some extra practice with your new skills, try out these exercises.

1. Make a new table with your own information, perhaps something like the names, ages, and birthdates of people you know.

2. Make your table accessible with a `summary` attribute and `scope` attributes. Use a `caption`.

3. Use styles to give your table an attractive appearance.

4. Experiment with the `border` property. Give the `td` element only `border-right` and `border-left` values. Or give the `td` element only `border-top` and `border-bottom` values. Or give the `thead` a thick `border-bottom`.

Summary

Recent advances in the use of CSS for page layout have meant big changes in the way tables are used on the Web. The recommended use for tables is for displaying tabular information. The `table` element is perfect for this task, since a table is basically a matrix of rows and columns.

A table is built with `tr`, `th`, and `td` elements that organize and display the data in cells. CSS can be used to determine table size, color, position, padding, border, alignment, and many other properties that contribute to the effectiveness and attractiveness of the display. CSS properties that were used for the first time in this chapter included `border-collapse` and `border-spacing`.

Tables present accessibility problems for users who try to glean the information in a table using an assistive browsing device. There are tools, including `summary`, `scope`, `caption`, and `headers` that designers can use to ensure that the table is easily understood with any Internet-capable device.

In Chapter 11, you will learn how to create forms so that you can collect data from your site visitors.

Chapter 11

Forms and Form Styles

This chapter is a bit different from the others in the book because you won't get all the foundation information you need about collecting information with forms by reading this chapter. Other chapters have helped you build that solid foundation, but forms generally require an associated script in order to execute the command to submit the data collected in the form fields.

Scripts and programming are beyond the scope of this book. You *will* learn in this chapter where to find some free scripts and helpful resources that will get you started on the subject of using scripts, but you won't learn everything you need to know about scripts in this book.

This chapter will help you continue to build on your solid base of XHTML and CSS, however, because you will learn how to create a form in XHTML, how to style it with CSS, and how to make sure that your form is easy to use and accessible.

Script Matters

Scripts that format and e-mail form data are often written in Perl and have the file extension `.pl`. Sometimes you see this as `.cgi` (for Common Gateway Interface). There are many places on the Internet that offer up free Perl and CGI scripts for various functions such as submitting e-mail or creating guest books. Consider using the scripts available from the open source outfit called Sourceforge. The Perl scripts in question are located at

```
http://nms-cgi.sourceforge.net/scripts.shtml
```

The script often used to submit form data is called FormMail. There is an extensive README file with each script at Sourceforge that explains in detail what needs to be done in your form and to your script in order to make it all work together.

TIP A book with a good chapter on using FormMail, including how to put it on your server and set permissions to execute it, is *Dreamweaver MX 2004 Savvy* by Christian Crumlish and Lucinda Dykes (Sybex, 2004).

Another possible source of scripts is here:

```
http://www.bebosoft.com/products/formstogo
```

This site provides software called Forms To Go that will generate a script for your forms. This is not a free service like that offered by Sourceforge, but it is inexpensive. You can select PHP, ASP, or Perl for the programming language of the script.

Some web hosting companies will let you use your version of FormMail.pl or some other form handling script. Others will not. Those who do not want you to use your own CGI scripts often provide a script located on their server that you are allowed to use. If the hosting company provides the script, they will give you the URL for the `action` attribute in your `form` element. More on the `action` attribute is coming in a minute.

Hosting companies are picky about this because the script that sends mail is actually an executable file. It can pose security risks or can be misused to send spam e-mail if it is not handled with the proper security.

NOTE See Chapter 12 for an explanation on how to use your FTP software to set permissions to execute a file.

Learn the XHTML

In the following exercises, you will make one main form with an example of each type of `form` element. You will make two forms that demonstrate a single concept that differs from the way the form was constructed in the main form.

On the CD, you will find two files: `ch11_forms_start.html` and `ch11_forms_finished.html`. If you use the beginning provided with the start page, then your forms will look similar to the finished page when the chapter is completed. The top section of the finished page is shown in Figure 11.1.

If you open the finished page in the browser, you will see that the three separate `form` elements have been color coded to make them stand out from each other. The styles used to accomplish that color coding and set a width for the three sections of the page are embedded in the head of both the start and the finished pages. Listing 11.1 shows the complete `ch11_forms_start.html` page. The page uses three `div` elements with named `id` attributes to establish structure for the colors and width of the containers that will hold each of the three forms.

LISTING 11.1: The *ch11_forms_start.html* Page

```
<!DOCTYPE html PUBLIC "-//W3C//DTD XHTML 1.0 Transitional//EN"
  "http://www.w3.org/TR/xhtml1/DTD/xhtml1-transitional.dtd">
<html xmlns="http://www.w3.org/1999/xhtml">
<head>
<title>Ch11: Forms Start Page</title>
<style type="text/css">
#script {
  background: #FFC;
  border: 1px dotted #3FF;
  width: 80%;
}
#mailto {
  background: #CDE8B7;
  border: 1px dotted #606;
  margin-top: 2em;
  width: 80%;
}
#table {
  background: #C2CDE8;
  border: 1px dotted #C03;
  margin-top: 2em;
```

```
    width: 80%;
}
</style>
</head>

<body>
<div id="script">
  <h1>A Script Example</h1>
</div>

<div id="mailto">
  <h1>An Email Example using a mailto action</h1>
</div>

<div id="table">
  <h1>A Table Layout Example using a label for attribute</h1>
</div>
</body>
</html>
```

FIGURE 11.1
The top of the finished forms page

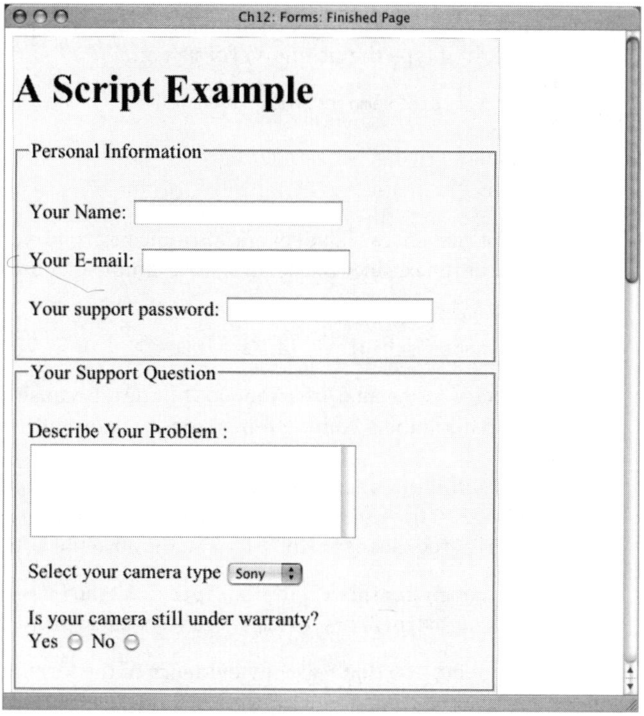

FIGURE 11.2
The start page
in the browser

FIGURE 11.2
The start page
in the browser

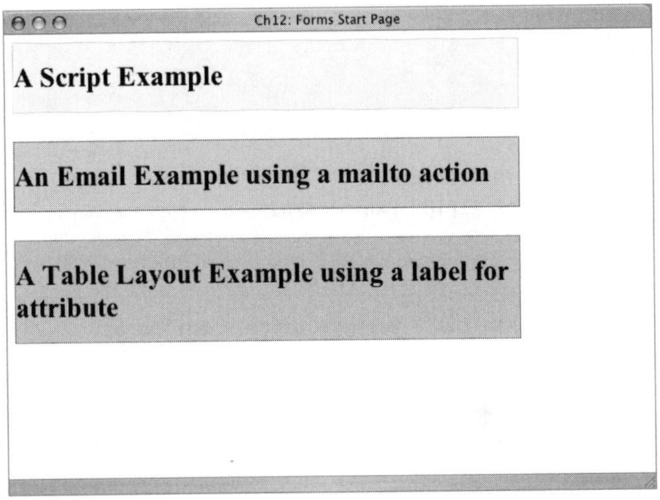

In the browser, the start page should look like Figure 11.2.

The main form will be contained by the div id="script" element.

The *form* Element

Following the <h1>A Script Example</h1>, type the opening **<form>** tag, then press Enter (Return) a few times and type the closing **</form>** tag:

```
<h1>A Script Example</h1>
<form>

</form>
```

The form element can have several attributes: method, action, name, and id. You will give it the name and id of scriptex, since this form is the example that uses a script. Add these to your form element, like this:

```
<form name="scriptex" id="scriptex">
```

The choices for method are either post or get. Because get limits the amount of data and the manner of formatting the incoming e-mail, post is normally used. Add method="post" to your form attributes.

The final attribute is action, which points to the location of the script. It might be a relative link such as action="../cgi-bin/somescript.pl", or it might be an absolute link such as action="http://www.example.com/somescript.pl". Use the absolute URL in your example form:

```
<form name="scriptex" id="scriptex" method="post"
   action="http://www.example.com/somescript.pl">
```

At this point, you don't see any evidence of the form in the browser because none of the visible form elements nor the submit button are there yet. And, of course, the action will not execute because it is an example URL and not a real URL.

Hidden Fields

Speaking of things you don't see in the browser, forms often use hidden fields, so you'll add one to this form. Following the opening form element, type this hidden form element:

```
<input name="recipient" type="hidden" value="someone@somewhere.com" />
```

As you continue creating form elements, you will see that many form elements are input elements. Each input element is given a type attribute, in this case, type="hidden".

TIP A name is assigned to each form element. When you receive the data that the user typed in the form, the e-mail is formatted in what are called *name-value pairs*. That is to say, you see the name of the form element and the value that the user typed or selected. It is good practice to give form elements names that will help you interpret the data you received from it in the form of name-value pairs. For example, a form element asking for a first name to be input could use name="firstname", or a form element asking for postal code input could use name="zipcode". Do not use spaces in form element names.

The hidden field you typed uses name="recipient" because the e-mail address listed in the value attribute will be the e-mail address that receives the submitted form data.

TEXT BOXES

Enough with the things you can't admire in the browser! Make a text box asking for the user's name.

There are two parts to the form elements that ask for user input, the label and the form element itself. In the scriptex form, the label element will enclose the entire form element.

To create a one-line text box, type **<input type="text" />**. You also need to name this element, and since it will be asking for a person's name, name it "name". With that added, you have <input type="text" name="name" />. Finally, you need to enclose the form element in the label element.

The label element has two parts: the label tag with the for attribute, coupled with an id matching the value of the for attribute in the input element. Since this input form is asking for a name, you can use the value "name" in the for attribute. Type this before the input element: **<label for="name">**. Next, add the id to the input element that matches the value of the for attribute, making the input element now read thus:

```
<input type=text" name="name" id="name" />
```

The value of the for attribute and the id attribute *must match*. The value of the name attribute does not have to be the same as the value used for the label and id, although it is in this example. Type the closing **</label>** tag after the input element. Note that the input element is an empty element.

The complete code is

```
<label for="name">Your Name: <input type="text" name="name" id="name" /></label>
```

NOTE My friends at www.knowbility.org inform me that label without the for attribute is fully supported by the aural screen readers Jaws, Window Eyes, and Home Page Reader. As of this writing, however, the accessibility validators will not give a form an acceptable rating without the for attribute. (See Chapter 12 for information about validators.) When using a table layout for a form, the for attribute *is* required because the label text is in a different table cell from the form element—I will address table layouts later in this chapter. To help you achieve acceptable validation results, you'll use the for attribute for all form labels.

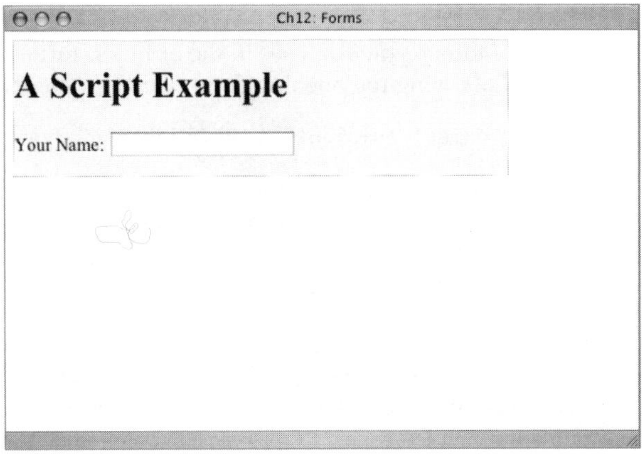

FIGURE 11.3
A text box with label is your first visible element

Now you can take a look in the browser because you finally have a form element you can see. Your text box should look similar to Figure 11.3.

You could use a `<br />` to move down to the next line for the next text box, but mark up each one in a p element instead. That way they will be spaced out a bit more. Do this:

```
<p><label>Your Name: <input type="text" name="name" /></label></p>
```

To make a text box asking for the user's e-mail, you use the same formatting, except the label will say Your E-mail: and the name will be "email". Use email as the value of the for and id attributes as well.

```
<p><label for="email">Your E-mail: <input type="text" name="email" id="email" />
    </label></p>
```

PASSWORD BOXES

Make one more text box so you can use `type="password"`. With a password box, when the user types something in the form field, only asterisks appear. This prevents other people from reading the password information. Make the label read **Your support password:**. Make the for and id attribute values "password". Use `input type="password"` and think of a great name for this form element, such as `name="password"`. All that, together with the p element, will look like this:

```
<p><label for="password">Your support password: <input type="password"
    name="password" id="password" /></label></p>
```

If you look at that in the browser, your view should be similar to Figure 11.4. For even more thrills, try typing in the browser password box to see if asterisks appear.

The *fieldset* Element

One of the most useful elements to become a recent addition to the form designer's options is the fieldset element. The fieldset element is used to organize form elements into related groups. The default appearance of a fieldset element is to box in the group of form elements and provide a legend that identifies the particular grouping.

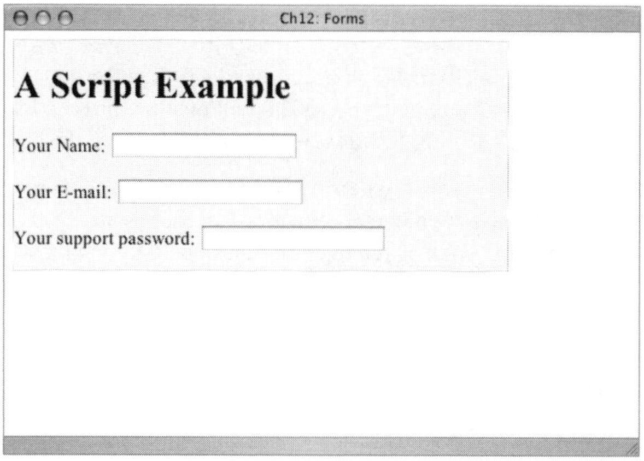

FIGURE 11.4
Three text boxes
are complete.

You now have three form elements asking for personal information about the user, so enclose them in a fieldset element.

Before the first p element in your form, type **<fieldset>**. Following the closing p tag after the third p element, type **</fieldset>**. That contains all three of your existing form elements in the fieldset, but you need to add the legend. After the opening fieldset element, type **<legend>Personal Information</legend>**. The completed fieldset element should look like this:

```
<fieldset><legend>Personal Information</legend>
    <p><label for="name">Your Name: <input type="text" name="name"
    id="name" /></label></p>
    <p><label for="email">Your E-mail: <input type="text" name="email"
    id="email" /></label></p>
    <p><label for="password">Your support password: <input type="password"
    name="password" id="password" /></label></p>
</fieldset>
```

With that in place, the view in the browser will be like Figure 11.5.

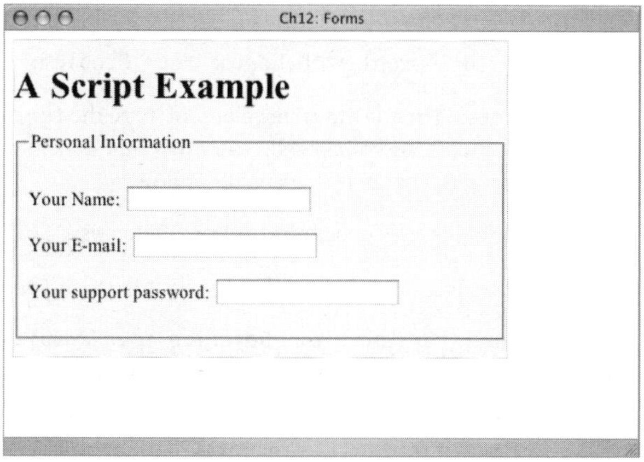

FIGURE 11.5
The personal informa-
tion fieldset organizes
the form elements.

ADDITIONAL TEXT BOX ATTRIBUTES

Several optional attributes can be used with text boxes. If you use `value="somevalue"` with an `input type="text"` element, the `value` will display in the `form` element before the user begins typing their own input. The initial value is replaced by whatever the user types.

You can use `size="n"` where *n* is the desired width of the box in characters, such as 30 or 40. The default size for a text box is 20 characters in width, but the size does not limit the number of characters that can actually be typed in the box. If you have an input box asking for a street address that is the default 20 characters in width and the user's address required more than 20 characters, the complete address can still be typed in the box as needed.

You can use `maxlength="n"` where *n* is the maximum number of characters that can be typed in a box. Sometimes this is useful when you are asking for information that has a specific number of characters such as a postal code or a social security number.

You can help your users understand what they need to type with `size` and `maxlength` in situations such as asking for a three-digit area code. A form such as the following gives helpful clues establishing the fact that only three digits should be entered in the form field:

```
<input type="text" size="3" maxlength="3" ...
```

The *textarea* Element

If you want a `form` element that allows for several lines of text to be entered, you want a `textarea` element. Before you make a `textarea` element, add another `fieldset` to organize this new section of the form. Type this:

```
<fieldset><legend>Your Support Question</legend>

</fieldset>
```

The next few `form` elements you learn will be enclosed in this `fieldset`.

A `textarea` can be as large as you want. You will make a rather small one in this exercise. Again, to help with line spacing, start by typing a **<p></p>** element. Nested inside the p element, type the label:

```
<label for="problem">Describe Your Problem: </label>
```

Finally, nested inside the `label` element, type the `textarea`. You will give a size in `cols` (for columns) and `rows` right off the bat as well. You must name the element; you are asking them to describe a problem, so use `name="problem"`. Type the following:

```
<textarea name="problem" cols="30" rows="5" id="problem"></textarea>
```

I added a `<br />` after the label too, but that isn't required. Here is the complete snippet:

```
<p><label for="problem">Describe Your Problem:<br />
  <textarea name="problem" cols="30" rows="5" id="problem"></textarea></label></p>
```

TIP   Notice that the `textarea` element requires a closing tag.

If you look at your page in the browser you should see the page shown in Figure 11.6, with one exception: your page won't have anything typed in the `textarea` element. I typed a couple of paragraphs there for the screen shot so you could see that a scrollbar automatically appears when the user types more than the `cols="30"` and `rows="5"` size will accommodate.

Of course, you can adjust the size values of the `cols` and `rows` attributes to suit your needs.

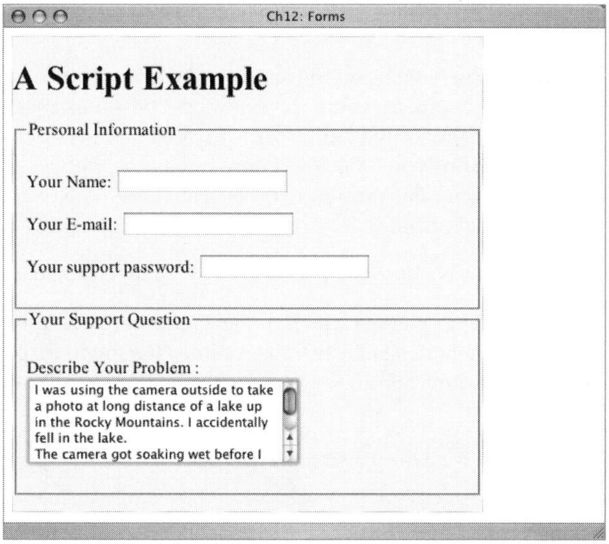

FIGURE 11.6
A `textarea` with a long response typed in it automatically generates a scrollbar.

The *select* Menu

The `select` element will be nested in the current `fieldset`, immediately following the `textarea` element. Start by typing this:

```
<p><label for="camera">Select your camera type</label></p>
```

The rest of the `select` menu will be nested in the `label` element. A `select` element contains several `option` elements. Start with just one:

```
<p>
  <label for="camera">Select your camera type
    <select name="camera" id="camera">
      <option value="sony">Sony</option>
    </select>
  </label>
</p>
```

Notice that the entire `select` menu uses `name="camera"`. Each individual option will have a different `value`. Add `option` elements for Kodak, Polaroid, and Canon, like this:

```
<p>
  <label for="camera">Select your camera type
```

```
<select name="camera" id="camera">
  <option value="sony">Sony</option>
  <option value="kodak">Kodak</option>
  <option value="polaroid">Polaroid</option>
  <option value="canon">Canon</option>
</select>
</label>
</p>
```

After you have listed the last `option`, close the `select` element and close the `label` element as well. Take a look at that in the browser. You should see results like Figure 11.7.

You are probably familiar with `form` elements like this that list all 50 states or numerous country codes in forms you have filled out yourself on websites.

If you want one `option` to be selected when the user first sees the `form` element, you can use the attribute `selected="selected"`, like this:

```
<option value="sony" selected="selected">Sony</option>
```

The `select` element can have several other attributes that are not needed in this example. One is `size="n"` where *n* is the number of lines the menu displays at one time. When the size is more than 1, a scrollbar may be added to allow the user to see all of the options. That code would look something like this:

```
<select name="camera" size="2">
```

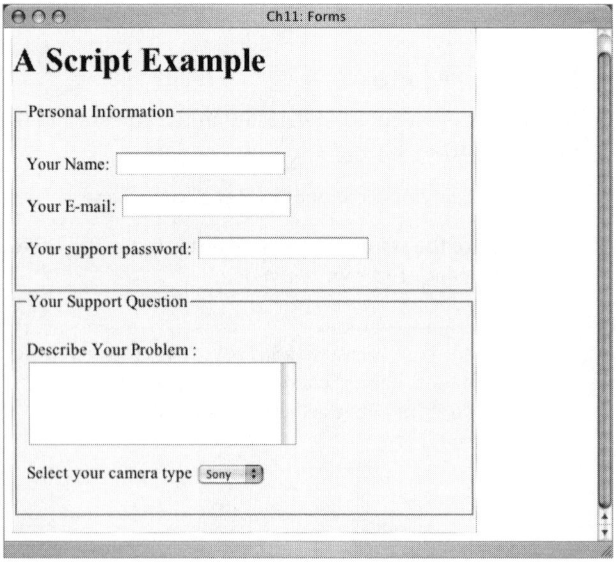

FIGURE 11.7
The `select` menu
`form` element

You may want to allow users to select more than one option from an option menu. The `multiple` attribute is used for this, as in:

```
<select name="camera" size="2" multiple="multiple">
```

If users are allowed to select more than one option, you need to add a note somewhere near the select menu instructing them how to do it. Normally this is accomplished by holding down the Ctrl key (the Command key on a Mac) while clicking the desired options.

Radio Buttons

Radio buttons allow a variety of responses to a question, only one of which may be selected at a time. You will make a set of radio buttons that say Yes and No. If the user selects Yes and then changes the selection to No, the Yes radio button will automatically become deselected.

Each radio button in the set has the same `name` attribute. If you asked the user, "Is your camera still under warranty?" you could use `name="warranty"` for every radio button in the set. However, each radio button in the set gets an individual `value`. In the example, this is the code:

```
<p>Is your camera still under warranty?<br />
  <label for="yes">Yes <input name="warranty" type="radio" value="Yes"
    id="yes" /></label>
  <label for="no">No <input name="warranty" type="radio" value="No"
    id="no" /></label>
</p>
```

The preceding snippet includes the `p` element, a `br` after the question, and a `label` for each of the radio buttons. In the browser, you should see a page similar to Figure 11.8.

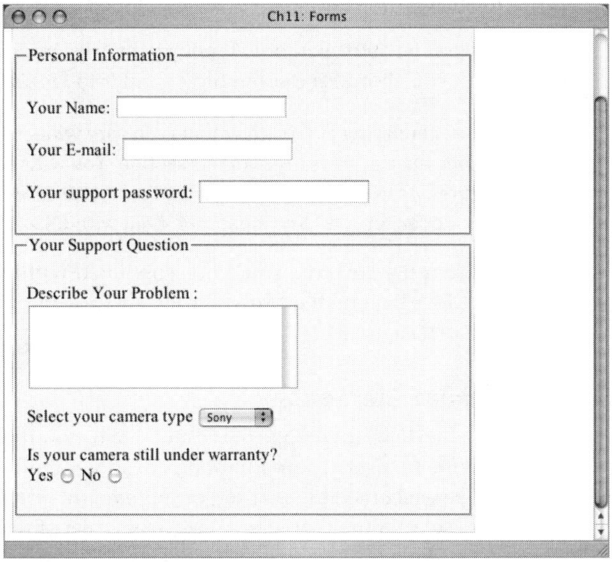

FIGURE 11.8
In a set of radio buttons, only one may be selected.

Letting Visitors Upload Files

A page like this might include an option for users to upload a photograph as an example of the problem with the camera. To make this happen, the following attribute would have to be included in the opening form element: enctype="multipart/form-data". This attribute specifies the content type used to submit the form to the server. In the example, with the enctype attribute added, the form element is

```
<form name="scriptex" id="scriptex" method="post"
   action="http://www.example.com/somescript.pl" enctype="multipart/form-data">
```

TIP   The method must be post for uploading files.

The particular form element you need for the user to be able to upload a file is input type="file". A complete form element of this type might be:

```
<label for="photo">Select a photo from your computer:<br />
   <input type="file" name="photo" id="photo" /></label>
```

A browse button automatically appears next to the form field when using the input type="file" attribute. The user browses their computer to find the file. When it is selected, the location of the file on the user's computer appears as a directory path in the form field box. If you ever sell something on eBay and upload a photo of the item you are selling, this is how it is coded on the eBay web page.

An explanatory paragraph telling the user what is being requested as an uploaded file might be helpful in making the form more useable. The completed upload section might look like this:

```
<p>Do you have a photograph taken with your camera that shows an example
   of the problem? If so, you can upload it.</p>
<p><label for="photo">Select a photo from your computer:<br />
   <input type="file" name="photo" id="photo" /></label></p>
```

The way a file input element is rendered varies widely depending on operating system and browser, but you should see something similar to Figure 11.9.

TIP   Because rendering of form elements can vary widely, a variety of browsers will be used for the screenshots illustrating the text in this section. You will notice those slight differences in rendering in the figures. As the designer, you have no control over the way the different operating systems and browsers render certain form elements, even with CSS.

That finishes the area that should be contained within the fieldset element for "Your Support Question." Move beyond the fieldset terminating tag, and you will create one last fieldset for the checkbox form element.

The *checkbox* Elements

Businesses often take advantage of the fact that users are submitting a form to establish a way to keep in contact with the user. There might be questions about whether special offers or product information would be welcomed by the user, or there might be an offer to receive a regular newsletter. Often the user will select more than one option from a set of related choices. You need a form element that allows for multiple options to be selected. That form element is the checkbox.

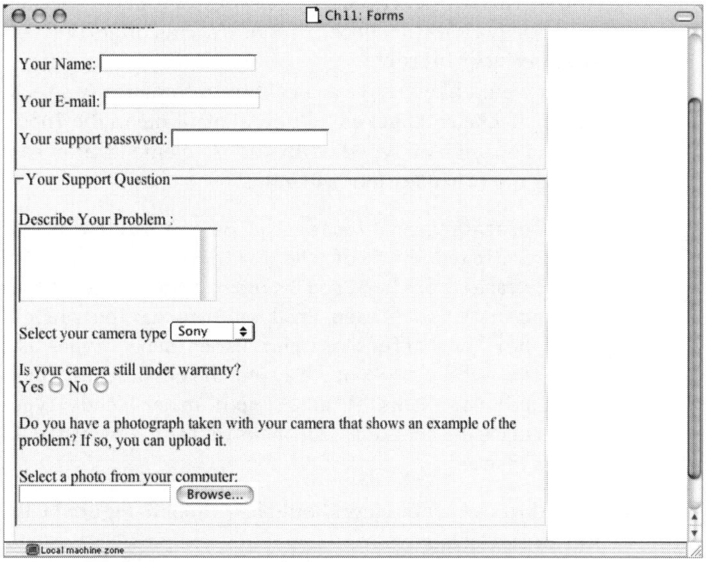

FIGURE 11.9
A file input form element automatically has a Browse button.

Before you add the checkbox, create one more `fieldset` element to set off the last section of the form. The `legend` should be something that lets the user know what the section is about. Type the following, pressing Enter (Return) a time or two before typing the closing tag:

```
<fieldset><legend>Please send me the following information</legend>

</fieldset>
```

The new `fieldset` element will be the container for the checkboxes. Some explanatory text might be good to begin:

```
<p>Indicate which of the following you would like to receive:</p>
```

Like radio buttons, checkboxes are grouped. The set of related checkboxes all have the same `name` and a unique `value`. Since you are asking what you can send the user, use `name="send"` for the group name.

A `checkbox` element looks like this:

```
<input name="groupname" type="checkbox" value="uniquevalue" />
```

It makes sense to have the text in the label appear after the checkbox, so with a label added, the element would look like this:

```
<label for="box"><input name="groupname" type="checkbox" value="uniquevalue"
    id="box" />Label text</label>
```

TIP   The order of the attributes does not matter. For example, the checkbox element could be coded as `<input type="checkbox" name="somename" value="somevalue" />` instead of in the order shown in the example.

You will make three checkboxes, asking for users to select whether they want to receive new product information (`value="newProd"`), money saving offers (`value="offers"`), and a monthly tips newsletter (`value="newsletter"`).

If you would like to have a checkbox automatically selected when the user sees the form, use the attribute `checked="checked"`. Put that attribute in the `input` element for Monthly Tips Newsletter.

When you get it all typed, with `<br />` elements after each checkbox, the whole new section including the `fieldset` looks like this:

```
<fieldset><legend>Please send me the following information</legend>
   <p>Indicate which of the following you would like to receive:</p>
   <p><label for="newProd"><input name="send" type="checkbox" value="newProd"
     id="newProd" />New Product Information</label><br />
   <label for="offers"><input name="send" type="checkbox" value="offers"
     id="offers" />Money Saving Offers</label><br />
   <label for="newsletter"><input name="send" type="checkbox" value="newsletter"
     checked="checked" id="newsletter" />Monthly Tips Newsletter</label></p>
</fieldset>
```

In the browser, your view should be similar to Figure 11.10. Note that the Monthly Tips Newsletter checkbox is selected.

FIGURE 11.10
Users may select more than one checkbox.

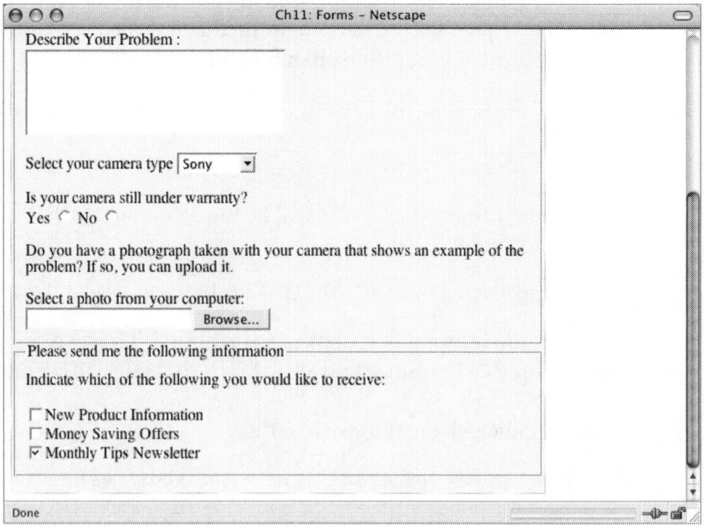

The *tabindex* Attribute

Users can move from one form field to the next with the Tab key, in a manner very similar to what was discussed in Chapter 7.

As with links, the `tabindex` attribute can be used with `form` elements to alter the normal tab order of form fields in the flow of the XHTML. To change the tab order, use `tabindex="n"` as an attribute of a `form` element, where *n* is a number.

The tabindex attribute is not needed in this form. I caution you to use it only when it is absolutely needed to make the page more usable and understandable. Make sure the user moves from one form field to another in the most logical manner when changing the tab order in any way.

The Submit Button

The last element to include in this form example is the submit button. The submit button is another input element, with the attribute type="button". The text that you use for the attribute value (e.g., value="Send Form") is the text that appears on the button.

The element looks like this:

```
<input name="submit" type="button" value="Submit" />
```

In the browser, you see a page like the one in Figure 11.11.

TIP   A label is not needed on a button. The control creates the needed text.

The size of the submit button will change depending on the assigned value. For example, change to this:

```
value="Send this baby on its way"
```

The browser then displays a page like Figure 11.12.

The form is complete! The terminating </form> and </div> elements should be immediately after your new submit button.

Before you move on to using CSS to style this page, there are a couple of other things about XHTML for forms that you need to know. You won't make a large form for the following examples, merely enough for you to learn the new information.

TIP   Data from forms can be sent directly to a database with the proper script.

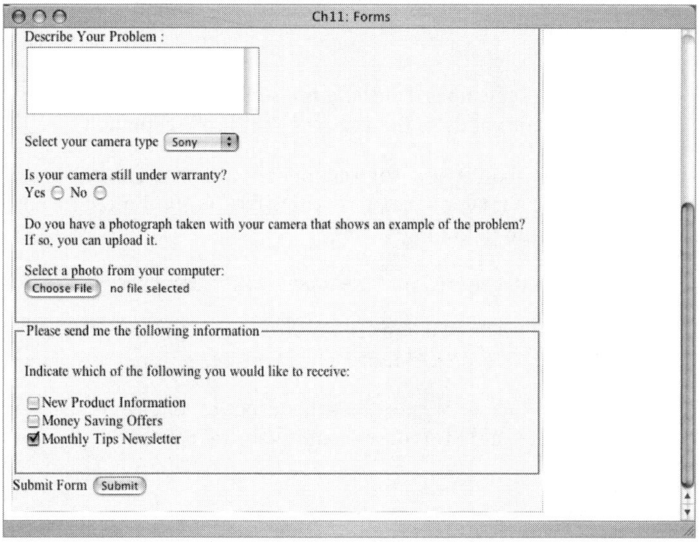

FIGURE 11.11
The user must press Submit to send the form.

FIGURE 11.12
Note the text on
the submit button.

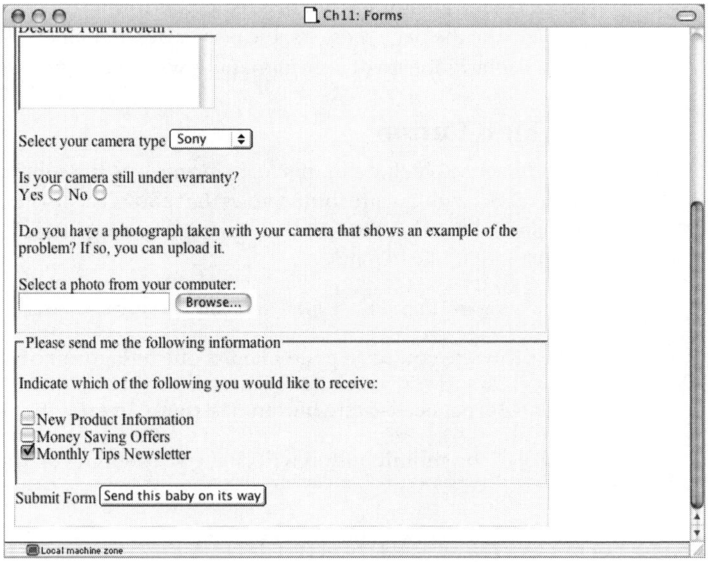

Using a *mailto* Action

If you don't have a script, you can still collect information by pointing to your e-mail address in the form `action` attribute.

On the page `ch11_forms_start.html`, find this code:

```
<div id="mailto">
  <h1>An Email Example using a mailto action</h1>

</div>
```

NOTE   Remember that there is a style rule in `ch11_forms_start.html` that sets a background color and width for the `div id="mailto"` section.

You will put a new `form` element in this `div`. The key to using `mailto` in the `action` attribute is this attribute: `enctype="text/plain"`. The method must be `post`.

Type the following:

```
form name="mailex" method="post" enctype="text/plain"
```

Add the action, using your own e-mail address in the `mailto:` value. Press Enter (Return) a couple of times and type **</form>**. The complete snippet looks like this:

```
<form name="mailex" method="post" enctype="text/plain"
  action="mailto:someone@example.com">

</form>
```

That is the only difference in what you need to do between the script submission and the e-mail submission forms. However, you can use first two text boxes from the earlier form so there is something to see here. Remember that an ID must be unique on the page, so the `for` and `id` attributes will have to change a bit to use the same two form fields:

```
<p><label for="name2">Your Name:
  <input type="text" name="name" id="name2" /></label></p>
<p><label for="email12">Your Email:
  <input type="text" name="email" id="email12" /></label></p>
```

Add a submit button:

```
<p><input type="submit" name="Submit" value="Submit" /></p>
```

In your browser, you should see results like Figure 11.13. There is no visible difference in this form, but when you press the Submit button the effect is to open an e-mail document containing the data from the name-value pairs in the form.

A form using `action="mailto:someone@somewhere.com"` may seem like the solution to all your problems—after all, no script is needed. However, there are two issues with this method. First, some older browsers don't know what to do with `enctype="text/plain"`, and this won't work with them. Secondly, the formatting of the e-mail leaves a lot to be desired in terms of readability.

If I put my name and a silly e-mail address in this form and press Submit, Figure 11.14 shows what would be sent in my default e-mail application. If there were more form fields in this form, they would all be formatted in this hard-to-read manner.

Using a `mailto action` is fine if you just want a small amount of information, but for processing large amounts of data, a script becomes necessary.

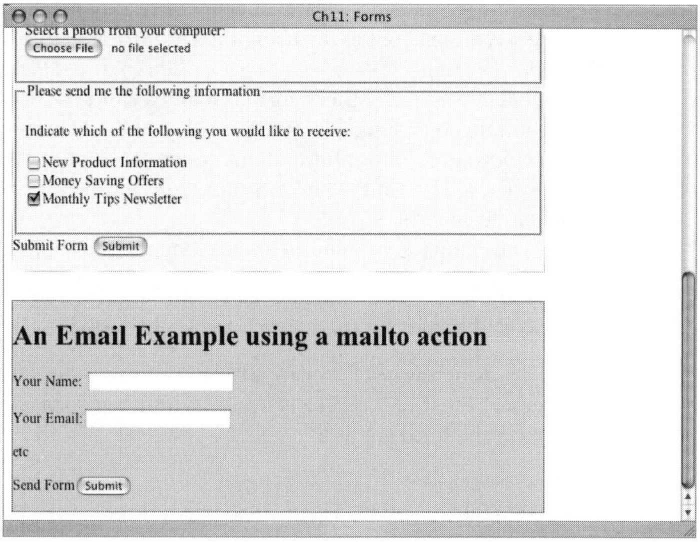

FIGURE 11.13
The action in this form is a `mailto`.

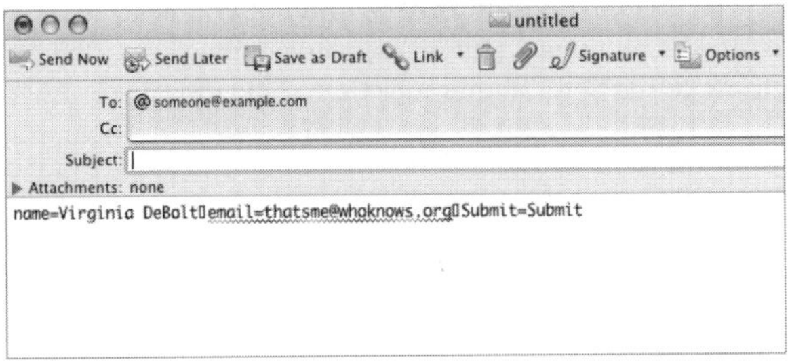

FIGURE 11.14

A formatted e-mail from a `mailto` submission

Using a Table to Lay Out a Form

In the first two forms you made, the `for` attribute isn't strictly necessary according to the standards specification. The specifications say that the `label` is all that is required. As an example, without the `for` attribute and its matching `id`, one of the previous `form` elements would be:

```
<label><input name="send" type="checkbox" value="newsletter"
  checked="checked" />Monthly Tips Newsletter</label>
```

This is another case where W3C recommendations and reality bump heads. Because of that, most people include the `for` attribute in their markup for every `label` element. Keep an eye on the accessibility news, because that may change.

Even more accessibility issues arise when a table is used to lay out a form. Designers lay out forms in a table so they can achieve a uniform alignment of text and `form` elements. However, separating the `label` from the `input` element by putting these two items in two different `td` elements creates a disconnect in logic for some types of screen readers. This is where the `label for="somename"` markup really shines, because it creates a logical connection between the information in the two table cells. In the table layout `form` you are about to do, using the `for` attribute is the only way to logically connect the `label` to the `input` element.

It is debatable as to whether a form is really a valid use for a data table. I will leave that issue alone and concentrate on making sure you know how to do it accessibly. What usually happens is the table uses two columns. In one column there is some text telling the user what to type into the form, perhaps their name. Then in the next column there is the input `form` element. The two parts of the form are in separate `td` cells.

Here is an example, in a couple of `td` elements, showing how it's done:

```
<td><label for="email">Your Email:</label></td>
<td><input type="text" name="email" id="email" /></td>
```

If you are using the `ch11_forms_start.html` page, find the `div="table"` section of the page. The `table` element must be completely nested within the `form` element, so before you can build the table, you must get the form started:

```
<div id="table">
  <h1>A Table Layout Example using a label for attribute </h1>
```

```
<form name="tableex" method="post"
  action="http://www.example.com/somescript.pl">

</form>
```

This will be another incomplete example just to let you learn the basics. The table will need three rows with two columns: a row for Name, a row for Email, and a row for Submit. (In order to have unique id values for this example, the numeral 3 was appended to the name and e-mail IDs.)

Instead of walking you through the table row by row, the entire div is shown in Listing 11.2. Use it to complete the last form. Change the values for width, summary, or border according to your own ideas.

LISTING 11.2: The Entire *div id="table"* Element

```
<div id="table">
  <h1>A Table Layout Example using a label for attribute </h1>
  <form name="tableex" method="post"
    action="http://www.example.com/somescript.pl">
  <table width="90%"  border="0"
    summary="layout table containing labeled form fields">
    <tr>
      <td width="30%">
      <label for="name3">Your Name:</label></td>
      <td width="70%"><input type="text" name="name" id="name3" /></td>
    </tr>
    <tr>
      <td><label for="email3">Your Email:</label></td>
      <td><input type="text" name="email" id="email3" /></td>
    </tr>
    <tr>
      <td><label for="submit">Submit:</label></td>
      <td><input type="submit" name="submit" id="submit" value="Submit" /></td>
    </tr>
  </table>
  </form>
</div>
```

Compare your results in the browser with Figure 11.15. Note carefully the capitalization of "Submit" vs. "submit".

That completes the third form and gives you the basic knowledge of how to build any type of form element you might need.

You can compare your finished page with ch11_forms_finished.html from the CD or with the complete page in Listing 11.3.

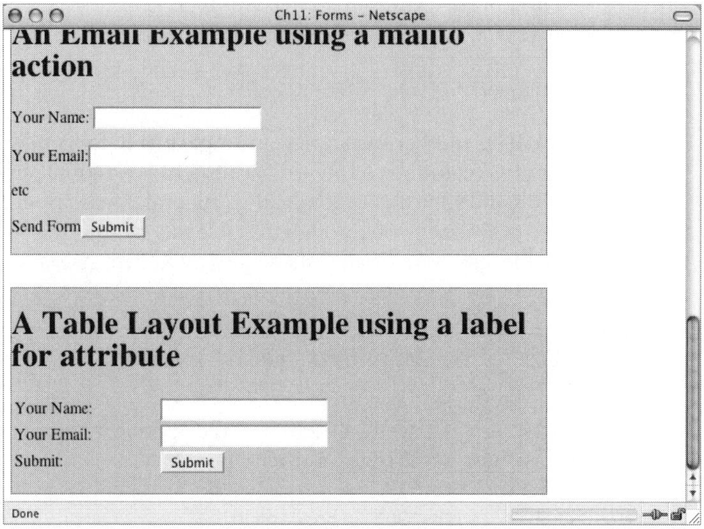

FIGURE 11.15
A form in a layout table must have the for attribute with the label element.

LISTING 11.3: *ch11_forms_finished.html*

```
<!DOCTYPE html PUBLIC "-//W3C//DTD XHTML 1.0 Transitional//EN"
  "http://www.w3.org/TR/xhtml1/DTD/xhtml1-transitional.dtd">
<html xmlns="http://www.w3.org/1999/xhtml">
<head>
<title>Ch11: Forms: Finished Page</title>
<style type="text/css">
#script {
  background: #FFC;
  border: 1px dotted #3FF;
  width: 80%;
}
#mailto {
  background: #CDE8B7;
  border: 1px dotted #606;
  margin-top: 2em;
  width: 80%;
}
#table {
  background: #C2CDE8;
  border: 1px dotted #C03;
  margin-top: 2em;
  width: 80%;
}
</style>
</head>
```

```
<body>
<div id="script">
  <h1>A Script Example</h1>
  <form name="scriptex" id="scriptex" method="post"
    action="http://www.example.com/somescript.pl" enctype="multipart/form-data">
  <input name="recipient" type="hidden" value="someone@somewhere.com" />
  <fieldset><legend>Personal Information</legend>
    <p><label for="name">Your Name: <input type="text" name="name" id="name" />
      </label></p>
    <p><label for="email">Your E-mail: <input type="text" name="email"
      id="email" /></label></p>
    <p><label for="password">Your support password: <input type="password"
      name="password" id="password" /></label></p>
  </fieldset>

  <fieldset><legend>Your Support Question</legend>
    <p><label for="problem">Describe Your Problem: <br />
      <textarea name="problem" cols="30" rows="5" id="problem">
      </textarea></label></p>
    <p><label for="camera">Select your camera type
        <select name="camera" id="camera">
          <option value="sony" selected="selected">Sony</option>
          <option value="kodak">Kodak</option>
          <option value="polaroid">Polaroid</option>
          <option value="canon">Canon</option>
        </select>
      </label></p>
    <p>Is your camera still under warranty?<br />
      Yes <input name="warranty" type="radio" value="Yes" />
      No <input name="warranty" type="radio" value="No" /></p>
    <p>Do you have a photograph taken with your camera that shows an example of
      the problem? If so, you can upload it.</p>
    <p><label for="photo">Select a photo from your computer:<br />
      <input type="file" name="photo" id="photo" /></label></p>
  </fieldset>

  <fieldset><legend>Please send me the following information</legend>
    <p>Indicate which of the following you would like to receive:</p>
    <p><label for="newProd"><input name="send" type="checkbox" value="newProd"
      id="newProd" />New Product Information</label><br />
    <label for="offers"><input name="send" type="checkbox" value="offers"
      id="offers" />Money Saving Offers</label><br />
    <label for="newsletter"><input name="send" type="checkbox" value="newsletter"
      checked="checked" id="newsletter" />Monthly Tips Newsletter</label></p>
  </fieldset>

  <input name="submit" type="button" value="Submit" />
  </form>
```

```
    </div>

    <div id="mailto">
      <h1>An Email Example using a mailto action </h1>
      <form name="mailex" method="post"  enctype="text/plain"
        action="mailto:someone@example.com">
        <p><label for="name2">Your Name:<input type="text" name="name" id="name2" />
          </label></p>
        <p><label for="email2">Your Email:<input type="text" name="email"
          id="email2" /></label></p>
        <p>etc</p>
        <p><input type="submit" name="Submit" value="Submit" /></p>
      </form>
    </div>

    <div id="table">
      <h1>A Table Layout Example using a label for attribute </h1>
      <form name="tableex" method="post"
        action="http://www.example.com/somescript.pl">
        <table width="90%"  border="0"
          summary="layout table containing labeled form fields">
          <tr>
            <td width="30%">
            <label for="name3">Your Name:</label></td>
            <td width="70%"><input type="text" name="name" id="name3" /></td>
          </tr>
          <tr>
            <td><label for="email3">Your Email:</label></td>
            <td><input type="text" name="email" id="email3" /></td>
          </tr>
          <tr>
            <td><label for="submit">Submit: </label></td>
            <td><input type="submit" name="submit" id="submit" value="Submit" /></td>
          </tr>
        </table>
      </form>
    </div>
    </body>
    </html>
```

Learn the CSS

Certain things about form elements fall into the realm of browser control rather than web designer control. If you are using z-index on a page to position elements one atop another, form controls are always going to be on top of everything else. Form element controls should and do remain consistently rendered by browsers. This is really about usability and accessibility—if designers were allowed to use CSS to completely change the way form controls looked, the form might become difficult or confusing to use.

Even so, there is still plenty you can do with `background-color`, `color`, `font`, `border`, `padding`, `text-align`, and other CSS properties to make a form's looks remain in keeping with your overall site design and color scheme.

Open up a new blank document in your text editor and save it using the filename `ch11_forms.css`. Then add a link to the still blank stylesheet to the XHTML document containing your form. Add the `link` element immediately following the `title` element in your document so that it comes before the embedded `style` element in the document `head`. If you save the CSS page in the same folder as the XHTML page, the link should look like this:

```
<link href="ch11_forms.css" rel="stylesheet" type="text/css" />
```

TIP Inserting the link to the external stylesheet before the embedded `style` element means that the embedded styles will be in closer proximity to the styled elements.

Styling the *fieldset*

The `fieldset` elements are bumping into one another vertically. A `margin-bottom: 1em` rule would separate them a bit. And they are of the same `width` as the `form` element. Reduce them a bit to width: 90%.

NOTE The `fieldset` element *could* be given a `background-color` value, but since this `form` is already in a `div` with a `background-color`, I won't add that. The `background-color` for a `fieldset` might be a very effective CSS rule on a different page, however.

The two rules I suggest are

```
fieldset {
  margin-bottom: 1em;
  width: 90%;
}
```

With that in your stylesheet, your browser should display a page similar to Figure 11.16.

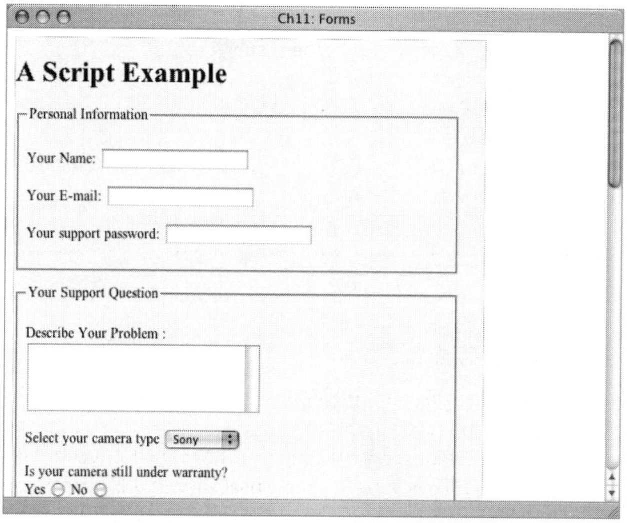

FIGURE 11.16
`margin-bottom` and width applied to the `fieldset`

The Legend

Styling the font and the color of the legend is easy enough. Use bold and a priority list of sans-serif fonts for the font-weight and font-family. Changing the color to blue (or #00F) would look good. I think a little added letter-spacing would look good, too, perhaps just 0.1em:

```
legend {
  font-weight: bold;
  font-family: Arial, Helvetica, sans-serif;
  color: #00F;
  letter-spacing: 0.1em;
}
```

Depending on your browser, that rule should make the legend look like Figure 11.17. The same style in the Opera browser (Figure 11.18) demonstrates the point that form elements display differently at the discretion of the browser maker.

FIGURE 11.17
The legend with a style added

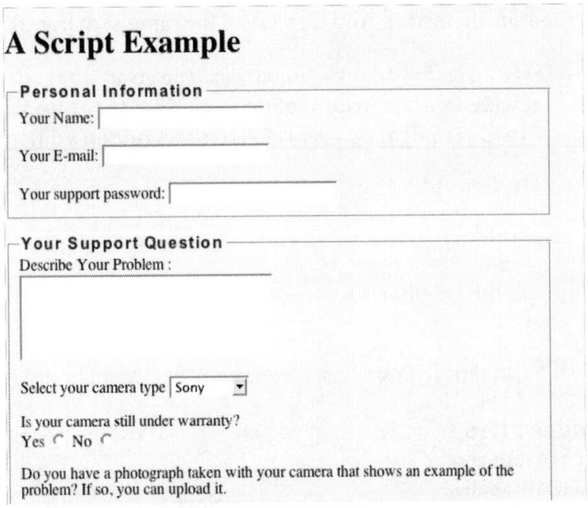

FIGURE 11.18
The legend as rendered by the Opera browser

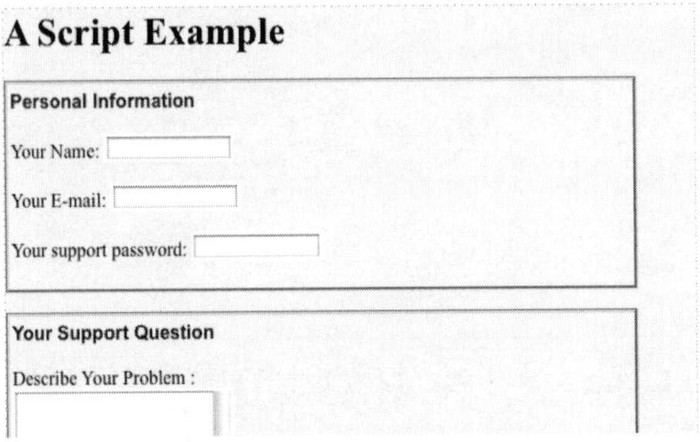

Paragraphs and Labels

Most of the form elements are in p elements. Furthermore, most of the p elements have label elements. On this page, if you styled the p elements, you would, in effect, be styling the label descendants as well. There are paragraphs on the page that don't have the <p><label></label></p> structure. This is one example to watch:

```
<p>Indicate which of the following you would like to receive:</p>
```

In a real-world situation where a form is a part of a site and requires navigation, banner areas, footer areas, and other site features incorporated on the page, the structure is more complex. Styling the p elements might or might not affect label elements; furthermore, styling for the p and label elements might need to be different on a real-world page.

I'll treat the p and label elements differently here to give the CSS a more real-world feel.

Start with p. Make it font-size: medium and font-family: Verdana, Arial, Helvetica, sans-serif. Verdana is different enough from the Arial you used elsewhere to make the appearance of the p easy to distinguish visually. Here's the rule:

```
p {
    font: medium Verdana, Arial, Helvetica, sans-serif;
}
```

As you can see in Figure 11.19, both p and the descendant label elements are Verdana with this rule in effect.

Make enough of a change in the rule for label to see a difference visually. Make the font-size: small and change back to Arial for the font-family. Like this:

```
label {
    font: small Arial, Helvetica, sans-serif;
}
```

FIGURE 11.19
The p element with a medium Verdana font style

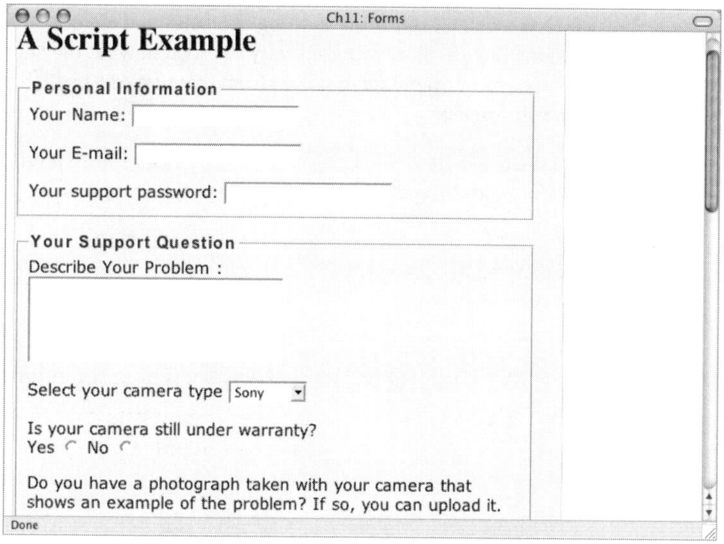

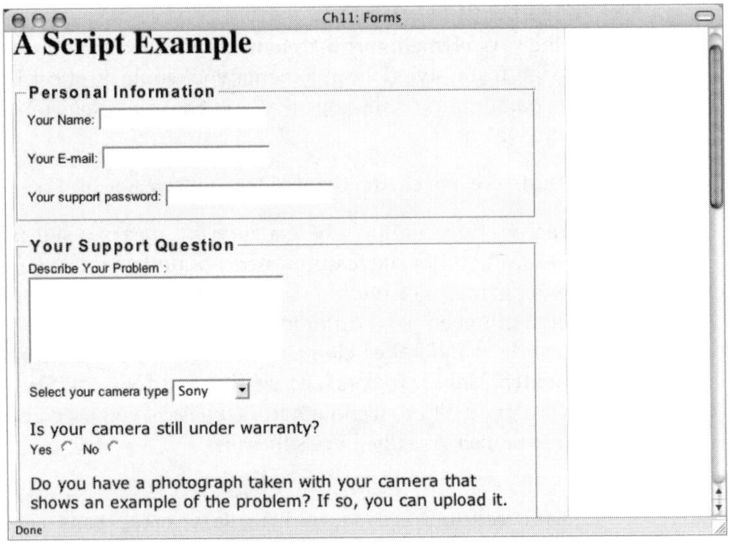

FIGURE 11.20
A different style rule in effect for p and `label`

FIGURE 11.20

You should notice a difference between the p and the `label` elements now, similar to what you see in Figure 11.20.

The Background Color of a *form* Element

It is possible to change the `background-color` on `input`, `select`, `textarea`, and other `form` elements. You can do one, just for the practice, although it may not look very good on this page, and you may not see any change at all depending on the browser you are using.

Since the largest `form` element on the page that will show the effect of `background-color` is the `textarea` element, write a style for it.

WARNING   I don't recommend using CSS rules that are not uniformly implemented in all browsers as a good practice. Since browsers vary so much in what they do with `background-color` on `form` elements, I recommend staying away from that property until the browsers come into alignment with the specifications.

If you write a style for `color` in the `textarea` element, it will affect the color of the text that the user types in the field. Here is an example of a rule for `textarea`:

```
textarea {
  background-color: #CCC;
  color: #009;
}
```

Look at the results in the browser and try typing something in the `textarea` field yourself to see the color (Figure 11.21).

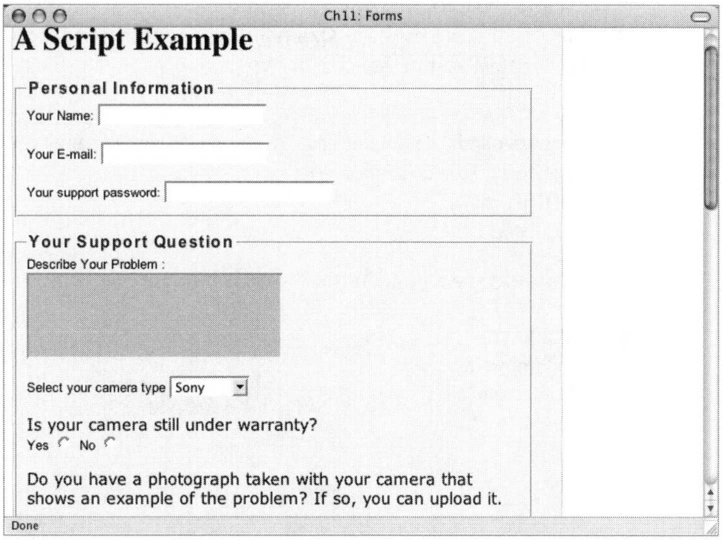

FIGURE 11.21
A background color and a
color may appear for the
`textarea` element.

The Script Example's Background

An interesting graphic background would be fun on this page. Find `camera.jpg` on the CD and save it in the same folder with your XHTML document. Anything on the page can have a graphic background, including the `body` element, the various `div` elements, the `form` elements, or the `fieldset` elements. Just to pick one and see how it works, use the `camera.jpg` image as a `background-image` for the `div id="script"` element.

As you recall, there is already an embedded `style` element in the document `head` that contains some style rules for the `#script` selector. They are

```
#script {
   background: #FFC;
   border: 1px dotted #3FF;
   width: 80%;
}
```

The new rule adding a `background-image` to the `#script` element could be written in the external stylesheet. However, the rule in the embedded `style` comes in the Cascade *after* the external stylesheet so it has to be changed to get rid of the yellow background color. It also makes sense to keep all the rules affecting the `#script` selector in one place, so make the changes to the rule in the embedded `style` element and not on the external stylesheet.

First, change the background color to `transparent`:

```
#script {
   background: transparent;
   border: 1px dotted #3FF;
   width: 80%;
}
```

Next add the URL, like this: url(camera.jpg). A repeat-y would work best for this element, so add that. Finally, set the background-position for left top. The complete changed #script selector rule, written in shorthand, is now:

```
#script {
  background: transparent url(camera.jpg) repeat-y left top;
  border: 1px dotted #3FF;
  width: 80%;
}
```

You should see a page in the browser like the one shown in Figure 11.22.

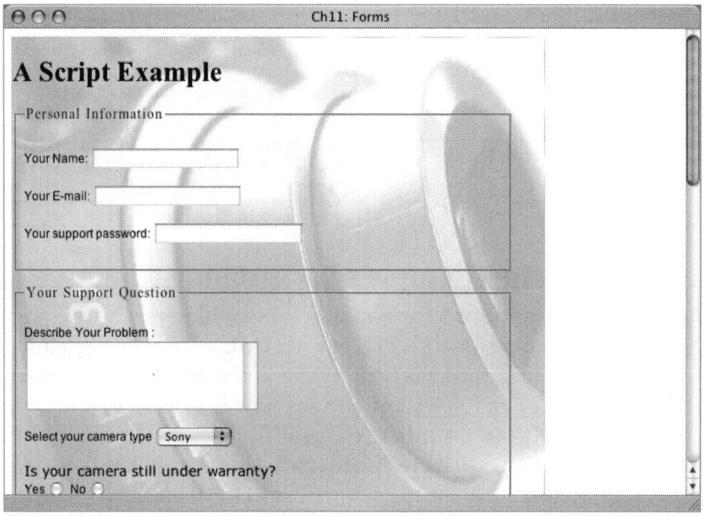

FIGURE 11.22
A background image in
the #script element

Real World Example

Molly Holzschlag of molly.com is a leading writer on web topics. She has over 20 books to her credit. She is the technical editor of this book, a fact that makes me both proud to be working with her and grateful for her expert help.

Her site can be held up as a good example in almost any chapter of this book, so while you are looking at her forms be sure you take time to appreciate the rest of what you see at molly.com. Molly likes to take small polls and surveys regularly. This means that most of her pages contain at least two form elements: one for the search box and one for the survey choices.

Figure 11.23 shows an example of what the main page of molly.com looked like on a particular day. The survey form is attractive, clear, usable and accessible, which all adds up to the perfect form example.

FIGURE 11.23
There are two `form` elements on this page at `molly.com`.

Challenge Yourself

Take some time to experiment with the CSS described in this chapter. Try out some ideas of your own, and see if you can make the changes suggested here.

1. Style the `legend` elements on this page using a black background color and a white font color.

2. Write `fieldset` rules that use `padding`, `border`, or `margin`.

3. Try using the `camera.jpg` graphic as a background for the entire page or for a different div such as `#mailto`.

4. Style the `#table form` selector: perhaps a border, a background, or some padding.

5. Style the `h1` elements on the page.

Summary

A form can be submitted by e-mail without an associated script. However, most of the time a script is needed to help process the form data being submitted. There are sources for free form processing scripts on the Internet.

The essential attributes of the form element include method and action. Individual form elements you learned to create include fieldset, legend, input, textarea, select, radio button, checkbox, and the submit button. Form elements need a label. The label for markup should be used for clarity and usability.

Any CSS rules you have learned up to this point for font, background, color, border, padding, alignment, position, and width can be used to write styles for forms. However, certain things about the appearance and function of form elements remain in the control of the browser as a means of ensuring accessibility and usability in forms.

In Chapter 12, you will learn how to put the web pages you make in a place where the rest of the world can see them! You are ready for the World Wide Web.

Chapter 12

Publishing and Testing Your Pages

You can make web pages 24 hours a day, but until you move them from your computer onto a server that can be reached on the World Wide Web, no one else will see what you have done.

This chapter will be an excursion into the world of *FTP (File Transfer Protocol)*. FTP transfers files from one computer to another. You will learn how to find a server space, or a *web host*, where your files can be put (by FTP) and seen by anyone who visits your pages.

There are places on the Internet that give you free space for a web page, usually in exchange for some ad space on your pages. You will learn how to find and use free web space. You will also learn how to get your own domain name and server space for your domain.

This chapter will show you how to register your site with the search engines and how to create special files that are placed on the server to manage your site.

After your pages are on a server, test them carefully for function, validity, accessibility and display quality. Several resources for testing your site are provided.

Finding Free Server Space

The companies that offer server space are called web hosts or web hosting companies. These companies usually have hundreds of servers. For a small monthly fee you can get space on one of these servers that will be for your exclusive use and will serve your web pages to any visitors to your URL.

You don't have to spend any money to try your new web design skills, however. These places have free web hosting plans:

- `http://www.netfirms.com/`
- `http://geocities.yahoo.com/`
- `http://www.tripod.lycos.com/host`

You have to look carefully for the free option, but they have one. While there are drawbacks and irritations (chiefly unwanted advertising) involved with using one of the free hosting sites, it does give you some practice getting your pages and images where they can be seen. If you are not ready for your own domain but just want to learn how to post pages on the web, free hosting is a good first step. You can learn the basics of using FTP and revising pages and re-uploading them and make sure images show up and links work properly. You can check your pages with various testing strategies that will be detailed in the following paragraphs. In brief, the free services are a good first step.

If you pick one of the companies listed previously, you need to read their instructions on how to manage your account and use FTP. The free hosting plans may include a browser-based interface that lets you upload files and see your server space in a browser window rather than with a separate FTP application as described in the next section. There will also be information there telling you what the URL for your pages will be so other people can find them.

Another free option you may have is with your *Internet service provider (ISP)*. Your ISP is the company you pay for your Internet connection service and e-mail account at your home. There are a multitude of choices among ISPs, but some of the larger ones include Earthlink, SBC Yahoo!, Roadrunner, AOL, and MSN. Sometimes your ISP provides you with a small amount of space on a server as part of your package. If that is the case with your ISP, there should be information on their website telling you how to FTP to your space and what your URL will be.

If you don't want to use one of the free hosting plans, see the section later in this chapter that explains how to buy a domain name and find a host for your domain.

Using FTP Software

There are trial versions of several FTP software tools on the CD accompanying this book. The File Transfer Protocol is really rather simple. You can *put* files somewhere, or you can *get* files from somewhere.

If you are familiar with using the command prompt on Windows or the terminal window on Mac OS X, you can FTP directly from that interface. You don't need any particular software tool. However, using a software tool such as those provided on the CD often makes much more sense visually to nonprogrammers who aren't familiar with command-line work.

FTP software tools are very easy to use and often let you drag and drop files from a window representing your computer to a window representing the server.

When you sign up for web hosting, you receive an e-mail from the hosting company with your FTP information, including the FTP address, your username, your password, and the directory path. You'll need this information when setting up your FTP software to connect to the server. Look at Figure 12.1 to examine the way you use the information in your FTP software.

Figure 12.1 shows an FTP application called Transmit. Other FTP tools may look slightly different or use slightly different terms. However, the basic information the tool needs will be the same no matter what terms are used or how the software looks.

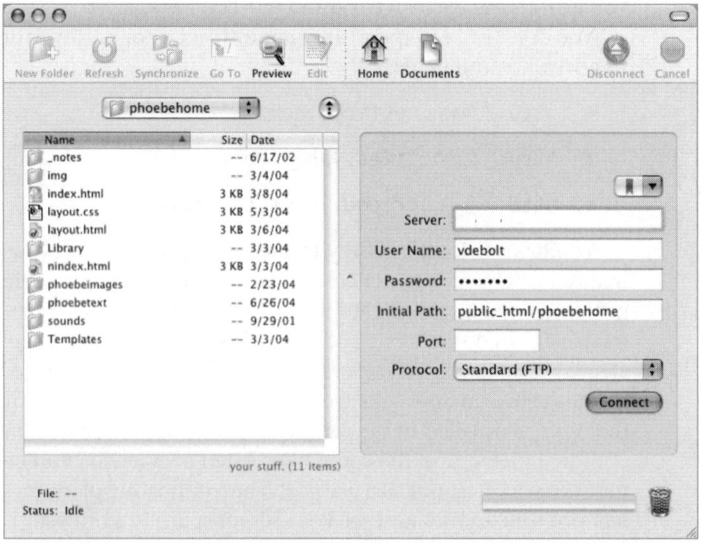

FIGURE 12.1

The server connection information screen in the Transmit 2 FTP tool

In Figure 12.1, you see your own computer on the left side. Transmit calls it "your stuff." Other tools may call it "local" or "your computer." In the figure, the view on the left side shows a particular folder on the computer. The folder name is phoebehome. The connection to be made will be to the server where the files from the folder phoebehome will be put.

Look at the right side of the figure. The server information goes here. (In this figure, the server name has been blanked out.) You put the FTP address in the form field where it says Server. Other tools might label this box FTP Address or URL. The information you put here depends on the particular server; it might be something like ftp.*example*.com or www.*example*.com or even a server number. When you open a web hosting account, the address that goes in the server form field will be sent to you with the initial e-mail from the hosting company.

Next are form fields where you enter your username and password. These two fields probably use the same terms no matter what software you are using.

The Initial Path form field might be called Directory or Directory Path in a different FTP tool. The information you put in this field is the name of the folder that contains your files. Most of the time, servers use names such as public_html, www, or htdocs for this path name. This is another important piece of information that is sent to you in the initial e-mail you receive from the hosting company when you open an account.

In the example in Figure 12.1, there is a subfolder in the path. The main site is located in public_html, but this particular set of files will be put into a subfolder called phoebehome.

There's also a field where a port number could be entered; a port number is not needed in this case, so it is blank. (In most situations, the default port is used to FTP, and there is no need to indicate any other choice.) A select menu has been set for Standard FTP. This particular software allows you to choose between standard FTP and secure FTP for the file transfers. Secure FTP is used for encrypted file transfers, which you most likely won't need for simple web page transfers.

The Transmit 2 FTP software does not have a form field for proxy server, but some FTP tools do. If you are working for a company that requires you to use a proxy server to get to the WWW, they will provide you with the address of the proxy server. As with the port number, if you don't need to enter a proxy address, simply leave it blank.

When all the information regarding the server has been filled in, click the Connect button. Other FTP software might label this button Choose or OK. If you did everything properly, when you click this button, you should be connected to the server.

After you connect, the view changes to show you the files on the server, as in Figure 12.2.

The first time you connect, there may not be any files on the server, or there may be one file there named index.html that the hosting company put in that space. This file usually says something like "Coming Soon" and is meant to be overwritten by your own index.html page.

Figure 12.2 shows a website that already has files and folders uploaded from the local computer (your stuff) to the remote computer (their stuff). Notice that not everything from the *your stuff* side was uploaded to the *their stuff* side. For example, there are folders called Library and Templates that were used in the making of this site, but that are not needed on the server. Also notice that the folder names that are on the server exactly match the folder names in the local site folder. Your links will break and your images may not display if you don't match up filenames, subfolder names, and structure exactly.

To copy a file from your computer to the server, simply drag and drop the file (or an entire folder when you first upload a folder) from the local side to the remote side. This is known in FTP lingo as *put*.

FIGURE 12.2
Local files are on the
left and remote files
are on the right.

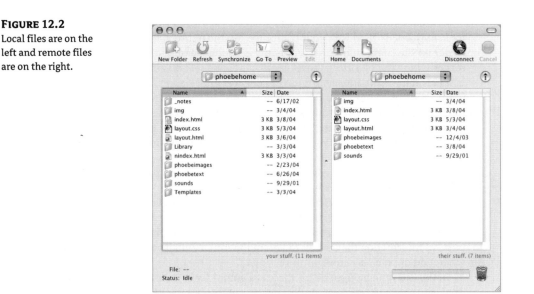

TIP   Before you put a file, be sure to save it.

If there was already an index.html file on the server and you revise it or create a new index.html page and put it on the server, it will overwrite the existing index.html file on the server.

Files can also be copied from the server to your computer. Simply drag and drop a file from the remote window into the local window. This is known in FTP lingo as *get*.

WARNING   When you get a file from the server and bring it to your computer, it overwrites the existing file you have by that name on your computer.

To transfer files to or from an individual subfolder, simply double-click to open the folder on both your computer and the server, then drag and drop the individual files. Figure 12.3 shows a view inside one of the subfolders in the example site.

To recap the work process, you do the following to publish a website:

1.   Create the XHTML, CSS, and image files on your computer.

2.   Use FTP software to transfer the completed files to a server.

3.   Launch a browser and look at your page on the WWW.

4.   If needed, edit or revise your files and upload the changed version to the server.

TIP   If you forget to put a needed file on the server, the user will see some sort of error such as a "File Not Found" message or an icon representing a missing image. This will also happen if you don't match the site structure on the server with your local site structure.

FIGURE 12.3
A view inside a subfolder on the local side and the server side

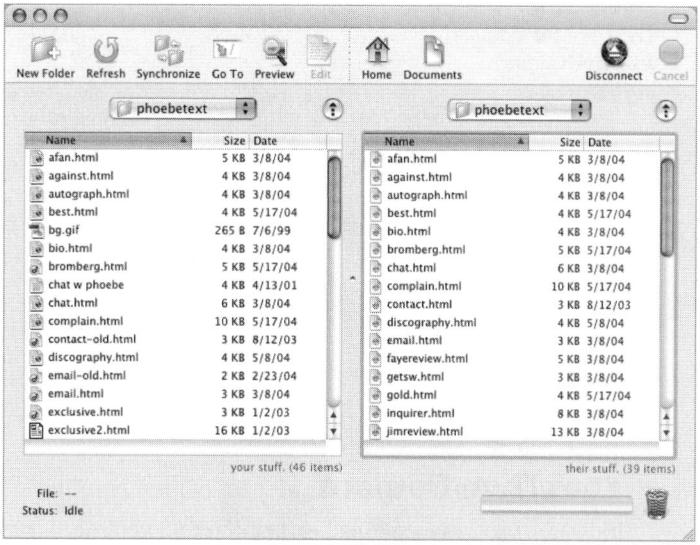

Setting Permissions

Most FTP software has the capability to *set permissions*, which means you can specify who has permission to read a file, write to a file, and execute a file. Permissions can also be set on an entire folder.

For XHTML or CSS files, there is no need to set permissions. To make a form submit, however, you must set permissions on the script used with the form so that it can be executed.

TIP See Chapter 11 for more on forms.

A script is often kept in a special directory on the web server called `cgi-bin`. The `cgi-bin` directory is at the same level as the `public_html` or the www directory. Therefore, if your FTP connection information is set to open in the `public_html` or www directory, you won't be able to see the `cgi-bin` directory or to upload files into it. If you are uploading a script, you need to temporarily leave the FTP connection directory field blank so you are able to see the `cgi-bin` directory when you connect to the server. The `cgi-bin` directory is often the only place you are allowed to store executable files such as scripts, and it is the directory where you will be working if you need to set permissions.

Permission is given to an individual user, a group of users, or to the whole world when specifying who can read, write, or execute a file.

In your FTP software, you can look at the properties (or choose Get Info) for an individual file or folder to see options such as those shown in Figure 12.4.

As you can see in Figure 12.4, this individual HTML file is set to let the world read it, but only the user (that's you) can write it. This is the normal setting. The only time you need to think about setting permissions is when you want to change the normal setting.

TIP An XHTML file won't execute, but a script will.

FIGURE 12.4
Setting permissions for
an individual file

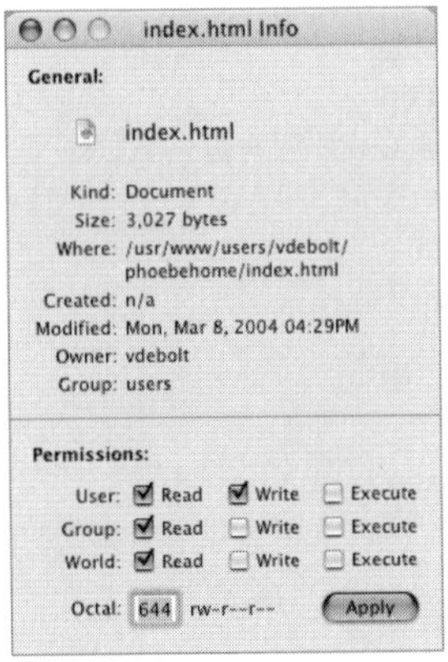

Your Own Domain

If the free services mentioned earlier don't fill your needs permanently, you can purchase web hosting services and your own domain name.

You can buy a domain name fairly inexpensively. A domain name is the part of a web address after the www; for example, in www.sybex.com, "sybex" is the domain name. There are a multitude of companies that will register your domain name. Often the same company that provides web hosting space for you will provide a domain name registration service as well. If you used any of the free hosting plans described at the beginning of the chapter, you probably noticed that the companies were selling hosting and domain name registration as you searched for the offer of free hosting space.

Some popular domain name registration and web hosting companies with good reputations are

◆ www.godaddy.com

◆ www.pairnic.com with www.pair.com

◆ www.register.com

Sometimes people feel that a local company will provide more accessible customer support, so you might check the reputations of the local companies in your area when you make a decision about hosting and domain name registration.

Many of the big-name Internet companies that you might already be familiar with, such as Yahoo!, also provide hosting and domain name registration.

Any domain name registration company, or registrar, will let you search *whois*, the index of names that are already registered, to see if a name you want is available.

Although it is not necessary, it is often easier to sign up for both web hosting and domain name registration with the same company. That way, all your information is available in one location.

The domain registrar must know the *DNS (Domain Name Server)* information about your server, or web host, so that the domain name can be associated with the correct server. When someone types www.*yourdomain*.com in their browser location bar, the DNS information is what connects that someone to your particular server out of all the millions of servers that are delivering web pages to the Internet.

Testing the Site

As you are designing the site, you check pages on your local computer. But it is also important to test everything about the site once it is on the Internet. Sometimes things seem to work on your local computer but are broken on a server. All sorts of problems may arise, including these and other major or minor disasters:

◆ Incorrect file paths

◆ Incorrect links

◆ Site organization not being copied properly when you upload to the server

◆ Forgotten files that never get uploaded

◆ Filenames with spaces or typos in them

Make it a habit to check every page of a site after you put it on the WWW. Check all the links, look for missing images, play any sound files, check to make sure the styles are working: test everything. If something is not working right, you need to find it and fix it immediately.

If an image does not appear, try these troubleshooting steps:

◆ Check the file path.

◆ Make sure the image is on the server in the place the `src` attribute points to.

◆ Make sure you are using a JPEG, GIF, or PNG file format instead of one that a browser won't display.

If a page cannot be found, check that the page is on the server in the place the `href` attribute points to and make sure the file has the correct file extension.

If you included sound or any type of multimedia such as Flash with your page, verify that the file plays when it is supposed to play. Check on the server to be sure the sound files or other multimedia files are in the place where they are supposed to be. If a special plug-in is needed to play multimedia files, have it installed in your browser.

Test the site in a variety of browsers and with different operating systems if you can. If you don't have access to more than one computer and operating system, send out a request to your colleagues and friends asking them to check the site using their systems. If they find something wrong, ask them to send you a screen shot and tell you what browser, what operating system, and what screen resolution they used to view the site.

TIP A for-fee service called Browser Cam (`www.browsercam.com`) will send you a screen shot of your web page using any operating system or browser you want tested.

The Validators

An important part of testing your site is making sure you have valid code. XHTML is valid when it follows the rules for the DTD declared in the page's DOCTYPE declaration. You can use the free validation services offered by the W3C to check your XHTML and your CSS for correctness.

The XHTML validator is at `http://validator.w3.org/`. The CSS validator is at `http://jigsaw.w3.org/css-validator/`. In both validators, you simply enter the URL of your XHTML or CSS file on the server and let the tool check your page.

CHARACTER ENCODING AND VALIDATION

Use the validators while still in the design process to test your markup and style rules. When you are sure you are writing correct and valid pages, it is easier to get pages to display as you want. Validation helps you spot your problems early. If you don't have the page on a server yet, the W3C lets you upload a file from your computer using one of those dandy `input type="file"` forms you learned about in Chapter 11. The character encoding is added to the web page on the server, so if you upload a file from your computer for validation and there is an error about character encoding, don't worry.

If you get an error about character encoding when testing a page using a URL from your server, then you need to check with the hosting company to see what type of encoding is set on the server. If for some reason the server does not have encoding set, you can add a `meta` element to your page to give your page this common character encoding for English: `iso-8859-1`. The `meta` element goes in the document head. It is

```
<meta http-equiv="Content-Type" content="text/html; charset=iso-8859-1"/>
```

The tool reports back with a detailed list of any problems you have in your code. It points out the exact line where the problem is and gives some rather minimal help in explaining what you need to do to correct the error.

Sometimes the validator results contain a message that is not entirely clear. I have learned to pick out the key phrase from such messages and search on it in Google. I can usually quickly find something that helps me understand what the message means and what I need to do with the code to fix it.

Make changes to your original file, upload it to the server, and then run the validator again. Do this as many times as you need to until every error has been corrected.

Accessibility Testing

When you have tested all your links and pages yourself and you have used the HTML and CSS validators to make sure your code is pristine, you still have one more important test of your site. You need to test for accessibility.

A great deal of accessibility testing is done online using "Bobby" at

```
http://bobby.watchfire.com/bobby/html/en/index.jsp
```

Like the validators at the W3C, the Bobby tool checks an online page using a URL. You can select whether you want the page to be tested against the W3C's Web Accessibility Guidelines or against the U. S. Section 508 Guidelines.

The W3C guidelines evaluated by Bobby check that you do the following on your page:

1. Provide equivalent alternatives to auditory and visual content.

2. Don't rely on color alone.

3. Use markup and style sheets and do so properly.

4. Clarify natural language usage.

5. Create tables that transform gracefully.

6. Ensure that pages featuring new technologies transform gracefully.

7. Ensure user control of time-sensitive content changes.

8. Ensure direct accessibility of embedded user interfaces.

9. Design for device-independence.

10. Use interim solutions.

11. Use W3C technologies and guidelines.

12. Provide context and orientation information.

13. Provide clear navigation mechanisms.

14. Ensure that documents are clear and simple.

Each of these guidelines from the W3C has several checkpoints. Some checkpoints are assigned a priority. Bobby reports point out any problems with your page according to the priority level. If you have any Priority 1 problems, Bobby mentions them first. This is how the W3C explains the priorities:

Priority 1: A web content developer *must* satisfy this checkpoint. Otherwise, one or more groups will find it impossible to access information in the document. Satisfying this checkpoint is a basic requirement for some groups to be able to use web documents.

Priority 2: A web content developer *should* satisfy this checkpoint. Otherwise, one or more groups will find it difficult to access information in the document. Satisfying this checkpoint will remove significant barriers to accessing web documents.

Priority 3: A web content developer *may* address this checkpoint. Otherwise, one or more groups will find it somewhat difficult to access information in the document. Satisfying this checkpoint will improve access to web documents.

TIP The complete document on guidelines, checkpoints, techniques for each checkpoint, and priorities is at www.w3.org/TR/WCAG10.

When you read through the report written by Bobby, you should definitely fix any Priority 1 problems you have. Priority 2 and 3 problems require some judgment on your part as to whether or not they really require changes.

If a page fails to meet an accessibility requirement, Bobby points it out in no uncertain terms, such as, "This page does not meet the requirements for Bobby AAA Approved status. Below is a list of 1 Priority 1 error(s) found."

Beyond mentioning any failure to meet requirements, Bobby may generate a long list of things it calls "User Checks." Don't let them scare you. They aren't necessarily a problem. The User Checks point out areas that could *potentially* be a problem, and you are asked to make sure that no such problem exists on your page.

One of the Priority 1 issues Bobby may raise is, "If style sheets are ignored or unsupported, are pages still readable and usable?" Certain browsers may allow you to look at web pages with the CSS turned off. Of course, you can test this on your own pages by simply temporarily removing the links to any stylesheets and seeing how the page looks in the browser. Remember, it doesn't have to look good without CSS, it only has to be readable and usable.

You can test what your pages would look like in a text-only browser (even the images won't appear in this simulation) by using the Lynx viewer here:

```
http://www.delorie.com/web/lynxview.html
```

If you can read, understand, and navigate your page in a text-only browser, that is a good indication that the page will be usable in various accessibility devices such as screen readers.

TIP   A site with a variety of helpful accessibility tools is Accessify, at `http://www.accessify.com/tools-and-wizards/default.asp`.

Getting Help from Browser Extensions

Open source projects provide source code for software to programmers and developers who are interested in working to improve a software application. One of the better known such projects is Mozilla, at `www.mozilla.org`. This open source project created the Mozilla browser, which eventually becomes a version of the Netscape browser. Mozilla is also the source of the Firefox browser, which has Web Developer extensions that are very helpful in testing and debugging your web pages.

NOTE   Mozilla is a complete suite of products, including an advanced e-mail and newsgroup client, an IRC chat client, and HTML editing. Firefox is a web browser.

You can download the latest version of Firefox at `www.mozilla.org/products/firefox`. Once you have Firefox installed on your computer, you can download the Web Developer extensions at `update.mozilla.org/extensions/`. There are over 100 extensions for Mozilla and Firefox, but the ones you need are named Web Developer. With the Web Developer extensions installed in Firefox, you have a toolbar with invaluable help in testing and validating your pages.

See Figure 12.5 for a view of the Web Developer toolbar in Firefox.

Let's look at some of the tools available to you in some of the choices in the toolbar. Look at Figure 12.6 for an expanded view of the Validation menu.

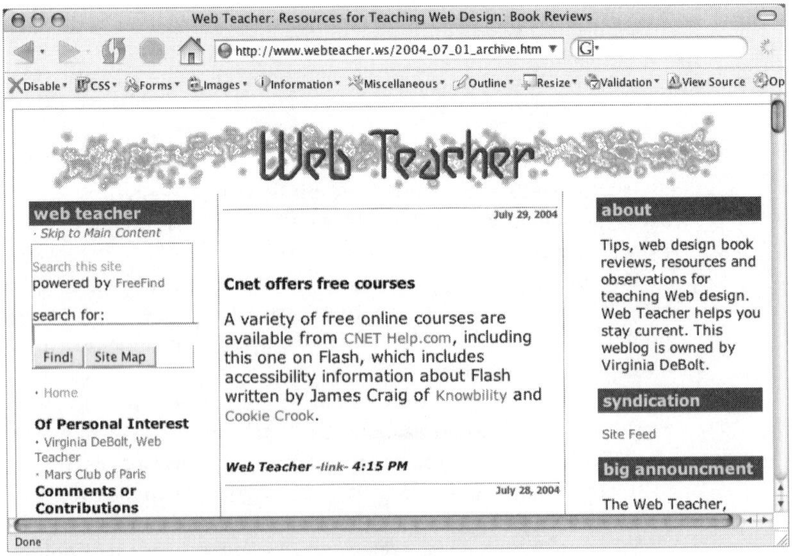

FIGURE 12.5
The Mozilla Web Developer extension toolbar appears under the address bar and has tools to check CSS, images, outline, validation, and more.

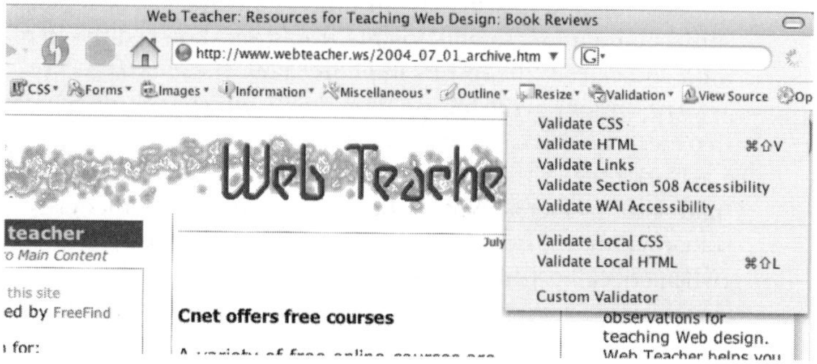

FIGURE 12.6
The Validation menu expanded

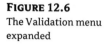

As you can see, there are built-in tools to validate CSS, HTML, links, and accessibility. The accessibility options include validation against the rules of Section 508 or the W3C's WAI (Web Accessibility Initiative) rules.

I selected the Validation ➢ Validate Section 508 Accessibility menu command, and my page was tested using the validation tool Cynthia Says. This tool is similar to the Bobby tool discussed earlier, although the report returned from Cynthia Says is slightly different from—and easier to interpret than—Bobby's. Figure 12.7 shows a bit of the Section 508 Validation Report, which is returned by opening the window in another tab, leaving my original page open in a tabbed window as well.

TIP   You can go straight to Cynthia Says at www.cynthiasays.com for accessibility validation if you do not have the Firefox Web Developer extensions.

Another of the useful tools can be seen in Figure 12.8, which shows the expanded Images menu.

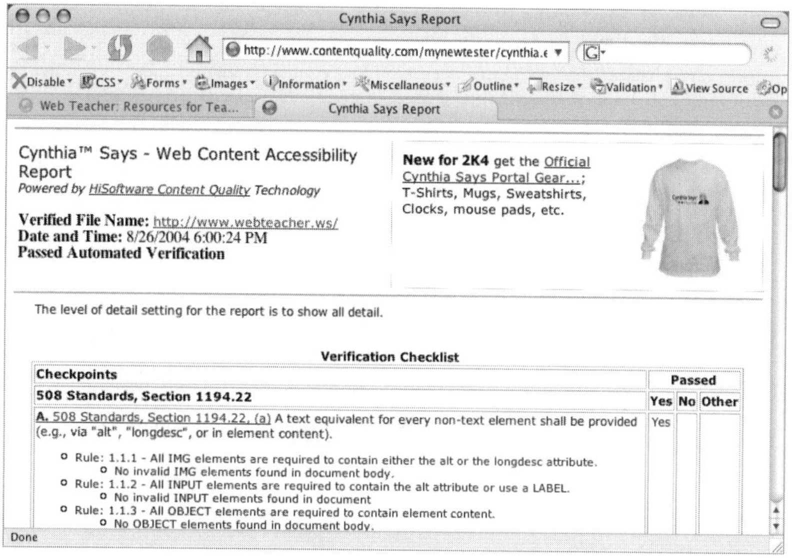

FIGURE 12.7
The results of the Section 508 Accessibility test are returned in a new tabbed window.

You can find missing alt attributes, hide images, or replace images with alt text to see what a user browsing without images visible would see. I picked the Replace Images with Alt Attributes option, and you can see the results in Figure 12.9.

The options in the Information menu, which include revealing all the div and class information on a page, are shown in Figure 12.10.

Under the Outline menu (Figure 12.11), you can outline block level elements, deprecated elements, and other elements. Notice the Outline Custom Elements menu option. You may have noticed that other menus also include an option to customize the tools to do whatever you particularly need done when checking your pages.

There is also a Disable menu in Firefox that allows you to disable the CSS or the colors on a web page.

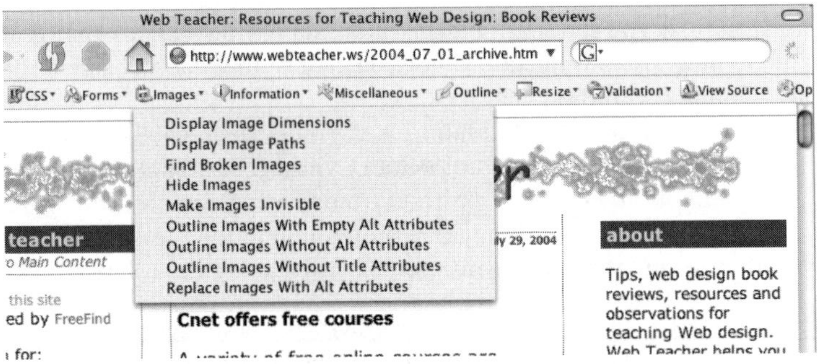

FIGURE 12.8
The expanded Images menu in the Firefox Web Developer toolbar

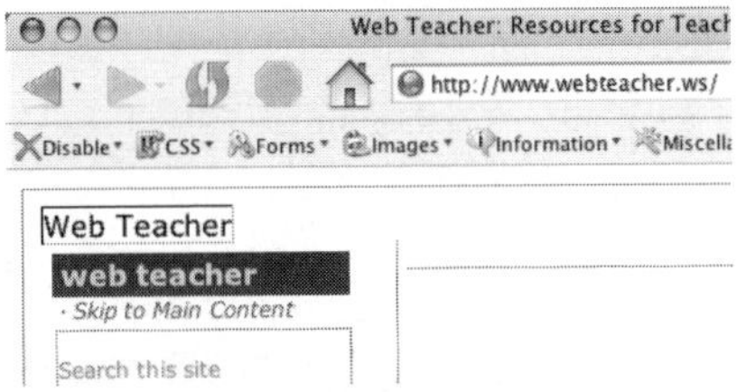

FIGURE 12.9
The graphic banner has been replaced by the alt text "Web Teacher" in a simple box

FIGURE 12.10
The expanded Information menu

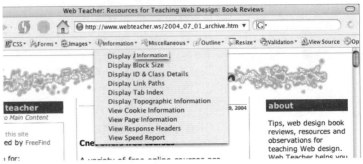

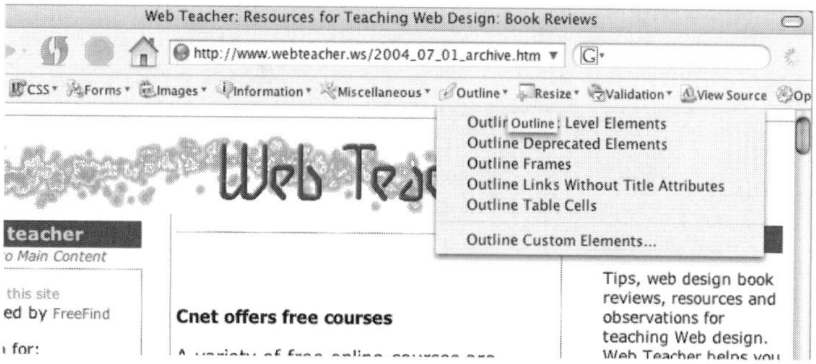

FIGURE 12.11

The Outline menu is expanded

One point about using Firefox and the other browsers I'm about to mention is that most of the time your page must be on a server. You cannot validate pages with tools like Cynthia Says while they are still on your hard drive.

You *can* test drive local XHTML and CSS files in Firefox (or any other browser) while the pages are still on your hard drive. You have been checking your pages that way throughout this book. Since Firefox is a browser that follows the standards quite well, it is a good browser to use as your test browser when you are first planning and designing your pages.

If you are a Mac user, the Safari browser has what it calls enhancements that include a Debug menu. Some of the options, including the Show Tree options to determine page structure, are shown in Figure 12.12.

Netscape includes a Tools menu with a JavaScript debugger and other tools, as shown in Figure 12.13.

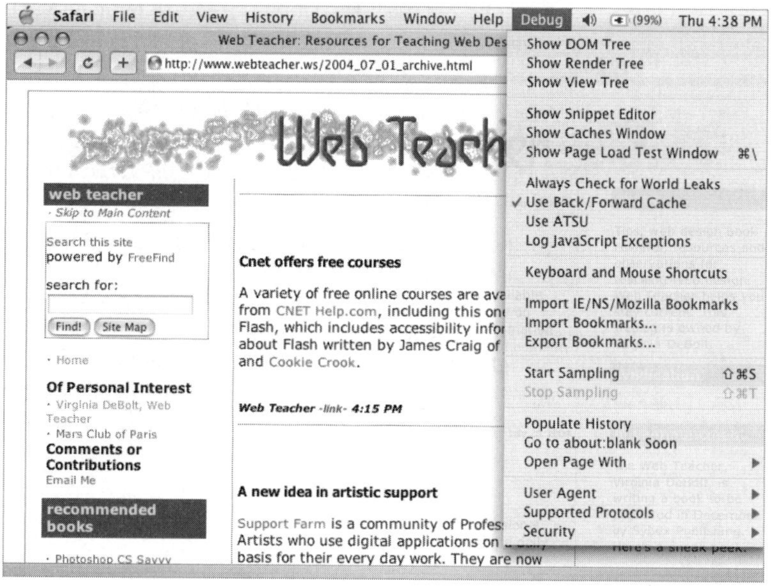

FIGURE 12.12

The Safari browser with Debug enhancements installed

FIGURE 12.13
Netscape tools for web development

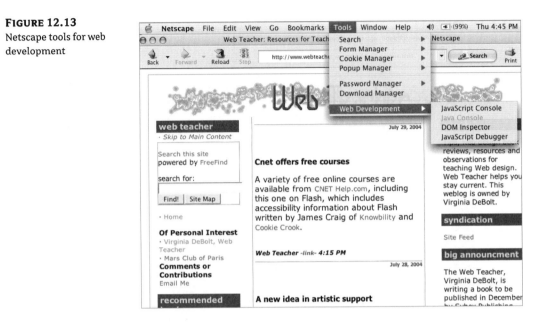

The Document Object Model (DOM)

You may have noticed the acronym DOM on some of the menus shown in the browser tools. DOM is the *Document Object Model*. The DOM is a way to manage XHTML document structure by treating elements on the page as objects that can be assigned behaviors, attributes, and content.

The W3C describes it at www.w3.org/DOM like this:

> *The Document Object Model is a platform- and language-neutral interface that will allow programs and scripts to dynamically access and update the content, structure, and style of documents. The document can be further processed and the results of that processing can be incorporated back into the presented page.*

Looking at the DOM tree gives you a tree outline of a document's structure, which might help you decipher questions of inheritance or document flow.

Figure 12.14 is a view of the DOM tree for www.webteacher.ws, using Safari's Debug menu. When Netscape shows the DOM tree, the results are more informative; see Figure 12.15. You can see information in the right panel explaining the item highlighted in the left panel. The highlighted item in the left panel says "LINK." The right panel shows that the link is to a stylesheet.

FIGURE 12.14

A Safari-generated DOM tree reveals the structure of a document

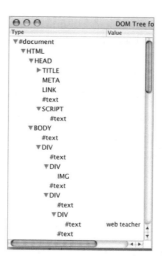

FIGURE 12.15

Netscape's DOM tree view gives more information about the page content

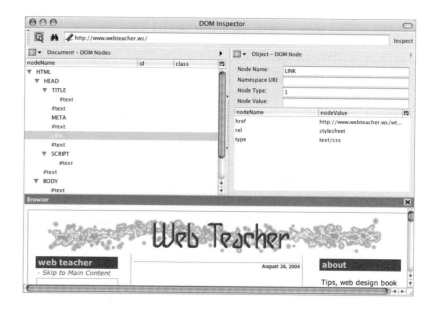

Telling the Search Engines You Are There

Before you even think about going to the search engines and registering your site with them, you need to make your site search engine–friendly. I've mentioned a few tips for search engines previously, but here are some tips that will help make your pages show up fairly well in the search engines:

- ◆ Have a good page title that gives information about content on the page.

- ◆ Have an h1 element at the top of the page that contains words describing the contents of the page.

- ◆ Use text with important keywords early in the page. If your site is filled with movie reviews, then "movie reviews" would be considered a keyword in your content.

- ◆ Use alt text for images.

- ◆ Use link text that describes what the link is about.

- ◆ Use description and keyword meta tags in the document head, for example:

    ```
    <meta name="description" content="Write a sentence describing your site." />
    <meta name="keywords" content="keyword, keyword phrase, keyword, keyword phrase" />
    ```

- ◆ Use simple, easy-to-navigate, and valid code.

There are also some things you should not do if you want good search engine results:

- ◆ *Don't* use images in place of text or well-written content. Images provide no information to your most important blind users: the search engines.

- ◆ *Don't* use Flash or other multimedia in place of well-written content.

- ◆ *Don't* use link text such as "Click Here" that provides no information about the link.

The search engines "index" your pages, which means they read the contents of the page and keep an index of what it is about. When a user does a search, the search engine looks through the indexed databanks of relevant content and returns sites that have contents that match the search term. If a user searches for "movie reviews" and your page has content saying "movie reviews," the search engine will add your site to the search results the user sees.

TIP If other sites are linked to your site, the search engines will generally find it simply by following links.

When you first launch a site, no one is linked to your site, so the search engines don't know you are available on the Web. You can go directly to the search engines and directories and register your site. It may take a while before you see results when you search, but the search engines should get it indexed within a few weeks.

Many search engines use the Open Directory at http://dmoz.org/. If you register there, you will be included in All the Web, AltaVista, Gigablast, Google USENET, Google, HotBot, Lycos, Teoma, WiseNut, and Yahoo!. Registering in the Open Directory is free. As soon as you open the main page at dmoz.org you see a "Suggest URL" link, but don't use it until you have drilled down in the directory structure and located the directory topic that most closely matches your content. This process can be somewhat inexact depending on your site's topic, but you should attempt to get in the right area before suggesting your URL.

For example, if you are registering a site containing movie reviews, you might select Arts > Movies > Reviews. There are even finer-grained options when you reach that point, or you might decide that this is the moment to click Suggest URL. If you click Suggest URL here, you will be adding your site to the Category: Arts: Movies: Reviews directory. You will be asked for your URL and your site description and to agree to some terms of use. Being in a certain category of the directory does not limit how you show up in the search engine results. Suppose you wrote about Cameron Diaz in a review of a movie. Someone who searched for "Cameron Diaz" in one of the search engines using Open Directory might see your site in the search results, even though they weren't searching for movie reviews.

There are more specialized search engines for some topics. If you are writing content on one of these topics, you probably know about the search engines on that particular topic. For example, there is a specialized chemistry search engine at www.chemindustry.com. If your site is about chemistry, you should register with both dmoz.org and chemindustry.com.

If your site is well planned using the preceding points and you are registered with the major search engines, there is no need to pay anyone who promises to register you with hundreds of search engines.

Paying for ad placement with the search engines themselves is a different matter. It is worthwhile to consider paid ads or keyword ads with some of the search engines if you are selling a product and want your site to appear in the advertising section when search results are displayed related to your keywords.

KEEPING SEARCH ENGINE ROBOTS OUT

Search engines create indexes by using machines called *robots* to index everything on your site. If you have something on your site that you don't want indexed or don't want to show up in search engine results, you can exclude the search engine robots from indexing certain directories.

There are all sorts of reasons why you might not want certain parts of your site indexed by search engines. Perhaps you have a directory called test on your server where you try out new designs before you are ready to make them live. Perhaps you have a directory called temp on your server where you put things temporarily, such as a screen shot you took for a friend or a photo of something you are selling on eBay. Perhaps you have a directory on your server called baby where you put photos of your kids so your grandmother in Tennessee can see them, but you don't want the general public to know they are there.

If you have a situation like that, you can use a robots exclusion file, which must be named robots.txt, to list directories that robots should not enter.

To exclude robots from the directories suggested in the previous examples, create a text file named robots.txt and include only this information:

```
User-agent: *

Disallow: /test

Disallow: /temp

Disallow: /baby
```

This exclusion uses a wildcard (*) to exclude all robots from visiting URLs starting with test, temp, and baby. Put that file in the top-level directory of your website, and no robots will index those sections of your site.

Understanding Your Audience

You need to know what people are looking for when they come to your site so you can make the information they seek easy to find. Once you understand what your users want, you must make sure your site provides that information in an easy to find manner so you can entice your visitors to return to the site again. For example, if you write a new movie review every week, returning visitors will want easy access to the new reviews as well as easy access to the older reviews that are still available. It helps you to know whether visitors are entering the site directly on a page with an older review, or if they are heading for the page with the newest review.

Most servers provide some sort of service that tracks and analyzes use. These statistical tools give you the number of times a page has been visited, the URL your visitors came from, the words used in searches that led to your page, the browser your visitors use, and sometimes even the screen resolution of the visitor. Pay attention to the statistics for your site, because it helps you understand your visitors.

One of the hosting companies I use provides a statistical analysis tool called Webalizer as part of the hosting package. Figure 12.16 shows a Webalizer chart of the top 15 browsers and operating systems that visited my site in June 2004.

The majority of the visitors to my site use Windows and Internet Explorer. Mac shows up in a couple of spots, and the search engine bots (for robot) even get counted.

You don't get any personal information from these statistical tools. You do get a good idea about what people are looking for when they visit and what equipment they are using to view your site. That knowledge about your audience can help you make decisions about site design and site content. For example, I don't see anyone visiting my site using Netscape 4.x, so it is probably safe for me to forget about making sure my styles work in Netscape 4 the next time I update the site.

If your hosting company does not provide you with enough information when you use the analysis tools that come with your hosting package, there are many such tools available on the Internet that you can install and use.

FIGURE 12.16

The hosting company can provide all sorts of statistics regarding the visitors to your site.

Top 15 of 531 Total User Agents		
#	Hits	User Agent
1	5212	15.08%	Mozilla/4.0 (compatible; MSIE 6.0; Windows NT 5.1; .NET CLR 1
2	4552	13.17%	Mozilla/4.0 (compatible; MSIE 6.0; Windows NT 5.1)
3	1561	4.52%	Mozilla/4.0 (compatible; MSIE 6.0; Windows NT 5.0)
4	1414	4.09%	Mozilla/4.0 (compatible; MSIE 6.0; Windows 98)
5	1078	3.12%	Mozilla/4.0 (compatible; MSIE 6.0; Windows NT 5.0; .NET CLR 1
6	844	2.44%	msnbot/0.11 (+http://search.msn.com/msnbot.htm)
7	601	1.74%	Mozilla/4.0 (compatible; MSIE 6.0; Windows NT 5.1; FunWebProd
8	435	1.26%	Mozilla/5.0 (Macintosh; U; PPC Mac OS X; en-us) AppleWebKit/1
9	392	1.13%	Mozilla/2.0 (compatible; Ask Jeeves/Teoma)
10	366	1.06%	Mozilla/4.0 (compatible; MSIE 5.0; Windows 98; DigExt)
11	363	1.05%	Googlebot/2.1 (+http://www.googlebot.com/bot.html)
12	335	0.97%	contype
13	308	0.89%	Mozilla/5.0 (Windows; U; Windows NT 5.1; en-US; rv:1.6) Gecko
14	287	0.83%	Mozilla/4.0 (compatible; MSIE 5.22; Mac_PowerPC)
15	286	0.83%	Mozilla/4.0 (compatible; MSIE 5.01; Windows NT 5.0)

A HANDY SERVER CONTROL FILE

Many web hosting companies use Apache servers. When you open an account with a web hosting company, you should be given information about the type of server the account will be using. In case you missed it, you can use the form labeled "What's that site running?" at uptime.netcraft.com and find out the type of server being used on any site.

If your site uses an Apache server, there is a very handy file called .htaccess (the leading period must be included in the filename) that can control all sorts of things. The .htaccess file (or "distributed configuration file") provides a way to make configuration changes on a per-directory basis. The .htaccess file, containing one or more directives, is placed in a particular document directory on the server, and the directives apply to that directory and all its subdirectories.

You can read the entire .htaccess tutorial from Apache here:

```
http://httpd.apache.org/docs/howto/htaccess.html
```

A more complete tutorial appears here:

```
http://wsabstract.com/howto/htaccess.shtml
```

You can do many things with .htaccess directives, but I only want to show you one in particular here. That directive relates to the file users see if they request a filename on your site that does not exist. This can happen because the user made a typo when entering the filename in the browser location bar or if you deleted something that was there for a while and the search engines picked it up and linked to it before you deleted it.

If you don't create a custom error document, the server provides one in the form of a 404 error page that basically says, "The file you are looking for does not exist on this server."

A custom error page—or a custom 404 page, in this case—tells the user that the file does not exist on the server, but it can provide helpful links to the site menu or other ways for the user to find a way back into your site navigation or home page. To see an example of a custom 404 page, go to www.amazon.com/oops.html. This page does not exist, so you will see the custom 404 page Amazon.com has designed.

If you create a custom 404 page and put it on your Apache server in a folder called errors with the filename notfound.html, then the directive in the .htaccess file will read:

```
ErrorDocument 404 /errors/notfound.html
```

That is the entire content of the .htaccess file if you only have this one directive. Save it as text (but without any .txt file extension; it must be saved as .htaccess with no file extension) and put it in the top level directory on the site.

You can use .htaccess directives to password-protect certain directories on a site or to do many other useful chores.

Summary

It isn't enough to create a web page. You must also put it on a server so that it can be seen on the World Wide Web. The most common way to put the files that make up your website on a server is with the File Transfer Protocol, or FTP.

When you open an account with a web hosting company and are given server space for your website, you receive information from the company that tells you the necessary facts for making an FTP connection to your server. Use that information in your FTP software to make a connection to the server and then put the XHTML, CSS, and images that make up your site on the server.

You can update your site at any time by editing your XHTML or CSS pages and then uploading them again by FTP to your server.

If you want your own domain name and server space, you will have to pay for it. It is possible to find free hosting. With free hosting, you may have ads added to your pages or popping up when your pages are viewed, but free hosting does give you a chance to practice and learn at no cost.

Testing your site is important to your success. Once your files are on the server, find your URL in a browser and test everything about your site to be sure it is working properly. Test the site yourself with as many browsers and Internet devices are you possibly can. Validate your XHTML and CSS using the free tools provided by the W3C. Check your pages for accessibility using the free tools provided by Bobby.

After your site is posted on the Web, you need to register with the search engines so that they know you are there and can send people your way. As time passes and you begin receiving visitors to your site, check the server statistics to learn about your audience. Knowing your audience will help you fine-tune your site over time.

Chapter 13

CSS for Weblogs

Publishing your thoughts and information with a weblog, or *blog*, is increasingly popular. In the beginning, blogs were like online journals, with people spilling out thoughts that might have previously been written in some more private format such as a diary. But weblogs have come a long way since then and are now used for all sorts of purposes.

Your local newspaper sports writer might use a blog to provide information and reflections on local sports that didn't make it into the newspaper but are of interest to the paper's readers. Your favorite band may have a blog on their site that makes it easy to add updated news about concerts and tours.

If your cell phone takes pictures, it can e-mail photos directly to a *moblog* (for "mobile weblog"). These have been used for everything from documenting a person's life in photos to sending in photos and locations of potholes to a city road administration blog.

Naturally, some of my favorite weblogs are on the topic of web design. I learn a lot reading Thoughts from Eric (Eric Meyer) at `www.meyerweb.com`. I enjoy reading Molly Holzschlag's blog at `www.molly.com`. Digital Web Magazine at `www.digital-web.com` uses a weblog with numerous contributors to provide the latest web design news tidbits. Shirley Kaiser, at `www.brainstormsandraves.com` has many posts about web topics. My own weblog, Web Teacher, is at `www.webteacher.ws`. I use my blog to keep track of helpful resources for teaching and learning web-related topics. It is rather like a gigantic annotated set of bookmarks for me.

Advantages of Weblogging

There are several disadvantages to using a weblog format to publish your content, the primary one being that the information tends to get disorganized over time. The main linking system is to archives of previous posts, which are organized in monthly or weekly increments by date. In other words, it doesn't replace a traditional website with well thought out main navigation categories that lead to subsections on particular topics. Some weblog software, however, allows you to categorize posts by topic, which is a good organizational aid.

The advantages of weblogs are what draw people into using them, so I'll detail a few of the advantages for you:

Ease of use   You can publish to a weblog using only a browser from any Internet-connected device or even, as I mentioned earlier, a cell phone with e-mail capability.

Preexisting designs   Most blogging companies provide professionally designed templates to hold your content. This chapter will show you how to modify a template using your XHTML and CSS skills.

If you are happy using one of the provided template designs, you don't need to know anything about HTML or CSS to create an attractive blog.

NOTE   My son asked me the other day to help him set up a weblog for the fantasy football teams he and his buddies pick and track every week. He was surprised to learn that he really doesn't need help, since one of the readymade templates provided is fine for what he needs (he's not trying to draw many visitors or use the blog in a portfolio).

Web practice and experience   As a person interested in HTML and CSS, or if you intend to pursue employment with your XHTML and CSS skills, you may want to include a weblog in your portfolio or resume. In that case, it's important to show a weblog that you successfully created or modified to fit your requirements.

Group participation   A weblog can be under the control of a single individual, or many people can be allowed to post to it. Some weblogs allow your users to comment on your posts, which can lead to some lively discussions, or even a book, as with www.simplebits.com, where Dan Cederholm used comments from his weblog in the book *Web Standards Solutions: The Markup and Style Handbook*.

Low cost   A final important advantage is that some weblog companies provide free hosting.

Where to Sign Up for a Weblog

Lately I've been hearing good reviews of the weblog tool WordPress (www.wordpress.org). It is free with a focus on web standards and usability. I've also heard good things about the weblog tool Type-pad (www.typepad.com) although it is not free.

In 2001, I signed up with Blogger (www.blogger.com) and have been happy enough to stay with it since. The examples in the chapter are based on Blogger, but the ideas can be used with almost any other weblog tool as well. Blogger has a free version and provides free hosting for your blog on BlogSpot.

There are other companies offering weblog services or software that have good reputations, including Movable Type (www.movabletype.org) and Greymatter (www.noahgrey.com/greysoft).

Check out all of these options and make a choice that is best for what you are trying to accomplish with your weblog.

What to Look for in Weblog Software

Weblog software must be customizable. You must be able to make changes to both the HTML and the CSS. You need access to the HTML used in the template, and you need to be able to use HTML in your posts. You need access to the stylesheets, and you need the option of making them either external or embedded stylesheets, or both.

Good help files and directions must be available. Read through the help files (they may be called something else, like Knowledge Base or FAQ) to see if they are clear and complete enough to get you going. It's also a good idea to be sure that you have a way to make e-mail contact with technical support questions.

Once those two requirements—customization and help—are satisfied, the other features will be based on your personal choice. Some things you might take into consideration are

♦   How much the service costs

♦   Whether you can add the weblog to an existing site or a new domain

♦   Whether you want to let users comment on your posts

♦   Whether you want to let other people besides yourself post to the blog

♦   Whether you can organize your posts into categories

Getting Started with a Blog

Before you can customize a weblog, you have to either get the software (if you are using a tool such as Movable Type), or sign up for an account with the weblog provider of choice (if you are using a blog hosting company like Blogger) and get the basic setup done. On the theory that free hosting is the best choice for you while you are in the learning stages, I'll step you quickly through some of the basics of starting a new Blogger weblog to be published free on BlogSpot. Once you have some experience with this, you can move on to WordPress or Movable Type and take complete creative control over your weblog.

The process begins at `www.blogger.com`. If you don't already have an account, follow the onscreen directions to get one. After you sign in, you are offered the opportunity to Create a Blog (Figure 13.1).

Give the blog a name, and select a URL (Figure 13.2). The URLs hosted free on BlogSpot will always be `http://`*somename*`.blogspot.com`, where *somename* is the URL you make up.

Next, you select one of the templates (Figure 13.3). These are actually wonderful templates created by CSS gurus such as Dave Shea (`www.mezzoblue.com`) and Douglas Bowman (`www.stopdesign.com`). I love orange, so I picked one called Sand Dollar by Jason Sutter (Figure 13.4). However, since you are going to be customizing the look, it doesn't really matter which one you pick.

WEBLOG EXAMPLES BY TOOL

What weblogging software or provider do some interesting weblogs use?

♦   Brainstorms and Raves at `www.brainstormsandraves.com` uses Movable Type.

♦   Molly.com at `www.molly.com` uses WordPress.

♦   Stop Design at `www.stopdesign.com` uses Movable Type.

♦   Thoughts from Eric at `www.meyerweb.com` uses WordPress.

♦   Web Teacher at `www.webteacher.ws` uses Blogger.

♦   All in the Head at `www.allinthehead.com` uses Textpattern.

♦   Design by Fire at `www.designbyfire.com` uses Movable Type.

FIGURE 13.1
After signing in to your account at Blogger, select the option to Create a Blog.

FIGURE 13.2
The new blog needs an name and a URL, which you create.

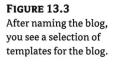

FIGURE 13.3
After naming the blog, you see a selection of templates for the blog.

FIGURE 13.4
Scrolling through the available templates, I find something orange that catches my eye. This template is named Sand Dollar.

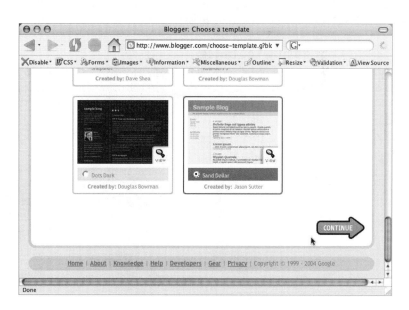

FIGURE 13.5
You can now start publishing posts on your new blog.

That is all it takes to be ready to start posting (Figure 13.5). Create at least one post and publish it so there will be something to see when you begin customizing.

Configuring Your Blog

There are some other setup chores to do. The work space for your blog has four main menu items: Posting, Settings, Template, and View Blog. Each of these main items has several secondary level navigation options, such as those you see under the Settings tab (Figures 13.6, 13.7, and 13.8).

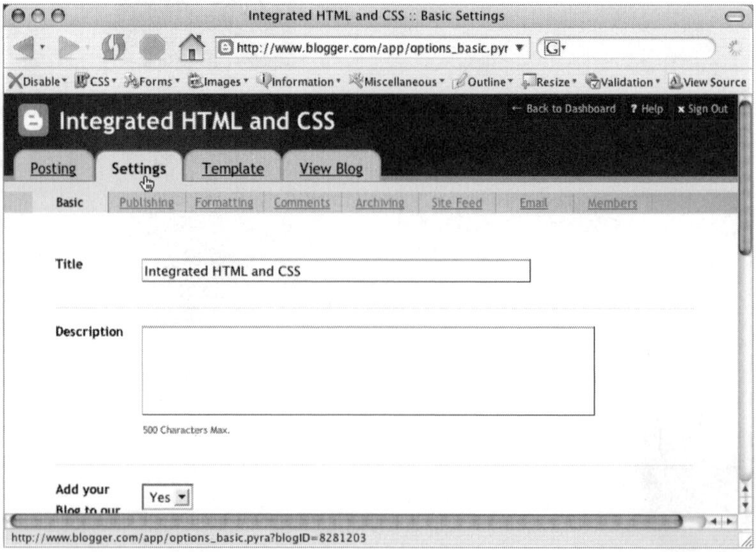

FIGURE 13.6
The Basic Settings ask for a blog description, which becomes part of every page of your weblog.

FIGURE 13.7
In the Formatting Settings, you set up how you want things such as dates to be formatted.

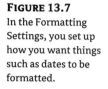

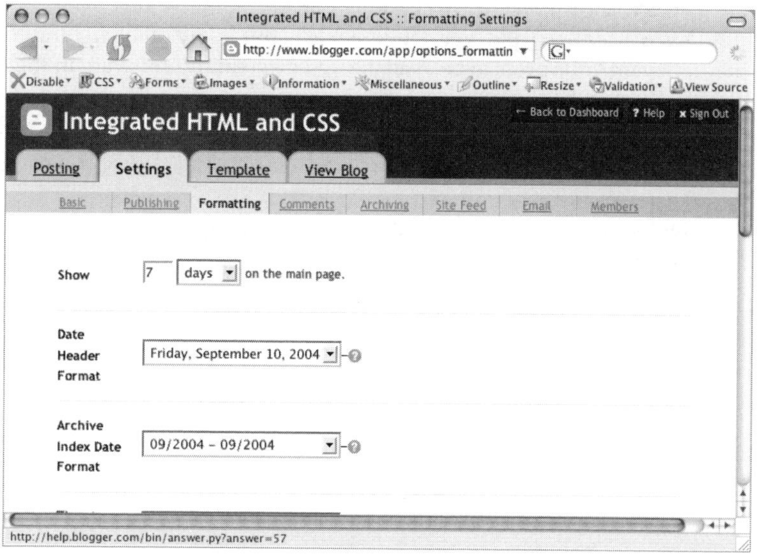

NOTE   The International Standard for the representation of dates and times is ISO 8601. You can see W3C-suggested date and time formats at www.w3.org/TR/NOTE-datetime.

FIGURE 13.8
Decide whether you want to allow comments on your posts and set up the rules for that under the Comments Settings.

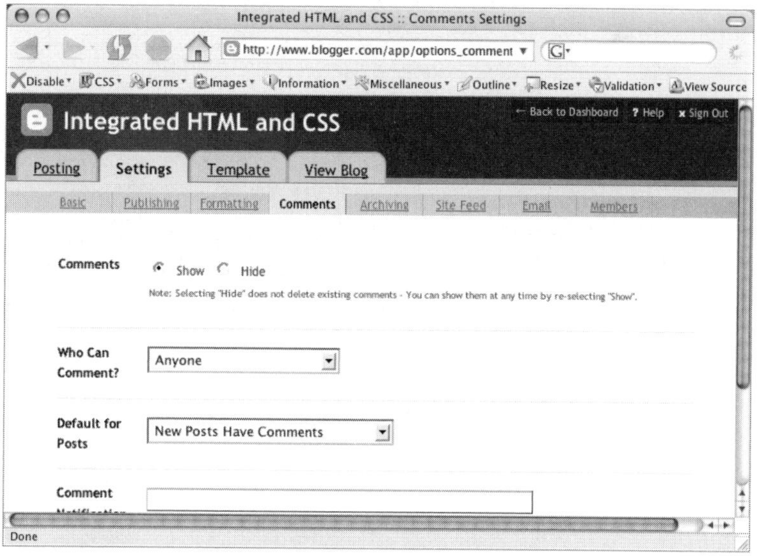

Site feeds are valuable for sites that are popular and have a wide audience. Blogger uses Atom (www.atomenabled.org). Blogger describes site feeds by saying, "When a regularly updated site such as a blog has a feed, people can subscribe to it using software for reading syndicated content called a "newsreader." People like using readers for blogs because it allows them to catch up on all their favorites at once. Like checking e-mail." Another very popular site feed tool is RSS (Really Simple Syndication). Blogger does not use it, but many other weblog companies do. Decide whether you want your posts to be available to newsreading software in the Site Feed section (Figure 13.9).

TIP   You can read more about RSS at `http://rss.userland.com`.

The rules specifying who can post to the blog are under the Members option. (Figure 13.10).

FIGURE 13.9
People who subscribe to your site feed get a notice in their news-reader each time you publish a new post.

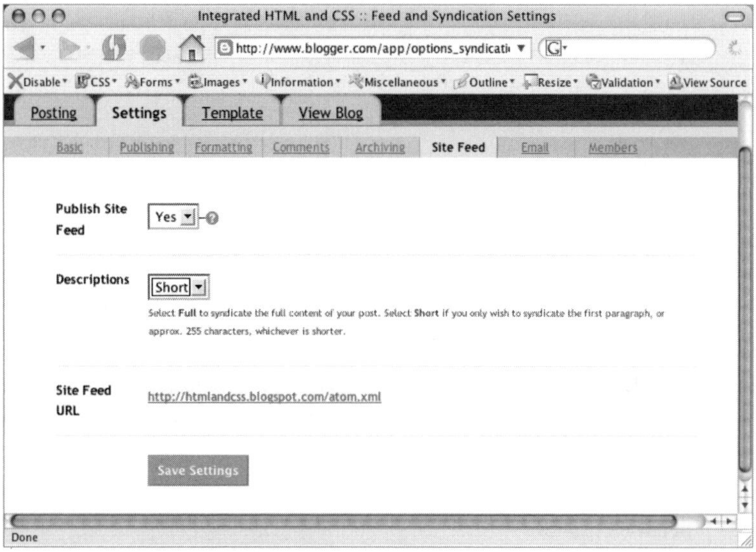

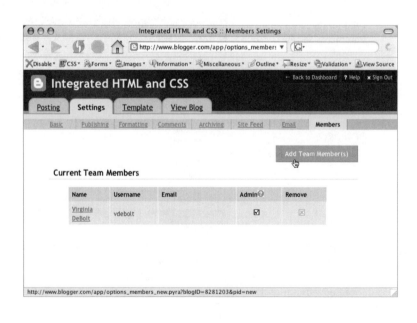

FIGURE 13.10
The only person allowed to write posts will be me, but I have allowed anyone to comment on my posts so users can still have a say.

Posting to Your Blog

Once you have all the settings to your liking, you can visit your URL—in my case www.htmlandcss
.blogspot.com—and look at your post (Figure 13.11). If you see an error, you can go back to Blogger
and edit your post (Figures 13.12 and 13.13).

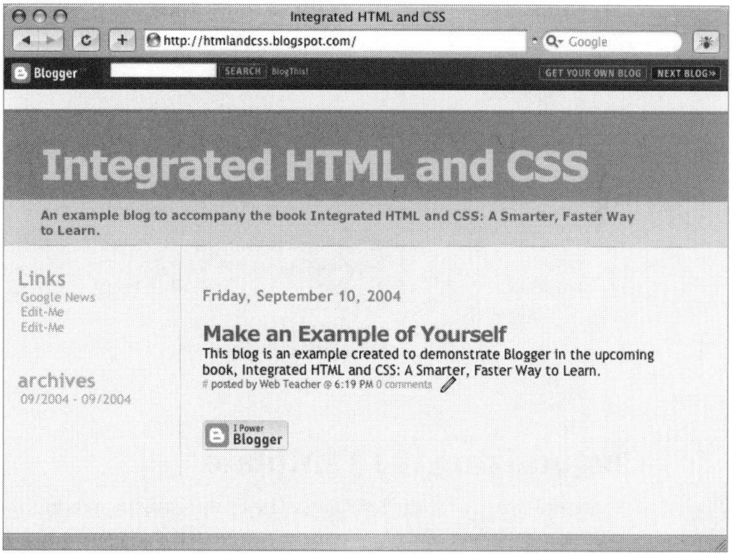

FIGURE 13.11

The first post appears at
the designated URL on
BlogSpot just as planned.

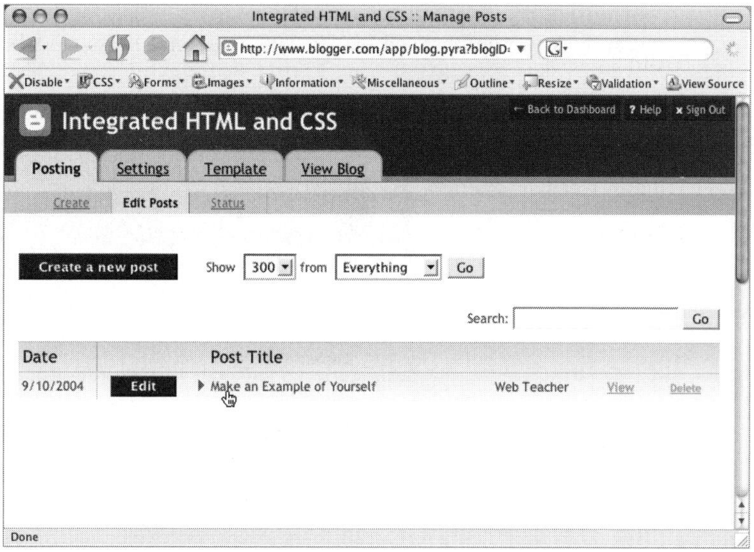

FIGURE 13.12

You can edit or
delete posts at any
time after they have
been published.

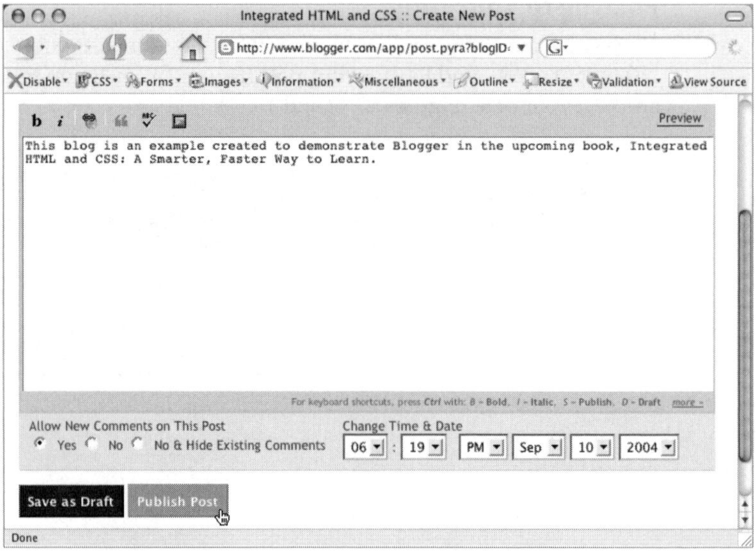

FIGURE 13.13
When creating or editing posts, you can preview your post, save it as a draft, or publish (or republish) it.

FIGURE 13.13
When creating or editing posts, you can preview your post, save it as a draft, or publish (or republish) it.

Customizing the Template

You are now ready for the template. The template is in an editable form field that you are free to modify, save, and republish. Since you cannot see all of it in Figure 13.14, I have put a copy on the accompanying CD called `template_start.html`. Excerpts from the template are also shown in Listing 13.1. In the listing, highlighted items indicate special Blogger codes that can be moved around some in the document but must not be deleted; bracketed ellipses mark omissions. In particular, I left out the embedded style because I'll present that completely a little later in a more readable format than the template uses.

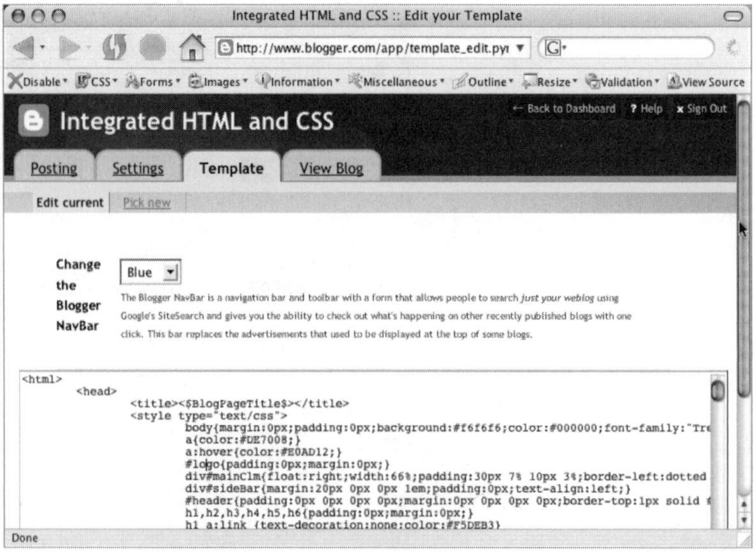

FIGURE 13.14
The template can be edited and saved under the Template menu.

LISTING 13.1:   The Template for Blogger's Sand Dollar Design

```
<html>
<head>
    <title><$BlogPageTitle$></title>
    <style type="text/css">
        body{margin:0px;padding:0px;background:#f6f6f6;color:#000000;
            font-family:"Trebuchet MS",Trebuchet,Verdana,Sans-Serif;}
        [...]
    </style>
    <$BlogMetaData$>
</head>
<body>
<div id="header">
    <h1>
        <ItemPage><a href="<$BlogURL$>"></ItemPage>
        <$BlogTitle$>
        <ItemPage></a></ItemPage>
    </h1>
    <p id="description"><$BlogDescription$></p>
</div>

<!-- Main Column -->
<div id="mainClm">

    <!-- Blog Posts -->
    <Blogger>
        <BlogDateHeader>
            <h3><$BlogDateHeaderDate$></h3>
        </BlogDateHeader>
        <a name="<$BlogItemNumber$>"> </a>
        <BlogItemTitle><h2><BlogItemURL><a href="<$BlogItemURL$>"></BlogItemURL>
            <$BlogItemTitle$><BlogItemURL></a></BlogItemURL></h2></BlogItemTitle>
        <div class="blogPost">
            <$BlogItemBody$><br />
            <div class="byline">[...]</div>
        </div>
        <ItemPage>
        <div class="blogComments">
            <BlogItemCommentsEnabled><a name="comments"></a>Comments:
                <BlogItemComments>
                <div class="blogComment">
                    <a name="<$BlogCommentNumber$>"></a>
                    <$BlogCommentBody$><br />
                    <div class="byline">[...]</div>
                    <$BlogCommentDeleteIcon$>
                </div>
                </BlogItemComments>
```

```
        <$BlogItemCreate$>
        </BlogItemCommentsEnabled><br /> <br />
        <a href="<$BlogURL$>">&lt;&lt; Home</a>
    </div>
    </ItemPage>
  </Blogger>
<!-- In accordance to the Blogger terms of service, please leave this button
     somewhere on your blogger-powered page. Thanks! -->
      <p><a href="http://www.blogger.com"><img width="88" height="31"
        src="http://buttons.blogger.com/bloggerbutton1.gif" border="0"
        alt="This page is powered by Blogger. Isn't yours?" /></a></p>
</div>

<!-- Sidebar -->
<div id="sideBar">
  <$BlogMemberProfile$>
  [...]
  <h6>archives</h6>
  <ul>
      <BloggerArchives><li><a href='<$BlogArchiveURL$>'><$BlogArchiveName$></a></
li></BloggerArchives>
      <!-- Link to the front page, from your archives -->
      <script type="text/javascript">if (location.href.indexOf("archive")!=-1)
document.write("<li><strong><a href=\"<$BlogURL$>\">Current Posts</a></strong></
li>");</script>
    </ul>
</div>
</body>
</html>
```

Anything that begins and ends with $, such as <$BlogURL$> represents a macro variable—one of the placeholders that makes Blogger work and brings parts of your page out of a database and puts it in the document as it is generated. You can change the locations of these things in the source order, but you cannot delete them. Otherwise, everything in the embedded styles and the markup is fair game for your customization.

Working in the template-editing window (Figure 13.14) is rather difficult because there is no line wrapping. I find it much easier to select the entire template, copy it, and paste it into a text editor. I make any changes I want in the text editor and paste them back into the template-editing window.

Changing the DOCTYPE Declaration

The first thing I noticed about the template was that it didn't have a DOCTYPE declaration. There are XHTML tags in the markup—for example,
—but without a proper DOCTYPE declaration, the XHTML syntax causes errors from the HTML validator. The validator goes into a tizzy and decides for itself to try HTML 4.01 Transitional as the DOCTYPE, which will not validate (Figure 13.15). You also don't want any DOCTYPE switching that will cause the document to render in quirks mode, so a proper XHTML Transitional DOCTYPE declaration is the first change to make, which you do in just a minute.

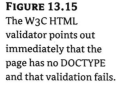

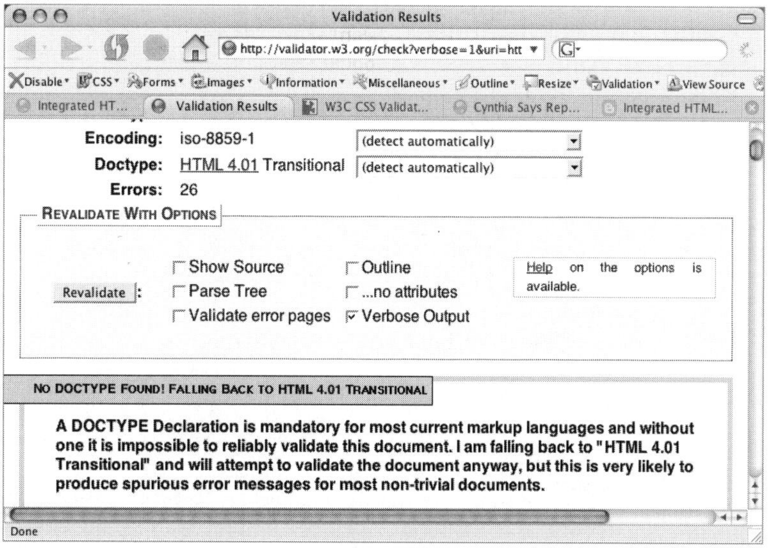

FIGURE 13.15
The W3C HTML validator points out immediately that the page has no DOCTYPE and that validation fails.

Paste the template into a text editor. You have the `template_start.html` document on the CD so you can work along. Immediately Save As by a new name so that the original document is still there just in case you make a mess of things and want to go back to the original. Save the working version as `template_finish.html`.

You can open either `template_start.html` or `template_finish.html` from your local computer in the browser. The Blogger tags will show up as text because the page isn't in the proper place to pull the info from the Blogger database. However, as you can see in Figure 13.16, the effects of the embedded styles in terms of layout, colors and fonts are apparent.

FIGURE 13.16
Working on the template on your local machine lets you see any changes to the CSS, but the Blogger tags are displayed as plain text.

The first change to make to the template is to change `<html>` to

```
<!DOCTYPE html PUBLIC "-//W3C//DTD XHTML 1.0 Transitional//EN"
  "http://www.w3.org/TR/xhtml1/DTD/xhtml1-transitional.dtd">
<html xmlns="http://www.w3.org/1999/xhtml">
```

If you make that one change in Blogger's template editing window, save the changes, and republish the blog, you can run the validator again. You'll still get errors, but some you cannot change in your customization efforts because Blogger is responsible for them (Figure 13.17).

If you decide to publish a blog of your own, I urge you to keep working on the HTML until you manage to get it through the validator successfully However, in the interests of getting to the CSS, I'm going to drop the discussion of it for now and move on. (Valid code may not be possible using the free hosting on BlogSpot, but if you go beyond this first step as a blogger, you need to strive for valid code.)

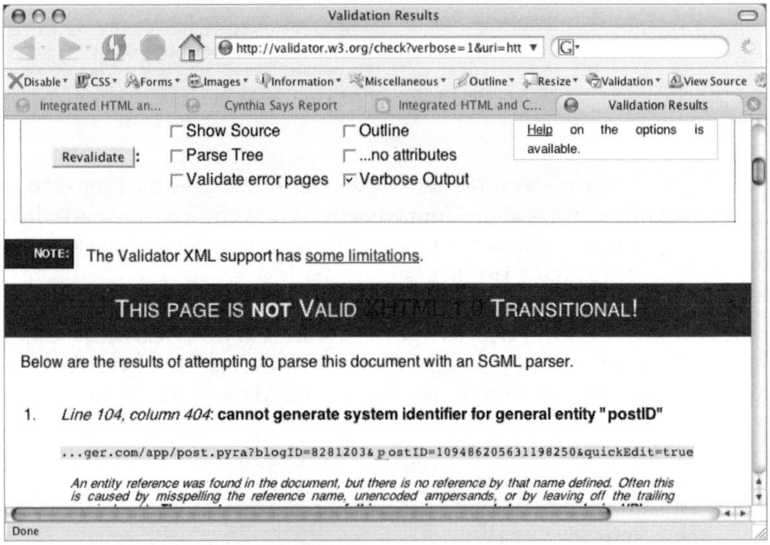

FIGURE 13.17
A valid DOCTYPE helps, but the document is still not passing the validation test.

Learn the CSS

Take a close look at the embedded styles in the template. In Listing 13.2, you see only the `style` element. The rules have been reformatted for easier reading, and comments have been inserted to help you identify what the styles are controlling. If you would like to insert this entire section of reformatted and commented styles into `template_finish.html` in place of the `style` element already there, it is provided for you on the accompanying CD in a file called `formatted_styles.txt`. It makes finding and changing specific CSS rules much easier.

LISTING 13.2:   Selected Blogger Template Styles, Reformatted and Commented

```
<style type="text/css">
/*  Settings for the body  */
body {
  margin:0px;
  padding:0px;
  background:#f6f6f6;
  color:#000000;
  font-family:"Trebuchet MS",Trebuchet,Verdana,Sans-Serif;
}
/*  Link colors  */
a {
  color:#DE7008;
}
a:hover {
  color:#E0AD12;
}
[...]
/*  This is the right column where the blog posts go.  */
div#mainClm {
  float:right;width:66%;
  padding:30px 7% 10px 3%;
  border-left:dotted 1px #E0AD12;
}
/*  This is the column on the left side where the profile, links,
    and archives go.  */
div#sideBar {
  margin:20px 0px 0px 1em;
  padding:0px;
  text-align:left;
}
/*  This is at the top where the blog title and blog description go.  */
#header {
  padding:0px 0px 0px 0px;
  margin:0px 0px 0px 0px;
  border-top:1px solid #eeeeee;
  border-bottom:dotted 1px #E0AD12;
  background:#F5E39E;
  color:white;
}
/*  A series of heading rules. Note the lack of a semicolon after the final
    rule declaration in some of the following. The semicolon is not required on
    the last declaration but is good practice and I suggest you add them.  */
```

```css
h1,h2,h3,h4,h5,h6 {
  padding:0px;
  margin:0px;
}
h1 a:link {
  text-decoration:none;
  color:#F5DEB3
}
h1 a:visited {
  text-decoration:none;
  color:#F5DEB3
}
h1 {
  padding:25px 0px 10px 5%;
  border-top:double 3px #BF5C00;
  border-bottom:solid 1px #E89E47;
  color:#F5DEB3;
  background:#DE7008;
  font:bold 300% Verdana,Sans-Serif;
  letter-spacing:-2px;
}
h2 {
  color:#9E5205;
  font-weight:bold;
  font-family:Verdana,Sans-Serif;
  letter-spacing:-1px;
}
[...]
/*  The rules for the list in the sidebar  */
#sideBar ul {
  margin:0px 0px 33px 0px;
  padding:0px 0px 0px 0px;
  list-style-type:none;
  font-size:95%;
}
#sideBar li {
  margin:0px 0px 0px 0px;
  padding:0px 0px 0px 0px;
  list-style-type:none;
  font-size:95%;
}
/*  The rules for the description  */
#description {
  padding:0px;
  margin:7px 12% 7px 5%;
  color:#9E5205;
  background:transparent;
  font:bold 85% Verdana,Sans-Serif;
```

```
}
/*  Two rules for the appearance of the posts  */
.blogPost {
  margin:0px 0px 30px 0px;
  font-size:100%;
}
.blogPost strong {
  color:#000000;
  font-weight:bold;
 }
/* A series of rules for the anchor tags in the unordered list in the sidebar */
#sideBar ul a {
  padding:2px;
  margin:1px;
  width:100%;
  border:none;
  color:#999999;
  text-decoration:none;
}
#sideBar ul a:link {
  color:#999999;
}
#sideBar ul a:visited {
  color:#999999;
}
#sideBar ul a:active {
  color:#ff0000;
}
#sideBar ul a:hover {
  color:#DE7008;
  text-decoration:none;
}
[...]
```

You can change anything in that `style` element. You can change styles, add styles, remove styles, or completely start from scratch with a whole new layout the way I did with the three-column layout on Web Teacher (`www.webteacher.ws`). (Because Web Teacher has its own domain, it does not use BlogSpot free hosting.)

For the purposes of the demonstration example, it will be enough to change the color scheme of the header with a two-column layout of elements. A few changes in color scheme will give you a basic understanding of how to customize the CSS.

A New Color Scheme

The new colors will be based on the colors on the cover of this book. Instead of a photo of my face, I filled out my Blogger profile with a photo of the book cover (Figure 13.18).

FIGURE 13.18
The book image
shows up on BlogSpot
as my profile.

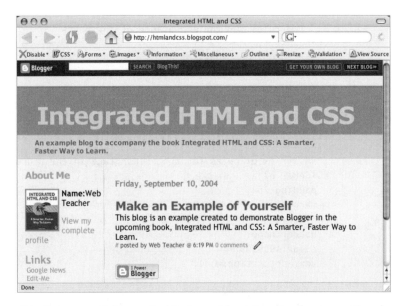

FIGURE 13.18
The book image
shows up on BlogSpot
as my profile.

As I bid a fond farewell to the orange, I change the h1 element foreground color to a yellow from the book's cover, #C93, and the background-color to a shade of red from the cover, #C03.

To help you stay oriented to what you are changing, I'll show you the entire style rule, with the changes highlighted, like this:

```
h1 {
    padding:25px 0px 10px 5%;
    border-top:double 3px #BF5C00;
    border-bottom:solid 1px #E89E47;
    color: #C93;
    background: #C03;
    font: bold 300% Verdana, Sans-Serif;
    letter-spacing:-2px;
}
```

The next change is to a couple of colors in the header div. I change the background-color to #C93, the yellow shade just mentioned. I will change the white value for color to a slightly off-white from the book cover, #FEFEFE:

```
#header {
    padding:0px 0px 0px 0px;
    margin:0px 0px 0px 0px;
    border-top:1px solid #eeeeee;
    border-bottom:dotted 1px #E0AD12;
    background:#C93;
    color: #FEFEFE;
}
```

The color in the description needs to change to #FEFEFE as well:

```
#description {
    padding:0px;
    margin:7px 12% 7px 5%;
    color:#FEFEFE;
    background:transparent;
    font:bold 85% Verdana,Sans-Serif;
}
```

TIP You can see the color changes on your computer if you are working along. The completed changes are also viewable at www.htmlandcss.blogspot.com.

The h2 element has a color set at #9E5205; however, the h2 element rule in the $BlogItemTitle$ is overridden by the color #DE7008 set for the a elements. In order to change the color of the $BlogItemTitle$, I must change the a element color to #C93:

```
a {
    color:#C93;
}
```

The blogComments should be #C93 as well:

```
.blogComments {
    padding:0px;
    color:#C93;
    font-size:110%;
    font-weight:bold;
    font-family:Verdana,Sans-Serif;
}
```

The words "Links" and "archives" in the left column are h6 element. They will be color: #C93 also:

```
h6 {
    color:#C93;
    font-size:140%;
}
```

The sidebar link colors also need to be changed. I'll stick with the yellow (#C93) except for a:active, which I'll make red (#C03). It may be hard to detect in black and white (Figure 13.19), but you should be able to see the new color rules in effect when looking at your changes in the browser.

```
#sideBar ul a {
    padding:2px;
    margin:1px;
    width:100%;
    border:none;
    color:#C93;
```

```
        text-decoration:none;
    }
    #sideBar ul a:link {
        color:#C93;
    }
    #sideBar ul a:visited {
        color:#C93;
    }
    #sideBar ul a:active {
        color:#C03;
    }
    #sideBar ul a:hover {
        color:#C93;
        text-decoration:none;
    }
```

FIGURE 13.19
You should be able to see the new color rules in effect when looking at your changes in the browser.

The "View Source" Secret to Blogger Modifications

If you are working on the template on your local computer, you see Blogger tags, as in Figures 13.16 or 13.19. When you are working this way, you sometimes cannot tell which CSS selectors are connected to specific things on the page that are generated on BlogSpot when the page is viewed. You have to do a bit of detective work.

The secret to figuring out what CSS rule is in use is to save the template, paste it into the Blogger template-editing window (refer back to Figure 13.14), and republish the blog. Then visit your blog on the web and use View Source. With View Source, you don't see mysterious things like $BlogDescription$, you see the actual HTML that is included on the page in place of the Blogger tags in the template.

Using the browser's View Source command, I can see that the words "About Me" in the sidebar are h2 elements assigned to the class sidebar-title. I would like these words to match the h6 style for color and size of the other headings (Links, Archives) in the sidebar, so I change the rule in the template to this:

```
h2.sidebar-title {
    color:#C93;
    margin:0px;
    padding:0px;
    font-size:140%;
}
```

Now the colors and size match, but the font-weight of the h2 used for "About Me" is greater than that of the h6 elements used for "Links" and "archive." The HTML in the "About Me" heading is out of reach, but I can change the HTML in the Links and Archives headings from h6 to h2, giving my sidebar headings a uniform look. I also want a capital letter A on "archives":

```
<h2>Links</h2>
    <ul>
        <li><a href="http://www.webteacher.ws/">Web Teacher</a></li>
        <li><a href="http://www.vdebolt.com/">Virginia DeBolt</a></li>
        <li><a href="http://www.sybex.com/">Sybex Computer Books</a></li>
    </ul>
<h2>Archives</h2>
```

Of course, there are many more changes I could make in margin, padding, border, and other properties used in the styles for this template. These examples should be sufficient to get you started with your own weblog modifications.

BLOGGING RESOURCES

Several books have been published that are solely devoted to the topic of blogging. These include:

◆ *Blogging: Genius Strategies for Instant Web Content* by Biz Stone.

◆ *Who Let the Blogs Out? A Hyperconnected Peek at the World of Weblogs* by Biz Stone. Biz Stone works for Blogger, so this book may contain good tips for Blogger users.

◆ *The Weblog Handbook: Practical Advice on Creating and Maintaining Your Blog* by Rebecca Blood.

◆ *Blog On: Building Online Communities with Weblogs* by Todd Stauffer.

There are also books specific to certain weblog types, such as *Sams Teach Yourself Movable Type in 24 Hours* by Porter Glendenning and Molly Holzschlag. And there is a chapter about the styling of Eric Meyer's blog, "Thoughts from Eric," in *More Eric Meyer on CSS* by Eric Meyer.

Blog This!

Your browser has a bookmarks toolbar (Internet Explorer calls it a Favorites Bar) that you can keep visible. If you don't see it in your browser, simply select it using the browser's View menu. Blogger provides a *bookmarklet* called "BlogThis!" (Figure 13.20) that you can insert into your browser's bookmark toolbar. A bookmarklet is a bit of JavaScript that creates a link like a normal bookmark (or favorite) but also has a brief script to produce a particular action when the link is clicked. The BlogThis! bookmarklet allows you to publish your post from a pop-up window without going to www.blogger.com. (See Figure 13.21.)

To find the bookmarklet to put a BlogThis! link in your toolbar, sign in to your Blogger account. Go to Blogger Help and choose Blogger Basics ➤ Posting and Editing ➤ What Is BlogThis!. Find the BlogThis! link and simply drag and drop onto your bookmarks bar.

FIGURE 13.20
Look at the BlogThis! item in the bookmark bar.

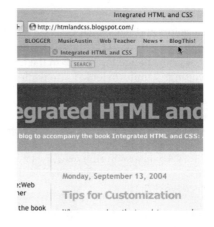

FIGURE 13.21
Clicking BlogThis! while visiting any web page automatically creates a link to the page and opens up a pop-up window where you can write your post about the page.

Challenge Yourself

Here are some ways to test your skills at styling a blog:

1. Pick any of the weblog tools, such as WordPress, Blogger, or Movable Type, and try out a weblog for yourself. As a first step, try modifying one of their templates.

2. Design a template of your own and publish it as your weblog. Be sure that any specific requirements for the weblog tool you are using, such as the Blogger tags in the examples in this chapter, are included in your template.

Summary

Weblogs are popular because they are easy and flexible. Sites sometimes include weblogs as a part of the overall site plan. Sometimes a site is built completely as a weblog.

You can use what you know about HTML and CSS to take the basic elements the weblog software or hosting company requires for a blog and add your own designs and modifications to make a unique and distinctive blog.

Chapter 14

Design Basics

Creating a web page is a form of visual communication. There are exceptions to this, of course, but most of the time website creators are concerned with appearance and how the visual elements work together to convey their message.

In this chapter you will explore a few of the basic design ideas that can make your web pages more successful. Design is a huge topic, so this chapter narrows things down significantly and focuses only on a few major concepts related to web page design.

Refer to the "Making Your Web Pages Easy to Use" section of the color insert in the center of this book to see sites that are examples of good usability demonstrate the design principles discussed in this chapter. Refer also to the "Real World Examples" near the end of most chapters to reexamine those sites in terms of the design principles in this chapter.

Layout

Web pages open at the top-left of the page (for languages such as English). The height from the top and the width from the left within the user's view of the page depends entirely on the device being used to display the page. Web page layouts are top heavy—the most important information needs to be at the top of the page. The term often used—borrowed from the newspaper world—is to put the main content "above the fold." In terms of a newspaper, the big stories must be at the top of the page so that they can be seen on the news stands before the page is unfolded. In terms of a web page, the concept of being above the fold refers to that part of the page the user sees before scrolling.

The above-the-fold logic leads to page designs like Figure 14.1, where site identification and main navigation are clustered near the top left of the page.

The idea of putting the main design elements near the top of a design doesn't necessarily apply to other types of design such as art or advertising or textiles, but it is important in web page layout.

Visual Hierarchy

In order to communicate effectively, the design must establish a visual hierarchy for the viewer.

One way to establish hierarchy is to create a focal point. The focal point draws the viewer's attention by being strong in the sense that it dominates the page. It screams, "Look here! This is the most important thing on the page!" Focal points are created with contrast: in size, color, texture, balance, or form, as shown in Figure 14.2.

FIGURE 14.1
Important elements need to be seen at a glance with no scrolling, so the important elements are often clustered near the top left of a page.

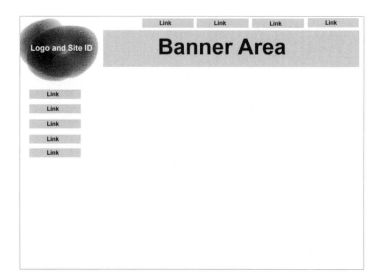

FIGURE 14.2
Several types of contrast create this focal point: light and dark, size and shape, variety, color, and alignment.

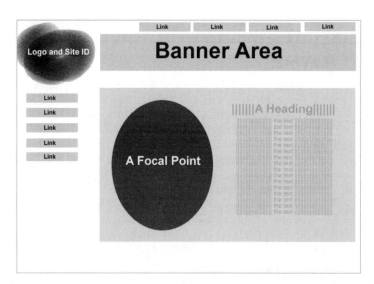

Headings are important in setting up a visual hierarchy. The six possible heading elements in XHTML are one way to create hierarchy. An h1 is of more importance in the visual hierarchy than an h2.

The heading must lead the eye directly to the related content. Robin Williams, in her wonderful book *The Non-Designer's Design Book* (listed in the resources section at the end of the chapter), calls this idea "proximity." Items that are related to one another must be in close proximity to one another. Without the help of proximity to lead the eye from one element to the element related to it, the visual hierarchy falls apart and any sense of what the page is about begins to get fuzzy. As you see in Figure 14.3, it appears that the heading is related to the element below it, when, in fact, it is related to the text quite some distance away.

It isn't enough to merely put the heading above the related content. It must look related by proximity as well. For example, in Figure 14.4, the B heading looks as if it is related to the text right above it! Figure 14.5 shows an arrangement that is easier to understand.

FIGURE 14.3
If the heading is not in close proximity to the text it heads, then the visual hierarchy of the page is muddled and the user can't make sense of your organization.

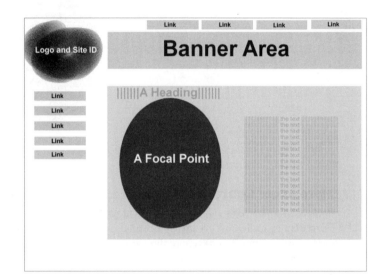

FIGURE 14.4
The heading and the text it heads appear unrelated by proximity in this arrangement.

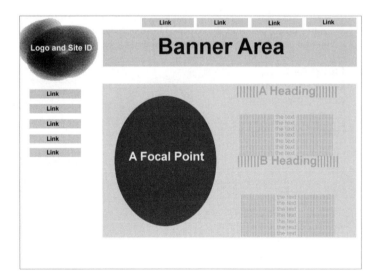

FIGURE 14.5
This layout creates a much more understandable visual hierarchy, with the headings in close proximity to the text they head.

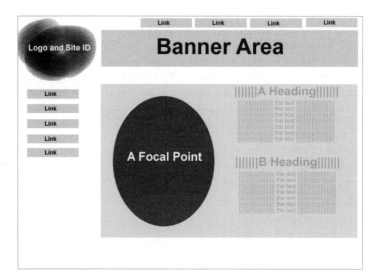

More About Contrast

Contrast is also used in web pages to create rollover effects and current page indicators (Figure 14.6). Current page indicators are an important aspect of the visual hierarchy of the page, because they help users stay grounded as to where they are and where they can go next.

Contrast can be created with form or variety as well—creating difference creates contrast. The simple addition of a different form by one of the links (Figure 14.7) is enough contrast to create a current page indicator.

You need to consider contrast when you make your choices for the site's color scheme. It is particularly important that the contrast between the color in the background and the color of the foreground text be great enough to be distinguishable even by the color-blind users of your site.

FIGURE 14.6
Contrast is used to create a current page indicator.

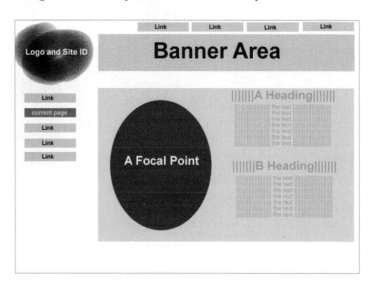

If you use background images, the contrast between any colors, patterns, or textures in the background and colors in the foreground text must be sufficient or the text becomes difficult to see.

Headings, of course, are meant to contrast in size from the text they head. You can create contrast with typefaces or fonts, as well. In Figure 14.8, the playful nature of the font in A Heading is quite a contrast from the staid sans-serif of the remaining fonts on the page.

Don't get carried away with typefaces and use eight or ten on a page, however. Remember the need for consistency in your pages, which is achieved through repetition.

FIGURE 14.7

The diamond shape next to one link creates a contrasting element distinguishing it from the other links.

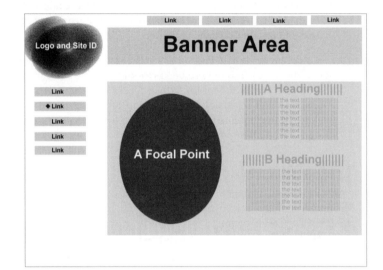

FIGURE 14.8

The use of typography and various fonts can create focal points and contrast and can add to a sense of visual hierarchy and emphasis.

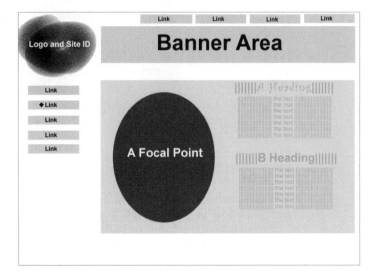

Repetition

Pages in your site have to be consistently designed. The placement of elements on the page, the location of the navigation, the colors used, the fonts used—all these things must be consistent throughout the site. This consistency is achieved partly through repetition. Repetition ties things together that aren't connected by proximity. For example, in Figure 14.9, the repetition of the same font for several elements on the page such as logo, banner, and headings ties the page together in a consistent design.

TIP   An unusual font such as the fanciful one in Figure 14.9 probably has to be inserted on the page as an image. You should not assume that the average viewer of your page will have such a specialized font installed on their computer.

You see repetition in Figure 14.9 in the size and shape of the links, both on the left main menu area and at the upper right where one presumes the site utilities would be.

You don't want the footer to be a focal point (Figure 14.10), so design it with minimal contrast elements: small sizes, lighter colors, and repeating use of the less showy font used on the page.

Adding the footer to the page in alignment with other page elements brings up another important design basic—alignment.

FIGURE 14.9
Use repetition in font, or size, or color or placement to create a consistent design from page to page.

Alignment

The choices in terms of alignment are left, right, centered, and—for text—justified. In Figure 14.10, the paragraph areas called "the text" are justified. In the real world, using justified text on the web is chancy. Not all browsers implement it correctly, and it can lead to strange, large gaps between words in some situations, making the text hard to read and odd looking.

In terms of reading words in English, left-aligned text (or ragged-right text, as it is also called), like that in Figure 14.11, is easier to read than either centered or right-aligned text.

FIGURE 14.10

Repeat design elements such as fonts in the footer, but do so in ways that decrease the emphasis on that part of the design.

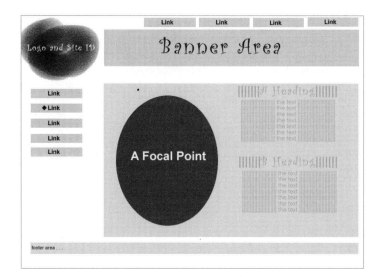

FIGURE 14.11

The paragraph text is left aligned, as is every other element on the page except the navigation at the upper right. The navigation in the upper right is aligned right.

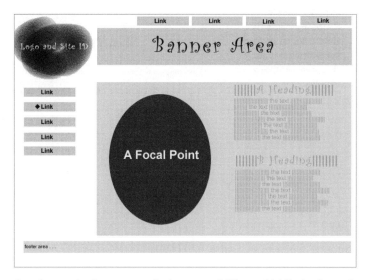

If I change the layout so that the text in the paragraphs is centered (Figure 14.12), the footer is centered on the page, and the navigation on the upper right is centered within the right column. The design no longer seems to hang together or look unified, and things seem accidentally placed on the page.

I have seen sites where every single thing on the page was centered down the same center line. This is very difficult to read, and makes establishing a visual hierarchy next to impossible. You can see what I mean in Figure 14.13, where a text-heavy page you are familiar with is centered.

Right alignment can be effective in small doses for contrast or variety—perhaps with headings or the navigation at the upper right, but most elements, especially paragraphs, would be hard to read, as in Figure 14.14.

Link
Link
Link
Link
Logo and Site ID
Banner Area
Link
Link
Link
Link
Link
A Focal Point
footer area . . .

FIGURE 14.12
Centering the paragraph text, the footer, and the top navigation does not look good and makes the paragraph text very hard to read.

Ch 6 Start
Ten Tips for New Web Page Designers
After teaching HTML at the local community college for a few semesters, I have learned to anticipate the mistakes new web page creators make. Here are ten tips to help you avoid falling into the newbie sinkhole of ugly, irritating ignorance.
1. Never leave anyone alone with only the back button for company.
Taking some poor innocent user to one of your web pages and leaving him or her stuck there with no way out except the back button is as bad as stranding someone in the Sahara with nothing but a bag of salty pretzels. Why would anyone want to go back to a page they have already seen? They want to move on to new content, not read the same old stuff again. Nothing but a "Back to Home Page" link is just as bad. Imagine going to the mall and being forced to go back to the main entrance each time you wanted to look in a different store. You might do it once, you might even do it twice, but before long you'd be on the road again looking for a friendlier place to shop.
To quote Steve Krug from Don't Make Me Think: A Common Sense Approach to Web Usability:
I think we talk about Web navigation because "figuring out where you are" is a much more pervasive problem on the Web than in physical spaces. We're inherently lost when we're on the Web, and we can't peek over the aisles to see where we are. Web navigation compensates for this missing sense of place by embodying the site's hierarchy, creating a sense of "there."
Navigation isn't just a feature of a Web site; it is the Web site, in the same way that the building, the shelves, and the cash register are Sears. Without it, there's no there there.
2. Backgrounds need to be unnoticeable.

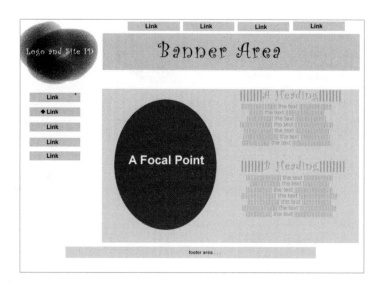

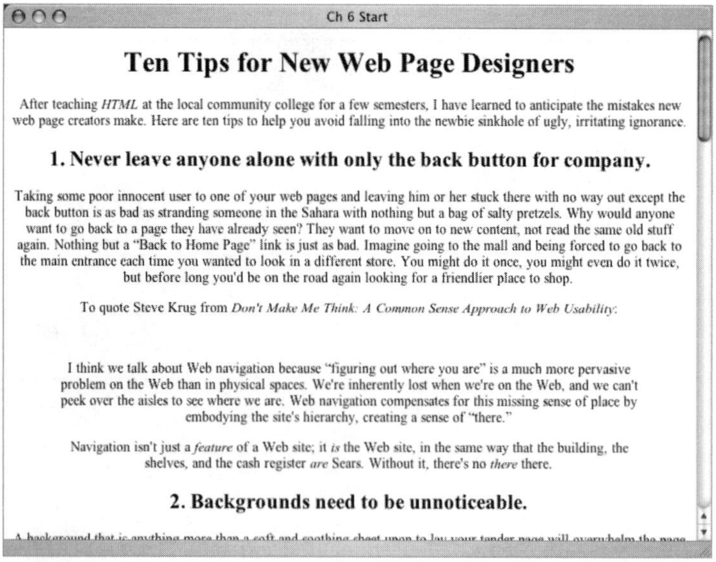

FIGURE 14.13
Centering elements should not be avoided in every situation, but for this page, centering is a very bad idea.

For this example page, left alignment for everything but the top navigation works best. Note that left alignment does not mean that everything is lined up on the left side of the page. It simply means that most of the elements on the page share left alignment, and further, the various elements are sitting on shared imaginary alignment lines. The eye connects elements along these invisible lines. I've added some lines to Figures 14.15 and 14.16 so you can see where elements repeatedly use the same lines to establish unity in the design.

To wind up the case for alignment, look at a page (Figure 14.17) that has no common alignment or shared lines of alignment. Eek, what a mess!

FIGURE 14.14
Making everything right aligned looks planned and organized, but the paragraphs are hard to read. Use right alignment in small doses.

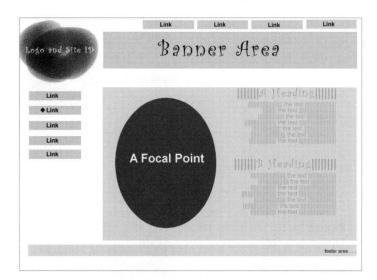

FIGURE 14.15
Heavy lines mark the places on the page where elements are visually connected to other elements by their shared left alignment.

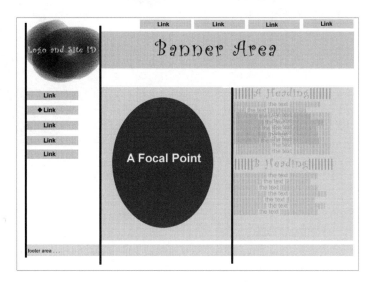

FIGURE 14.16
Several elements on the page are visually connected by the same line on the right.

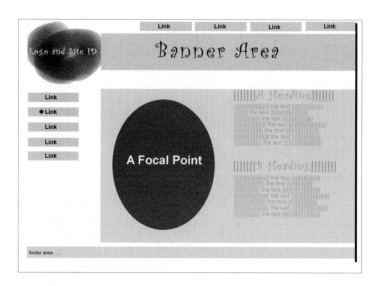

FIGURE 14.17
An alignment nightmare, which serves to show you what a difference a line makes, even an invisible line.

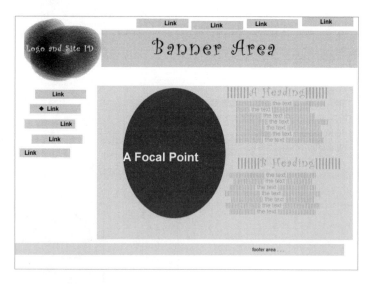

Resources

If you would like to extend your knowledge of design, here are some suggestions to get you started. General design resources include:

- Dimitri's Design Lab on WebReference.com at www.webreference.com/dlab
- Communication Arts Network at www.commarts.com

- The Smithsonian's Cooper-Hewitt National Design Museum at `www.ndm.si.edu`
- The Principles of Universal Design at

  `http://www.pbs.org/pov/pov2004/freedommachines/special_universal.html`

Typography resources include:

- Planet Typography at `www.planet-typography.com`
- Web Style Guide: Typography at `www.webstyleguide.com/type`

Resources for inspiration include:

- Cool Home Pages at `www.coolhomepages.com`
- Linkdup at `www.linkdup.com`
- Net Diver at `www.netdiver.net`
- Moluv's Picks at `www.moluv.com`
- Lynda.com's list of inspirational sites at `www.lynda.com/resources/inspiration`

Color resources include:

- Web Whirlers at `www.webwhirlers.com/colors/wizard.asp`
- HTML Basics: Choosing a Color at

  `http://www.devx.com/projectcool/Article/19817/page/1`

- Color Schemer Online at `www.colorschemer.com/online.html`
- Palette Man at `www.wire-man.com/paletteman`
- VisiCheck simulates color blindness at `www.vischeck.com`

Other helpful books include:

- *The Non-Designers Design Book* by Robin Williams (Peachpit Press, 2004)
- *The Non-Designers Web Book* by Robin Williams (Peachpit Press, 1998)
- *Fresh Styles for Web Designers: Eye Candy from the Underground* by Curt Cloninger (New Riders, 2001)
- *The Web Design WOW Book* by Jack Davis and Susan Merritt (Peachpit Press, 1998)
- *Color for Websites: Digital Media Design* by Molly Holzschlag (Rotovision, 2001)

Real World Examples

The first of these two examples is one of the few real-world websites in this book where I'm not suggesting you visit the site to learn more about web coding. Instead, The Mirror Project at www.mirrorproject.com was selected as an example because it exemplifies the design principles discussed in this chapter particularly well.

The Mirror Project is a fascinating community site. Photos are sent in by members taken of themselves as reflections—not just reflections in mirrors, but in any reflective surface such as puddles, the side of a truck, a doll's eye, or an oven door. The site is all about the images, and the navigation is organized around browsing through the images in various ways. (See Figures 14.18 and 14.19.)

Inner pages repeat the color scheme of the home page. All inner pages are consistent in design and layout, keeping the focus on the photos.

A second well-designed example is Sundog at www.sundog.net a company in North Dakota that helps develop e-business processes and solutions. Their website not only demonstrates good design principles such as above-the-fold layout, effective visual hierarchy, contrast, and repetition, but also uses valid XHTML and CSS and passes accessibility tests. Their home page is shown in Figure 14.20. The home page uses a small Flash movie, demonstrating a valid and accessible use of Flash with an XHTML Strict DOCTYPE—something I have not often seen.

FIGURE 14.18
The home page of The Mirror Project shows attention to color, contrast, size, alignment, and layout above the fold and emphasizes the images in the visual hierarchy of the page.

FIGURE 14.19
An inner page of The Mirror Project where the focal point is a particular photo sent in by a community member. Note the careful alignment of the menu items on the right.

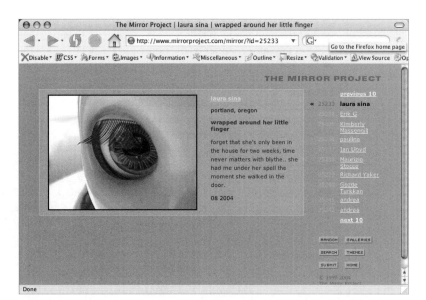

FIGURE 14.20
With a large graphic as a focal point, Sundog still manages to get the main navigation choices and the utility navigation (upper right) above the fold.

On the inner pages, such as the Solutions page shown in Figure 14.21, Sundog uses a different image, but the navigation details remain consistent. Layout, typography, and other details are repeated in the same manner as the home page as well.

FIGURE 14.21
The inner pages at Sundog maintain a consistent look, even though the main graphic is changed. Notice the current page indicator uses contrast in both size and color to distinguish itself.

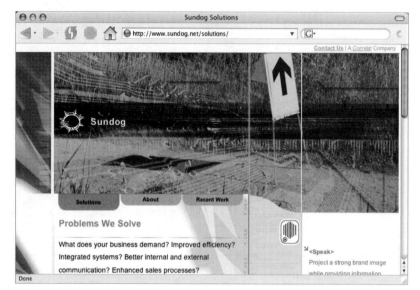

Summary

In this chapter, you dipped a toe into the ocean of design by looking at some of the factors that are important in designing web pages. You learned about above-the-fold layout and about creating visual hierarchy through size, placement, contrast, and headings. You discovered more about the importance of consistent design, or repetition in design. In addition, you learned about the importance of careful alignment of page elements to create unity in your designs.

Glossary

Italicized terms serve as cross-references to other glossary entries.

This section defines and explains many of the terms, standards, formats, and philosophies that are mentioned throughout this book. It also defines a few of the key jargon terms that you'll encounter.

Symbols

@import

A directive to the browser to import and use a particular stylesheet.

A

absolute link

Links in a website can be *relative* or absolute. Absolute links list the complete *URL* for a document and include a protocol, a server, and a filename. `http://www.sybex.com/` is an absolute link.

absolute positioning

A method of removing an element from the *document flow* and positioning it with regard to its *containing block*.

ancestor

An element two or more levels above the element it contains. The contained elements are known as *descendant elements*.

attribute

May be assigned to an *element* as part of the element's *opening tag*. The attribute must have a *value* assigned. Attributes assign certain *properties* to the element.

B

block-level element

An element that automatically begins on a new line and is followed by an automatic line break.

blog

A contraction of *weblog*. A weblog is a personal website that is easily updated on a daily basis.

bookmarklet

Creates a link like a normal bookmark (or favorite) but also has a brief script to produce a particular action when the link is clicked.

box model

Every element on a page generates a rectangular box. The box model is a visual model that browsers use to interpret visual directives. The box includes its content as well as optional padding, border, and margin. The box model is a standard specification; however, some browsers misinterpret the specifications with regard to the model.

browser

A software program used for finding and displaying various kinds of Internet resources, including web pages.

C

cache

A folder on your computer where the browser stores downloaded stylesheets, images, and web pages that have already been viewed. Once a *CSS* file is stored in cache, it does not have to be downloaded again the next time it is needed.

cascade

An application hierarchy—a means of determining in which order style sheets and style rules will be applied to a given page.

Cascading Style Sheets (CSS)

Style rules that define the visual appearance or positioning of structured XHTML. Styles can be located either on the page or stored in a separate (`.css`) file. The Cascade determines the order of precedence of style rules based on their location.

character entity

Symbols, marks, and characters used in writing that are not available on a standard keyboard. These entities are entered on a web page with a special code. Also known as *special characters*.

child element

If an element falls exactly one level within another, the two elements have a parent-child relationship.

class

1. A name assigned as a specific *attribute* used to apply a style.
2. A CSS selector for which style rules can be written.

closing tag

Terminates the element and consists of a forward slash and the element name. XHTML elements are contained within *opening tags* and closing tags. In *empty elements*, there are no closing tags. Instead, the terminating forward slash is contained within the element tag.

color code

Color for a web page is expressed with special color codes. Colors can be expressed with hexadecimal color codes (for example, #FF0000), with *RGB* numeric codes (for example, 255,0,0), or with RGB percentage codes (for example, 100%, 0%, 0%). There are 17 colors that can be identified by name (for example, red). A *web-safe color*, which consists of matched pairs of hexadecimal numbers or letters such as #FF0000, can be expressed in shorthand. For example, the matched pairs of #FF0000 expressed in shorthand are #F00.

comments

A syntactical device that provides information, identifies particular areas of a document, or annotates a document in various ways. Comments can be used in both XHTML and CSS and are a way of telling the browser, "Don't display this."

containing block

A *block-level element* that contains the element in question. It can be another element within the XHTML or the initial containing block, which is always the `html` element.

contextual selectors

Used to create rules for *elements* based on an element's relationship to the ancestor from which it is descended. Also known as *descendant selectors*.

CSS

See *Cascading Style Sheets*.

D

declaration

Consists of a *property* and a property *value*. A CSS rule is made of a *selector* and a declaration block. A declaration block contains one or more declarations.

default

A default display is the browser's built-in interpretation of what the element should be. You can change the default display with element attributes and *values* or with *CSS* rules.

deprecated element

An element that has been dropped from the current *DTD* but was available in previous DTDs is considered deprecated. Deprecated elements can be used with transitional DOCTYPES, but not with *strict* DOCTYPES.

descendant element

An element contained within another element. For example, an element on a web page might be a descendant of the body element.

descendant selector

See *contextual selectors*.

DNS

See *Domain Name Server*.

DOCTYPE declaration

A declaration placed at the beginning of an XHTML page stating the language and language version of the document. The DOCTYPE declaration may include the *URI* to the particular *DTD* in use on the page.

DOCTYPE switching

Some browsers may change from *standards mode* to *quirks mode*, depending on the document's *DOCTYPE declaration*. If the *URI* to a specific *DTD* is not included in the DOCTYPE declaration, certain browsers switch to rendering in quirks mode.

Document Object Model (DOM)

The browser's interface that allows elements on a web page to be treated as objects that can be manipulated with CSS or scripts.

Document Type Definition (DTD)

The DTD sets out the elements and attributes that are allowed in a particular version of XHTML. There are three DTDs for XHTML: *transitional*, *strict*, or *frameset*.

DOM

See *Document Object Model*.

Domain Name Server (DNS)

Maps a domain name to a server on the Internet in order to find a specific website.

dots per inch (dpi)

DPI expresses the number of dots a printer can print per inch, or that a monitor can display.

dpi

See *dots per inch*.

DTD

See *Document Type Definition*.

document flow

Describes the direction in which a document is read. Normally, a document in English flows from top to bottom and from left to right.

E

element

A semantic structure in markup that is used to structure content within a document. Text marked up as a paragraph is a p element. A nonempty element includes an *opening tag*, the content of the element such as text or other elements, and a *closing tag*. An *empty element* has no closing tag, but has a forward slash before the final bracket.

embedded style

Style rules contained in the head element of a particular XHTML document. Also called *internal style*.

empty element

An *element* that contains no text. In empty elements, there is no *closing tag*. In XHTML, closure is required, so the terminating forward slash is contained within the element tag.

Extensible Hypertext Markup Language (XHTML)

HTML is coded format language used for creating hypertext documents on the World Wide Web. XHTML is an extensible version of HTML written to XML specifications.

Extensible Markup Language (XML)

An extensible text markup language for interchange of structured data on the World Wide Web.

external stylesheet

A text document containing style rules. It is linked to an XHTML page to control the presentation of the page.

F

File Transfer Protocol (FTP)

Transfers files to or from another computer or server.

fixed positioning

A method of positioning an element in a fixed position in the viewport.

frameset

One of three *DTDs* for XHTML. Used only when the website is constructed with frames, that is, when two or more XHTML pages are loaded into a single browser window, each in a separate frame. The frameset is a single document that sets up the arrangement of the windows to display the various XHTML pages in a site.

FTP

See *File Transfer Protocol*.

G

GIF

See *Graphic Interchange Format*.

Graphic Interchange Format (GIF)

One of the image formats displayed by web browsers.

H

HTML

See *Hypertext Markup Language*.

HTTP

See *Hypertext Transfer Protocol*.

hypertext

Text that contains links to other documents.

Hypertext Markup Language (HTML)

A markup language used to create web pages.

Hypertext Transfer Protocol (HTTP)

A web protocol used to transfer *hypertext* documents from one computer to another.

I

ID

A unique name assigned to an *element*.

image optimization

A range of techniques used to reduce the file size of an image so that it downloads quickly.

inheritance

Reflects the fact that *elements* in an XHTML document are nested within one another in a relationship that is referred to as *parent* and *child* or *ancestral* and *descendant*.

inline element

Elements contained in the flow of a line of text. There is no line break following an inline element.

inline style

Style rules written as an *attribute* of a particular *element* on a page.

internal style

See *embedded style*.

Internet

The Internet is a collection of connected computer networks. The World Wide Web (WWW) is part of the Internet but is not the Internet itself. The Internet includes many parts besides the WWW, such as e-mail.

Internet Service Provider (ISP)

The company providing Internet service to a home or business.

ISP

See *Internet Service Provider*.

J

Joint Photographers Expert Group (JPEG)

One of the image formats displayed by web browsers.

JPEG

See *Joint Photographers Expert Group*.

M

media attribute

Specifies the media where the document is to be rendered (e.g., graphical displays, television screens, handheld devices, speech-based browsers, braille-based tactile devices, etc.). Assigning a media attribute to a stylesheet assigns the rules in the linked stylesheet to only a specific medium such as print.

mouseover

A special effect on a web page created when the mouse is passed over or held over an element. A mouseover effect can be used to change a color or a graphic, for example.

O

opening tag

Identifies the *element* that follows. Opening tags may contain *attributes* and *values* that define the element. See also *closing tag*.

P

page

An individual XHTML document. Websites are constructed of related web pages.

parent element

If an *element* contains another element, and the second element is nested exactly one level within the containing element, the containing element is the parent of the nested (or *child*) element.

permissions

Rule set on a server for files and folders that specifies who has permission to read, write, or execute files.

pixel

The smallest element of a graphics display. One pixel makes one dot on a computer monitor.

Portable Network Graphic (PNG)

One of the image formats displayed by web browsers.

PNG

See *Portable Network Graphic*.

point

A measure of font size used in print.

prolog

Part of an XHTML document that precedes the head element. The prolog includes an optional XML declaration as well as the *DOCTYPE declaration* for the document.

property

A CSS *declaration* consists of a property and a *value*. Property is a characteristic of the element. The property and its value describe the effect you want the related *selector* to have.

protocol

A protocol is a machine-to-machine detail used to specify the scheme being used to exchange information. Some of the protocols used with websites are HTTP, FTP, and mailto.

pseudo element

Fictional *elements*. Certain things that don't exist in a document, such as the state of a particular link, can be styled by creating pseudo elements.

Q

quirks mode

When a browser interprets a web page using its own particular set of rules (as opposed to the standard rules) it is referred to as quirks mode.

R

red, green, and blue (RGB)

The colors on a computer screen. Different levels of red, green, and blue create different colors.

RGB

See *red, green, and blue.*

relative link

Links that are written to be a pathway from the page in a site where the link is anchored to the page where the source document is located. Links within a website can be relative or *absolute.*

relative positioning

An element offset by the amount specified from its position in the normal *document flow.*

robot

A machine used to canvas everything found on the Internet and add it to a search engine database.

rollover

A special effect on a web page that creates a change in color or graphic when the mouse is in a position over a specific element.

S

selector

Used in a CSS stylesheet to determine which *elements* on a web page a style rule will apply to.

server

A computer that provides access to web pages, files, and programs.

site

A collection of web *pages* on a particular topic.

special characters

See *character entities.*

specificity

A means of conflict resolution in CSS that allows style rules to have importance based on a standardized algorithm that determines how specific that rule is. A more specific rule has more importance than a less specific rule and would therefore be applied over the less specific rule.

standards mode

When a browser interprets a web page using the standards and specifications set by the *W3C*, it is using standards mode.

strict

A *DTD* that allows the use of a limited set of elements.

structure

Semantic markup applied to content such as headings, lists, paragraphs, tables, block quotes, and links. Text can also be structured with *class* and *ID* attributes.

style

A rule determining the presentation of a particular *element* on a web *page.*

stylesheet

A text document containing one or more *style* rules. A stylesheet may be linked or imported into any number of XHTML documents. Style rules may also be embedded in an individual document.

syntax

The formal rules determining how XHTML or CSS will be written.

T

tag

An HTML/XHTML markup command. A tag is a code used to give an *element* its name.

transitional

An XHTML *DTD* that allows elements found in the strict DTD but also allows elements from previous versions of a DTD that are no longer included in the strict DTD.

U

Uniform Resource Indicator (URI)

Points out the location of a resource. URI is an umbrella term including *URLs* and other types of resource indicators.

Uniform Resource Locator (URL)

Points out the location of a resource.

URI

See *Uniform Resource Indicator*.

URL

See *Uniform Resource Locator*.

V

valid

Valid markup follows the specifications of a particular *DTD*.

validate

To check the syntax of a document against the standard specifications. Tools used for this purpose are called validators.

value

The specific option selected for a property or attribute. A CSS *declaration* consists of *properties* and values. XHTML elements can be assigned *attributes* and values. The value for the property color, for example, might be a hexadecimal *color code* such as #3366FF. In CSS, a value must be followed by a semicolon (;). In XHTML, all values must be enclosed in quotation marks.

viewport

The view in the browser window.

visual formatting model

In this model, each element generates zero or more boxes according to the *box model*.

W

W3C

See *Worldwide Web Consortium*.

web-safe color

One of a limited set of colors that should display uniformly across all platforms.

website

A collection of various related files such as HTML, images, scripts, and other resources found at a particular *URL* on the World Wide Web.

whitespace

That part of a page that contains no characters or images.

whois

A searchable database of domain name registrations.

Worldwide Web Consortium (W3C)

A group of experts who work to develop specifications and guidelines for web technologies.

X

XHTML

See *Extensible Hypertext Markup Language*.

XML

See *Extensible Markup Language*.

XML declaration

An *XML* declaration tells a browser the version of XML that is used on a web page.

Index

Note to the reader: Throughout this index **boldfaced** page numbers indicate primary discussions of a topic. *Italicized* page numbers indicate illustrations. Page numbers beginning with "C" indicate the color section.

Get

Savvy™

Sybex introduces Savvy,™ a new series
of in-depth, premium graphics and web
books. Savvy books turn beginning and
intermediate level graphics professionals
into experts, and give advanced users a
meaningful edge in this competitive climate.

In-Depth Coverage. Each book contains
compelling, professional examples and illustrations
to demonstrate the use of the program in a working
environment.

Proven Authors. Savvy authors have the
first-hand knowledge and experience to deliver
useful insights, making even the most advanced
discussions accessible.

Sophisticated Package. Savvy titles have a
striking interior design, enhanced by high-quality,
coated paper for crisp graphic reproduction.

Flash™ MX 2004 Savvy
by Ethan Watrall
and Norbert Herber
ISBN: 0-7821-4284-2
US $44.99

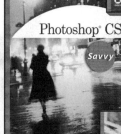

Photoshop® CS Savvy
by Stephen Romaniello
ISBN: 0-7821-4280-X
US $44.99

Maya™ 5 Savvy
by John Kundert-Gibbs,
Peter Lee, Dariush Derakhshani,
and Eric Kunzendorf
ISBN: 0-7821-4230-3
US $59.99

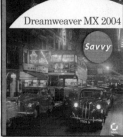

**Dreamweaver® MX
2004 Savvy**
by Christian Crumlish and
Lucinda Dykes
ISBN: 0-7821-4306-7
US $44.99

SYBEX®

www.sybex.com

Style. Substance. Sybex.